P9-BJW-088

1998 Edition

The Definitive Buyer's Guide to Car Safety, Fuel Economy, Maintenance, and Much More

by Jack Gillis

with Ashley B. Cheng and Karen Fierst

graphics and design by Amy B. Curran

foreword by Clarence M. Ditlow
Center for Auto Safety

HarperPerennial
A Division of HarperCollins*Publishers*

Riverside Community College
Library
4800 Magnolia Avenue

TL162 .G55
Gillis, Jack.
The car book

The difficult and complex process of buying a car has been made easier this year because a new person has stepped in to lead collection and analysis of the information you need to make a smart, sensible and reliable choice: Ashley Cheng. Ashley takes over as co-author for the 18th edition of The Car Book and joins computer graphics maven Amy Curran to seamlessly compile and package more information than we've ever before presented. Thanks to his cool-headed management style, expertise and willingness to work hard, Ashley was able to assemble one of the most complex consumer guides available—all with grace and style. Amy's ability to make graphical sense out of all of this data is the key ingredient in successfully providing this important information to the American car buyer. These two professionals worked together like precise gears in a Swiss watch—keeping perfect time all the way. They were able to accomplish this increasingly complex feat with the competent assistance of super-intern Ailis Aaron (University of North Carolina). Ailis performed tirelessly as our main researcher, number cruncher, and fact checker extraordinaire. Also assisting Ashley was the newest member of the team, Sharon Guttman, who helped with research, copyediting, data collection and photo selection.

As has been the case for 13 years, the experience and institutional knowledge of Car Book veteran Karen Fierst was the icing on the cake. But, alas, it has come time for Karen to blow out the candles. As she moves on to new challenges, we are confident that her considerable accomplishments and contributions will only grow bigger and better. To you, Karen, I say: Todah and Shalom.

Many, many talented professionals enabled Ashley and Amy to successfully accomplish this effort. This year's edition would not have been possible without essential contributions from many talented individuals. Most significant was Clarence Ditlow and the staff of the Center for Auto Safety. In addition, valuable insight and information was provided by safety expert David Biss, president of Automotive Safety Analysis; legal expert Phil Nowicki, president of Nowicki and Associates; Carolyn Gorman of the Insurance Information Institute; Martha Casey, U.S. EPA; Pete Packer, Runzheimer International; Kim Hazelbaker, Highway Loss Data Institute; Debbie Bindeman, Insurance Services Organization. Very special thanks go to my friend and terrific literary agent, Stuart Krichevsky.

As always, the most important factor in being able to bring this information to the American car buyer for 18 years is the encouragement, support, and love from my brilliant and beautiful wife, Marilyn Mohrman-Gillis.

J.G.

As Always,

for Marilyn &
Katie, John, Brian, and Brennan

THE CAR BOOK *(1998 edition)*. Copyright© 1998, 1997, 1996, 1995, 1994, 1993, 1992, 1991, 1990, 1989, 1988, 1987, 1986, 1985, 1984, 1983, 1982, 1981 by Jack Gillis. All rights reserved. Printed in the United States of America. No part of this book may be used or reproduced in any manner whatsoever without written permission except in the case of brief quotations embodied in critical articles and reviews. For information, address HarperCollins Publishers, Inc., 10 East 53rd Street, New York, NY 10022.

HarperCollins books may be purchased for educational, business, or sales promotional use. For information, please write: Special Markets Department, HarperCollins Publishers, Inc., 10 East 53rd Street, New York, NY 10022.

ISSN: 0893-1208
ISBN: 0-06-273-447-4
97 98 99 CW 5 4 3 2 1

Cover design ©Gillis and Associates.
Photo credits: Chrysler Corporation, Dodge Division; Ford Motor Corporation; General Motors Corporation, Buick Division; General Motors Corporation, Chevrolet Division; Mitsubishi Motor Sales of America, Inc.; Volvo Cars of North America
Cover Photo of Jack Gillis: Donna Cantor-MacLean

Contents

Foreword

by Clarence M. Ditlow,
Executive Director, Center for Auto Safety

The rise of *The Car Book* since the first edition in 1981 contrasts with the demise of safety regulations over the same period. The federal agencies no longer enforce safety and consumer protection laws because they view protecting the profits of auto companies as more important than protecting the lives and pocketbooks of consumers. If one doesn't have *The Car Book*, one is lost in the car jungle without a guide, surrounded by safety hazards and consumer scams.

Today, when it comes to motor vehicle safety, the motto is: Let the buyer beware. A perfect example is the airbag. Overall, airbags are real lifesavers, particularly in higher speed crashes where seatbelts alone will not save an occupant. But when it comes to protecting out-of-position occupants and small adults, all airbags are not created equal. Some auto companies, like Honda, put very good airbags in their cars. They are designed to reduce injuries to small adults and out-of-position occupants. But because the National Highway Traffic Safety Administration (NHTSA) failed to set a standard that required protecting small children and people leaning toward the dash, particularly in low speed crashes, some companies installed less safe airbags. If NHTSA had set a tough, protective airbag standard, Chrysler would not have used a horizontally deploying airbag in its minivan that has killed 11 passengers. Instead, they would have used a vertically deploying airbag mounted in the top of the dash, like Honda's, which has not killed or injured anyone.

Although the Center for Auto Safety (CAS) has repeatedly called on NHTSA to set a standard for the rear hatches of minivans, the agency refused to do so until 37 people had been killed when the rear hatch popped open on Chrysler minivans. Among the victims was 6 year old Sergio Jimenez who was ejected out the rear hatch of his parent's Dodge Caravan in 1994 after it was hit by a Honda going 10 miles per hour. Shocked by Chrysler's knowledge of the defect and its Washington lobbying to kill a safety recall, a Charleston, SC jury hit Chrysler with a $250 million punitive damage message to recall, rather than stonewall.

The 1998 model year mark's the 25th anniversary of the introduction of the most lethal defect in U.S. auto history, General Motors' full size pickups with side saddle gas tanks. These vehicles have killed 1,600 people in fire crashes, over 20 times as many as the infamous Ford Pinto. Tragically, many victims of GM's pickups are people in other cars who have the misfortune of striking a GM pickup at speeds as low as 20 miles per hour. In 1984, a GM vice president called a $23 safety shield for the pickups "a probably easy fix," but GM refused to install it even though the company made $13 billion in profits on these side-saddle pickups. Even today, GM's pickups are the most lethal defect on the road with 68 more people killed in fire crashes in 1996 alone and 148 since U.S. Transportation Secretary Federico Pena let GM off the hook without a recall in December 1994. The families of GM pickup victims were so upset by this decision that they have launched a national petition campaign to recall the trucks, which will be on the road crashing and burning until well into the 21st century.

The Federal Trade Commission (FTC) after years of protecting motorists from non-safety defects like rust and exposing secret warranties under Chairman Mike Pertschuk through the early 1980's now looks the other way on secret warranties and lets auto companies force consumers to pay for engineering mistakes. Even though the Big Three (Chrysler, GM and Ford) had secret warranties on peeling paint because they omitted a primer layer to save money, the FTC said it was okay not to tell consumers. In fact, states are often more aggressive in pursuing automotive abuses than federal agencies. When California caught Chrysler reselling bought back lemons without notifying the next purchaser, it moved to suspend Chrysler from doing business in the state for 45 days. On the other hand, when Consumers for Auto Reliability and Safety asked the FTC to establish a regulation to prevent lemon laundering, they simply set up a task force to study the problem.

Consumers need to get mad and tell the auto companies to fire the lawyers and lobbyists, who make loopholes, and hire more engineers to make better cars. Until the car companies wake up and realize that they need to treat consumers fairly and give them safe cars to ride or lose sales and lawsuits, consumers need the *1998 Car Book*. It can help save your life and tell you how to become a better consumer.

Introduction

For 18 years, *The Car Book* has been your single source for hard-to-find information essential to purchasing a safe, reliable and economical car. In 1980, when the government began releasing crash tests results, *The Car Book* was the first to provide you with this valuable and life-saving information. And now, in 1998, we're once again your source for the first-ever government *side* crash test results.

A tragedy occurred last September when the first properly belted child was killed by a passenger-side airbag. Safety advocates, auto makers and government officials are frantically working together to implement the best possible solution: smart airbags.

Unfortunately, we will not see smart airbags until 2000. Until then, auto makers will be de-powering the passenger-side airbags on their vehicles. Beware — de-powered airbags can still be fatal to out-of-position children (children who are not sitting up straight and properly buckled in). Worse, de-powered airbags lowers the protection for adult passengers.

In other words, always buckle up and put your children in back.

There is some good news for 1998. Dealers have finally learned that if they want your business, you need to be treated with respect. Smarter dealers are replacing sleazy sales techniques with informed personnel and fixed prices. Auto makers are also changing direction. Last year, car prices peaked at the highest point ever, averaging well over $22,000. For '98, some auto makers have held the line on price increases. In fact, the newly redesigned 1998 Honda Accord costs up to $900 less than last year's model!

Last year, we were among the first to introduce you to the future of travel, GM's EV1, the first-ever electric car to be available on the market. For '98, Honda joins the electric car parade with the EV Plus. We've devoted a car page each to both of these futuristic vehicles.

With the addition of side crash test ratings, you now have in your hands the best arsenal of facts available to help you wade through the useless claims and exaggerated hype from auto companies. Use the information in *The Car Book* wisely and there is no reason why your car shouldn't last over 100,000 miles. To help make your selection easy to do, we've completely updated the 18th edition of *The Car Book* with more data and information than ever!

Your continued use of the information in *The Car Book* dramatically influences how car companies build their cars. In fact, in the last 25 years, even though the number of vehicles on the road has more than doubled, the fatality rate has dropped by an astonishing 66 percent! Now, however, with increased speed limits, we may see that decline slow down. Buying for safety is one way to protect you and your loved ones.

How does today's consumer buy safety? Many consumers mistakenly believe that handling and performance are the key elements in the safety of a car. While an extremely unresponsive car could

Missing Safety: Minivans

Minivans, pickups, and sport utility vehicles continue to be the fastest growing vehicle types. Minivans are convenient because few station wagons are large enough to hold growing families. If you are interested in one of these vehicles, be warned: They do not have to meet all of the safety standards applied to passenger cars. Even though thousands of Americans buy these vehicles for family and non-commercial use, the National Highway Traffic Safety Administration has been slow to require safety improvements.

Minivans, pickups and sport utility vehicles were finally required to provide roofs strong enough to support the vehicle's weight if it rolls over and contain reinforcement beams in the doors to protect occupants in side crashes in 1995. By 1999, these vehicles must meet the same side impact standards as passenger cars. However, these vehicles are not yet required to have bumpers that meet any kind of strength requirements. Most importantly, these vehicles are not yet required to provide any automatic crash protection, in the form of either automatic belts or airbags. Automatic crash protection requirements are currently being phased in, but will not become standard until next year.

Because of their popularity with car buyers, we've included minivans in *The Car Book*. We also compile *The Truck, Van and 4x4 Book*, which provides hundreds of facts about these popular vehicles, including sport utility vehicles.

cause an accident, most new cars meet basic handling requirements. In fact, many people actually feel uncomfortable driving high performance cars because the highly responsive steering, acceleration, and suspension systems can be difficult to get used to. But the main reason handling is overrated as a safety measure is that automobile collisions are, by nature, accidents. Once they've begun, they are beyond human capacity to prevent, no matter how well your car handles. So the key to protecting yourself is to purchase a car that offers a high degree of crash protection.

As our concern for safety has influenced car makers' attitudes, so have our demands for quality. The result—U.S. cars in the '90s continue to be better built than those of the '80s. And, because we're demanding that companies stand behind their products, we're seeing better warranties, too. Since *The Car Book* began comparing warranties in 1986, a number of car makers have told us that they've been forced to improve their warranties now that consumers can tell the difference.

Consumers are learning that they can get better-performing and safer cars by buying the ones with good safety records, low maintenance costs, long warranties, and insurance discounts. Use the "Buying Guide" to compare cars, and read the chapters to learn more about each model. This year, the "Buying Guide" is loaded with new and important information. You'll find everything from crash test results to an ease-of-parking rating.

The "safety" chapter rates crash safety, describes your options for protection, and is where you'll find vital information on airbags, the detailed frontal and the all-new side crash test results, tips on avoiding unsafe child seats, and a review of safety belt and child seat laws.

The "fuel economy" chapter uncovers the money-saving gas misers and offers advice on some products to avoid.

The "maintenance" chapter allows you to compare those inevitable repair costs *before* you buy. You'll also find advice on dealing with mechanics and how to make your car last longer.

The "warranties" chapter offers a critical comparison of the new warranties and lets you know the best and worst before you get into trouble down the road. If you do have trouble, we'll let you know which companies offer roadside assistance and we'll tip you off to secret warranties.

The "insurance" chapter will help you save money on an expense that is often forgotten in the showroom.

Because most of us can't tell one tire from another, we've included the "tire" chapter to help you select the best.

The "complaint" chapter provides a road map to resolving inevitable problems quickly and efficiently. We provide consumers with their only access to about 300,000 car complaints on file with the U.S. government. Thanks to the efforts of the Center for Auto Safety, we continue to include this otherwise unavailable information.

Review the "showroom strategies" chapter for tips on getting the best price—for many of us one of the hardest and most distasteful aspects of car buying.

Finally, our "ratings" chapter provides a detailed review of each of the 1998 cars and minivans. These pages provide, at a glance, an overview of all the criteria you need to make a good choice. Here, you'll be able to quickly assess key features and see how the car you're interested in stacks up against its competition so you can make sure your selection is the best car for you. Car prices have more than doubled since 1980, so we've also included the percent of *dealer* markup to help you negotiate the very best price.

The information in *The Car Book* is based on data collected and developed by our staff, the U.S. Department of Transportation, and the Center for Auto Safety. With all of this data in hand, you'll find some great choices for 1998. *The Car Book* will guide you through the trade-offs, promises, facts, and myths to the car that will best meet your needs.

—*Jack Gillis*

Questions, Comments

If you have any suggestions, questions, or comments, you may e-mail us at JAGillis@aol.com

BUYING GUIDE

The Buying Guide provides an overall comparison of the 1998 cars in terms of safety, fuel economy, maintenance, insurance costs, warranty, complaint ratings, and other key items. The cars are arranged by size class based on weight.

Based on these comparisons, we have developed *The Car Book*'s Best Bets for 1998—these vehicles rated tops when all of these categories were considered. In general, there are five key steps to buying a car.

1 Narrow your choice down to a particular class of car–sports, station wagon, minivan, sedan, large luxury, or economy car. These are general classifications and some cars may fit into more than one category. In most cases, *The Car Book* presents the vehicles by size class.

2 Determine what features are really important to you. Most buyers consider safety on the top of their list, which is why the "safety" chapter is right up front in *The Car Book*. Airbags, power options, ABS, and the number of passengers, as well as "hidden" elements such as maintenance and insurance costs, should be considered at this stage in your selection process.

3 Find 3 or 4 cars that meet the needs you outlined above *and* your pocketbook. It's important not to narrow your choice down to one car because then you lose all your bargaining power in the showroom. In fact, because cars today are more similar than dissimilar, it's not hard to keep three or four choices in mind. On the car rating pages in the back of the book, we suggest some competitive choices for your consideration. For example, if you are interested in the Honda Accord, you should also consider the Toyota Camry and Ford Taurus.

4 Make sure you take a good, long test drive. The biggest car buying mistake most of us make is to overlook those nagging problems that seem to surface only after we've brought the car home. Spend at least an hour driving the car without a dealer in the car. If a dealership won't allow you to test drive a car without a dealer, go somewhere else. This includes time on the highway, parking, taking the car in and out of your driveway or garage, sitting in the back seat, and using the trunk or storage area. Whatever you do, *don't talk price until you're ready to buy!*

5 This is the stage most of us dread–negotiating the price. While price negotiation is a car buying tradition, a few car makers and dealers are trying to break tradition by offering so called "no-haggle pricing." Since they're still in the minority and, because it's almost impossible to establish true competition between dealers as individuals, we offer a new means to avoid negotiating altogether by using the non-profit CarBargains pricing service.

Now that you have a quick guide to the steps necessary in making a good choice, use the tables that follow to quickly review the new cars and the pages in the back for a detailed critique of each model. See the "showroom strategies" chapter for more details on getting the best price.

In This Chapter...

Using the Buying Guide

The "Buying Guide" will allow you to quickly compare the 1998 models.

To fully understand these summary charts, it is important to read the appropriate section of the book. You will note that here and throughout the book, some of the charts contain empty boxes. This indicates that data were unavailable at the time of printing.

Here's how to understand what's included in the "Buying Guide."

Page Reference: The page in the back of the book where you'll find all the details for this car.

Overall Rating: This is the "bottom line." It shows how well this car stacks up on a scale of 1 to 10 when compared to all others on the market. The overall rating considers safety, maintenance, fuel economy, warranty, insurance costs and complaints. Due to the importance of crash tests, cars with no results as of our publication date cannot be given an overall rating. More recent results may be available from the Auto Safety Hotline at 1-800-424-9393 (see page 77).

Car Book Crash Test Rating: This indicates how well the car performed in the U.S. Government's 35-mph frontal crash test program. We have analyzed and compared all of the crash test results to date and have given them a rating from *very good* to *very poor*. These ratings allow you to compare the test results of one car with another. A car with a poor rating may have done well according to government injury ratings, but still be among the worst performers of cars being offered in 1998.

Airbags: Here we tell you if the car is equipped with dual and side airbags, dual with optional side airbags, or only dual airbags.

Daytime Running Lights: Daytime running lights are a low-cost method of reducing your chances of being in a crash by increasing the visibility of your vehicle. Studies have shown that daytime running lights can reduce crashes by up to 40 percent. Here we indicate if daytime running lights are *standard*, *optional* or *none*.

Fuel Economy: This is the EPA-rated fuel economy for city and highway driving measured in miles per gallon. A single model may have a number of fuel economy ratings because of different engine and transmission options. We have included the figure for what is expected to be the most popular model.

Repair Rating: This rating is based on nine typical repairs after the warranty expires and the cost of following the manufacturer's preventive maintenance schedule during the warranty period.

Warranty Rating: This is an overall assessment of the car's warranty when compared to all other warranties. The rating considers the important features of each warranty, with emphasis on the length of the basic and powertrain warranties.

Best Bets for 1998

Based on information in the *Buying Guide*, this list shows the highest-rated cars in each of the size categories. Ratings are based on expected performance in eight important categories (crash tests, safety features, fuel economy, maintenance and repair costs, warranties, insurance costs, and complaints), with the heaviest emphasis on crash test performance and complaints.

Subcompact
Saturn SL/SW (10)
Subaru Impreza (9)
Toyota Paseo (9)
Nissan Sentra (8)
Suzuki Swift (8)
Toyota Tercel 2dr. (8)

Compact
BMW 3 Series (10)
Subaru Legacy (9)
Volkswagen Golf (8)
Volkswagen Jetta (8)
Ford Contour (7)
Mercury Mystique (7)

Intermediate
Audi A4 (10)
Mercedes Benz C-Class (8)
Mercury Sable (8)

Intermediate (cont.)
Buick Century (7)
Ford Taurus (7)
Mazda Millenia (7)

Large
Cadillac DeVille (10)
Infiniti I30 (10)
Pontiac Bonneville (10)
Acura TL (9)
Buick LeSabre (9)
Lexus ES300 (9)
Oldsmobile 88 (9)

Minivan
Isuzu Oasis (10)
Honda Odyssey (7)
Nissan Quest (6)
Oldsmobile Silhouette (5)
Pontiac Trans Sport (5)

Complaint Index: This rating is based on the number of complaints about that car on file at the U.S. Department of Transportation. The complaint index will give you a general idea of experiences others have had with models which are essentially unchanged for this model year. All-new vehicles for 1998 are given an *average* complaint rating as it is unknown how many complaints they will receive.

Insurance Cost: Many automobile insurance companies use ratings based on the car's accident and occupant injury history to determine whether or not the insurance premium of a car should be *discounted* or *surcharged*. (Your insurance company may or may not participate in a rating program.) If the car is likely to receive neither, we label it *regular*.

Parking Index: This rating of *very easy* to *very hard* is an indicator of how much difficulty you will typically have parking. If you regularly parallel park, or find yourself maneuvering in and out of tight spaces, this can be an important factor in your choice of a car. This rating is based on the car's wheelbase, length, and turning circle.

Typical Price: This price range will give you a general idea of the "sticker," or asking price of a car. It is based on the lowest to highest retail price of the various models, and it does not include options or the discount that you should be able to negotiate using a service such as CarBargains (see page 92).

TIP

Typical Operating Costs

As you can probably guess, buying a 1998 luxury car rather than an economy model will cost considerably more—not only due to higher initial cost, but also higher fuel, maintenance, tire replacement, insurance and finance costs. Also, higher priced cars often decrease faster in value.

The table below shows the *annual* operating costs for fifteen popular cars. Costs include operating expenses (fuel, oil, maintenance and tires) and ownership expenses (insurance, depreciation, financing, taxes, and licensing) and are based on keeping the car for 3 years, driving 20,000 miles per year.

	Annual Costs*		
Vehicle	**Operating**	**Ownership**	**Total**
Mercedes 320 S	$2,740	$14,585	$17,325
Lincoln Town Car Exec.	$2,680	$12,158	$14,838
Cadillac DeVille	$2,890	$11,811	$14,701
Buick Riviera	$2,510	$10,122	$12,632
Oldsmobile Aurora	$2,710	$9,701	$12,411
Buick LeSabre Ltd	$2,330	$8,348	$10,678
Mercury Grand Marquis GS	$2,490	$8,023	$10,513
Nissan Maxima GXE	$2,280	$7,720	$10,000
Dodge Intrepid	$2,330	$7,076	$9,406
Ford Taurus SE	$2,240	$6,934	$9,174
Chevy Lumina	$2,240	$6,444	$8,684
Toyota Camry CE	$1,960	$5,988	$7,948
Dodge Neon	$1,860	$5,689	$7,549
Honda Accord DX	$1,890	$5,334	$7,224
Saturn SL2	$1,960	$5,149	$7,109
Chevy Metro LSi	$1,640	$5,153	$6,793

Source: Runzheimer International, Rochester, Wisconsin.
*Costs are based on four-door models, with automatic transmission, power steering, power disc brakes, air conditioning, tinted glass, AM-FM stereo, body side molding, cruise control, left-hand remote control mirror, rear window defogger, pulse windshield wipers, ABS, dual air bags and tilt-steering.

Car	See Pg.	Overall Rating[1] Poor ⇔ Good	Crash Test	Airbags	Daytime Running Lights	Fuel Economy	Repair Rating
Subcompact							
Chevrolet Metro	125	1	Good	Dual Only	Standard	44/49	Poor
Dodge/Plym. Neon	137	1	Average	Dual Only	None	29/39	Very Good
Ford Escort	143	4	Average	Dual Only	None	28/37	Very Good
GM EV1	147		No Test	Dual Only	Standard		
Honda Civic	150	7	Very Good	Dual Only	None	33/38	Average
Honda EV Plus	151		No Test	Dual Only	None		
Hyundai Accent	154	7	Average	Dual Only	None	28/36	Very Good
Kia Sephia	161		No Test	Dual Only	None	28/34	Average
Mazda Miata	170	4	Average	Dual Only	None	23/29	Average
Mazda Protege	173		No Test	Dual Only	None	30/37	Average
Mercury Tracer	180	6	Average	Dual Only	None	28/37	Very Good
Mitsubishi Mirage	185		No Test	Dual Only	None	33/40	Poor
Nissan Sentra	190	8	Good	Dual Only	None	30/40	Average
Saturn SC	207		No Test	Dual Only	Standard	28/39	Good
Saturn SL/SW	208	10	Very Good	Dual Only	Standard	28/39	Good
Subaru Impreza	209	9	Good	Dual Only	None	23/30	Good
Suzuki Esteem	211		No Test	Dual Only	Standard	30/37	Poor
Suzuki Swift	212	8	Good	Dual Only	Standard	39/43	Poor
Toyota Paseo	217	9	Good	Dual Only	None	21/37	Poor
Toyota Tercel	219	7	Average[2]	Dual Only	None	32/39	Poor
Compact							
Acura Integra	103	6	Average	Dual Only	None	31/25	Very Poor
BMW 3-Series	108	10	Good	Dual/Opt. Side	None	32/23	Good
BMW Z3	110	8	No Test	Dual Only	None	32/23	Good
Chevrolet Cavalier	122	8	Good	Dual Only	Standard	37/25	Good
Chevrolet Prizm	127		No Test	Dual/Opt. Side	Standard	37/31	Poor
Chrysler Sebring	132	2	Very Good	Dual Only	None	31/22	Good
Dodge Avenger	134	4	Very Good	Dual Only	None	32/22	Good
Eagle Talon	139	2	Good	Dual Only	None	33/22	Good
Ford Contour	141	7	Good	Dual Only	None	35/24	Good
Honda Prelude	153		No Test	Dual Only	None	27/22	Poor
Hyundai Elantra	155	5	Average	Dual Only	None	32/24	Very Good
Hyundai Tiburon	157		No Test	Dual Only	None	30/22	Very Good

[1]Due to the importance of crash tests, cars with no crash test results as of publication date cannot be given an overall rating.
[2]Data given for sedan; frontal crash test for coupe is Good for an overall rating of 8.

Warranty	Complaint Rating	Insurance Rating	Parking Index	Typical Price $	Overall Rating* Poor ⇔ Good	See Pg.	Car
							Subcompact
Very Poor	Very Poor	Surcharge	Very Easy	8-11,000		125	Chevrolet Metro
Very Poor	Very Poor	Surcharge	Easy	10-12,000		137	Dodge/Plym. Neon
Very Poor	Average	Surcharge	Very Easy	11-15,000		143	Ford Escort
	Average		Very Easy	33-34,000		147	GM EV1
Very Poor	Average	Surcharge	Very Easy	10-14,000		150	Honda Civic
	Average		Easy	53-54,000		151	Honda EV Plus
Poor	Poor	Discount	Very Easy	8-10,000[2]		154	Hyundai Accent
Average	Average	Regular	Very Easy	9-11,000[2]		161	Kia Sephia
Very Poor	Very Good	Regular	Very Easy	19-20,000[2]		170	Mazda Miata
Very Poor	Poor	Surcharge	Easy	12-16,000		173	Mazda Protege
Very Poor	Average	Regular	Very Easy	11-13,000		180	Mercury Tracer
Average	Average	Surcharge	Very Easy	10-14,000		185	Mitsubishi Mirage
Poor	Average	Surcharge	Easy	11-17,000		190	Nissan Sentra
Poor	Average	Regular	Average	12-14,000		207	Saturn SC
Poor	Good	Regular	Average	10-14,000		208	Saturn SL/SW
Poor	Good	Regular	Very Easy	15-18,000		209	Subaru Impreza
Very Poor	Good	Regular	Very Easy	11-14,000		211	Suzuki Esteem
Very Poor	Very Good	Surcharge	Very Easy	9-10,000		212	Suzuki Swift
Very Poor	Very Good	Discount	Very Easy	13-18,000[2]		217	Toyota Paseo
Very Poor	Good	Discount	Very Easy	11-13,000[2]		219	Toyota Tercel
							Compact
Average	Good	Regular	Easy	16-20,000[2]		103	Acura Integra
Good	Good	Surcharge	Easy	21-34,000		108	BMW 3-Series
Good	Good	Regular	Very Easy	29-37,000		110	BMW Z3
Very Poor	Average	Discount	Easy	11-16,000		122	Chevrolet Cavalier
Very Poor	Average	Regular	Easy	12-14,000[2]		127	Chevrolet Prizm
Very Poor	Very Poor	Regular	Hard	16-21,000		132	Chrysler Sebring
Very Poor	Very Poor	Regular	Hard	14-18,000		134	Dodge Avenger
Very Poor	Very Poor	Discount	Average	14-21,000		139	Eagle Talon
Very Poor	Poor	Regular	Average	14-16,000		141	Ford Contour
Very Poor	Average	Discount	Easy	23-28,000[2]		153	Honda Prelude
Poor	Poor	Discount	Very Easy	11-13,000[2]		155	Hyundai Elantra
Poor	Average	Regular	Easy	13-15,000[2]		157	Hyundai Tiburon

[1]Due to the importance of crash tests, cars with no crash test results as of publication date cannot be given an overall rating.

[2]Based on 1997 prices.

Car	See Pg.	Overall Rating[1] Poor ⇔ Good	Crash Test	Airbags	Daytime Running Lights	Fuel Economy	Repair Rating
Compact (cont.)							
Mazda 626	169		No Test	Dual Only	None	34/26	Average
Mercury Mystique	178		Good	Dual Only	None	35/24	Good
Mitsubishi Eclipse	183		Good	Dual Only	None	33/23	Good
Mitsubishi Galant	184		Good	Dual Only	None	30/23	Average
Oldsmobile Achieva	192		Very Good	Dual Only	Standard	32/22	Average
Pontiac Grand Am	201		Very Good	Dual Only	Standard	33/23	Average
Pontiac Sunfire	203		Good	Dual Only	Standard	37/25	Average
Subaru Legacy	210		Very Good	Dual Only	None	30/23	Good
Toyota Celica	215		No Test	Dual Only	None	35/29	Poor
Toyota Corolla	216		No Test	Dual/Opt. Side	Standard	38/31	Poor
Volkswagen Golf	220		Average	Dual/Opt. Side	Standard	31/24	Very Good
Volkswagen Jetta	221		Average	Dual/Opt. Side	Standard	31/24	Very Good
Intermediate							
Audi A4	106		Very Good	Dual & Side	None	23/32	Good
BMW 5 Series	109		No Test	Dual & Side	None	18/26	Good
Buick Century	111		Good	Dual Only	Standard	20/29	Good
Buick Regal	114		Good	Dual Only	Standard	19/30	Good
Cadillac Catera	116		No Test	Dual Only	Standard	18/25	Good
Chevrolet Camaro	121		Very Good	Dual Only	Standard	18/27	Average
Chrysler Cirrus	129		No Test	Dual Only	None	20/30	Good
Chrysler Concorde	130		No Test	Dual Only	None	21/30	Good
Dodge Intrepid	136		No Test	Dual Only	None	21/30	Very Good
Dodge Stratus	138		No Test	Dual Only	None	26/37	Very Good
Eagle Vision	140		No Test	Dual Only	None	19/27	Very Good
Ford Mustang	144		Good[2]	Dual Only	None	20/30	Average
Ford Taurus	145		Very Good	Dual Only	None	20/28	Good
Honda Accord	149		No Test	Dual Only	None	25/31	Average
Hyundai Sonata	156		Average	Dual Only	None	21/28	Very Good
Mazda Millenia	171		Very Good	Dual Only	None	20/27	Poor
Merc-Benz C-Class	174		Good	Dual & Side	None	23/30	Very
Mercury Sable	179		Very Good	Dual Only	None	20/28	Good
Nissan 240SX	186		Average	Dual Only	None	22/28	Poor
Nissan Altima	187		No Test	Dual Only	None	24/31	Good

[1]Due to the importance of crash tests, cars with no crash test results as of publication date cannot be given an overall rating.
[2]Data given for coupe; frontal crash test for convertible is Very Good for an overall rating of 5.

Warranty	Complaint Rating	Insurance Rating	Parking Index	Typical Price $	Overall Rating[1] Poor ⇔ Good	See Pg.	Car
							Compact (cont.)
Very Poor	Average	Regular	Easy	15-24,000		169	Mazda 626
Very Poor	Average	Regular	Average	16-18,000		178	Mercury Mystique
Average	Very Poor	Discount	Average	15-25,000		183	Mitsubishi Eclipse
Average	Poor	Discount	Easy	15-26,000		184	Mitsubishi Galant
Poor	Very Good	Regular	Easy	17-18,000		192	Oldsmobile Achieva
Very Poor	Good	Regular	Easy	14-17,000		201	Pontiac Grand Am
Very Poor	Good	Discount	Average	12-20,000		203	Pontiac Sunfire
Poor	Average	Regular	Easy	19-23,000		210	Subaru Legacy
Very Poor	Very Good	Surcharge	Easy	17-24,000[2]		215	Toyota Celica
Very Poor	Average	Regular	Very Easy	11-15,000		216	Toyota Corolla
Very Good	Average	Surcharge	Very Easy	13-14,000		220	Volkswagen Golf
Very Good	Average	Surcharge	Very Easy	14-15,000		221	Volkswagen Jetta
							Intermediate
Very Good	Very Good	Regular	Average	23-31,000		106	Audi A4
Good	Average	Regular	Average	39-54,000		109	BMW 5 Series
Very Poor	Average	Discount	Hard	18-20,000		111	Buick Century
Very Poor	Average	Discount	Hard	20-24,000		114	Buick Regal
Good	Average	Surcharge	Easy	29-34,000		116	Cadillac Catera
Very Poor	Poor	Surcharge	Hard	16-21,000		121	Chevrolet Camaro
Very Poor	Very Poor	Regular	Average	19-20,000		129	Chrysler Cirrus
Very Poor	Average	Regular	Hard	20-21,000[2]		130	Chrysler Concorde
Very Poor	Average	Regular	Hard	19-23,000[2]		136	Dodge Intrepid
Very Poor	Poor	Regular	Average	14-18,000		138	Dodge Stratus
Very Poor	Poor	Discount	Hard	20-25,000[2]		140	Eagle Vision
Very Poor	Average	Surcharge	Hard	15-20,000		144	Ford Mustang
Very Poor	Average	Regular	Hard	18-22,000		145	Ford Taurus
Very Poor	Average	Regular	Average	15-22,000		149	Honda Accord
Poor	Poor	Discount	Easy	14-19,000[2]		156	Hyundai Sonata
Very Poor	Good	Regular	Average	29-37,000		171	Mazda Millenia
Average	Good	Discount	Easy	30-36,000		174	Merc-Benz C-Class
Very Poor	Average	Discount	Hard	19-23,000		179	Mercury Sable
Poor	Poor	Discount	Very Easy	18-25,000[2]		186	Nissan 240SX
Poor	Average	Regular	Average	14-20,000		187	Nissan Altima

[1]Due to the importance of crash tests, cars with no crash test results as of publication date cannot be given an overall rating.

[2]Based on 1997 prices.

Car	See Pg.	Overall Rating[1] Poor ⇔ Good	Crash Test	Airbags	Daytime Running Lights	Fuel Economy	Repair Rating
Intemediate (cont.)							
Nissan Maxima	188		Average	Dual/Opt. Side	None	22/27	Poor
Oldsmobile Cutlass	194		Good	Dual Only	Standard	20/29	Good
Oldsmobile Intrigue	195		Good	Dual Only	Standard	19/30	Good
Plymouth Breeze	197		No Test	Dual Only	None	26/37	Good
Pontiac Firebird	200		Very Good	Dual Only	Standard	19/30	Average
Pontiac Grand Prix	202		Good	Dual Only	Standard	20/29	Good
Saab 900	205		Good	Dual Only	Standard	22/28	Average
Saab 9000	206		Good	Dual Only	Standard	21/27	Average
Toyota Avalon	213		Very Good	Dual & Side	None	21/31	Poor
Toyota Camry	214		Good	Dual/Opt. Side	None	23/31	Poor
VW Passat	222		No Test	Dual & Side	Standard	23/32	Good
Volvo C70/S70/V70	223		No Test	Dual & Side	Standard	20/28	Poor
Large							
Acura CL	102		No Test	Dual Only	None	23/29	Poor
Acura RL	104		No Test	Dual Only	None	19/25	Very Poor
Acura TL	105		Good	Dual Only	None	20/25	Very Poor
Audi A6	107		No Test	Dual & Side	None	17/28	Good
Buick LeSabre	112		Good	Dual Only	Standard	19/30	Good
Buick Park Avenue	113		Average	Dual Only	Standard	19/28	Good
Buick Riviera	115		Average	Dual Only	Standard	18/27	Average
Cadillac DeVille	117		Very Good	Dual & Side	Standard	17/26	Average
Cadillac Eldorado	118		No Test	Dual Only	Standard	17/26	Average
Cadillac Seville	119		Average	Dual & Side	Standard	17/26	Average
Chevrolet Lumina	123		Very Good	Dual Only	Standard	20/29	Good
Chevrolet Malibu	124		Good	Dual Only	Standard	23/32	Average
Chevrolet Monte Carlo	126		Good	Dual Only	Standard	20/29	Good
Chrysler LHS	131		Good	Dual Only	None	17/26	Good
Ford Crown Victoria	142		Very Good	Dual Only	None	17/25	Average
Infiniti I30	158		Average	Dual/Opt. Side	None	21/28	Poor
Infiniti Q45	159		No Test	Dual & Side	None	18/23	Poor
Lexus ES300	162		Good	Dual & Side	None	19/25	Average
Lexus GS300/400	163		No Test	Dual & Side	None	20/25	Average
Lexus LS400	164		No Test	Dual & Side	None	19/25	Poor

[1]Due to the importance of crash tests, cars with no crash test results as of publication date cannot be given an overall rating.

Warranty	Complaint Rating	Insurance Rating	Parking Index	Typical Price $	Overall Rating[1] Poor ⇔ Good	See Pg.	Car
							Intermediate (cont.)
Poor	Good	Regular	Easy	21-27,000		188	Nissan Maxima
Poor	Average	Regular	Average	17-20,000		194	Oldsmobile Cutlass
Poor	Average	Regular	Average	20-23,000		195	Oldsmobile Intrigue
Very Poor	Very Good	Regular	Average	14-15,000		197	Plymouth Breeze
Very Poor	Poor	Surcharge	Average	18-26,000		200	Pontiac Firebird
Very Poor	Average	Discount	Average	18-21,000		202	Pontiac Grand Prix
Good	Very Poor	Surcharge	Easy	24-37,000		205	Saab 900
Good	Poor	Regular	Average	38-40,000		206	Saab 9000
Very Poor	Average	Regular	Average	24-29,000		213	Toyota Avalon
Very Poor	Average	Regular	Average	16-23,000		214	Toyota Camry
Very Good	Average	Regular	Average	20-21,000		222	VW Passat
Very Good	Average	Regular	Easy	26-39,000		223	Volvo C70/S70/V70
							Large
Average	Average	Regular	Hard	22-23,000[2]		102	Acura CL
Average	Very Good	Regular	Average	41-42,000[2]		104	Acura RL
Average	Very Good	Discount	Average	28-33,000[2]		105	Acura TL
Very Good	Average	Regular	Hard	32-34,000		107	Audi A6
Very Poor	Good	Discount	Hard	22-26,000		112	Buick LeSabre
Very Poor	Average	Discount	Hard	30-36,000		113	Buick Park Avenue
Very Poor	Poor	Discount	Hard	32-33,000		115	Buick Riviera
Good	Average	Discount	Very Hard	37-43,000		117	Cadillac DeVille
Good	Average	Discount	Hard	38-43,000		118	Cadillac Eldorado
Good	Average	Discount	Hard	40-46,000[2]		119	Cadillac Seville
Very Poor	Very Poor	Discount	Average	17-20,000		123	Chevrolet Lumina
Very Poor	Average	Regular	Average	15-19,000		124	Chevrolet Malibu
Very Poor	Poor	Regular	Average	17-21,000		126	Chevrolet Monte Carlo
Very Poor	Poor	Discount	Hard	30-31,000[2]		131	Chrysler LHS
Very Poor	Poor	Discount	Very Hard	21-24,000[2]		142	Ford Crown Victoria
Very Good	Very Good	Regular	Easy	28-33,000		158	Infiniti I30
Very Good	Average	Discount	Average	47-50,000[2]		159	Infiniti Q45
Good	Average	Discount	Average	30-31,000		162	Lexus ES300
Good	Average	Regular	Average	36-45,000		163	Lexus GS300/400
Good	Very Good	Surcharge	Average	52-53,000		164	Lexus LS400

[1]Due to the importance of crash tests, cars with no crash test results as of publication date cannot be given an overall rating.
[2]Based on 1997 prices.

Car	See Pg.	Overall Rating[1] Poor ⇔ Good	Crash Test	Airbags	Daytime Running Lights	Fuel Economy	Repair Rating
Large (cont.)							
Lexus SC300/400	165		No Test	Dual Only	None	19/24	Average
Lincoln Continental	166		No Test	Dual Only	None	17/25	Poor
Lincoln Mark VIII	167		Very Good	Dual Only	None	18/26	Average
Lincoln Town Car	168		No Test	Dual Only	None	17/25	Good
Merc-Benz E-Class	175		No Test	Dual & Side	None	21/29	Very Poor
Mercury Cougar	176		Very Good	Dual Only	None	18/26	Average
Mercury Gr. Marquis	177		Very Good	Dual Only	None	17/25	Average
Mitsubishi Diamante	182		No Test	Dual Only	None	18/26	Very
Oldsmobile 88	191		Good	Dual Only	Standard	19/29	Good
Oldsmobile Aurora	193		Average	Dual Only	Standard	17/26	Average
Pontiac Bonneville	199		Good	Dual Only	Standard	19/28	Good
Volvo S90/V90	224		No Test	Dual & Side	Standard	18/26	Poor
Minivan							
Chevrolet Astro	120		Poor	Dual Only	Standard	16/21	Good
Chevrolet Venture	128		Good	Dual Only	Standard	18/25	Good
Chrys. Town and Cntry	133		Good	Dual Only	None	17/24	Very Good
Dodge Caravan	135		Good	Dual Only	None	20/25	Very Good
Ford Windstar	146		Very Good	Dual Only	None	18/25	Good
GMC Safari	148		Poor	Dual Only	Standard	16/21	Good
Honda Odyssey	152		Good	Dual Only	None	20/24	Poor
Isuzu Oasis	160		Good	Dual Only	None	21/26	Poor
Mazda MPV	172		Very Good	Dual Only	None	16/21	Poor
Mercury Villager	181		Good	Dual Only	None	17/23	Good
Nissan Quest	189		Good	Dual Only	None	17/23	Good
Oldsmobile Silhouette	196		Good	Dual & Side	Standard	18/25	Good
Plymouth Voyager	198		Good	Dual Only	None	20/25	Very Good
Pontiac Trans Sport	204		Good	Dual & Side	Standard	18/25	Good
Toyota Sienna	218		No Test	Dual Only	None	18/24	Very Poor

[1]Due to the importance of crash tests, cars with no crash test results as of publication date cannot be given an overall rating.

Warranty	Complaint Rating	Insurance Rating	Parking Index	Typical Price $	Overall Rating[1] Poor ⇔ Good	See Pg.	Car
							Large (cont.)
Good	Very Good	Surcharge	Average	40-53,000		165	Lexus SC300/400
Average	Average	Regular	Very Hard	37-38,000		166	Lincoln Continental
Average	Average	Regular	Hard	37-40,000		167	Lincoln Mark VIII
Average	Average	Regular	Very Hard	27-44,000[2]		168	Lincoln Town Car
Average	Very Good	Discount	Average	41-46,000		175	Merc-Benz E-Class
Very Poor	Average	Regular	Average	18-19,000[2]		176	Mercury Cougar
Very Poor	Poor	Discount	Very Hard	23-25,000[2]		177	Mercury Gr. Marquis
Average	Average	Regular	Average	27-34,000		182	Mitsubishi Diamante
Poor	Good	Discount	Hard	22-25,000		191	Oldsmobile 88
Good	Average	Surcharge	Very Hard	34-36,000		193	Oldsmobile Aurora
Very Poor	Good	Discount	Hard	22-30,000		199	Pontiac Bonneville
Very Good	Average	Regular	Easy	34-36,000		224	Volvo S90/V90
							Minivan
Very Poor	Average	Discount	Hard	20-23,000		120	Chevrolet Astro
Very Poor	Average	Regular	Average	20-23,000		128	Chevrolet Venture
Very Poor	Very Poor	Discount	Hard	26-35,000		133	Chrys. Town and Cntry
Very Poor	Very Poor	Discount	Average	17-23,000		135	Dodge Caravan
Very Poor	Very Poor	Surcharge	Very Hard	20-30,000		146	Ford Windstar
Very Poor	Poor	Discount	Hard	20-23,000		148	GMC Safari
Very Poor	Very Good	Discount	Average	23-26,000[2]		152	Honda Odyssey
Good	Very Good	Discount	Average	23-26,000[2]		160	Isuzu Oasis
Very Poor	Poor	Regular	Average	23-29,000		172	Mazda MPV
Very Poor	Poor	Discount	Hard	20-27,000		181	Mercury Villager
Poor	Average	Discount	Hard	21-27,000[2]		189	Nissan Quest
Poor	Average	Regular	Average	23-28,000		196	Oldsmobile Silhouette
Very Poor	Very Poor	Regular	Average	17-23,000		198	Plymouth Voyager
Very Poor	Average	Regular	Average	20-24,000		204	Pontiac Trans Sport
Very Poor	Average	Regular	Hard	21-28,000		218	Toyota Sienna

[1]Due to the importance of crash tests, cars with no crash test results as of publication date cannot be given an overall rating.
[2]Based on 1997 prices.

Corporate Twins

"Corporate twin" is a term for similar cars sold under different names. In many cases, the cars are identical, such as the Dodge and Plymouth Neon. Sometimes the difference is in body style and luxury items, as with the Buick Regal and Pontiac Grand Prix. Generally, twins have the same mechanics, engine, drive train, size, weight, and internal workings. In addition to corporate twins, there are what we call "Asian cousins." These are Asian imports marketed under a U.S. name. In most cases, the main difference is the name plate and price; sometimes you will find differences in style.

Twins

Chrysler

Dodge Caravan
Plymouth Voyager

Chrysler Town & Country
Dodge Grand Caravan
Plymouth Grand Voyager

Chrysler Cirrus
Dodge Stratus
Plymouth Breeze

Chrysler Concorde
Dodge Intrepid

Chrysler Sebring
Dodge Avenger

Dodge Neon
Plymouth Neon

Volkswagen
VW Golf
VW Jetta

Toyota
Lexus ES 300
Toyota Camry

Nissan
Infiniti I30
Nissan Maxima

Ford

Ford Crown Victoria
Lincoln Town Car
Mercury Grand Marquis

Ford Escort
Mercury Tracer

Ford Taurus
Mercury Sable

Ford Contour
Mercury Mystique

General Motors

Buick Park Avenue
Buick Riviera
Cadillac Seville
Oldsmobile Aurora

Buick Century
Buick Regal
Oldsmobile Intrigue
Pontiac Grand Prix

Buick LeSabre
Oldsmobile 88
Pontiac Bonneville

Chevrolet Venture
Oldsmobile Silhouette
Pontiac Trans Sport

Chevrolet Astro
GMC Safari

Chevrolet Lumina
Chevrolet Monte Carlo

Chevrolet Camaro
Pontiac Firebird

Chevrolet Malibu
Oldsmobile Cutlass

Chevrolet Cavalier
Pontiac Sunfire

Oldsmobile Achieva
Pontiac Grand Am

Asian Cousins

Chevrolet Metro-*Suzuki Swift*
Chevrolet Prizm-*Toyota Corolla*
Chry. Sebring/Dodge Avenger-*Mitsubishi Galant*
Eagle Talon-*Mitsubishi Eclipse*
Honda Odyssey-*Isuzu Oasis*
Mercury Villager-*Nissan Quest*

SAFETY

For most of us, safety is one of the most important factors in choosing a new car, yet it is one of the most difficult items to evaluate. To provide the greatest possible protection, a car should have a variety of safety features including dual airbags, side airbags, safety belt adjusters and pretensioners, 4-wheel anti-lock brakes (ABS) and built-in child safety seats.

Another key factor in occupant protection is how well the car performs in a crash test. In order for you to easily use the government crash tests, we have analyzed the results and presented them in a easy-to-understand format. In the past, crash tests have measured protection in a frontal crash. The government is now testing the performance of cars in *side* crash tests. Where available, we have included these results on the following charts.

Also in this chapter, you'll find a review of the current safety features in this year's models including ABS and a state-by-state list of the safety belt and child restraint laws. We also provide a detailed look at an important, and often overlooked, safety feature—the child safety seat. Our section on children and airbags is a must-read for any parent.

Crash Test Program: In 1979, the U.S. Department of Transportation began a crash test program to compare the occupant protection of cars called the New Car Assessment Program. These crash tests show significant differences in how well various vehicles protect belted occupants in crashes.

In the frontal crash test, an automobile is sent forward into a concrete barrier at 35-mph, causing an impact similar to two identical cars crashing head on at 35-mph. The car contains electronically monitored dummies in the driver and passenger seats. This electronic data is analyzed to measure the impact of such a collision on a human being.

For the new side crash tests, a moving barrier is smashed into the vehicle on both sides at 38.5-mph. This test simulates a typical intersection collision between two vehicles. The dummies in the side crash tests are also electronically monitored and the data collected measures the impact on a human being.

Note that in both crash tests, the dummies are securely belted. Therefore, these test results do not apply to unbelted occupants.

To make it easy for you to use this important data to compare vehicles, we have analyzed and presented the results using our *Car Book Crash Test Index*. Using this Index, you can easily compare the crash test performance among vehicles.

It is best to compare the results within the same weight class, such as compacts to compacts. Do not compare cars with differing weights. For example, a subcompact that is rated "Good" may not be as safe as a large car with the same rating.

We rate the crash test results of each car relative to all of the cars ever crash tested to give you a better idea of the true top performers among the '98 models and identify those cars which have room for improvement.

The Car Book's crash test rating is intended to stimulate competition. You, the buyer, now know which are the best performers. Manufacturers who have chosen to build better performing cars will likely be rewarded with your decision to purchase their models.

1998 cars missing from this list have not been tested at the time of printing.

In This Chapter ...

Crash Tests: How the Cars Are Rated

A car's ability to protect you in a crash depends on its ability to absorb the force of impact rather than transfer it to the occupant. This is a function of the car's size, weight and, most importantly, design. Frontal and side crash tests measure the amount of crash forces transferred to the head, chest and legs of occupants in a 35-mph (frontal) or 38.5-mph (side) crash.

The table on the following pages indicate how this year's cars can be expected to perform in crash tests. They are listed by weight class, then alphabetically by manufacturer. We only included a vehicle if its design has not changed enough to dramatically alter previous results. Twins that are structurally the same, like the Dodge Caravan and Plymouth Voyager, can be expected to perform similarly.

The first column provides *The Car Book*'s overall Crash Test Index. This number represents all the forces measured by the test. Lower index numbers are better. The Index is best used to compare cars within the same size and weight class.

The second column provides an overall rating of *Very Good*, *Good*, *Average*, *Poor*, or *Very Poor*. These reflect the car's performance compared to all other models ever tested. The overall crash test ratings let you compare, at a glance, the performance of the cars you'll find in the showroom.

The next two columns indicate the likelihood of each occupant sustaining a life-threatening injury, based on the dummies' head and chest scores. Lower percentages mean a lower likelihood of being seriously injured. This information is taken directly from the government's analysis of the crash test results.

The last two columns indicate how the dummies' legs fared in the crash test. Legs labeled *Poor* did not meet the government's standards. Those that did meet the standards are rated *Moderate*, *Good*, and *Very Good*, reflecting performance relative to all other cars ever tested. The leg injury ratings are not weighted as heavily as the head and chest in determining overall performance.

Crash test results may vary due to differences in the way cars are manufactured, in how models are equipped, and in test conditions. There is no absolute guarantee that a car which passed the test will adequately protect you in an accident. Keep in mind that some two-door models may not perform exactly like their four-door counterparts.

Crash Tests: The Best

Here is a list of the best crash test performers among the 1998 cars for which crash test information is available. Lower Crash Test Index numbers indicate better performance. See the following tables for more results.

Front Tests

Subcompact
Honda Civic 4dr. (2113)
Honda Civic 2dr. (2344)
Saturn SL (2523)

Compact
Chrysler Sebring (1760)
Dodge Avenger (1760)
Oldsmobile Achieva 2dr. (2219)
Pontiac Grand Am 2dr. (2219)
Oldsmobile Achieva 4dr. (2233)
Pontiac Grand Am 4dr. (2233)
Subaru Legacy (2526)

Minivan
Ford Windstar (1671)
Mazda MPV (2405)

Intermediate
Chevrolet Camaro (1705)
Pontiac Firebird (1705)
Ford Mustang (1916)
Mazda Millenia (2085)
Toyota Avalon (2196)
Ford Taurus (2294)
Mercury Sable (2294)
Audi A4 (2385)

Large
Lincoln Mark VIII (1632)
Mercury Cougar (1632)
Ford Crown Victoria (1678)
Mercury Grand Marquis (1678)
Chevrolet Lumina (2173)
Cadillac DeVille (2515)

Side Tests

Compact
Ford Contour (1540)
Mercury Mystique (1540)

Large
Cadillac DeVille (1196)
Ford Crown Victoria (1485)
Mercury Grand Marquis (1485)

Crash Test Performance		Crash Test Index	Car Book Rating	Likelihood of Life Threatening Injury		Leg Injury Rating	
				Driver	Passenger	Driver	Passenger
Subcompact							
Chevrolet Metro	FRONT	3080	Good	15%	16%	Moderate	Good
Dodge/Plymouth Neon*	FRONT	3461	Average	19%	18%	Moderate	Good
Ford Escort*	FRONT	4389	Average	31%	18%	Moderate	Good
	SIDE	2734	Average	18%	14%	Moderate	Good
Honda Civic 2dr.*	FRONT	2344	Very Good	11%	12%	Good	Good
Honda Civic 4dr.*	FRONT	2113	Very Good	12%	10%	Good	Very Good
	SIDE	2557	Average	15%	14%	Moderate	Poor
Hyundai Accent	FRONT	3763	Average	30%	12%	Good	Good
Mazda Miata	FRONT	4053	Average	20%	23%	Good	Moderate
Mazda Protege	FRONT	—	—	29%	—	Very Good	Good
Mercury Tracer (Escort)*	FRONT	4389	Average	31%	18%	Moderate	Good
	SIDE	2734	Average	18%	14%	Moderate	Good
Nissan Sentra*	FRONT	2842	Good	16%	16%	Very Good	Good
Saturn SL/SW*	FRONT	2523	Very Good	13%	13%	Very Good	Good
	SIDE	3158	Average	18%	20%	Moderate	Good
Subaru Impreza	FRONT	2931	Good	15%	17%	Very Good	Good
Suzuki Swift (Metro)	FRONT	3080	Good	15%	16%	Moderate	Good
Toyota Paseo	FRONT	3099	Good	15%	19%	Good	Good
Toyota Tercel 2dr.	FRONT	3156	Good	15%	20%	Very Good	Good
	SIDE	2057	Good	15%	8%	Very Good	Very Good
Toyota Tercel 4dr.	FRONT	3705	Average	24%	17%	Good	Good
Compact							
Acura Integra	FRONT	3543	Average	16%	21%	Moderate	Good
BMW 3 Series	FRONT	3366	Good	19%	17%	Good	Good

Parentheses indicate actual model tested.
*A version of this vehicle is scheduled to be tested later this year. Results are expected to be similar.

HOW TO READ THE CHARTS:

1234 **Crash Test Index** is the overall numerical injury rating for front occupants in a frontal and side crash. *Lower numbers mean better performance.*

Very Good **Car Book Rating** shows how the vehicle compares among all cars tested to date. The range is very good, good, average, poor and very poor.

Note: Side crash ratings are included when available.

00% **Likelihood of Life Threatening Injury** is the chance that the occupants would be seriously injured in a frontal and side crash. *Lower percentages mean better performance.*

Good **Leg Injury Rating** indicates how well the occupants' legs would fare in a frontal and side crash among all cars tested to date.

Crash Test Performance		Crash Test Index	Car Book Rating	Likelihood of Life Threatening Injury		Leg Injury Rating	
				Driver	Passenger	Driver	Passenger
Compact (cont.)							
Chevrolet Cavalier 2dr.	*FRONT*	3295	Good	16%	20%	Good	Good
	SIDE	5496	Very Poor	49%	22%	Moderate	Good
Chevrolet Cavalier 4dr.*	*FRONT*	3264	Good	14%	21%	Good	Good
Chrysler Sebring (Avenger)	*FRONT*	1760	Very Good	9%	6%	Good	Moderate
Dodge Avenger	*FRONT*	1760	Very Good	9%	6%	Good	Moderate
Eagle Talon (Eclipse)*	*FRONT*	3013	Good	18%	13%	Good	Good
Ford Contour*	*FRONT*	2940	Good	10%	20%	Good	Good
	SIDE	1540	Very Good	11%	6%	Good	Good
Hyundai Elantra*	*FRONT*	4467	Average	21%	29%	Good	Moderate
Mercury Mystique (Contour)*	*FRONT*	2940	Good	10%	20%	Good	Good
	SIDE	1540	Very Good	11%	6%	Good	Good
Mitsubishi Eclipse*	*FRONT*	3013	Good	18%	13%	Good	Good
Mitsubishi Galant	*FRONT*	3050	Good	18%	14%	Moderate	Good
	SIDE	3420	Poor	16%	25%	Good	Good
Olds. Achieva (Gr. Am) 2dr.	*FRONT*	2219	Very Good	13%	9%	Good	Good
Olds. Achieva (Gr. Am) 4dr.	*FRONT*	2233	Very Good	10%	13%	Good	Good
	SIDE	4333	Very Poor	35%	19%	Good	Moderate
Pontiac Grand Am 2dr.	*FRONT*	2219	Very Good	13%	9%	Good	Good
Pontiac Grand Am 4dr.	*FRONT*	2233	Very Good	10%	13%	Good	Good
	SIDE	4333	Very Poor	35%	19%	Good	Moderate
Pontiac Sunfire (Cavalier) 2dr.	*FRONT*	3295	Good	16%	20%	Good	Good
	SIDE	5496	Very Poor	49%	22%	Moderate	Good
Pontiac Sunfire (Cavalier) 4dr.*	*FRONT*	3264	Good	14%	21%	Good	Good
Subaru Legacy*	*FRONT*	2526	Very Good	12%	15%	Good	Very Good

Parentheses indicate actual model tested.
*A version of this vehicle is scheduled to be tested later this year. Results are expected to be similar.

HOW TO READ THE CHARTS:

1234 **Crash Test Index** is the overall numerical injury rating for front occupants in a frontal and side crash. *Lower numbers mean better performance.*

Very Good **Car Book Rating** shows how the vehicle compares among all cars tested to date. The range is very good, good, average, poor and very poor.

00% **Likelihood of Life Threatening Injury** is the chance that the occupants would be seriously injured in a frontal and side crash. *Lower percentages mean better performance.*

Good **Leg Injury Rating** indicates how well the occupants' legs would fare in a frontal and side crash among all cars tested to date.

Note: Side crash ratings are included when available.

Crash Test Performance		Crash Test Index	Car Book Rating	Likelihood of Life Threatening Injury		Leg Injury Rating	
				Driver	Passenger	Driver	Passenger
Compact (cont.)							
Volkswagen Golf (Jetta)*	FRONT	3940	Average	21%	22%	Good	Good
Volkswagen Jetta*	FRONT	3940	Average	21%	22%	Good	Good
Intermediate							
Audi A4	FRONT	2385	Very Good	14%	9%	Good	Good
Buick Century (Grand Prix)*	FRONT	3193	Good	20%	14%	Good	Good
Buick Regal (Grand Prix)*	FRONT	3193	Good	20%	14%	Good	Good
Chevrolet Camaro	FRONT	1705	Very Good	8%	9%	Good	Very Good
	SIDE	2345	Good	17%	10%	Good	Moderate
Chrysler Cirrus (Stratus)*	FRONT	—	—	30%	—	Good	Good
	SIDE	3094	Average	12%	25%	Moderate	Good
Dodge Stratus*	FRONT	—	—	30%	—	Good	Good
	SIDE	3094	Average	12%	25%	Moderate	Good
Ford Mustang*	FRONT	2758	Good	12%	15%	Good	Good
Ford Mustang conv.	FRONT	1916	Very Good	9%	8%	Good	Good
Ford Taurus*	FRONT	2294	Very Good	11%	11%	Good	Good
	SIDE	2430	Good	11%	17%	Good	Good
Hyundai Sonata	FRONT	4034	Average	25%	20%	Moderate	Good
	SIDE	4235	Very Poor	29%	25%	Moderate	Good
Mazda Millenia	FRONT	2085	Very Good	11%	8%	Good	Good
Mercedes-Benz C-Class*	FRONT	3420	Good	19%	19%	Good	Good
Mercury Sable (Taurus)*	FRONT	2294	Very Good	11%	11%	Good	Good
	SIDE	2430	Good	11%	17%	Good	Good
Nissan 240SX	FRONT	3669	Average	28%	15%	Very Good	Very Good
Nissan Maxima*	FRONT	3741	Average	18%	25%	Good	Good
	SIDE	1857	Good	10%	11%	Good	Good
Olds. Cutlass (Malibu)	FRONT	2715	Good	17%	12%	Good	Good
	SIDE	3698	Poor	27%	18%	Moderate	Good
Olds. Intrigue (Grand Prix)*	FRONT	3193	Good	20%	14%	Good	Good
Plymouth Breeze (Stratus)	FRONT	—	—	30%	—	Good	Good
	SIDE	3094	Average	12%	25%	Moderate	Good
Pontiac Firebird (Camaro)	FRONT	1705	Very Good	8%	9%	Good	Very Good
	SIDE	2345	Good	17%	10%	Good	Moderate
Pontiac Grand Prix*	FRONT	3193	Good	20%	14%	Good	Good

Parentheses indicate actual model tested.
*A version of this vehicle is scheduled to be tested later this year. Results are expected to be similar.

Crash Test Performance		Crash Test Index	Car Book Rating	Likelihood of Life Threatening Injury		Leg Injury Rating	
				Driver	Passenger	Driver	Passenger
Intermediate (cont.)							
Saab 900	FRONT	2868	Good	15%	15%	Good	Good
Saab 9000	FRONT	2736	Good	12%	17%	Good	Very Good
Toyota Avalon*	FRONT	2196	Very Good	13%	11%	Very Good	Good
Toyota Camry*	FRONT	2853	Good	17%	14%	Good	Very Good
	SIDE	2344	Good	15%	12%	Good	Good
Large							
Acura TL	FRONT	3017	Good	17%	15%	Good	Very Good
Buick LeSabre*	FRONT	2673	Good	12%	15%	Good	Good
Buick Park Avenue (Aurora)	FRONT	4380	Average	23%	26%	Good	Good
Buick Riviera (Aurora)	FRONT	4380	Average	23%	26%	Good	Good
Cadillac DeVille	FRONT	2515	Very Good	14%	12%	Good	Good
	SIDE	1196	Very Good	6%	7%	Good	Good
Cadillac Seville	FRONT	4380	Average	23%	26%	Good	Good
Chevrolet Lumina*	FRONT	2173	Very Good	9%	13%	Good	Good
	SIDE	1793	Good	7%	13%	Very Good	Moderate
Chevrolet Malibu	FRONT	2715	Good	17%	12%	Good	Good
	SIDE	3698	Poor	27%	18%	Moderate	Good
Chevrolet Monte Carlo	FRONT	3049	Good	16%	17%	Good	Good
Chrysler LHS	FRONT	3107	Good	20%	13%	Good	Good
Ford Crown Victoria*	FRONT	1678	Very Good	8%	8%	Good	Good
	SIDE	1485	Very Good	9%	7%	Good	Good
Infiniti I30 (Maxima)	FRONT	3741	Average	18%	25%	Good	Good
	SIDE	1857	Good	10%	11%	Good	Good

Parentheses indicate actual model tested.
*A version of this vehicle is scheduled to be tested later this year. Results are expected to be similar.

HOW TO READ THE CHARTS:

1234 **Crash Test Index** is the overall numerical injury rating for front occupants in a frontal and side crash. *Lower numbers mean better performance.*

Very Good **Car Book Rating** shows how the vehicle compares among all cars tested to date. The range is very good, good, average, poor and very poor.

00% **Likelihood of Life Threatening Injury** is the chance that the occupants would be seriously injured in a frontal and side crash. *Lower percentages mean better performance.*

Good **Leg Injury Rating** indicates how well the occupants' legs would fare in a frontal and side crash among all cars tested to date.

Note: Side crash ratings are included when available.

Crash Test Performance		Crash Test Index	Car Book Rating	Likelihood of Life Threatening Injury		Leg Injury Rating	
				Driver	Passenger	Driver	Passenger
Large (cont.)							
Lexus ES300 (Camry)	FRONT	2853	Good	17%	14%	Good	Very Good
	SIDE	2344	Good	15%	12%	Good	Good
Lincoln Mark VIII	FRONT	1632	Very Good	8%	7%	Good	Good
Mercury Cougar	FRONT	1632	Very Good	8%	7%	Good	Good
	SIDE	4071	Poor	20%	30%	Poor	Very Good
Mercury Gr. Marq. (Cr. Vic.)*	FRONT	1678	Very Good	8%	8%	Good	Good
	SIDE	1485	Very Good	9%	7%	Good	Good
Oldsmobile 88 (LeSabre)	FRONT	2673	Good	12%	15%	Good	Good
Oldsmobile Aurora	FRONT	4380	Average	23%	26%	Good	Good
Pontiac Bonneville (LeSabre)*	FRONT	2673	Good	12%	15%	Good	Good
Minivan							
Chevrolet Astro	FRONT	5091	Poor	25%	34%	Moderate	Good
Chevrolet Venture*	FRONT	3227	Good	17%	17%	Moderate	Good
Chrys. T&C (Caravan)*	FRONT	2996	Good	20%	11%	Moderate	Good
Dodge Caravan*	FRONT	2996	Good	20%	11%	Moderate	Good
Ford Windstar*	FRONT	1671	Very Good	9%	7%	Good	Good
GMC Safari (Astro)	FRONT	5091	Poor	25%	34%	Moderate	Good
Honda Odyssey	FRONT	2889	Good	16%	15%	Good	Very Good
Isuzu Oasis (Odyssey)	FRONT	2889	Good	16%	15%	Good	Very Good
Mazda MPV	FRONT	2405	Very Good	13%	11%	Good	Good
Mercury Villager	FRONT	3248	Good	11%	22%	Good	Moderate
Nissan Quest (Villager)	FRONT	3248	Good	11%	22%	Good	Moderate
Olds. Silhouette (Venture)*	FRONT	3227	Good	17%	17%	Moderate	Good
Plymouth Voyager (Caravan)*	FRONT	2996	Good	20%	11%	Moderate	Good
Pontiac Tr. Sport (Venture)*	FRONT	3227	Good	17%	17%	Moderate	Good

Parentheses indicate actual model tested.
*A version of this vehicle is scheduled to be tested later this year. Results are expected to be similar.

Automatic Crash Protection

The concept of automatic protection is not new—automatic fire sprinklers in public buildings, automatic release of oxygen masks in airplanes, purification of drinking water, and pasteurization of milk are all commonly accepted forms of automatic safety protection. Ironically, of all the products we buy, the one most likely to kill us has only recently been equipped with automatic safety protection. In fact, we often incorporate better technology in safely transporting electronic equipment, eggs, and china than we do in packaging humans in automobiles.

Over twenty years ago, in cooperation with the federal government, the automobile industry developed two basic forms of automatic crash protection: airbags and automatic safety belts. These devices will not prevent all deaths, but they will cut in half your chances of being killed or seriously injured in a car accident.

The idea behind automatic crash protection is to protect people from what is called the "second collision" when the occupant comes forward and collides with the interior of their own car. Because the "second collision" occurs within milliseconds, and because so many people do not use seat belts, providing automatic rather than manual protection dramatically improves the chances of escaping injury.

Federal law now requires all new cars to be equipped with some form of automatic crash protection that will protect the driver and front seat passenger in a 30-mph frontal collision into a fixed barrier and a 33.5-mph side collision. To meet the standard, auto makers now opt for airbags and no longer use automatic belts.

Airbags: Hidden in the steering wheel hub and the right side of the dashboard, airbags provide unobtrusive and effective protection in frontal crashes. When needed, they inflate instantly to cushion the driver and the front seat passenger. By spreading crash forces over the head and chest, airbags protect the body from violent contact with the hard surfaces of the car. Cars with airbags also provide manual seat belts to protect occupants in nonfrontal crashes and to keep them in the best position to benefit from an airbag. However, airbags offer protection in frontal crashes even if the safety belt is not fastened.

Side airbags work the same way, except they come out of the doors in order to spread crash forces across the driver or passenger's legs, side and arms.

Should I Turn My Airbag Off? In short, no. Approximately, 2,500 people have been saved by airbags. In spite of the tragic stories you have no doubt heard, airbags save lives. If properly belted, an airbag will reduce your risk of a serious head injury by 75 percent!

Because of concern for their children's safety, parents may be considering turning off their airbag—a far better alternative is to keep your children in the back seat and keep the airbag ready to save a larger passenger.

De-Powered Airbags: In an effort to lower the number of improperly buckled children killed by airbag deployment, the government is allowing auto makers to de-power their airbags for new models. As a result, almost all the auto makers are de-powering their airbags on 1998 models, which has safety advocates concerned. Please be warned: de-powered airbags can still be fatal to out-of-position children (children who are not sitting upright and properly buckled in). Additionally, de-powering airbags lowers the amount of protection for adults. De-powering airbags, unfortunately, is weak solution to a serious problem.

Airbag Cutoff Switches: One option presently available is the airbag cutoff switch. The government will only allow a cutoff switch

A Note for Pregnant Women:

The American College of Obstetricians and Gynecologists strongly urges pregnant women to always wear a safety belt, including on the ride to the hospital to deliver the baby! In a car crash, the most serious risk to an unborn baby is that the mother may be injured. Obstetricians recommend that the lap and shoulder belts be used, with the lap belt as low as possible on the hips, under the baby.

When packing your things for the hospital, make sure you include an infant car safety seat to bring your baby home. As the American Academy of Pediatrics says, "Make the first ride a safe ride!"

in vehicles without a back seat like the F-Series and C/K Series Pickups. However, the cutoff switch has it's own danger—it only takes that one time to forget to turn the airbag back on when an adult sits in the seat for tragedy to occur.

Smart Airbags: The solution to airbag concerns lies with smart airbags. Mercedes-Benz already offers a special child seat system which, when installed in the passenger-side seat, has a sensor that emits an electronic signal to turn the airbag off. It will even inform you if you've installed the seat improperly. When the seat is removed, the airbag turns back on.

Most auto makers are developing smart airbag systems which will differentiate between an adult, a child, a rear-facing child seat or an empty seat, using various heat, ultrasonic sound wave and infrared sensors. Not only will smart airbags save lives, but by preventing the passenger-side airbag from deploying when the seat is empty, they will save thousands in repair costs. When will they be available? Probably not before the year 2000, but we hope the car companies will prove us wrong.

Consumers with questions about airbags often find dealers do not know the facts about these safety devices. Here are the correct answers to typical airbag questions from the Insurance Institute for Highway Safety:

Is the gas that inflates airbags dangerous? Nitrogen, which makes up 79.8 percent of the air we breathe, is the gas that inflates the bags. A solid chemical, sodium azide, generates this nitrogen gas. Sodium azide does not present a safety hazard in normal driving, in crashes, or in disposal. In fact, occupants of the car will never even come in contact with the sodium azide.

Will airbags inflate by mistake? Airbags will inflate only in frontal impacts equivalent to hitting a solid wall at about 10-mph or higher. They will not inflate when you go over bumps or potholes or when you hit something at low speed. Even slamming on your brakes will not cause the airbags to inflate unless you hit something.

In the unlikely event of an inadvertent airbag deployment, you would not lose control of the car. Airbags are designed to inflate and deflate in fractions of a second. GM tested driver reaction by inflating airbags without warning at speeds of up to 45-mph. GM reported that "without exception, the drivers retained control of the automobile."

Will airbag systems last very long? Airbags are reliable and require no maintenance. Only one part moves, the device that senses the impact, so there is nothing to wear out. They work throughout the life of the car although some manufacturers suggest inspections at anywhere from two to ten years.

In a study of 228 cars in which airbags were deployed, 40 had traveled more than 40,000 miles. One car had traveled almost 115,000 miles at the time of the crash. In every case, the airbags worked as they were designed to.

Are airbags reliable? According to the U.S. Department of Transportation, airbags have saved over 2,500 lives since they were introduced in the early 1980s. General Motors installed airbags in over 10,000 cars from 1974 to 1976. These cars traveled over 600 million miles, and the death and injury rate of the occupants was 50 percent lower than the rate for non-airbag cars. Studies of the operation of the airbags reported no cases of failure to deploy or malfunction of the inflator. This reliability rate (99.995 percent) is far higher than that of such safety features as brakes, tires, steering, and lights, which show failure rates of up to 10 percent.

Will airbags protect occupants without seat belts? Airbags are designed to protect unbelted front-seat *adult* in 30-mph frontal crashes into a wall. However, airbags are *not* designed to protect unbelted children or elderly. Equipping cars with airbags reduced the average injury severity for adults in serious frontal crashes by 64 percent, even though over 80 percent of the occupants were unbelted. The best protection, however, is provided by a combination of airbags and lap and shoulder safety belts. With airbags and seat belts, you'll be protected in the event of side impact and roll-over crashes, as well as in frontal crashes.

Airbag Deployment

In the fall of 1997, the Center for Auto Safety (CAS) revealed major differences in passenger-side airbag design which may affect their safety. The study found auto manufacturers generally chose one of two methods to deploy passenger-side airbags, vertically or horizontally. The horizontally deploying airbags shoot straight out of the dashboard toward the passenger. Vertically deploying airbags move upward towards the windshield and reflect off the windshield towards the passenger. According to CAS, all passenger-side airbag deaths have been from horizontally deploying airbags and there have been no deaths from vertically deploying airbags. It appears that vertically deploying airbags may be more effective.

Based on data collected by CAS and responses received from auto companies, we have listed below those manufacturers who have chosen to use vertically deploying airbags. Some models may be missing due to lack of information available — the government presently does not require auto companies to disclose this information.

It is our hope that with the implementation of smart airbags, the information presented here will become obsolete. Please note that while no deaths have occurred due to vertically deploying airbags, you still must keep your children in the back seat, even with a vertically deploying passenger-side airbag. And whoever does sit up front, *always* buckle up and sit back.

Vertically Deploying Passenger Side Airbags

Acura CL
Acura Integra
Acura RL
Acura TL
BMW 3 Series
BMW 5 Series
BMW Z3
Buick Riviera
Chevrolet Cavalier
Chevrolet Malibu
Ford Taurus
Honda Accord
Honda Civic
Honda Odyssey
Honda Prelude
Lexus ES300
Lexus GS300/400
Lexus LS400
Lexus SC300/400
Mercedes-Benz C-Class
Mercedes-Benz E-Class
Mercury Sable
Nissan 240SX
Nissan Sentra
Oldsmobile Aurora
Oldsmobile Cutlass
Pontiac Sunfire
Saab 900
Subaru Impreza
Subaru Legacy
Toyota Camry
Toyota Celica
Toyota Sienna
Toyota Tercel
Volvo C70/S70/V70
Volvo S90/V90

Saved by the Airbag

Do airbags save lives? Here is how Kathleen Jones Carlisle of Blacksburg, VA, and one of over 2,500 people who've been saved by airbags, described her experience:

"On Wednesday, August 21, 1996, while traveling at approximately 55 mph, another car swerved into my lane. I braced for impact, closed by eyes and prayed. Immediately upon impact my seat belt pinned me tightly to my seat and my airbag exploded. I slowly opened my eyes. I couldn't believe I was alive. I could not move, but I was able to carefully glance around to see I was in one piece. My red 1991 Mercury Capri sustained a head-on collision and I was alive to tell the world. I later learned the driver of the car who hit me died horribly at the scene. He wasn't wearing his seat belt, nor did he have an airbag."

Kathleen is a member of Advocates for Highway and Auto Safety's "Saved by the Airbag" group. If you or someone you know has been protected from death and/or serious injury by an airbag, please call Cathy Hickey at 1-800-659-BAGS (2247) to find out how you can help promote the lifesaving benefits of airbags.

Children and Airbags

Will airbags protect children? Studies of actual crashes indicate that children can be protected by airbags—but only if they are properly buckled up! A deploying airbag can be deadly to an unrestrained child. Properly buckling your child has never been more important now that virtually all cars and minivans, and most trucks and sport utilities, offer airbags on the passenger's side where children often sit.

According to government estimates, airbags have saved the lives of approximately 2,500 people. However, to date, 55 children under the age of 9 have been killed by the deployment of an airbag. The National Highway Traffic Safety Administration estimates about one child per month is killed by airbag deployment and, if certain measures are not implemented, the number could increase to one per week.

Remember—*most children killed by airbags are not properly belted.* The majority of the children killed were either completely unrestrained or improperly restrained. To protect the occupant, an airbag must inflate in a fraction of a second before the occupant hits the dashboard. For an full-size adult, the result is coming forward into a cushion of air. For a child who isn't properly buckled, it can be deadly, especially if the child is standing up or leaning on the dashboard.

How to Best Protect Your Child (and Yourself)

Never place a rear-facing child seat in front of a passenger side airbag. The best spot for your children is in the center of the back seat. If you do not have a back seat, here are some tips for keeping your child (and yourself) safe while seated in an airbag seat:

- ☑ Push the seat as far back as it will go.
- ☑ Make sure your child is sitting up straight and not leaning forward against the dash.
- ☑ If you are an adult, sit at least 10-12 inches away from the steering wheel. In the passenger side, slide the seat back as far as it will go.
- ☑ Do not let your child play with any sharp objects like toys or lollipops. A sudden stop and the pop could be forced down the child's throat or a severe cut could result from a toy.

For tips on how to use a child seat and how to properly buckle up your child, see pages 34-40.

Young Drivers

Each year, teenagers accounted for about 14 percent of highway deaths. According to the Insurance Institute for Highway Safety (IIHS), the highest driver death rate per 100,000 people is among 18 year olds. Clearly, parents need to make sure their children are fully prepared to be competent, safe drivers before letting them out on the road. All states, except Conneticut and New Hampshire, issue learner's permits. However, only 29 states and the District of Columbia *require* permits before getting a driver's license. It isn't difficult for teenagers to get a license and only nine states prohibit teenagers from driving during night and early morning. Call your MVA for your state's young driver laws.

Anti-Lock Brakes

After airbags, one of the best safety features available is an anti-lock braking system (ABS). ABS shortens stopping distance on dry, wet, and even icy roads by preventing wheel lock-up and keeps you from skidding out of control when you "slam" on the brakes.

The ABS works by sensing the speed of each wheel. If one or more of the wheels begins to lock up or skid, it releases that wheel's brakes, allowing the wheel to roll normally again, thus stopping the skid. When the wheel stops skidding, the hydraulic pressure is reapplied instantly. This cycle can be repeated several times per second, keeping each wheel at its optimum braking performance even while your foot keeps pushing on the brake pedal. Although ABS is typically connected to all four wheels, in some light trucks and vans it is connected to only the rear wheels.

The ABS is only active when it senses that the wheels are about to lock up. When an ABS is active, you may notice that the brake pedal pulsates slightly. This pulsation is normal, and it indicates that the brakes are being released and reapplied. *Don't pump your brakes*—the ABS is doing it for you. If there is a failure in the ABS, the vehicle reverts to its conventional braking system and a warning light indicates that the ABS needs repair.

Note: Using tires other than the ones originally on the vehicle may affect the anti-lock braking system. If you are planning to change the size of the tires on your vehicle, first consult your owner's manual.

You'll find ABS on all 1998 models, but mostly as an option.

Don't Buy Add-On ABS Brakes

Adding "so-called" ABS brakes to your car can be dangerous. These products use a variety of deceptive names that incorporate the letters ABS, such as ABS-Trax (Automotive Breakthrough Science—the company's name) and Brake-Guard ABS (Advanced Braking System). These add-on systems "have virtually no effect on stopping distances, vehicle stability or control," according to government tests. You should *not* purchase or install these systems. Only *electronic* ABS systems are capable of preventing wheel skid in panic braking situations. Currently, true electronic anti-lock brakes are only available as factory installed systems.

What Happens in a Collision

A car crash typically involves two collisions. First, the car hits another object and second, the occupant collides with the inside of the car. Injuries result from this *second collision.* The key to surviving an auto accident is protecting yourself from the second collision. Always wearing your safety belt is the most important defense while having an airbag is a very close second. The whole purpose of the airbag is to protect you in this second collision.

Upon impact, in a typical 35-mph crash, the car begins to crush and slow down. Within 1/10 of a second, the car comes to a stop, but the person keeps moving forward at 35-mph. 1/50 of a second after the car has stopped, the unbelted person slams into the dashboard or windshield.

According to government reports prepared before the widespread use of belts and airbags, these were the major causes of injury in the *second collision:*

Steering wheel	27%
Instrument panel	11%
Side (doors)	10%
Windshield	5%
Front roof pillar	4%
Glove box area	3%
Roof edges	3%
Roof	2%

About 60 percent of occupants killed or injured in auto crashes would have been saved from serious harm had they been wearing safety belts. Yet many Americans do not use these life-saving devices.

Safety belts are particularly important in minivans, 4x4s and pickups because there is a greater chance of being killed or seriously injured in a rollover accident. The simple precaution of wearing your belt greatly improves your odds of survival.

Why don't people wear their belts? They simply don't know the facts. Once you know the facts, you should be willing to buckle up.

While most safety advocates welcome the passage of safety belt usage laws, the ones passed to date are weak and generally unenforced. In addition, most of the laws are based on "secondary" enforcement—meaning that you cannot be stopped for failing to wear your belt. If you are stopped for another reason and the officer notices you don't have your belt on by the time he or she reaches the vehicle, you may be fined. In states with "primary" enforcement, you can be stopped for not wearing a safety belt. Yet, in many cases the fines are less than a parking ticket. In Arkansas, however, you can get a $10 credit toward a primary violation if you are wearing a seat belt and in Wyoming, a $5 credit.

Another unusual feature of these laws is that most of them allow drivers to avoid buckling up if they have a doctor's permission. This loophole was inserted to appease those who were not really in favor of the law. However, many doctors are wondering if they will be held responsible for the injuries of unbuckled patients. In fact, the State of New York Medical Society cautions doctors never to give medical dispensation from the law because "no medical condition has yet been found to warrant a medical exemption for seat belt use."

Even though most state laws are weak, they have heightened awareness and raised the level of usage. Belt use in states that have passed a safety belt law tends to rise sharply after the law is enacted. However, after the law has been on the books a few months, safety belt use drops.

The tables on the following pages describe the current safety belt laws. In some cases, the driver is responsible for all or some of the passengers as noted; otherwise, occupants are responsible for themselves. All states are listed, even those that do not yet have safety belt laws. We hope that the blank following New Hampshire will soon be filled with new laws.

Safety Belt Myths and Facts

Myth: *"I don't want to be trapped by a seat belt. It's better to be thrown free in an accident."*

Fact: The chance of being killed is 25 times greater if you're ejected. A safety belt will keep you from plunging through the windshield, smashing into trees, rocks, or other cars, scraping along the ground, or getting run over by your own or another's vehicle. If you are wearing your belt, you're far more likely to be conscious after an accident to free yourself and other passengers.

Myth: *"Pregnant women should not wear safety belts."*

Fact: According to the American Medical Association, "Both the pregnant mother and the fetus are safer, provided the lap belt is worn as low on the pelvis as possible."

Myth: *"I don't need it. In case of an accident, I can brace myself with my hands."*

Fact: At 35 mph, the impact of a crash on you and your passengers is brutal. There's no way your arms and legs can brace you against that kind of collision; the speed and force are just too great. The force of impact at only 10 mph is roughly equivalent to the force of catching a 200-pound bag of cement dropped from a first floor window.

Myth: *"I just don't bellieve it will ever happen to me."*

Fact: Every one of us can expect to be in a crash once every 10 years. For one out of 20 of us, it will be a serious crash. For one out of 60 born today, it will be fatal.

Safety Belt Laws

	Law Applies To:	Driver Fined For:	Enforcement	Max. Fine 1st Offense
Alabama	Front seat only	6 year olds and up	Secondary	$25
Alaska*	All occupants	16 year olds and up	Secondary	$15
Arizona	Front seat only	5 year olds and up	Secondary	$10
Arkansas	Front seat only	5 year olds and up	Secondary	$25[1]
California*	All occupants	16 year olds and up	Primary	$202
Colorado	Front seat only	4 year olds and up	Secondary	$15
Connecticut	Front seat only	4 year olds and up	Primary	$15
Delaware	Front seat only	All occupants	Secondary	$240
Dist. of Columbia	All occupants	All occupants	Primary	$50**
Florida	Front seat only	6 year olds and up	Secondary	$25
Georgia	All occupants	4 to 17 year olds	Primary	$15[2]
Hawaii	Front seat only	4 year olds and up	Primary	$20
Idaho	Front seat only	4 year olds and up	Secondary	$5
Illinois	Front seat only	6 year olds and up	Secondary	$25
Indiana	Front seat only	5 year olds and up	Secondary	$25
Iowa	Front seat only	6 year olds and up	Primary	$10
Kansas	Front seat only	14 year olds and up	Secondary	$10
Kentucky*	All occupants	Over 40 inches	Secondary	$25
Louisiana	Front seat only	13 year olds and up	Primary	$25[1]
Maine	All occupants	Over 4 years old	Secondary	$50
Maryland	Front seat only	16 year olds and up	Primary	$25
Massachusetts*	All occupants	12 year olds and up	Secondary	$25
Michigan	All occupants	4 to 15 year olds	Secondary	$25
Minnesota	All occupants	3 to 10 year olds[3]	Secondary	$25
Mississippi	Front seat only	4 year olds and up	Secondary	$25
Missouri	Front seat only	4 year olds and ups	Secondary	$10

* In these states driver can be held liable in court for *all* passengers.
**Driver gets 2 points on license.
See next page for footnotes.

Safety Belt Laws

	Law Applies To:	Driver Fined For:	Enforcement	Max. Fine 1st Offense
Montana*	All occupants	4 years old and up	Secondary	$20
Nebraska	Front seat	5 year olds and up	Secondary	$25
Nevada*	All occupants	5 year olds and up	Secondary	$25
New Hampshire	No law			
New Jersey	Front seat only	5 year olds and up	Secondary	$20
New Mexico	Front seat only	11 year olds and up	Primary	$25
New York	Front seat[4]	16 year olds and up	Primary	$50
North Carolina	Front seat only	12 year olds and up	Primary	$25
North Dakota	Front seat	3 year olds and up	Secondary	$20
Ohio	Front seat only	4 year olds and up	Secondary	$25[7]
Oklahoma	Front seat only	All occupants	Primary	$20
Oregon*	All Occupants	16 year olds and up	Primary	$50
Pennsylvania	Front seat only	4 year olds and up	Secondary	$10
Rhode Island*	All Occupants	13 year olds and up	Secondary	None
South Carolina	All Occupants[5]	6 year olds and up	Secondary	$10
South Dakota	Front seat	5 year olds and up	Secondary	$20
Tennessee	Front seat only	13 year olds and up	Secondary	$50
Texas	Front seat only	4 year olds and up	Primary	$50
Utah	Front seat only	10 year olds and up	Secondary	$10
Vermont*	All occupants	13 year olds and up	Secondary	$10
Virginia	Front seat only	16 year olds and up	Secondary	$25
Washington*	All occupants	All occupants	Secondary	$66
West Virginia	Front seat[6]	9 year olds and up	Secondary	$25
Wisconsin	All occupants[5]	4 year olds and up	Secondary	$10
Wyoming	Front seat only	3 year olds and up	Secondary	None[1]

* In these states driver can be held liable in court for *all* passengers.
1 In Arkansas, reward for buckling up is a $10 reduction in primary violation fine; in Wyoming, a $5 reduction. In Louisiana, 10% reduction in fine for moving violation.
2 $25 fine if driver is a minor. In Georgia, driver is responsible for 18 year olds and those in front seat.
3 Parent driver is responsible for all occupants in front seat.
4 Driver responsible for 4 to 10 year olds riding in rear seat.
5 Covers rear seat occupants where shoulder belts are available.
6 Driver responsible for occupants 9 to 17 years old in rear seat.
7 $15 passenger fine.

Child Safety Seats

How many times have you gone out of your way to prevent your children from being injured by keeping household poisons out of reach, watching carefully as they swam, or keeping a good grip on their hand while crossing a street or parking lot? Probably quite often. Yet, parents ignore the biggest danger of all when they allow their children to lay down in the back of a minivan or roam unrestrained in their car. Ironically, it's your automobile that poses the greatest threat to your child's health.

Child safety seats are the best and only reliable way to protect your child in a vehicle. Automobiles crashes remain the leading cause of death in children over one year old. Sadly, over 100,000 children are injured unnecessarily each year. Research on the effectiveness of child safety seats has found that they reduce the risk of fatal injury by 69% for infants (less than one year old) and by 47% for toddlers (1-4 years old) if used correctly.

Never place a child in your lap. At 30 mph, a crash or sudden stop will wrench a ten pound child from your arms with a force of nearly 300 pounds! If you aren't wearing a seat belt, then your own body will be thrown forward with enough force to crush your child against the dashboard or the back of the front seat.

Hand-Me-Down Seats: To insure that a secondhand child seat will adequately protect your child, see if its identification stickers, belt instructions and date of manufacture are still visible. Only use seats less than 5 years old. Make sure no parts or instructions are missing. Most importantly, know the history of the child seat—never use seats that have been in crashes, no matter how perfect they look.

Buying Tips: Purchasing a new child seat for your child is always money well spent. Many vehicles now have built-in child seats which are an excellent option. Child seats with an automatic retracting harness and a shield are typically the easiest to use. Here are some additional tips when shopping for a child safety seat:

☑ Try before you buy. Your car's seat belts and the shape of its seats will determine which child seats fit your car so make sure it can be properly installed.

☑ Determine how many straps or buckles must be fastened to use a child seat. The less complicated the seat, the less chance for misuse. The easiest seats require only one strap or buckle after fastening the seat belt around the child seat.

☑ Make sure the seat is wide enough for growth and bulky winter clothes. If possible, let your child sit in the seat to measure for fit.

☑ Is your child comfortable? Can your child move his or her arms freely, sleep in the seat, or see out a window?

Locking Clips

Locking clips come with most child safety seats and are needed if the latch plate on the car's seat belt slides freely along the belt. If you don't properly install the locking clip, the child seat can move or tip over. Look for *heavy-duty locking clips*, available at Ford, Toyota and Nissan dealers. The safest way to use a heavy-duty locking clip is to pull the seat belt entirely out and attach the clip so the child seat is secure with no retracting involved. For more information, contact Safety Belt Safe at 800-745-SAFE.

Register Your Child Seat

Last year, the U.S. Department of Transportation recalled millions of child safety seats for serious safety defects. Tragically, most parents never heard about these recalls and the majority of these problem seats are still being used. You can do two things to protect your children—first, call the Auto Safety Hotline at 800-424-9393 and find out if your seat has been recalled. If so, they will tell you how to contact the manufacturer for a resolution. Second, make sure you fill out the registration card that must come with all new seats. This will enable the company to contact you should there be a recall. If you currently own a seat, ask the Hotline for the address of your seat's manufacturer and send them your name, address and seat model, asking them to keep it on file for recall notices.

Child Safety Seat Types

There are six types of child seats: *infant-only, convertible, toddler-only, child/booster, booster* and *built-in*.

Infant-Only Seats: Infant-only seats can be used from birth until your baby reaches a weight of 17-20 pounds. This type of seat must be installed facing the rear in a semi-reclined position. In a collision, the crash forces are spread over the baby's back, the strongest body surface. The seat's harness should come from below the child's shoulders in the rear-facing position.

One benefit of an infant-only seat is that you can easily install and remove the seat with the baby in place. Most infant car seats can also be used as household baby seats. Caution: Some household baby seats look remarkably similar to infant safety seats. These are not crash worthy and should *never* be used as car safety seats.

Convertible Seats: Buying a convertible seat can save you the expense of buying both an infant and a toddler seat. Most convertible seats can be used from birth until the child reaches four years and 40 pounds. When used for an infant, the seat faces rearward in a semi-reclined position. When the child is at least a year old and 20 pounds or more, the frame can be adjusted upright and the seat turned to face forward.

As with any safety seat, it is extremely important that the straps fit snugly over the child's shoulders. A good way to ensure that the straps are adjusted correctly is to buy a seat with an automatically adjusting harness. Like a car safety belt, these models automatically adjust to fit snugly on your child.

Convertible seats come in three basic types:

The *five-point harness* consists of two shoulder and two lap straps that converge at a buckle connected to a crotch strap. These straps are adjustable, allowing for growth and comfort.

The *T-shield* has a small pad joining the shoulder belts. With only one buckle, many parents find this the simplest and easiest-to-use type of convertible seat; but, it will not fit newborns properly.

The *tray shield* is another convenient model, since the safety harness is attached to the shield. As the shield comes down in front of the child, the harness comes over the child's shoulders. The shield is an important part of the restraint system, but like the T-shield, it will not fit small infants.

Toddler-Only Seats: These are really booster child seats and they may take the place of convertible seats when a child is between 20 and 30 pounds. Weight and size limits vary greatly among seats.

Child/Booster Seats: Some manufacturers are now making a variety of combination child/booster seats. For example, one model can be converted from a 5-point harness to a high-backed, belt-positioning booster seat. They can be used for children ranging from 20 to 40 pounds, making them a very economical choice.

Booster Seats: Booster seats are used when your child is too big for a convertible seat, but too small to use safety belts. Most car lap/shoulder belts do not adequately fit children with a seating height less than 28". Booster seats can be used for children over 30 pounds and come in three types:

Belt-positioning booster seats raise the child for a better fit with the car's safety belts. If your child is under 3 years old, do not use belt-positioning booster seats because your child may be able to unbuckle him or herself.

The *removable-shield booster seat* can be used with a lap/shoulder belt with the shield removed, or with a lap belt with the shield on. This seat can be adapted to different cars and seating positions, making it a good choice.

The *shield-type booster seat* has a small plastic shield with no straps and can be used only with lap belts. Typically, the safety belt fastens in front of the shield, anchoring it to the car. Most safety experts recommend using these seats until a child is 4 years old and 40 pounds.

Built-in Seats: Chrysler, Ford, GM, Volvo and other auto companies offer the option of a fold-out toddler seat on some of their models. These seats are only for children older than one and come as either a five-point harness or a booster with 3-point belt; however, the 3-point booster is not recommended for children under 3 years old. This built-in seat is an excellent feature because it is always in the car and does not pose the problem of compatability that often occurs with separate child seats.

Name of Seat	Price	Comments
Infant Safety Seats		
Century Assura 565 Series	$29-39	3-pt.; up to 20 lbs., correct recline indicator
Century Assura Premiere	$49-59	3-pt.; separate base stays in car; can be used without base; correct recline indicator
Cosco Arriva	$35-55	3-pt.; up to 22 lbs.; detachable base with some models
Cosco Dream Ride Plus	$59	3-pt.; up to 17-20 lbs. (depending on mfg date); use as car seat rear facing; converts to swing
Cosco TLC	$20-25	3-pt.
Evenflo Joy Ride	$25-45	3-pt.; harness adjuster located in compartment behind seat.
Evenflo On My Way	$55-65	3-pt.; detachable base; can use without base
Evenflo Travel Tandem	$45-55	3-pt.; separate base stays in car; can be used without base; harness adjuster behind seat.
Gerry Guard with Glide	$50-55	3-pt.; use as glider in house; must be converted to in-car position
Gerry Secure Ride	$40	3-pt.; tilt-indicator
Kolcraft Travel About	$60-70	3-pt.; detachable base; can use without base
Kolcraft Infant Rider	$50-60	3-pt.
Kolcraft Rock 'N Ride	$30-35	3-pt.; no harness height adjustment
Convertible Safety Seats		
Babyhood Baby Sitter	$89-99	5-pt.
Century 1000 STE, 1500 Prestige	$49-75	5-pt.; adjustable crotch strap positions
Century 2000 STE, 2500 Prestige	$59-85	T-shield; adjustable crotch strap positions
Century 3000 STE, 3500 Prestige	$69-89	Tray shield; 5-position adjustable shield
Century Smart Move	$109-139	5-pt./ Tray shield; adjustable shield grows with child
Cosco Regal Ride	$65-85	5-pt./ T-shield/ Tray shield; use rear-facing up to 22 lbs.
Cosco Touriva 5-pt.	$40-60	5-pt./ T-Shield/ Tray shield; use rear facing up to 22 lbs.
Early Development Guardian Comfort	$80-100	5-pt./ T-shield/ Tray shield; harness designed like vehicle seat belts; lock upon impact.

Based on data collected by the American Academy of Pediatrics.

Name of Seat	Price	Comments
Convertible Seats (cont.)		
Evenflo Champion	$50-70	Tray shield; optional tether available
Evenflo Scout	$39-60	5-pt./ T-shield; optional tether available
Evenflo Trooper	$60-70	5-pt./ Tray shield; adjustable shield; optional tether available
Evenflo Ultara I	$80-100	Tray shield; adjustable shield; optional tether available
Evenflo Ultara V	$80-100	5-pt.; optional tether available
Gerry One-Click	$80-90	Tray shield; automatic harness adjustment; optional tether available
Gerry Pro-Tech	$60-65	5-pt.; optional tether available
Kolcraft Auto-Mate	$50-60	5-pt.; requires 2-handed operation
Safeline Sit 'N Stroll	$159-169	5-pt.; converts to stroller
Toddler-Only Vests and Built-In Seats		
Chrysler Built-In Seat	$100-200	5-pt. (20-65 lbs.); 2 built in option in minivans; one seat available in most sedans
E-Z-On Vest	$74-90	4-pt. (25+ lbs.); tether strap must be installed in vehicle
Ford Built-In	$135-240	5-pt. (20-60 lbs.); two seats optional in minivans; one seat optional in Explorer, Escort, and Tracer
GM Built-In	N/A	5-pt. (20-40 lbs., Booster 40-60 lbs.); seats optional in minivans and some sedans.
Little Cargo Travel Vest	$39-49	5-pt. (25-40 lbs.); simplified strap-buckle system; auto lap belt attached through padded stress plate
Booster		
Century Breverra Classic	$49-59	High-backed; use 5-point shield with lap belt only; remove shield when using vehicle lap/shoulder belt
Cosco Grand Explorer/Adventurer	$20-35	Must use shield if vehicle has lap belts only; use as a belt-positioning booster with lap/shoulder belt
Evenflo Sidekick	$20-30	Must use shield if vehicle has lap belts only; use as a belt-positioning booster with lap/shoulder belt
Gerry Evolution	$54-60	High-backed; optional tether available

Based on data collected by the American Academy of Pediatrics.

Tips for Using Your Child Safety Seat

The incorrect use of child safety seats has reached epidemic proportions. A stunning 95% of parents misuse their child's safety seat. Problems fall into two categories: incorrect installation of the seat and incorrect use of the seat's straps to secure the child. In most cases, the car's safety belt was improperly routed through the seat.

Incorrect use of a child safety seat prevents lifesaving protection and may even contribute to further injury. In addition to following your seat's installation instructions, here are some important usage tips:

☑ The safest place for the seat is the center of the back seat.

☑ Use a locking clip when needed. Check the instructions that come with your seat and those in your car owner's manual.

☑ Keep your child rear-facing for at least a year.

☑ Regularly check the seat's safety harness and the car's seat belt for a tight, secure fit because the straps will stretch on impact.

☑ Don't leave sharp or heavy objects or groceries loose in the car. Anything loose can be deadly in a crash.

☑ In the winter, dress your baby in a legged suit to allow proper attachment of the harness. If necessary, drape an extra blanket over the seat after your baby is buckled.

☑ Be sure all doors are locked.

☑ Do not give your child lollipops or ice cream on a stick while riding. A bump or swerve could jam the stick into his or her throat.

Seat Belts for Kids: How long should children use car seats? For school age children, a car seat is *twice* as effective in preventing injury than an adult lap and shoulder harness — use a booster as long as possible. Most children can start using seat belts at 65 pounds and when tall enough for the shoulder belt to cross the chest, not the neck. The lap section of the belt should be snug and as low on the hips as possible. If the shoulder belt does cross the face or neck, use a booster.

Never:

☒ Use the same belt on two children.

☒ Move a shoulder belt behind a child's back or under an arm.

☒ Buckle in a pet or any large toys with the child.

☒ Recline a seat with a belted child.

☒ Use a twisted seat belt. The belt must be straight and flat.

☒ Use pillows or cushions to boost your child.

☒ Place a belt around you with a child in your lap. In an accident or sudden stop, your child would absorb most of the crash force.

Buckled Up = Better Behavior

Medical researchers have concluded that belted children are better behaved. When not buckled up, children squirm, stand up, complain, fight, and pull at the steering wheel. When buckled into safety seats, however, they displayed 95 percent fewer incidents of bad behavior.

When buckled up, children feel secure. In addition, being in a seat can be more fun because most safety seats are high enough to allow children to see out the window. Also, children are less likely to feel carsick and more likely to fall asleep in a car seat.

Make the car seat your child's own special place, so he or she will enjoy being in it. Pick out some special soft toys or books that can be used only in the car seat to make using the seat a positive experience.

Set a good example for your child by using your own safety belt every time you get in the car.

Rear-Facing Child Safety Seats

Never use a rear-facing child safety seat in a seating position that has an airbag. To deploy fast enough to protect adult occupants, an airbag inflates with enough force to potentially cause serious head and chest injuries to a child in a rear-facing safety seat. And remember, airbags do not take the place of child safety seats.

Child Restraint Laws

Every state now requires children to be in safety seats or buckled up when riding in automobiles. The following table provides an overview of the requirements and penalties in each state. Note that most states use the child's age to define the law, although some states have height or weight requirements as well. Also, in most states, the laws are not limited to children riding with their parents, but require that any driver with child passengers makes sure those children are buckled up.

	Law Applies To:	Children Covered Through:	Max. Fine 1st Offense	Safety Belt OK:
Alabama	Resident drivers	5 yrs.	$10	4-5 yrs.
Alaska	All drivers	15 yrs.	$50	4-15 yrs.
Arizona	All drivers	4 yrs.	$50	No
Arkansas	Resident drivers	4 yrs. or 40 lbs.	$100	4 yrs.
California	All drivers	15 yrs.	$100	4-15 yrs.[5]
Colorado	All drivers	15 yrs.	$56	4-15 yrs., <40 lbs.
Connecticut	All drivers	15 yrs. or 40 lbs.	$90	4-15 yrs., <40 lbs.
Delaware	All drivers	15 yrs.	$29	4-15 yrs.
Dist. of Columbia	All drivers	16 yrs.	$55	4-16 yrs.
Florida	All drivers	5 yrs.	$60	4-5 yrs.
Georgia	All drivers	4 yrs.	$50	3-4 yrs.
Hawaii	All drivers	3 yrs.	$200	3 yrs. only
Idaho	All drivers	3 yrs. or 40 lbs.	$52	No
Illinois	All drivers	5 yrs.	$25	4-5 yrs.
Indiana	Resident drivers	4 yrs.	$500	3-4 yrs.
Iowa	Resident drivers	5 yrs.	$10	3-5 yrs.
Kansas	All drivers	13 yrs.	$20	4-13 yrs.
Kentucky	All drivers	Under 40 inches	$50	No
Louisiana	Resident drivers	4 yrs.	$50	3-4 yrs. in rear
Maine	All drivers	18 yrs.	$55	4-18 yrs.
Maryland	All drivers	15 yrs.	$25	4-15 yrs., <40 lbs.
Massachusetts	All drivers	11 yrs.	$25	5-11 yrs.
Michigan	All drivers	3 yrs.	$10	1-3 yrs. in rear
Minnesota	All drivers	3 yrs.	$50	No
Mississippi	Resident drivers	3 yrs.	$25	No

Child Restraint Laws

	Law Applies To:	Children Covered Through:	Max. Fine 1st Offense	Safety Belt OK:
Missouri	All drivers	3 yrs.	$25	No
Montana	Resident drivers[1]	3 yrs. or 40 lbs.	$25	2-3 yrs.
Nebraska	Resident drivers	4 yrs.	$25	4 yrs., <40 lbs.
Nevada	All drivers	4 yrs. or 40 lbs.	$100	No
New Hampshire	All drivers	17 yrs.	$25	4-17 yrs.
New Jersey	All drivers	4 yrs.	$25	1/2-4 yrs. in rear
New Mexico	All drivers	10 yrs.	$25	1-4 yrs. in rear[2]
New York	All drivers	15 yrs.[3]	$100	4-9 yrs. in rear[2]
North Carolina	All drivers	11 yrs.	$25	4-11 yrs.
North Dakota	All drivers	10 yrs.	$20	3-10 yrs.
Ohio	Resident drivers	3 yrs. or <40 lbs.	$100	No
Oklahoma	Resident drivers	5 yrs.	$25	4-5 yrs.
Oregon	All drivers	15 yrs. or >40 lbs.	$50	4-15 yrs.
Pennsylvania	All drivers	3 yrs.	$25	No
Rhode Island	All drivers	12 yrs.	$30	3-12 yrs.[4]
South Carolina	Resident drivers	5 yrs.	$25	1-5 yrs. in rear[5]
South Dakota	All drivers	4 yrs.	$20	2-4 yrs.
Tennessee	All drivers	12 yrs.	$50	4-12 yrs.
Texas	All drivers	3 yrs.	$50	2-3 yrs.
Utah	All drivers	9 yrs.	$75	2-9 yrs.
Vermont	All drivers	12 yrs.	$25	5-12 yrs.
Virginia	All drivers	3 yrs.	$50	4-15 yrs.
Washington	All drivers	9 yrs.	$47	3-9 yrs.
West Virginia	All drivers	8 yrs.	$20	3-8 yrs.
Wisconsin	All drivers	7 yrs.	$75	4-7 yrs.
Wyoming	All drivers[1]	2 yrs.[6]	$25	1-2 yrs.[6]

[1] In own car only.
[2] 5-10 year olds in all seats.
[3] 9 year olds in rear.
[4] Under 5 years in rear.
[5] 4-5 year olds in front seat.
[6] If no space for child restraint.

FUEL ECONOMY

A car's fuel efficiency affects both our environment and our wallets—which is why comparative mileage ratings are an important factor to most consumers. To save money and the environment, the first and most obvious step is to select a car that gets high mileage, so we've included the Environmental Protection Agency's fuel economy ratings for all 1998 vehicles. We also discuss numerous factors that affect your car's fuel efficiency, and caution you against the many products that falsely promise more gas mileage.

Using EPA ratings is an excellent way to incorporate fuel efficiency in selecting a new car. By comparing these ratings, even among cars of the same size, you'll find that fuel efficiency varies greatly. One compact car might get 36 miles per gallon (mpg) while another gets only 22 mpg. If you drive 15,000 miles a year and you pay $1.20 per gallon for fuel, the 36 mpg car will save you $319 a year over the "gas guzzler."

Octane Ratings: Once you've purchased your car, you'll be faced with choosing the right gasoline. Oil companies spend millions of dollars trying to get you to buy so-called higher performance or high octane fuels. Because high octane fuel can add considerably to your gas bill, it is important that you know what you're buying.

The octane rating of a gasoline is *not* a measure of power or quality. It is simply a measure of the gas's resistance to engine knock, which is the pinging sound you hear when the air and fuel mixture in your engine ignites prematurely during acceleration.

The octane rating appears on a yellow label on the fuel pump. Octane ratings vary with different types of gas (premium or regular), in different parts of the country (higher altitudes require lower octane ratings), and even between brands (Texaco's gasolines may have a different rating than Exxon's).

Determining the Right Octane Rating for Your Car: Using a lower-rated gasoline saves money. Most cars are designed to run on a posted octane rating of 87. The following procedure can help you select the lowest octane level for your car.

1 Have your engine tuned to exact factory specifications by a competent mechanic, and make sure it is in good working condition.

2 When the gas in your tank is very low, fill it up with your usual gasoline. After driving 10 to 15 miles, find a safe place to come to a complete stop and then accelerate rapidly. If your engine knocks during acceleration, switch to a higher octane rating. If there is no knocking sound, wait until your tank is very low and fill up with a lower rated gasoline. Repeat the test. When you determine the level of octane that causes your engine to knock during the test, use gasoline with the next highest rating.

Note: Your engine may knock when accelerating a heavily loaded car uphill or when the humidity is low. This is normal and does not call for a higher-octane gasoline.

In This Chapter . . .

Factors Affecting Fuel Economy

Fuel economy is affected by a number of factors that you can consider before you buy.

Transmission: Manual transmissions are generally more fuel-efficient than automatic transmissions. In fact, a 5-speed manual transmission can add up to 6.5 miles per gallon over a three-speed automatic. However, the incorrect use of a manual transmission wastes gas, so choose a transmission that matches your preference. Many transmissions now feature an overdrive gear, which can improve a vehicle's fuel economy by as much as 9 percent for an automatic transmission and 3 percent for a manual transmission.

Engine: The size of your car's engine greatly affects your fuel economy. The smaller your engine, the better your fuel efficiency. A 10-percent increase in the size of an engine can increase fuel consumption by 6 percent.

Cruise Control: Cruise control can save fuel because driving at a constant speed uses less fuel than changing speeds frequently.

Air Conditioning: Auto air conditioners add weight and require additional horsepower to operate. They can cost up to 3 miles per gallon in city driving. At highway speeds, however, an air conditioner has about the same effect on fuel economy as the air resistance created by opening the windows.

Trim Package: Upgrading a car's trim, installing soundproofing, and adding undercoating can increase the weight of a typical car by 150 pounds. For each 10 percent increase in weight, fuel economy drops 4 percent.

Power Options: Power steering, brakes, seats, windows, and roofs reduce your mileage by adding weight. Power steering alone can cause a 1-percent drop in fuel economy.

Here are some tips for after you buy:

Tune-Up: If you have a 2- to 3- mpg drop over several fill-ups that is not due to a change of driving pattern or vehicle load, first check tire pressure, then consider a tune-up. A properly tuned engine is a fuel saver.

Tire Inflation: For maximum fuel efficiency, tires should be inflated to the pressure range found on the label in your door well. The tire's maximum pressure may not be suitable for your car. Be usre to check the tire pressure when the tires are cold before you've driven a long distance.

Short Trips: Short trips can be expensive because they usually involve a "cold" vehicle. For the first mile or two before the engine gets warmed up, a cold vehicle only gets 30 to 40 percent of the mileage it gets a full efficiency.

Using Oxyfuels

Today's gasoline contains a bewildering array of ingredients touted as octane boosters or pollution fighters. Some urban areas with carbon monoxide pollution problems are requiring the use of oxygen-containing components (called oxyfuels) such as ethanol and MTBE (methyl-tertiary-butylether). The use of these compounds is controversial. Some auto companies recommend their use; others caution against them. Most companies approve the use of gasoline with up to 10-percent ethanol, and all approve the use of MTBE up to 15 percent. Many companies recommend against using gasoline with methanol, alleging that it will cause poorer driveability, deterioration of fuel system parts, and reduced fuel economy. These companies may not cover the cost of warranty repairs if these additives are used, so check your owner's manual and warranty to determine what additives are covered. Also check the gas pump, as many states now require the pump to display the percentage of methanol and ethanol in the gasoline.

Products That Don't Work

Hundreds of products on the market claim to improve fuel economy. Not only are most of these products ineffective, some may even damage your engine.

Sometimes the name or promotional material associated with these products implies they were endorsed by the federal government. *In fact, no government agency endorses any gas saving products.* Many of the products, however, *have* been tested by the U.S. EPA.

Of the hundreds of so-called gas saving devices on the market, only five tested by the EPA have been shown to *slightly* improve your fuel economy without increasing harmful emissions. Even these, however, offer limited savings because of their cost. They are the Pass Master Vehicle Air Conditioner P.A.S.S. Kit, Idalert, Morse Constant Speed Accessory Drive, Autotherm, and Kamei Spoilers. We don't recommend these products because the increase in fuel economy is not worth the investment in the product.

Do NOT Buy These Devices

Purported gas-saving devices come in many forms. Listed below are the types of products on the market. Under each category are the names of devices actually reviewed or tested by the EPA for which there was *no evidence of any improvement in fuel economy.*

AIR BLEED DEVICES
ADAKS Vacuum Breaker Air Bleed
Air-Jet Air Bleed
Aquablast Wyman Valve Air Bleed
Auto Miser
Ball-Matic Air Bleed
Berg Air Bleed
Brisko PCV
Cyclone - Z
Econo Needle Air Bleed
Econo-Jet Air Bleed Idle Screws
Fuel Max
Gas Saving Device
Grancor Air Computer
Hot Tip
Landrum Mini-Carb
Landrum Retrofit Air Bleed
Mini Turbocharger Air Bleed*
Monocar HC Control Air Bleed
Peterman Air Bleed*
Pollution Master Air Bleed
Ram-Jet
Turbo-Dyne G.R. Valve

DRIVING HABIT MODIFIERS
Fuel Conservation Device
Gastell

FUEL LINE DEVICES
Fuel Xpander
Gas Meiser I
Greer Fuel Preheater
Jacona Fuel System
Malpassi Filter King
Moleculetor
Optimizer
Petro-Mizer
Polarion X
Russell Fuelmiser
Super-Mag Fuel Extender
Wickliff Polarizer

FUELS AND FUEL ADDITIVES
Bycosin*
EI-5 Fuel Additive*
Fuelon Power Gasoline Fuel Additive
Johnson Fuel Additive*
NRG #1 Fuel Additive
QEI 400 Fuel Additive*
Rolfite Upgrade Fuel Additive
Sta-Power Fuel Additive
Stargas Fuel Additive
SYNeRGy-1
Technol G Fuel Additive
ULX-15/ULX-15D
Vareb 10 Fuel Additive*
XRG #1 Fuel Additive

IGNITION DEVICES
Autosaver
Baur Condenser*
BIAP Electronic Ignition Unit
Fuel Economizer
Magna Flash Ignition Ctrl. Sys.
Paser Magnum/Paser 500/ Paser 500 HEI
Special Formula Ignition Advance Springs*

INTERNAL ENGINE MODIFICATIONS
ACDS Auto. Cyl. Deactivation Sys.
Dresser Economizer*
MSU Cylinder Deactivation*

LIQUID INJECTION
Goodman Engine Sys. Model 1800*
Waag-Injection System*

MIXTURE ENHANCERS
Basko Enginecoat
Dresser Economizer
Electro-Dyne Superchoke*
Energy Gas Saver*
Environmental Fuel Saver*
Filtron Urethane Foam Filter*
Gas Saving and Emission Control Improvement Device
Glynn-50*
Hydro-Catalyst Pre-Combustion System
Lamkin Fuel Metering Device
Petromizer System
Sav-A-Mile
Smith Power and Deceleration Governor Spritzer*
Spritzer
Turbo-Carb
Turbocarb

OILS AND OIL ADDITIVES
Analube Synthetic Lubricant
Tephguard*

VAPOR BLEED DEVICES
Atomized Vapor Injector
Econo-Mist Vacuum Vapor Injection System
Frantz Vapor Injection System*
Hydro-Vac
Mark II Vapor Injection System*
Platinum Gasaver
POWER FUeL
Scatpac Vacuum Vapor Induction System
Turbo Vapor Injection System*
V-70 Vapor Injector

MISCELLANEOUS
Brake-Ez*
Dynamix
Fuel Maximiser
Gyroscopic Wheel Cover
Kat's Engine Heater
Lee Exhaust and Fuel Gasification EGR*
Mesco Moisture Extraction Sys.
P.S.C.U. 01 Device
Treis Emulsifier

* For copies of reports on these products, write Test and Evaluation Branch, U.S. EPA, 2565 Plymouth Rd., Ann Arbor, MI 48105. For the other products, contact the National Technical Information Service, Springfield, VA 22161 (703-487-4650).

Fuel Economy Ratings

Every year the Department of Energy publishes the results of the Environmental Protection Agency's (EPA) fuel economy tests in a comparative guide. In the past, millions of these booklets have been distributed to consumers who are eager to purchase fuel-efficient automobiles. However, the government has recently limited the availability of the guide. Because the success of the EPA program depends on consumers' ability to compare the fuel economy ratings easily, we have reprinted the EPA mileage figures for this year's misers and guzzlers.

1998 Fuel Economy Winners and Losers

The Misers	MPG City/Highway	Annual Fuel Cost[1]
Chevrolet Metro (1.0L/3/M5)	44/49	$407
Volkswagen Jetta (1.9L/4/M5)	40/49	$419
Volkswagen Passat (1.9L/4/M5)	39/50	$419
Volkswagen Passat Wgn (1.9L/4/M5)	39/50	$419
Chevrolet Metro (1.3L/4/M5)	39/43	$458
Suzuki Swift (1.3L/4/M5)	39/43	$458
Honda Civic HX (1.6L/4/M5)	36/44	$480
Honda Civic HX (1.6L/4/AV)	34/39	$521
Mitsubishi Mirage (1.6L/4/M5)	33/40	$521
Honda Civic (1.6L/4/M5)	32/37	$551
The Guzzlers[2]		
Mazda MPV 4WD (3.0L/5/L4)	15/19	$1,172
Chevrolet Astro 2WD (4.3L/6/L4)	16/20	$1,102
Chevrolet Astro AWD (4.3L/6/L4)	15/19	$1,102
GMC Safari 2WD (4.3L/6/L4)	16/20	$1,102
GMC Safari AWD (4.3L/6/L4)	15/19	$1,102
Lexus GS300/400 (3.0L/6/L5)	17/23	$1,105
Audi A6 Quattro (2.8L/6/L5)	17/26	$1,050
Cadillac Catera (3.0L/6/L4)	18/24	$1,050
Cadillac Deville (4.6L/8/L4)	17/26	$1,050
Cadillac Eldorado (4.6L/8/L4)	17/26	$1,050
Cadillac Seville (4.6L/8/L4)	17/26	$1,050
Chevrolet Camaro (5.7L/8/L4)	17/25	$1,050
Ford Mustang (4.6L/8/M5)	17/26	$1,050
Ford Taurus (3.0L/8/L4)	17/25	$1,050
Infiniti Q45 (4.1L/8/L4)	18/23	$1,050
Lincoln Continental (4.6L/8/L4)	17/24	$1,050
Lincoln Mark VIII (4.6L/8/L4)	17/26	$1,050
Mitsubishi Diamante (3.5L/6/L4)	18/24	$1,050
Oldsmobile Aurora (4.0L/8/L4)	17/26	$1,050
Pontiac Firebird (5.7L/8/L4)	18/24	$1,050
Volkswagen Passat Wgn (2.8L/6/L5)	17/26	$1,050
Volvo V90 (2.9L/6/L4)	18/25	$1,050

Based on 1998 EPA figures. (Engine size/number of cylinders/transmission type)
[1] Based on driving 15,000 miles per year.
[2] Based on popular models.

1998 EPA Figures

The following pages contain the EPA mileage ratings and the average annual fuel cost for most of the cars and many popular trucks sold in the United States. We have arranged the list in alphabetical order. After the car name, we have listed the engine size in liters, the number of cylinders, and some other identifiers: A = automatic transmission; L = lockup transmission; M = manual transmission.

The table includes the EPA city (first) and highway (second) fuel economy ratings. The city numbers will most closely resemble your expected mileage for everyday driving. The third column presents your average annual fuel cost. Reviewing this number will give you a better idea of how differences in fuel economy can affect your pocketbook. The amount is based on driving 15,000 miles per year.

Car (eng./trans.)	City	Hwy	Cost
Acura 3.0CL (3.0L/6/L4)	20	28	$ 816
Acura 2.5TL (2.5L/5/L4)	20	25	$ 956
Acura 3.2TL (3.2L/6/L4)	19	24	$1000
Acura 3.5RL (3.5L/6/L4)	19	25	$1000
Acura Integra (1.8L/4/L4)	24	31	$ 694
Acura Integra (1.8L/4/M5)	25	31	$ 669
Acura Integra (1.8L/4/M5)	25	31	$ 777
Audi A4 (1.8L/4/L5)	21	31	$ 876
Audi A4 (1.8L/4/M5)	23	32	$ 808
Audi A4 (2.8L/6/L5)	18	29	$ 956
Audi A4 (2.8L/6/M5)	20	29	$ 914
Audi A4 Avant (2.8L/6/L5)	18	29	$ 956
Audi A4 Avant Quattro (2.8L/6/L5)	17	27	$1000
Audi A4 Avant Quattro (2.8L/6/M5)	19	27	$ 956
Audi A4 Quattro (1.8L/4/L5)	19	27	$ 956
Audi A4 Quattro (1.8L/4/M5)	21	29	$ 876
Audi A4 Quattro (2.8L/6/L5)	17	27	$1000
Audi A4 Quattro (2.8L/6/M5)	19	27	$ 956
Audi A6 (2.8L/6/L5)	17	28	$1000
Audi A6 Quattro (2.8L/6/L5)	17	26	$1050
Audi A6 Wgn Quattro (2.8L/6/L4)	19	24	$1000
BMW 318i,318is (1.9L/4/L4)	22	31	$ 750
BMW 318i,318is (1.9L/4/M5)	23	32	$ 722
BMW 318ti (1.9L/4/L4)	22	31	$ 722
BMW 318ti (1.9L/4/M5)	23	32	$ 722
BMW 323i Convertible (2.5L/6/L4)	19	27	$ 853
BMW 323i Convertible (2.5L/6/M5)	20	30	$ 782
BMW 323is (2.5L/6/L4)	19	27	$ 853
BMW 323is (2.5L/6/M5)	20	30	$ 782
BMW 328i Convertible (2.8L/6/L4)	18	26	$ 892
BMW 328i Convertible (2.8L/6/M5)	20	28	$ 816
BMW 328i, 328is (2.8L/6/L4)	18	26	$ 892
BMW 328i, 328is (2.8L/6/M5)	20	28	$ 816
BMW 528i (2.8L/6/L4)	18	26	$ 892
BMW 528i (2.8L/6/M5)	20	28	$ 816
BMW 540i (4.4L/8/L5)	18	24	$ 938
BMW 540i (4.4L/8/M6)	15	24	$1042
BMW Z3 Roadster (1.9L/4/L4)	22	31	$ 722
BMW Z3 Roadster (1.9L/4/M5)	23	32	$ 722
BMW Z3 Roadster (2.8L/6/L4)	18	24	$ 938
BMW Z3 Roadster (2.8L/6/M5)	19	26	$ 892
Buick Century (3.1L/6/L4)	20	29	$ 816
Buick Lesabre (3.8L/6/L4)	19	30	$ 816
Buick Park Avenue (3.8L/6/L4)	19	28	$ 853
Buick Park Avenue (3.8L/6/L4)	18	27	$1000
Buick Regal (3.8L/6/L4)	19	30	$ 816
Buick Regal (3.8L/6/L4)	17	27	$1000
Buick Riviera (3.8L/6/L4)	18	27	$1000
Buick Skylark (2.4L/4/L4)	22	32	$ 722
Buick Skylark (3.1L/6/L4)	20	29	$ 816
Cadillac Catera (3.0L/6/L4)	18	24	$1050
Cadillac Deville (4.6L/8/L4)	17	26	$1050
Cadillac Eldorado (4.6L/8/L4)	17	26	$1050
Cadillac Seville (4.6L/8/L4)	17	26	$1050
Chev. Astro 2wd(cargo) (4.3L/6/l4)	16	21	$1042
Chev. Astro AWD(cargo) (4.3L/6/l4)	16	20	$1102
Chev. Astro 2wd(pass) (4.3L/6/L4)	16	20	$1102
Chev. Astro AWD(pass) (4.3L/6/l4)	15	19	$1102
Chev. Camaro (3.8L/6/L4)	19	29	$ 853
Chev. Camaro (3.8L/6/M5)	19	30	$ 816
Chev. Camaro (5.7L/8/L4)	17	25	$1050
Chev. Camaro (5.7L/8/M6)	18	27	$1000
Chev. Cavalier (2.2L/4/L3)	23	29	$ 722
Chev. Cavalier (2.2L/4/L4)	23	31	$ 722
Chev. Cavalier (2.2L/4/M5)	24	34	$ 669
Chev. Cavalier (2.4L/4/L4)	22	32	$ 722
Chev. Cavalier (2.4L/4/M5)	23	33	$ 722
Chev. Corvette (5.7L/8/L4)	17	25	$1050
Chev. Corvette (5.7L/8/M6)	18	27	$1000
Chev. Lumina (3.1L/6/L4)	20	29	$ 816
Chev. Lumina (3.8L/6/L4)	19	30	$ 816
Chev. Malibu (2.4L/4/L4)	23	32	$ 722
Chev. Malibu (3.1L/6/L4)	20	29	$ 816
Chev. Metro (1.0L/3/M5)	44	49	$ 407

Car (eng./trans.)	City	Hwy	Cost
Chev. Metro (1.3L/4/A3)	30	34	$585
Chev. Metro (1.3L/4/M5)	39	43	$458
Chev. Monte Carlo (3.1L/6/L4)	20	29	$816
Chev. Monte Carlo (3.8L/6/L4)	19	30	$816
Chev. Prizm (1.8L/4/L3)	28	33	$624
Chev. Prizm (1.8L/4/L4)	28	36	$606
Chev. Prizm (1.8L/4/M5)	31	37	$568
Chev. Venture FWD (3.4L/6/L4)	18	25	$892
Chrys. Cirrus (2.4L/4/L4)	21	30	$782
Chrys. Cirrus (2.5L/6/L4)	19	28	$853
Chrys. Concorde (3.2L/6/L4)	19	29	$853
Chrys. Sebring (2.0L/4/L4)	21	30	$782
Chrys. Sebring (2.0L/4/M5)	22	31	$750
Chrys. Sebring (2.5L/6/L4)	19	28	$853
Chrys. T & C 2wd (3.3L/6/L4)	18	24	$938
Chrys. T & C 2wd (3.8L/6/L4)	17	24	$986
Chrys. T & C (3.8L/6/L4)	16	23	$986
Dodge Avenger (2.0L/4/L4)	21	30	$782
Dodge Avenger (2.0L/4/M5)	22	32	$750
Dodge Avenger (2.5L/6/L4)	19	28	$853
Dodge Caravan 2wd (2.4L/4/L3)	20	26	$853
Dodge Caravan 2wd (3.0L/6/L3)	19	24	$892
Dodge Caravan 2wd (3.0L/6/L4)	19	26	$892
Dodge Caravan 2wd (3.3L/6/L4)	18	24	$938
Dodge Caravan 2wd (3.8L/6/L4)	17	24	$986
Dodge Caravan AWD (3.8L/6/L4)	16	23	$986
Dodge Intrepid (3.2L/6/L4)	19	29	$853
Dodge Neon (2.0L/4/L3)	24	33	$694
Dodge Neon (2.0L/4/M5)	29	41	$568
Dodge Stratus (2.0L/4/M5)	27	37	$606
Dodge Stratus (2.4L/4/L4)	21	30	$782
Dodge Stratus (2.5L/6/L4)	19	28	$853
Dodge Stratus (2.5L/6/L4)	19	29	$816
Eagle Talon (2.0L/4/L4)	21	30	$782
Eagle Talon (2.0L/4/L4)	19	25	$1000
Eagle Talon (2.0L/4/L4)	20	27	$914
Eagle Talon (2.0L/4/M5)	23	33	$722
Eagle Talon (2.0L/4/M5)	21	28	$876
Eagle Talon (2.0L/4/M5)	23	31	$808
Ford Contour (2.0L/4/L4)	24	32	$694
Ford Contour (2.0L/4/M5)	24	35	$669
Ford Contour (2.5L/6/L4)	21	30	$782
Ford Contour (2.5L/6/M5)	20	29	$816
Ford Escort (2.0L/4/L4)	25	34	$647
Ford Escort (2.0L/4/M5)	28	38	$585
Ford Escort Wgn (2.0L/4/L4)	25	34	$647
Ford Escort Wgn (2.0L/4/M5)	28	38	$585
Ford Escort Zx2 (2.0L/4/L4)	25	33	$669
Ford Escort Zx2 (2.0L/4/M5)	26	33	$647

Car (eng./trans.)	City	Hwy	Cost
Ford Mustang (3.8L/6/L4)	19	28	$853
Ford Mustang (3.8L/6/M5)	20	29	$782
Ford Mustang (4.6L/8/L4)	17	24	$938
Ford Mustang (4.6L/8/M5)	17	26	$1050
Ford Mustang (4.6L/8/M5)	17	25	$938
Ford Taurus (3.0L/6/L4)	19	28	$853
Ford Taurus (3.0L/6/L4)	18	27	$892
Ford Taurus (3.4L/8/L4)	17	25	$1050
Ford Taurus Wgn (3.0L/6/L4)	18	25	$938
Ford Taurus Wgn (3.0L/6/L4)	18	26	$892
Ford Windstar FWD Van (3.0L/6/L4)	18	25	$892
Ford Windstar FWD Wgn (3.0L/6/L4)	18	25	$892
GMC Safari 2wd(cargo) (4.3L/6/L4)	16	21	$1042
GMC Safari AWD(cargo) (4.3L/6/L4)	16	20	$1102
GMC Safari 2wd(pass) (4.3L/6/L4)	16	20	$1102
GMC Safari AWD(pass) (4.3L/6/L4)	15	19	$1102
Honda Accord (2.3L/4/L4)	22	29	$750
Honda Accord (2.3L/4/L4)	23	30	$722
Honda Accord (2.3L/4/M5)	24	31	$694
Honda Accord (2.3L/4/M5)	25	31	$694
Honda Accord (3.0L/6/L4)	20	28	$816
Honda Civic (1.6L/4/L4)	29	36	$585
Honda Civic (1.6L/4/L4)	28	35	$624
Honda Civic (1.6L/4/M5)	32	37	$551
Honda Civic (1.6L/4/M5)	30	35	$585
Honda Civic HX (1.6L/4/Av)	34	39	$521
Honda Civic HX (1.6L/4/M5)	36	44	$480
Honda Odyssey (2.3L/4/L4)	21	26	$816
Honda Prelude (2.2L/4/L4)	21	27	$876
Honda Prelude (2.2L/4/M5)	23	27	$876
Hyundai Accent (1.5L/4/L4)	27	35	$624
Hyundai Accent (1.5L/4/M5)	28	36	$585
Hyundai Elantra (1.8L/4/L4)	22	30	$750
Hyundai Elantra (1.8L/4/M5)	24	32	$694
Hyundai Elantra Wgn (1.8L/4/L4)	22	30	$750
Hyundai Elantra Wgn (1.8L/4/M5)	24	31	$694
Hyundai Sonata (2.0L/4/L4)	20	27	$816
Hyundai Sonata (2.0L/4/M5)	21	28	$782
Hyundai Sonata (3.0L/6/L4)	17	24	$938
Hyundai Tiburon (2.0L/4/L4)	22	29	$750
Hyundai Tiburon (2.0L/4/M5)	22	31	$750
Infiniti I30 (3.0L/6/L4)	21	28	$816
Infiniti I30 (3.0L/6/M5)	21	26	$816
Infiniti Q45 (4.1L/8/L4)	18	23	$1050
Isuzu Oasis (2.3L/4/L4)	21	26	$816
Kia Sephia (1.8L/4/L4)	23	31	$722
Kia Sephia (1.8L/4/M5)	24	31	$694
Lexus ES 300 (3.0L/6/L4)	19	27	$853
Lexus GS 300/GS 400 (3.0L/6/L5)	20	25	$956

Car (eng./trans.)	City	Hwy	Cost
Lexus GS 300/GS 400 (4.0L/8/L5)	17	23	$1105
Lexus LS 400 (4.0L/8/L5)	19	25	$1000
Lexus SC 300/SC 400 (3.0L/6/L4)	19	24	$1000
Lexus SC 300/SC 400 (4.0L/8/L5)	19	25	$1000
Lincoln Continental (4.6L/8/L4)	17	24	$1050
Lincoln Mark VIII (4.6L/8/L4)	17	26	$1050
Mazda 626 (2.0L/4/L4)	22	29	$ 782
Mazda 626 (2.0L/4/M5)	26	33	$ 647
Mazda 626 (2.5L/6/L4)	20	26	$ 914
Mazda 626 (2.5L/6/M5)	21	27	$ 876
Mazda Millenia (2.3L/6/L4)	20	28	$ 956
Mazda Millenia (2.5L/6/L4)	20	27	$ 956
Mazda MPV (3.0L/6/L4)	16	21	$1042
Mazda MPV 4x4 (3.0L/6/L4)	15	19	$1172
Mazda Protege (1.5L/4/L4)	25	32	$ 669
Mazda Protege (1.5L/4/M5)	30	37	$ 568
Mazda Protege (1.8L/4/L4)	23	30	$ 722
Mazda Protege (1.8L/4/M5)	26	32	$ 647
Merc.-Benz C230 (2.3L/4/L5)	23	30	$ 808
Merc.-Benz C280 (2.8L/6/L5)	21	27	$ 914
Merc.-Benz Cl500 (5.0L/8/L5)	15	22	$1168
Merc.-Benz Cl600 (6.0L/12/L5)	13	19	$1401
Merc.-Benz Clk320 (3.2L/6/L5)	21	29	$ 876
Merc.-Benz E300 Turbo. (3.0L/6/l5)	26	34	$ 599
Merc.-Benz E320 (3.2L/6/L5)	20	26	$ 956
Merc.-Benz E320 (3.2L/6/L5)	21	29	$ 876
Merc.-Benz E320 (3.2L/6/L5)	20	26	$ 956
Merc.-Benz E320 (3.2L/6/L5)	20	27	$ 914
Merc. Mystique (2.0L/4/L4)	24	32	$ 694
Merc. Mystique (2.0L/4/M5)	24	35	$ 669
Merc. Mystique (2.5L/6/L4)	21	30	$ 782
Merc. Mystique (2.5L/6/M5)	19	28	$ 853
Merc. Sable (3.0L/6/L4)	19	28	$ 853
Merc. Sable (3.0L/6/L4)	18	27	$ 892
Merc. Sable Wgn (3.0L/6/L4)	18	25	$ 938
Merc. Sable Wgn (3.0L/6/L4)	18	26	$ 892
Merc. Tracer (2.0L/4/L4)	25	34	$ 647
Merc. Tracer (2.0L/4/M5)	28	38	$ 585
Merc. Tracer Wgn (2.0L/4/L4)	25	34	$ 647
Merc. Tracer Wgn (2.0L/4/M5)	28	38	$ 585
Merc. Villager FWD Van (3.0L/6/L4)	17	23	$ 938
Merc. Villager FWD (3.0L/6/L4)	17	23	$ 938
Mitsu. Diamante (3.5L/6/L4)	18	24	$1050
Mitsu. Eclipse (2.0L/4/L4)	21	30	$ 782
Mitsu. Eclipse (2.0L/4/L4)	19	25	$1000
Mitsu. Eclipse (2.0L/4/L4)	20	27	$ 914
Mitsu. Eclipse (2.0L/4/M5)	23	33	$ 722
Mitsu. Eclipse (2.0L/4/M5)	21	28	$ 876
Mitsu. Eclipse (2.0L/4/M5)	23	31	$ 808

Car (eng./trans.)	City	Hwy	Cost
Mitsu. Eclipse Conv (2.0L/4/L4)	20	26	$ 956
Mitsu. Eclipse Conv (2.0L/4/M5)	23	31	$ 808
Mitsu. Eclipse Conv (2.3L/4/L4)	21	28	$ 816
Mitsu. Eclipse Conv (2.3L/4/M5)	22	30	$ 750
Mitsu. Galant (2.3L/4/L4)	22	28	$ 782
Mitsu. Galant (2.3L/4/M5)	23	30	$ 750
Mitsu. Mirage (1.5L/4/L4)	28	36	$ 606
Mitsu. Mirage (1.5L/4/M5)	33	40	$ 521
Mitsu. Mirage (1.8L/4/L4)	26	33	$ 647
Mitsu. Mirage (1.8L/4/M5)	29	36	$ 585
Nissan 240SX (2.4L/4/L4)	21	27	$ 914
Nissan 240SX (2.4L/4/M5)	22	28	$ 876
Nissan Altima (2.4L/4/L4)	22	30	$ 750
Nissan Altima (2.4L/4/M5)	24	31	$ 694
Nissan Maxima (3.0L/6/L4)	21	28	$ 782
Nissan Maxima (3.0L/6/M5)	22	27	$ 782
Nissan Sentra (1.6L/4/L4)	27	36	$ 624
Nissan Sentra (1.6L/4/M5)	29	39	$ 568
Nissan Sentra (2.0L/4/L4)	23	30	$ 722
Nissan Sentra (2.0L/4/M5)	23	31	$ 722
Nissan Quest (3.0L/6/L4)	17	23	$ 938
Oldsmobile 88 (3.8L/6/L4)	19	29	$ 816
Oldsmobile 88 (3.8L/6/L4)	18	27	$1000
Oldsmobile Achieva (2.4L/4/L4)	22	32	$ 722
Oldsmobile Achieva (2.4L/4/M5)	23	33	$ 722
Oldsmobile Achieva (3.1L/6/L4)	20	29	$ 782
Oldsmobile Aurora (4.0L/8/L4)	17	26	$1050
Oldsmobile Cutlass (2.4L/4/L4)	23	32	$ 722
Oldsmobile Cutlass (3.1L/6/L4)	20	29	$ 816
Oldsmobile Intrigue (3.8L/6/L4)	19	30	$ 816
Olds Silhouette FWD (3.4L/6/L4)	18	25	$ 892
Plymouth Breeze (2.0L/4/L4)	23	33	$ 722
Plymouth Breeze (2.0L/4/M5)	27	37	$ 606
Plymouth Breeze (2.4L/4/L4)	21	30	$ 782
Plymouth Neon (2.0L/4/L3)	24	33	$ 694
Plymouth Neon (2.0L/4/M5)	29	41	$ 568
Ply. Voyager 2wd (2.4L/4/L3)	20	26	$ 853
Ply. Voyager 2wd (3.0L/6/L3)	19	24	$ 892
Ply. Voyager 2wd (3.0L/6/L4)	19	26	$ 892
Ply. Voyager 2wd (3.3L/6/L4)	18	24	$ 938
Pontiac Bonneville (3.8L/6/L4)	19	28	$ 853
Pontiac Bonneville (3.8L/6/L4)	17	27	$1000
Pontiac Firebird (3.8L/6/L4)	19	29	$ 853
Pontiac Firebird (3.8L/6/M5)	19	30	$ 816
Pontiac Firebird (5.7L/8/L4)	18	24	$1050
Pontiac Firebird (5.7L/8/M6)	17	26	$1000
Pontiac Grand Am (2.4L/4/L4)	22	32	$ 722
Pontiac Grand Am (2.4L/4/M5)	23	33	$ 722
Pontiac Grand Am (3.1L/6/L4)	20	29	$ 816

Car (eng./trans.)	City	Hwy	Cost
Pontiac Grand Prix (3.1L/6/L4)	20	29	$816
Pontiac Grand Prix (3.8L/6/L4)	18	27	$1000
Pontiac Grand Prix (3.8L/6/L4)	19	30	$816
Pontiac Sunfire (2.2L/4/L3)	23	29	$722
Pontiac Sunfire (2.2L/4/L4)	23	31	$722
Pontiac Sunfire (2.2L/4/M5)	24	34	$669
Pontiac Sunfire (2.4L/4/L4)	22	32	$722
Pontiac Sunfire (2.4L/4/M5)	23	33	$722
Pont. Trans Sport FWD (3.4L/6/L4)	18	25	$892
Saturn SC (1.9L/4/L4)	27	37	$606
Saturn SC (1.9L/4/L4)	24	34	$669
Saturn SC (1.9L/4/M5)	26	36	$624
Saturn SC (1.9L/4/M5)	28	39	$585
Saturn SL (1.9L/4/L4)	27	37	$606
Saturn SL (1.9L/4/L4)	24	34	$669
Saturn SL (1.9L/4/M5)	28	39	$585
Saturn SL (1.9L/4/M5)	26	36	$624
Saturn SW (1.9L/4/L4)	27	34	$624
Saturn SW (1.9L/4/L4)	24	34	$669
Saturn SW (1.9L/4/M5)	26	36	$624
Saturn SW (1.9L/4/M5)	27	37	$606
Subaru Impreza AWD (2.2L/4/L4)	23	30	$722
Subaru Impreza AWD (2.2L/4/M5)	23	30	$750
Subaru Impreza AWD (2.5L/4/L4)	22	28	$782
Subaru Impreza AWD (2.5L/4/M5)	22	28	$782
Sub. Impreza Wgn AWD (2.2L/4/M5)	23	30	$750
Sub. Impreza Wgn AWD (2.2L/4/L4)	23	30	$722
Subaru Legacy (2.2L/4/L4)	24	31	$694
Subaru Legacy AWD (2.2L/4/L4)	23	30	$722
Subaru Legacy AWD (2.2L/4/M5)	23	30	$750
Subaru Legacy AWD (2.5L/4/L4)	21	26	$816
Subaru Legacy AWD (2.5L/4/M5)	21	27	$816
Subaru Legacy Wgn (2.2L/4/L4)	24	31	$694
Sub. Legacy Wgn AWD (2.2L/4/L4)	23	30	$750
Sub. Legacy Wgn AWD (2.2L/4/M5)	23	30	$750
Sub. Legacy Wgn AWD (2.5L/4/L4)	21	26	$816
Sub. Legacy Wgn AWD (2.5L/4/M5)	21	27	$816
Suzuki Esteem (1.6L/4/L4)	27	34	$647
Suzuki Esteem (1.6L/4/M5)	30	37	$568
Suzuki Esteem Wgn (1.6L/4/L4)	26	33	$647
Suzuki Esteem Wgn (1.6L/4/M5)	30	36	$585
Suzuki Swift (1.3L/4/A3)	30	34	$585
Toyota Avalon (3.0L/6/L4)	21	30	$782

Car (eng./trans.)	City	Hwy	Cost
Toyota Camry (2.2L/4/L4)	23	30	$722
Toyota Camry (2.2L/4/M5)	23	32	$694
Toyota Camry (3.0L/6/L4)	19	27	$853
Toyota Camry (3.0L/6/M5)	20	28	$816
Toyota Corolla (1.8L/4/L3)	28	33	$624
Toyota Corolla (1.8L/4/L4)	28	36	$606
Toyota Corolla (1.8L/4/M5)	31	38	$551
Toyota Paseo (1.5L/4/L4)	27	32	$647
Toyota Paseo (1.5L/4/M5)	29	35	$585
Toyota Paseo Conv. (1.5L/4/L4)	27	32	$647
Toyota Paseo Conv. (1.5L/4/M5)	29	34	$606
Toyota Sienna (3.0L/4/L4)	18	24	$892
Toyota Tercel (1.5L/4/L3)	29	33	$606
Toyota Tercel (1.5L/4/L4)	30	37	$568
Toyota Tercel (1.5L/4/M5)	31	39	$551
VW Golfi (2.0L/4/L4)	22	29	$782
VW Golf (2.0L/4/M5)	24	31	$722
VW Jetta (1.9L/4/M5)	40	49	$419
VW Jetta (2.0L/4/L4)	22	29	$782
VW Jetta (2.0L/4/M5)	24	31	$722
VW Jetta GLX (2.8L/6/L4)	18	25	$892
VW Jetta GLX (2.8L/6/M5)	19	26	$853
VW Passat (1.9L/4/L4)	31	44	$500
VW Passat (1.9L/4/M5)	39	50	$419
VW Passat (1.8L/4/L5)	21	31	$876
VW Passat (1.8L/4/M5)	23	32	$808
VW Passat (2.8L/6/L5)	18	29	$1000
VW Passat (2.8L/6/M5)	20	29	$914
VW Passat Wgn (1.9L/4/L4)	31	44	$500
VW Passat Wgn (1.9L/4/M5)	39	50	$419
VW Passat Wgn (1.8L/4/L5)	21	31	$876
VW Passat Wgn (1.8L/4/M5)	23	32	$808
VW Passat Wgn (2.8L/6/L5)	17	26	$1050
Volvo S70 (2.4L/5/M5)	20	29	$914
Volvo S70 (2.4L/5/L4)	20	28	$914
Volvo S70 (2.4L/5/L4)	19	27	$956
Volvo S70 (2.3L/5/M5)	19	25	$1000
Volvo S70 (2.3L/5/L4)	18	25	$1000
Volvo V70 (2.4L/5/M5)	20	29	$914
Volvo V70 (2.4L/5/L4)	20	28	$914
Volvo V90 (2.9L/6/L4)	18	25	$1050
Volvo V90 (2.9L/6/L4)	18	25	$1050

MAINTENANCE

After you buy a car, maintenance costs will be a significant portion of your operating expenses. This chapter allows you to consider and compare some of these costs *before* deciding which car to purchase. These costs include preventive maintenance servicing—such as changing the oil and filters—as well as the cost of repairs after your warranty expires. On the following pages, we compared the costs of preventive maintenance and nine likely repairs for the 1998 models. Since the cost of a repair also depends on the shop and the mechanic, this chapter includes tips for finding a good shop, communicating effectively with a mechanic, and extending the life of your car.

Preventive maintenance is the periodic servicing, specified by the manufacturer, that keeps your car running properly. For example, regularly changing the oil and oil filter. Every owner's manual specifies a schedule of recommended servicing for at least the first 50,000 miles, and the tables on the following pages estimate the cost of following this preventive maintenance schedule.

If for some reason you do not have an owner's manual with the preventive maintenance schedule, contact the manufacturer to obtain one.

Note: Some dealers and repair shops create their own maintenance schedules which call for more frequent (and thus more expensive) servicing than the manufacturer's recommendations. If the servicing recommended by your dealer or repair shop doesn't match what the car maker recommends, make sure you understand and agree to the extra items.

The tables also list the costs for nine repairs that typically occur during the first 100,000 miles. There is no precise way to predict exactly when a repair will be needed. But if you keep a car for 75,000 to 100,000 miles, it is likely that you will experience most of these repairs at least once. The last column provides a relative indication of how expensive these nine repairs are for many cars. Repair cost is rated as *Very Good* if the total for nine repairs is in the bottom fifth of all the cars rated, and *Very Poor* if the total is in the top fifth.

Most repair shops use "flat-rate manuals" to estimate repair costs. These manuals list the approximate time required for repairing many items. Each automobile manufacturer publishes its own manual and there are several independent manuals as well. For many repairs, the time varies from one manual to another. Some repair shops even use different manuals for different repairs. To determine a repair bill, a shop multiplies the time listed in its manual by its hourly labor rate and then adds the cost of parts.

Our cost estimates are based on flat-rate manual repair times multiplied by a nationwide average labor rate of $50 per hour. All estimates also include the cost of replaced parts and related adjustments, which are based on 1997 figures.

Prices in the following tables may not predict the exact costs of these repairs. For example, the labor rate for your area may be more or less than the national average. However, the prices will provide you with a relative comparison of maintenance costs for various automobiles.

In This Chapter...

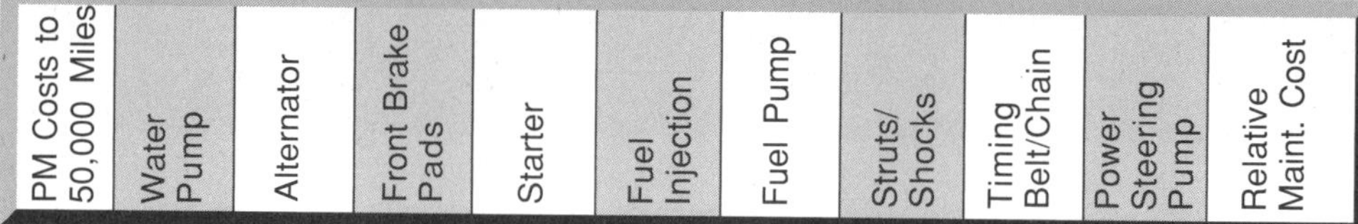

	PM Costs to 50,000 Miles	Water Pump	Alternator	Front Brake Pads	Starter	Fuel Injection	Fuel Pump	Struts/ Shocks	Timing Belt/Chain	Power Steering Pump	Relative Maint. Cost
Subcompact											
Chevrolet Metro	821	254	507	119	444	325	425	409	112	851	Vry. Pr.
Dodge/Plymouth Neon	733	200	310	137	232	136	302	149	174	270	Vry. Gd.
Ford Escort	690	263	290	103	285	80	142	284	128	159	Vry. Gd.
Honda Civic	924	184	319	109	250	168	223	320	134	248	Vry. Gd.
Hyundai Accent	371	184	298	79	298	107	195	218	162	384	Vry. Gd.
Kia Sephia	735	243	352	102	337	311	437	353	169	400	Poor
Mazda Miata	824	230	259	113	225	307	398	344	160	481	Average
Mazda Protege	824	253	262	121	238	316	379	308	178	599	Average
Mercury Tracer	690	179	317	103	285	80	153	274	128	159	Vry. Gd.
Mitsubishi Mirage	1090	213	284	125	211	174	386	310	126	623	Average
Nissan Sentra	756	183	389	99	286	163	143	264	582	281	Average
Saturn SC	919	138	201	94	179	138	267	176	278	243	Vry. Gd.
Saturn SL/SW	919	138	201	94	179	116	267	176	281	243	Vry. Gd.
Subaru Impreza	614	218	425	112	323	155	327	400	167	439	Average
Suzuki Esteem	821	237	779	113	331	281	473	422	184	614	Vry. Pr.
Suzuki Swift	821	259	311	126	283	256	423	462	185	646	Poor
Toyota Paseo	981	150	389	87	261	206	318	402	179	623	Average
Toyota Tercel	981	162	395	87	266	206	318	401	164	628	Average
Compact											
Acura Integra	1143	288	402	113	361	165	389	341	159	675	Poor
BMW 3 Series	327	177	383	123	444	167	267	535	436	301	Poor
BMW Z3	327	160	360	129	242	235	270	578	376	707	Poor
Chevrolet Cavalier	733	144	272	100	255	175	589	250	334	367	Average
Chevrolet Prizm	890	191	553	125	484	193	379	338	451	624	Vry. Pr.
Chrysler Sebring	716	215	300	135	518	131	245	166	224	332	Good
Dodge Avenger	716	205	233	135	551	129	250	191	204	313	Good
Eagle Talon	733	210	228	123	550	159	425	173	204	317	Average
Ford Contour	690	274	457	96	424	103	237	197	183	214	Good
Honda Prelude	926	226	432	109	301	158	407	339	200	635	Poor
Hyundai Elantra	371	169	298	76	298	104	185	250	152	369	Vry. Gd.
Average	**752**	**224**	**367**	**120**	**315**	**192**	**341**	**276**	**294**	**439**	

	PM Costs to 50,000 Miles	Water Pump	Alternator	Front Brake Pads	Starter	Fuel Injection	Fuel Pump	Struts/ Shocks	Timing Belt/Chain	Power Steering Pump	Relative Maint. Cost
Compact (cont.)											
Hyundai Tiburon	371	169	297	71	292	89	180	270	121	374	Vry. Gd.
Mazda 626	824	222	261	113	256	199	351	342	152	291	Good
Mercury Mystique	701	273	457	96	414	108	237	207	178	214	Good
Mitsubishi Eclipse	733	237	371	130	212	173	301	189	224	303	Good
Mitsubishi Galant	1042	253	310	130	231	187	258	213	204	357	Good
Oldsmobile Achieva	738	341	265	100	313	195	588	360	251	300	Poor
Pontiac Grand Am	738	341	265	125	313	180	453	327	281	341	Average
Pontiac Sunfire	738	144	272	100	247	185	589	260	279	367	Average
Subaru Legacy	595	218	329	112	443	155	306	334	167	248	Good
Toyota Celica	964	240	371	94	288	216	394	401	156	707	Poor
Toyota Corolla	890	213	394	109	284	216	307	416	131	663	Poor
Volkswagen Golf	213	275	450	123	397	161	367	185	96	276	Good
Volkswagen Jetta	213	275	450	123	397	161	367	185	96	276	Good
Intermediate											
Audi A4	0	277	590	175	371	220	276	245	192	440	Poor
BMW 5 Series	327	180	418	122	248	180	274	476	483	525	Poor
Buick Century	745	118	187	95	183	251	298	183	370	238	Vry. Gd.
Buick Regal	745	133	241	106	217	241	327	380	396	245	Good
Cadillac Catera	570	253	65	155	345	355	382	353	179	577	Average
Chevrolet Camaro	745	181	215	104	336	176	654	558	237	387	Poor
Chrysler Cirrus	716	257	323	143	256	134	246	131	210	333	Vry. Gd.
Chrysler Concorde	716	272	192	131	201	149	295	251	225	270	Vry. Gd.
Dodge Intrepid	716	90	242	131	202	126	305	271	232	270	Vry. Gd.
Dodge Stratus	716	231	328	143	222	132	246	131	189	319	Vry. Gd.
Eagle Vision	716	90	192	131	203	185	295	261	227	303	Vry. Gd.
Ford Mustang	757	267	349	130	364	145	233	185	359	380	Average
Ford Taurus	672	209	410	108	349	101	260	209	575	214	Average
Honda Accord	926	275	386	109	292	138	250	295	249	486	Average
Hyundai Sonata	371	239	304	83	169	89	203	208	240	508	Vry. Gd.
Mazda Millenia	822	275	531	241	288	324	477	453	246	911	Vry. Pr.
Average	**752**	**224**	**367**	**120**	**315**	**192**	**341**	**276**	**294**	**439**	

	PM Costs to 50,000 Miles	Water Pump	Alternator	Front Brake Pads	Starter	Fuel Injection	Fuel Pump	Struts/ Shocks	Timing Belt/Chain	Power Steering Pump	Relative Maint. Cost
Intermediate (cont.)											
Mercedes-Benz C-Class	1039	500	845	116	469	163	283	233	472	876	Vry. Pr.
Mercury Sable	672	196	392	108	322	126	260	209	553	238	Average
Nissan 240SX	738	168	323	115	401	195	349	543	719	399	Vry. Pr.
Nissan Altima	733	110	325	102	245	193	192	285	779	255	Average
Nissan Maxima	763	251	426	109	356	252	234	722	771	534	Vry. Pr.
Oldsmobile Cutlass	745	113	239	160	158	216	443	130	336	370	Good
Oldsmobile Intrigue	745	133	249	106	217	241	375	248	401	245	Good
Plymouth Breeze	716	220	328	143	222	137	246	141	183	334	Vry. Gd.
Pontiac Firebird	745	201	220	113	326	280	594	269	237	387	Average
Pontiac Grand Prix	745	133	249	106	217	241	375	248	401	245	Good
Saab 900	655	205	495	134	290	165	315	528	631	660	Vry. Pr.
Saab 9000	706	210	495	130	295	160	300	255	611	775	Vry. Pr.
Toyota Avalon	964	257	387	109	386	256	308	411	179	573	Poor
Toyota Camry	964	270	525	109	353	246	308	401	172	632	Poor
Volkswagen Passat	218	300	450	124	450	161	391	228	101	301	Average
Volvo C70/S70/V70	1148	242	568	114	322	141	306	216	160	492	Average
Large											
Acura CL	1142	249	371	119	382	141	237	310	145	747	Poor
Acura RL	1142	487	413	118	417	160	346	439	198	624	Vry. Pr.
Acura TL	1142	284	355	113	552	136	398	430	159	704	Poor
Audi A6	0	263	683	142	497	190	274	260	194	445	Poor
Buick LeSabre	751	236	280	114	234	163	294	238	267	387	Good
Buick Park Avenue	751	251	280	114	210	163	257	190	277	409	Good
Buick Riviera	751	231	274	109	321	168	477	196	272	382	Average
Cadillac DeVille	570	159	313	114	326	151	416	1291	756	343	Vry. Pr.
Cadillac Eldorado	570	164	282	114	321	151	558	1291	748	293	Vry. Pr.
Cadillac Seville	570	164	313	114	326	151	558	1291	756	343	Vry. Pr.
Chevrolet Lumina	751	133	249	96	217	241	265	252	356	240	Vry. Gd.
Chevrolet Malibu	745	321	262	160	316	185	443	338	347	251	Average
Chevrolet Monte Carlo	751	133	249	106	217	241	265	252	401	240	Good
Average	**752**	**224**	**367**	**120**	**315**	**192**	**341**	**276**	**294**	**439**	

	PM Costs to 50,000 Miles	Water Pump	Alternator	Front Brake Pads	Starter	Fuel Injection	Fuel Pump	Struts	Timing Belt	Power Steering Pump	Relative Maint. Cost
Large (cont.)											
Chrysler LHS	733	272	192	131	201	149	295	251	228	270	Vry. Gd.
Ford Crown Victoria	757	191	382	140	346	222	278	98	328	382	Average
Infiniti I30	745	255	439	109	287	248	315	767	601	508	Vry. Pr.
Infiniti Q45	745	154	505	115	374	324	350	299	1100	566	Vry. Pr.
Lexus ES300	745	256	472	111	258	259	313	500	179	626	Poor
Lexus GS300/400	745	276	480	110	300	309	374	156	191	685	Poor
Lexus LS400	745	364	532	116	515	344	380	213	255	737	Vry. Pr.
Lexus SC300/400	745	268	606	111	308	319	324	282	186	642	Poor
Lincoln Continental	745	228	431	180	343	154	361	859	483	357	Vry. Pr.
Lincoln Mark VIII	745	149	455	194	393	159	363	448	448	405	Poor
Lincoln Town Car	745	181	382	138	352	143	321	109	328	387	Good
Mercedes-Benz E-Class	1252	515	1035	113	454	202	259	279	785	798	Vry. Pr.
Mercury Cougar	742	213	437	149	348	178	269	289	361	395	Average
Mercury Grand Marquis	757	191	382	130	346	222	278	98	328	382	Average
Mitsubishi Diamante	1115	390	343	125	379	202	385	357	247	650	Poor
Oldsmobile 88	738	236	280	114	219	163	294	248	267	392	Good
Oldsmobile Aurora	760	154	372	114	301	156	531	213	486	397	Poor
Pontiac Bonneville	738	236	280	114	168	171	308	248	267	392	Good
Volvo S90/V90	1148	237	434	89	296	194	241	291	146	546	Average
Minivan											
Chevrolet Astro	694	260	273	108	266	192	356	117	236	390	Good
Chevrolet Venture	694	130	258	104	250	191	340	221	361	354	Good
Chrys. Town and Country	639	113	345	134	202	123	268	193	249	307	Vry. Gd.
Dodge Caravan	639	255	325	134	230	135	275	183	203	272	Vry. Gd.
Ford Windstar	617	325	447	106	338	161	281	259	631	263	Poor
GMC Safari	694	260	251	108	264	161	356	117	238	390	Good
Honda Odyssey	924	211	385	109	333	138	399	329	189	846	Poor
Isuzu Oasis	924	212	385	114	436	132	470	252	179	745	Poor
Mazda MPV	868	260	268	152	308	362	250	383	227	838	Poor
Mercury Villager	644	224	418	136	321	325	349	258	172	386	Average
Average	**752**	**224**	**367**	**120**	**315**	**192**	**341**	**276**	**294**	**439**	

	PM Costs to 50,000 Miles	Water Pump	Alternator	Front Brake Pads	Starter	Fuel Injection	Fuel Pump	Struts/ Shocks	Timing Belt/Chain	Power Steering Pump	Relative Maint. Cost
Minivan (cont.)											
Nissan Quest	644	245	336	131	259	359	250	272	240	508	Average
Oldsmobile Silhouette	694	134	252	115	269	186	458	216	365	357	Average
Plymouth Voyager	639	256	325	134	230	196	273	183	197	272	Vry. Gd.
Pontiac Trans Sport	694	134	257	115	274	171	335	221	365	357	Good
Toyota Sienna	964	270	525	109	353	246	308	401	172	632	Poor
Average	**752**	**224**	**367**	**120**	**315**	**192**	**341**	**276**	**294**	**439**	

Top Ten Things to Do on a Test Drive

The biggest mistake most of us make when buying a new car is not taking a good, long test drive. Plan on spending at least an hour to an hour and a half with the car, and include the following:

1. Take the car on a highway to review handling, acceleration, braking and wind noise.
2. Take the car on the bumpiest road you know.
3. Parallel park the car.
4. Pull the car in and out of your driveway and garage.
5. Sit in the passenger and back seats.
6. Put things in and out of the trunk or cargo space.
7. Look for blind spots.
8. Try the driver's seat in various positions.
9. Take a ride with other members of your family.
10. Make sure everyone tries on the seat belts.

Each year, about 25 percent of new car buyers buy "service contracts." Averaging around $380 in price, a service contract is one of the most expensive options you can buy. In fact, service contracts are a major profit source for many dealers.

A service contract is not a warranty. It is more like an insurance plan that, in theory, covers repairs that are not covered by your warranty or that occur after the warranty runs out.

Service contracts are generally a very poor value. The companies who sell contracts are very sure that, on average, your repairs will cost considerably less than what you pay for the contract—if not, they wouldn't be in business.

Tip: One alternative to buying a service contract is to deposit the cost of the contract into a savings account. If the car needs a major repair not covered by your warranty, the money in your account will cover the cost. Most likely, you'll be building up your down payment for your next car!

If you believe that you really need a service contract, contact an insurance company, such as GEICO. You can save up to 50-percent by buying from an insurance company.

Here are some important questions to ask before buying a service contract:

How reputable is the company responsible for the contract? If the company offering the contract goes out of business, you will be out of luck. Recently, a number of independent service contract companies have gone under, so be very careful about who you buy from. Check with your Better Business Bureau or office of consumer affairs if you are not sure of a company's reputation. Service contracts from car and insurance companies are more likely to remain in effect than those from independent companies.

Exactly what does the contract cover and for how long? Service contracts vary considerably—different items are covered and different time limits are offered. This is true even among service contracts offered by the same company. For example, Ford's plans range from 4 years/36,000 miles maximum coverage to 6 years/100,000 miles maximum coverage, with other options for only powertrain coverage.

If you plan to resell your car in a few years, you won't want to purchase a long-running service contract. Some service contracts automatically cancel when you resell the car, while others require a hefty transfer fee before extending privileges to the new owner.

Some automakers offer a "menu" format which lets you pick the items you want covered in your service contract. Find out if the contract pays for preventive maintenance, towing, and rental car expenses. If not written into the contract, assume they are not covered.

Finally, think twice before purchasing travel services offered in the contract. Such amenities are offered by auto clubs, and you should compare prices before adding them into your contract cost.

How will the repair bills be paid? It is best to have the service contractor pay bills directly. Some contracts require you to pay the repair bill, and reimburse you later.

Where can the car be serviced? Can you take the car to any mechanic if you have trouble on the road? What if you move?

What other costs can be expected? Most service contracts will have a deductible expense. Compare deductibles on various plans. Also, some companies charge the deductible for each individual repair while other companies charge per visit, regardless of the number of repairs made.

Turbocharging

A turbocharger is an air pump that forces more air into the engine for combustion. Most turbo chargers consist of an air compressor driven by a small turbine wheel that is powered by the engine's exhaust. The turbine takes advantage of energy otherwise lost and forces increased efficiency from the engine. Turbochargers are often used to increase the power and sometimes the fuel efficiency of small engines. Engines equipped with turbochargers are more expensive than standard engines. The extra power may not be necessary when you consider the added expense and the fact that turbocharging adds to the complexity of the engine.

Tips for Dealing with a Mechanic

Call around. Don't choose a shop simply because it's nearby. Calling a few shops may turn up estimates cheaper by half.

Don't necessarily go for the lowest price. A good rule is to eliminate the highest and lowest estimates; the mechanic with the highest estimate is probably charging too much, and the lowest may be cutting too many corners.

Check the shop's reputation. Call your local consumer affairs agency and the Better Business Bureau. They don't have records on every shop, but if their reports on a shop aren't favorable, you can disqualify it.

Look for certification. Mechanics can be certified by the National Institute for Automotive Service Excellence, an industry-wide yardstick for competence. Certification is offered in eight areas of repair and shops with certified mechanics are allowed to advertise this fact. However, make sure the mechanic working on your car is certified for the repair.

Take a look around. A well-kept shop reflects pride in workmanship. A skilled and efficient mechanic would probably not work in a messy shop.

Don't sign a blank check. The service order you sign should have specific instructions or describe your vehicle's symptoms. Signing a vague work order could make you liable to pay for work you didn't want. Be sure you are called for final approval before the shop does extra work.

Show interest. Ask about the repair. A mechanic may become more helpful just knowing that you're interested. But don't act like an expert if you don't really understand what's wrong. Demonstrating your ignorance, on the other hand, may set you up to be taken by a dishonest mechanic, so strike a balance.

Express your satisfaction. If you're happy with the work, compliment the mechanic and ask for him or her the next time you come in. You will get to know each other and the mechanic will get to know your vehicle.

Develop a "sider." If you know a mechanic, ask about work on the side—evenings or weekends. The labor will be cheaper.

Test drive, then pay! Before you pay for a major repair, you should take the car for a test drive. The few extra minutes you spend checking out the repair could save you a trip back to the mechanic. If you find that the problem still exists, there will be no question that the repair wasn't properly completed. It is more difficult to prove the repair wasn't properly made after you've left the shop.

TIP

Repair Protection By Credit Card

Paying your auto repair bills by credit card can provide a much-needed recourse if you are having problems with an auto mechanic. According to federal law, you have the right to withhold payment for sloppy or incorrect repairs. Of course, you may withhold no more than the amount of the repair in dispute.

In order to use this right, you must first try to work out the problem with the mechanic. Also, unless the credit card company owns the repair shop (this might be the case with gasoline credit cards used at gas stations), two other conditions must be met. First, the repair shop must be in your home state (or within 100 miles of your current address), and second, the cost of repairs must be over $50. Until the problem is settled or resolved in court, the credit card company cannot charge you interest or penalties on the amount in dispute.

If you decide to take action, send a letter to the credit card company and a copy to the repair shop, explaining the details of the problem and what you want as settlement. Send the letter by certified mail with a return receipt requested.

Sometimes the credit card company or repair shop will attempt to put a "bad mark" on your credit record if you use this tactic. Legally, you can't be reported as delinquent if you've given the credit card company notice of your dispute, but a creditor can report that you are disputing your bill, which goes in your record. However, you have the right to challenge any incorrect information and add your side of the story to your file.

For more information, write to the Federal Trade Commission, Credit Practices Division, 601 Pennsylvania Avenue, NW, Washington, DC 20580.

Keeping It Going

With the popularity of self-service gasoline stations, many of us overlook the simplest and most vital maintenance task of all: checking various items to prevent serious problems down the road. All it takes is about fifteen minutes a month to do the following checks. *Warning:* Many new vehicles have electric cooling fans that operate when the engine is off. Be sure to keep your hands away from the fan if the engine is warm.

Coolant: We'll start with the easiest fluid to check. Most vehicles have a plastic reservoir next to the radiator. This bottle will have "full hot" and "full cold" marks on it. If coolant is below "full cold" mark, add water to bring it up to that mark. (Anti-freeze should be used if you want extra protection in cold weather.) *Caution:* If vehicle is hot, do not open the radiator cap. Pressure and heat that can cause a severe burn may be released.

Brakes: The most important safety item on the vehicle is the most ignored. A simple test will signal problems. (With power brakes, turn on engine to test.) Push the brake pedal down and hold it down. It should stop firmly and stay about halfway to the floor. If the stop is mushy or the pedal keeps moving to the floor, you should have your brakes checked. Checking the brake fluid on most vehicles is also easy. Your owner's manual tells you where to find the fluid reservoir, which indicates minimum and maximum fluid levels. If you add your own brake fluid, buy it in small cans and keep them tightly sealed. Brake fluid absorbs moisture, and excess moisture can damage your brake system. Have the brakes checked if you need to replace brake fluid regularly.

Oil: A few years ago, the phrase "fill it up and check the oil" was so common that it seemed like one word. Today, checking the oil often is the responsibility of the driver. To check your oil, first turn off the engine. Find the dipstick (look for a loop made of flat wire located on the side of the engine). If the engine has been running, be careful, because the dipstick and surrounding engine parts will be hot. Grab the loop, pull out the dipstick, clean it off, and reinsert it into the engine. Pull it out again and observe the oil level. "Full" and "add" are marked at the end of the stick. If the level is between "add" and "full," you are OK. If it is below "add," you should add enough oil until it reaches the "full" line. To add oil, remove the cap at the top of the engine. You may have to add more than one quart. Changing your oil regularly (every 3000-5000 miles based on your driving habits) is the single most important way to protect your engine. Many owner's manuals also contain directions for doing so. Change the oil filter whenever you change the oil.

Transmission Fluid: An automatic transmission is a complicated and expensive item. Checking your transmission fluid level is easy and can prevent a costly repair job. As in the oil check, you must first find the transmission fluid dipstick. Usually it is at the rear of the engine and looks like a smaller version of the oil dipstick. To get an accurate reading, the engine should be warmed up and running. If fluid is below the "add" line, pour in one pint at a time, but do not overfill the reservoir.

While you check the fluid, also note its color. It should be a bright, cherry red. If it is a darker, reddish brown, the fluid needs changing. If it is very dark, nearly black, and has a burnt smell (like varnish), your transmission may be damaged. You should take it to a specialist.

Automatic transmission fluid is available at most department stores; check your owner's manual for the correct type for your vehicle.

Power Steering: The power steering fluid reservoir is usually connected by a belt to the engine. To check it, unscrew the cap and look in the reservoir. There will be markings inside; some vehicles have a little dipstick built in to the cap.

Belts: You may have one or more belts connected to your engine. A loose belt in the engine can lead to electrical, cooling, or even air conditioning problems. To check, simply push down on the middle of each belt. It should feel tight. If you can push down more than half an inch, the belt needs tightening.

Battery: If your battery has caps on the top, lift off the caps and check that fluid comes up to the bottom of the filler neck. If it doesn't, add water (preferably distilled). If it is very cold outside, add water only if you are planning to drive the vehicle immediately. Otherwise the newly added water can freeze and damage your battery.

Also, look for corrosion around the battery connections. It can prevent electrical circuits from being completed, leading you to assume your perfectly good battery is "dead." If cables are corroded, remove and clean with fine sandpaper or steel wool. The inside of the connection and the battery posts should be shiny when you put the cables back on. *Caution:* Do not smoke or use any flame when checking the battery.

Tires: Improperly inflated tires are a major cause of premature tire failure. Check for proper inflation at least once a month. The most fuel-efficient inflation level can be found on the information label in your driver's side door well. The maximum pressure listed on the tire may not be appropriate for your car. Since many gas station pumps do not have gauges, and those that do are generally inaccurate, you should invest in your own tire gauge.

Air Filter: Probably the easiest item to maintain is your air filter. You can usually check the filter by just looking at it. If it appears dirty, change it—it's a simple task. If you are not sure how clean your filter is, try the following: Once the engine warms up, put the vehicle in park or neutral and, with the emergency brake on, let the vehicle idle. Open the filter lid and remove the filter. If the engine begins to run faster, change the filter.

Battery Safety

Almost all motorists have had to jump start a vehicle because of a dead battery. But that innocent-looking battery can cause some serious injuries.

Batteries produce hydrogen gas when they discharge or undergo heavy use (such as cranking the engine for a long period of time). A lit cigarette or a spark can cause this gas to explode. Whenever you work with the battery, always remove the negative (or ground) cable first and reconnect it last; it is usually marked with a minus sign. This precaution will greatly reduce the chance of causing a spark that could ignite any hydrogen gas present.

For a safe jump start:

1. Connect each end of the red cable to the positive (+) terminal on each battery.
2. Connect one end of the black cable to the negative (-) terminal of the *good* battery.
3. Connect the other end of the black cable to exposed metal away from the battery of the vehicle being started.
4. To avoid damaging electrical parts, make sure the engine is idling before disconnecting the cables.

Saving Gasoline

A cold-running engine dramatically reduces fuel economy. Most engines operate efficiently at 180 degrees, and an engine running at 125 degrees can waste one out of every ten gallons of gas. Your engine temperature is controlled by a thermostat valve. A faulty thermostat can be a major cause of poor fuel economy. If you feel that your vehicle should be getting better mileage, have your thermostat checked. They are inexpensive and easy to replace.

WARRANTIES

Along with your new car comes a warranty, which is a promise from the manufacturer that the car will perform as it should. Most of us never read the warranty—until it is too late. In fact, because warranties are often difficult to read and understand, most of us don't really know what our warranties offer. This chapter will help you understand what to look for in a new car warranty, tip you off to secret warranties, and provide you with the best and worst among the 1998 warranties.

There are two types of warranties: one provided by the manufacturer and one implied by law.

Manufacturers' warranties are either "full" or "limited." The best warranty you can get is a full warranty because, by law, it must cover all aspects of the product's performance. Any other guarantee is called a limited warranty, which is what most car manufacturers offer. Limited warranties must be clearly marked as such, and you must be told exactly what is covered.

Warranties implied by law are warranties of merchantability and fitness. The "warranty of merchantability" ensures that your new car will be fit for the purpose for which it is used—that means safe, efficient, and trouble-free transportation. The "warranty of fitness" guarantees that if the dealer says a car can be used for a specific purpose, it will perform that purpose.

Any claims made by the salesperson are also considered warranties. They are called expressed warranties and you should have them put in writing if you consider them to be important. If the car does not live up to promises made to you in the showroom, you may have a case against the seller.

The manufacturer can restrict the amount of time the limited warranty is in effect. And in most states, the manufacturer can also limit the time that the warranty implied by law is in effect.

Through the warranty, the manufacturer is promising that the way the car was made and the materials used are free from defects, provided that the car is used in a normal fashion for a certain period after you buy it. This period of time is usually measured in both months and miles— whichever comes first is the limit.

In This Chapter...

While the warranty is in effect, the manufacturer will perform, at no charge to the owner, repairs that are necessary because of defects in materials or in the way the car was manufactured.

The warranty does not cover parts that have to be replaced because of normal wear, such as filters, fuses, light bulbs, wiper blades, clutch linings, brake pads, or the addition of oil, fluids, coolants, and lubricants. Tires, batteries, and the emission control system are covered by separate warranties. Options, such as a stereo system, should have their own warranties as well. Service should be provided through the dealer. A separate rust (corrosion) warranty is also included.

The costs for the required maintenance listed in the owner's manual are not covered by the warranty. Problems resulting from misuse, negligence, changes you make in the car, accidents, or lack of required maintenance are also not covered.

Any implied warranties, including the warranties of merchantability and fitness, are limited to 12 months or 12,000 miles. Also, the manufacturer is not responsible for other problems caused by repairs, such as the loss of time or use of your car, or any expenses they might cause.

In addition to the rights granted to you in the warranty, you may have other rights under your state laws.

To keep your warranty in effect, you must operate and maintain your car according to the instructions in your owner's manual. Remember, it is important to keep a record of all maintenance performed on your car.

To have your car repaired under the warranty, take it to an authorized dealer or service center. The work should be done in a reasonable amount of time during normal business hours.

Be careful not to confuse your warranty with a service contract. The *service contract* must be purchased separately while the warranty is yours at no extra cost when you buy the car. (See page 55 for more on service contracts.)

Corrosion Warranty: All manufacturers warrant against corrosion. The typical corrosion warranty lasts for six years or 100,000 miles, whichever comes first.

Some dealers offer extra rust protection at an additional cost. Before you purchase this option, compare the extra protection offered to the corrosion warranty already included in the price of the car—it probably already provides sufficient protection against rust.

Emission System Warranty: The emission system is warranted by federal law. Any repairs required during the first two years or 24,000 miles will be paid for by the manufacturer if an original engine part fails because of a defect in materials or workmanship, and the failure causes your car to exceed federal emissions standards. Major components, such as an onboard computer emissions control unit, are covered for eight years or up to 80,000 miles.

Using leaded fuel in a car designed for unleaded fuel will void your emission system warranty and may prevent the car from passing your state's inspection. Because an increasing number of states are requiring an emissions test before a car can pass inspection, you may have to pay to fix the system if you used the wrong type of fuel. Repairs to emission systems are usually very expensive.

Dealer Options & Your Warranty

Make sure that "dealer-added" options will not void your warranty. For example, some consumers who have purchased cruise control as an option to be installed by the dealer have found that their warranty is void when they take the car in for engine repairs. Also, some manufacturers warn that dealer-supplied rustproofing will void your corrosion warranty. If you are in doubt, contact the manufacturer before you authorize the installation of dealer-supplied options. If the manufacturer says that adding the option will not void your warranty, get it in writing.

Getting Warranty Service

Ford dealers are finally offering better warranty service to their customers! Now, most Ford dealers will perform warranty work on all Ford vehicles, regardless of where the vehicle was purchased. Previously, only the selling dealer was required to perform repairs under warranty. Individual Ford dealers can still set their own policy, however, so it is best to call and ask before taking your vehicle in for warranty service. GM, Japanese, and European car dealers also provide this service to their customers, and Chrysler "recommends" that dealers follow this policy.

Secret Warranties

If dealers report a number of complaints about a certain part and the manufacturer determines that the problem is due to faulty design or assembly, the manufacturer may permit dealers to repair the problem at no charge to the customer even though the warranty is expired. In the past, this practice was often reserved for customers who made a big fuss. The availability of the free repair was never publicized, which is why we call these *secret* warranties.

Manufacturers deny the existence of secret warranties. They call these free repairs "policy adjustments" or "goodwill service." Whatever they are called, most consumers never hear about them.

Many secret warranties are disclosed in service bulletins that the manufacturers send to dealers. These bulletins outline free repair or reimbursement programs, as well as other problems and their possible causes and solutions.

Service bulletins from many manufacturers may be on file at the National Highway Traffic Safety Administration. For copies of the bulletins on file, send a letter with the make, model and year of the car, and the year you believe the service bulletin was issued, to the NHTSA's Technical Reference Library, Room 5108, NHTSA, Washington, DC 20590. If you write to the government, ask for "service bulletins" rather than "secret warranties."

If you find that a secret warranty is in effect and repairs are being made at no charge after the warranty has expired, contact the Center for Auto Safety, 2001 S Street, NW, Washington, DC 20009. They will publish the information so others can benefit.

Disclosure Laws: Spurred by the proliferation of secret warranties and the failure of the FTC to take action, California, Connecticut, Virginia, and Wisconsin have passed legislation that requires consumers to be notified of secret warranties on their cars. Several other states have introduced similar warranty bills.

Typically, the laws require the following: Direct notice to consumers within a specified time after the adoption of a warranty adjustment policy; notice of the disclosure law to new car buyers; reimbursement, within a number of years after payment, to owners who paid for covered repairs before they learned of the extended warranty service; and dealers must inform consumers who complain about a covered defect that it is eligible for repair under warranty.

New York's bill has another requirement—the establishment of a toll-free number for consumer questions, despite opposition from Ford, GM, Toyota, and other auto manufacturers.

If you live in a state with a secret warranty law already in effect, write your state attorney general's office (in care of your state capitol) for information. To encourage passage of such a bill, contact your state representative (in care of your state capitol).

Secret Warranties Made Public

Due to past secret warranty problems, three auto companies are required to make their service bulletins public.

Ford: Information on goodwill adjustments is available through Ford's "defect line" at 800-241-3673.
General Motors: Bulletins are available from the past three years for a charge and free indexes to bulletins are available through GM dealers or call 800-551-4123.
Volkswagen: An index of all service bulletins can be ordered by calling 800-544-8021.

Uncovering Secret Warranties

Every auto company makes mistakes building cars. When they do, they often issue technical service bulletins telling dealers how to fix the problem. Rarely do they publicize these fixes, many of which are offered for free, called secret warranties. The Center for Auto Safety has published a new book called *Little Secrets of the Auto Industry*, a consumer guide to secret warranties. This book explains how to find out about secret warranties, offers tips for going to small claims court and getting federal and state assistance, and lists information on state secret warranty laws. To order a copy, send $16.50 to: Center for Auto Safety, Pub. Dept., 2001 S Street, NW, Washington, DC 20009.

Comparing Warranties

Warranties are difficult to compare because they contain lots of fine print and confusing language. The following table will help you understand this year's new car warranties. Because the table does not contain all the details about each warranty, you should review the actual warranty to make sure you understand its fine points. Remember, you have the right to inspect a warranty before you buy—it's the law.

The table provides information on five areas covered by a typical warranty:

The **Basic Warranty** covers most parts of the car against manufacturer's defects. The tires, batteries, and items you may add to the car are covered under separate warranties. The table describes coverage in terms of months and miles; for example, 36/36,000 means the warranty is good for 36 months or 36,000 miles, whichever comes first. This is the most important part of your warranty.

The **Powertrain Warranty** usually lasts longer than the basic warranty. Because each manufacturer's definition of the powertrain is different, it is important to find out exactly what your warranty will cover. Powertrain coverage should include parts of the engine, transmission, and drivetrain. The warranty on some luxury cars will often cover some additional systems such as steering, suspension, and electrical systems.

The **Corrosion Warranty** usually applies only to actual holes due to rust. Read this section carefully, because many corrosion warranties *do not* apply to what the manufacturer may describe as cosmetic rust or bad paint.

The **Roadside Assistance** column indicates whether or not the warranty includes a program for helping with problems on the road. Typically, these programs cover such things as lock outs, jump starts, flat tires, running out of gas and towing. Most of these are offered for the length of the basic warranty. Some have special limitations or added features, which we have pointed out. Because each one is different, check yours out carefully.

The last column contains the **Warranty Rating Index,** which provides an overall assessment of this year's warranties. The higher the Index number, the better the warranty. The Index number incorporates the important features of each warranty. In developing the Index, we gave the most weight to the basic and powertrain components of the warranties. The corrosion warranty was weighted somewhat less, and the roadside assistance features received the least weight. We also considered special features such as whether you had to bring the car in for corrosion inspections, or if rental cars were offered when warranty repairs were being done.

After evaluating all the features of the new warranties, here are this year's best and worst ratings.

1998 Warranties: The Best and The Worst

The Best		The Worst	
Volkswagen Passat	1800	Suzuki	670
Audi	1591	Honda	834
Infiniti	1518	Chrysler	932
Volkswagen	1470	Dodge	932
Volvo	1411	Eagle	932
BMW	1379	Plymouth	932
Lexus	1367		

The higher the index number, the better the warranty. See the table on the following pages for complete details.

Manufacturer	Basic Warranty	Powertrain Warranty	Corrosion Warranty	Roadside Assistance	Index	Warranty Rating
Acura	48/50,000	48/50,000	60/unlimited	48/50,000	1163	Average
Audi	36/50,000[1]	36/50,000	120/unlimited	36/50,000[2]	1591	Very Good
BMW	48/50,000[3]	48/50,000	72/unlimited[4]	48/50,000[2]	1379	Good
Buick	36/36,000	36/36,000	72/100,000	36/36,000	956	Very Poor
Cadillac	48/50,000	48/50,000	72/100,000	Lifetime[5,6]	1227	Good
Chevrolet	36/36,000	36/36,000	72/100,000	36/36,000	956	Very Poor
Chrysler	36/36,000	36/36,000	60/100,000	36/36,000	932	Very Poor
Dodge	36/36,000	36/36,000	60/100,000	36/36,000	932	Very Poor
Eagle	36/36,000	36/36,000	60/100,000	36/36,000	932	Very Poor
Ford	36/36,000	36/36,000	60/unlimited	36/36,000	942	Very Poor
Honda	36/36,000	36/36,000	60/unlimited	None	834	Very Poor
Hyundai	36/36,000	60/60,000	60/100,000	36/36,000[7]	1022	Poor
Infiniti	48/60,000	72/70,000	84/unlimited	48/unlimited	1518	Very Good
Isuzu	36/50,000	60/60,000	72/100,000	60/60,000	1228	Good
Kia	36/36,000	60/60,000	60/100,000	36/36,000[2]	1126	Average
Lexus	48/50,000	72/72,000	72/unlimited	48/50,000	1367	Good
Lincoln	48/50,000[8]	48/50,000	60/unlimited	48/50,000	1163	Average
Mazda	36/50,000	36/50,000	60/unlimited	36/50,000[9]	984	Very Poor
Mercedes-Benz	48/50,000	48/50,000	48/50,000	Lifetime	1179	Average
Mercury	36/36,000	36/36,000	60/unlimited	36/36,000	942	Very Poor
Mitsubishi	36/36,000	60/60,000	84/100,000	36/36,000	1124	Average
Nissan	36/36,000	60/60,000	60/unlimited	36/36,000[7]	1032	Poor
Oldsmobile	36/36,000	36/36,000	72/100,000	36/36,000[2]	1006	Poor
Olds Aurora	48/50,000	48/50,000	72/100,000	48/50,000[2]	1227	Good
Plymouth	36/36,000	36/36,000	60/100,000	36/36,000	932	Very Poor

[1] Includes all service, repairs and parts to 36/50,000.
[2] Covers trip interruption expenses.
[3] Includes all service, repairs and parts to 36/36,000.
[4] Inspection required every 2 years.
[5] <48/50,000=Free; >48/50,000=Small Charge.
[6] Covers trip interruption expenses up to 48/50,000 for a warranty failure.
[7] Limited roadside services.
[8] The basic warranty also includes car rental payments of a maximum of $30/day for 5 days (if car kept overnight for servicing).
[9] Millenia and MPV only.
[10] Suzuki Soft Tops have a 24/24,000 Basic Warranty on the soft top itself.
[11] Includes all service, repairs and parts to 24/24,000.

Manufacturer	Basic Warranty	Powertrain Warranty	Corrosion Warranty	Roadside Assistance	Index	Warranty Rating
Pontiac	36/36,000	36/36,000	72/100,000	36/36,000	956	Very Poor
Saab	48/50,000	48/50,000	72/unlimited	48/50,000[2]	1279	Good
Saturn	36/36,000	36/36,000	72/100,000	36/36,000[2]	1006	Poor
Subaru	36/36,000	60/60,000	60/unlimited	36/36,000	1086	Poor
Suzuki[10]	36/36,000	36/36,000	36/unlimited	None	670	Very Poor
Toyota	36/36,000	60/60,000	60/unlimited	Optional	978	Very Poor
Volkswagen	24/24,000[11]	120/100,000	72/unlimited	24/24,000[2]	1470	Very Good
VW Passat	24/24,000[11]	120/100,000	132/unlimited	24/24,000[2]	1800	Very Good
Volvo	48/50,000	48/50,000	96/unlimited	48/50,000[2]	1411	Very Good

[1] Includes all service, repairs and parts to 36/50,000.
[2] Covers trip interruption expenses.
[3] Includes all service, repairs and parts to 36/36,000.
[4] Inspection required every 2 years.
[5] <48/50,000=Free; >48/50,000=Small Charge.
[6] Covers trip interruption expenses up to 48/50,000 for a warranty failure.
[7] Limited roadside services.
[8] The basic warranty also includes car rental payments of a maximum of $30/day for 5 days (if car kept overnight for servicing).
[9] Millenia and MPV only.
[10] Suzuki Soft Tops have a 24/24,000 Basic Warranty on the soft top itself.
[11] Includes all service, repairs and parts to 24/24,000.

INSURANCE

Insurance is a big part of ownership expenses, yet it's often forgotten in the showroom. As you shop, remember that the car's design and accident history may affect your insurance rates. Some cars cost less to insure because experience has shown that they are damaged less, less expensive to fix after a collision, or stolen less.

This chapter provides you with the information you need to make a wise insurance purchase. We discuss the different types of insurance, offer special tips on reducing this cost, and include information on occupant injury, theft, and bumper ratings—all factors that can affect your insurance.

More and more consumers are saving hundreds of dollars by shopping around for insurance. In order to be a good comparison shopper, you need to know a few things about automobile insurance. First, there are six basic types of coverage:

Collision Insurance: This pays for the damage to your car after an accident.

Comprehensive Physical Damage Insurance: This pays for damages when your car is stolen or damaged by fire, floods, or other perils.

Property Damage Liability: This pays claims and defense costs if your car damages someone else's property.

Medical Payments Insurance: This pays for your car's occupants' medical expenses resulting from an accident.

Bodily Injury Liability: This provides money to pay claims against you and to pay for the cost of your legal defense if your car injures or kills someone.

Uninsured Motorists Protection: This pays for injuries caused by an uninsured or a hit-and-run driver.

A number of factors determine what these coverages will cost you. A car's design can affect both the chances and severity of an accident. A car with a well-designed bumper may escape damage altogether in a low-speed crash. Some cars are easier to repair than others or may have less expensive parts. Cars with four doors tend to be damaged less than cars with two doors.

The reason one car may get a discount on insurance while another receives a surcharge also depends upon the way it is traditionally driven. Sports cars, for example, are usually surcharged due, in part, to the typical driving habits of their owners. Four-door sedans and station wagons generally merit discounts.

Insurance companies use this and other information to determine whether to offer a *discount* on insurance premiums for a particular car, or whether to levy a *surcharge*.

Not all companies offer discounts or surcharges, and many cars receive neither. Some companies offer a discount or impose a surcharge on collision premiums only. Others apply discounts and surcharges on both collision and comprehensive coverage. Discounts and surcharges usually range from 10 to 30 percent. Allstate offers discounts of up to 35 percent on certain cars. Remember that one company may offer a discount on a particular car while another may not.

Check with your insurance agent to find out whether your company has a rating program. The "ratings" pages at the end of the book indicate the expected insurance rates for each of the 1998 models.

In This Chapter ...

No-Fault Insurance

One of the major expenses of vehicular accidents has been the cost of determining who is "at fault." Often, both parties hire lawyers and wait for court decisions, which can take a long time. Another problem with this system is that some victims receive considerably less than others for equivalent losses.

To resolve this, many states have instituted "no-fault" vehicle insurance. The concept is that each person's losses are covered by his or her personal insurance protection, regardless of who is at fault. Lawsuits are permitted only under certain conditions, usually restricted by the severity of the injuries.

While the idea is the same from state to state, the details of the no-fault laws vary. These variations include the amounts paid in similar situations, conditions of the right to sue, and the inclusion or exclusion of property damage.

Ironically, some no-fault states still permit lawsuits to determine who is at fault. Although the laws in each state may vary, here is a list of states with and without no-fault laws.

No-Fault States

Colorado	Massachusetts	New York
Florida	Michigan	North Dakota
Hawaii	Minnesota	Pennsylvania
Kansas	New Jersey	Utah
Kentucky		

States Without No-Fault

Alabama	Louisiana	Oregon
Alaska	Maine	Rhode Island
Arizona	Maryland	South Carolina
Arkansas	Mississippi	South Dakota
California	Missouri	Tennessee
Connecticut	Montana	Texas
Delaware	Nebraska	Vermont
District of Columbia	Nevada	Virginia
Georgia	New Hampshire	Washington
Idaho	New Mexico	West Virginia
Illinois	North Carolina	Wisconsin
Indiana	Ohio	Wyoming
Iowa	Oklahoma	

Insurance Injury Statistics

The insurance industry regularly publishes information about the accident history of cars currently on the road. The most reliable source of this rating information is the Highway Loss Data Institute (HLDI). These ratings, which range from very good to very poor, are based on the frequency of medical claims under personal injury protection coverages. A few companies will charge you more to insure a car rated poor than for one rated good.

A car's accident history may not match its crash test performance. Such discrepancies arise because the accident history includes driver performance. A sports car, for example, may have good crash test results but a poor accident history because its owners tend to drive relatively recklessly.

If you want more information about the injury history, bumper performance, and theft rating of today's cars, write to HLDI, 1005 North Glebe Road, Arlington, VA 22201.

Reducing Insurance Costs

After you have shopped around and found the best deal by comparing the costs of different coverages, consider other factors that will affect your final insurance bill.

Your Annual Mileage: The more you drive, the more your vehicle will be "exposed" to a potential accident. The insurance cost for a car rarely used will be less than the cost for a frequently used car.

Where You Drive: If you regularly drive and park in the city, you will most likely pay more than if you drive in rural areas.

Youthful Drivers: Usually the highest premiums are paid by male drivers under the age of 25. Whether or not the under-25-year-old male is married also affects insurance rates. (Married males pay less.) As the driver gets older, rates are lowered.

In addition to shopping around, take advantage of certain discounts to reduce your insurance costs. Most insurance companies offer discounts of 5 to 30 percent on various parts of your insurance bill. The availability of discounts varies among companies and often depends on where you live. Many consumers do not benefit from these discounts simply because they don't ask about them.

To determine whether you are getting all the discounts that you're entitled to, ask your insurance company for a complete list of the discounts that it offers.

Here are some of the most common insurance discounts:

Driver Education/Defensive Driving Courses: Many insurance companies offer (and in some cases mandate) discounts to young people who have successfully completed a state-approved driver education course. Typically, this can mean a $40 reduction in the cost of coverage. Also, a discount of 5-15 percent is available in some states to those who complete a defensive driving course.

Good Student Discounts: Many insurance companies offer discounts of up to 25 percent on insurance to full-time high school or college students who are in the upper 20 percent of their class, on the dean's list, or have a B or better grade point average.

Good Driver Discounts: Many companies will offer discounts to drivers with an accident and violation-free record.

Mature Driver Credit: Drivers ages 50 and older may qualify for up to a 10 percent discount, or a lower price bracket.

Sole Female Driver: Some companies offer discounts of 10 percent for females, ages 30 to 64, who are the only driver in a household, citing favorable claims experience.

Non-Drinkers and Non-Smokers: A limited number of companies offer incentives ranging from 10-25 percent to those who abstain.

Farmer Discounts: Many companies offer farmers either a discount of 10-30 percent or a lower price bracket.

Car Pooling: Commuters sharing driving may qualify for discounts of 5-25 percent or a lower price bracket.

Insuring Driving Children: Children away at school don't drive the family car very often, so it's usually less expensive to insure them on the parents' policy rather than separately. If you do insure them separately, discounts of 10-40 percent or a lower price bracket are available.

Don't Speed

Besides endangering the lives of your passengers and other drivers, speeding tickets will increase your insurance premium. It only takes one speeding ticket to lose your "preferred" or "good driver" discount, which requires a clean driving record. Two or more speeding tickets or accidents can increase your premium by 40% to 200%. Some insurers may simply drop your coverage. According to the Insurance Institute for Highway Safety (IIHS), you are 17% more likely to be in an accident if you have just one speeding ticket. Insurance companies know this and will charge you for it.

Desirable Cars: Premiums are usually much higher for cars with high collision rates or that are the favorite target of thieves.

Passive Restraints/Anti-Lock Brake Credit: Many companies offer discounts (from 10 to 30 percent) for automatic belts and air bags. Some large companies are now offering a 5 percent discount to owners of vehicles with anti-lock brakes.

Anti-Theft Device Credits: Discounts of 5 to 15 percent are offered in some states for cars equipped with a hood lock and an alarm or a disabling device (active or passive) that prevents the car from being started.

Account Credit: Some companies offer discounts of up to 10 percent for insuring your home and auto with the same company.

Long-Term Policy Renewal: Although not available in all states, some companies offer price breaks of 5-20 percent to customers who renew a long-term policy.

First Accident Allowance: Some insurers offer a "first accident allowance," which guarantees that if a customer achieves five accident-free years, his or her rates won't go up after the first at-fault accident.

Deductibles: Opting for the largest reasonable deductible is the obvious first step in reducing premiums. Increasing your deductible to $500 from $200 could cut your collision premium about 20 percent. Raising the deductible to $1,000 from $200 could lower your premium about 45 percent. The discounts may vary by company.

Collision Coverage: The older the car, the less the need for collision insurance. Consider dropping collision insurance entirely on an older car. Regardless of how much coverage you carry, the insurance company will only pay up to the car's "book value." For example, if your car requires $1,000 in repairs, but its "book value" is only $500, the insurance company is required to pay only $500.

Uninsured Motorist Coverage/ Optional Coverage: The necessity of both of these policies depends upon the extent of your health insurance coverage. In states where they are not required, consumers with applicable health insurance may not want uninsured motorist coverage. Also, those with substantial health insurance coverage may not want an optional medical payment policy.

Rental Cars: If you regularly rent cars, special coverage on your personal auto insurance can cover you while renting for far less than rental agencies offer.

Multi-Car Discount: Consumers insuring more than one car in the household with the same insurer can save up to 20 percent.

Tip: Expensive fender bender repairs can add up for both you and your insurance company. To reduce repairs, look for a car with bumpers that can withstand a 5-mph impact without damage. See page 68 for more information on bumpers.

Beep, Beep

As car instrument panels become more and more sophisticated, there is growing confusion about the location of horn buttons. There are no regulations requiring a standard location so manufacturers put them in various places around the steering wheel. On your test drive, make sure the horn button is easy to locate and use. When renting a car or driving an unfamiliar car, also be sure you know where the horn button is located. Proper use of a car horn can avoid serious accidents. Because of this, the Center for Auto Safety has been urging the government to standardize horn location since 1980. If you have experienced a problem due to a non-standard horn location, we urge you to contact the National Highway Traffic Safety Administration, Rulemaking Division, 400 7th St., SW, Washington, DC 20590 and the Center for Auto Safety, 2001 S Street, NW, Suite 410, Washington, DC 20009.

The risk of your vehicle being stolen is an important factor in the cost of your insurance. In fact, each year over 1.5 million vehicles are stolen. As a result, the market is flooded with expensive devices designed to prevent theft. Before you spend a lot of money on anti-theft devices, consider this: Of the vehicles stolen, nearly 80 percent were unlocked and 40 percent actually had the keys in the ignition. Most of these thefts are by amateurs. While the most important way to protect your vehicle is to keep it locked and remove the keys, this precaution will not protect you from the pros. If you live or travel in an area susceptible to auto thefts, or have a high-priced vehicle, here are some steps you can take to prevent theft.

Inexpensive Prevention:

☑ Replace door lock buttons with tapered tips. They make it difficult to hook the lock with a wire hanger. (But it will also keep you from breaking into your own vehicle!)

☑ Buy an alarm sticker (even if you don't have an alarm) for one of your windows.

☑ Buy an electric etching tool (about $15) and write your driver's license number in the lower corners of the windows and on unpainted metal items where it can be seen. Many police departments offer this service at no charge. They provide a sticker and enter the number into their records. The purpose of these identifying marks is to deter the professional thief who is planning to take the vehicle apart and sell the components. Since the parts can be traced, your vehicle becomes less attractive.

☑ Remove the distributor wire. This is a rather inconvenient, but effective, means of rendering your vehicle inoperable. If you are parking in a particularly suspect place, or leaving your vehicle for a long time, you may want to try this. On the top of the distributor, there is a short wire running to the coil. Removing the wire makes it impossible to start the vehicle.

A recently popular anti-theft device is a long rod that locks the steering wheel into place. It costs about $50 and requires a separate key to remove. Beware, however, that thieves now use a spray can of freon to freeze the lock, making it brittle enough to be smashed open with a hammer.

More Serious Measures:

☑ Cutting off the fuel to the engine will keep someone from driving very far with your vehicle. For around $125, you can have a fuel cutoff device installed that enables you to open or close the gasoline line to the engine. One drawback is that the thief will be able to drive a few blocks before running out of gas. If your vehicle is missing, you'll have to check your neighborhood first!

☑ Another way to deter a pro is to install a second ignition switch for about $150. To start your vehicle, you activate a hidden switch. The device is wired in such a complicated manner that a thief could spend hours trying to figure it out. Time is the thief's worst enemy, and the longer it takes to start your vehicle, the more likely the thief is to give up.

☑ The most common anti-theft devices on the market are alarms. These cost from $100 to $500 installed. Their complexity ranges from simply sounding your horn when someone opens your door to setting off elaborate sirens when someone merely approaches the vehicle. Alarms usually require a device such as a key or remote control to turn them on or off. Some people buy the switch, mount it on their vehicle, and hope that its presence will intimidate the thief.

The Highway Loss Data Institute regularly compiles statistics on motor vehicle thefts. In rating cars, they consider the frequency of theft and the loss resulting from the theft. The result is an index based on "relative average loss payments per insured vehicle year." The list below includes the most and least stolen cars among the 1998 models.

Auto Theft

Most Stolen		Least Stolen	
Mercedes-Benz S-Class	1033	Mercury Sable	12
Lexus GS300/400	695	Buick Regal	13
Lexus LS400	552	Saab 900	13
Lexus SC300/400	491	Buick Park Avenue	13
Chevrolet Corvette (conv.)	437	Buick Regal	14
BMW 3-Series	433	Mercury Tracer	19
Chevrolet Corvette	416	Buick LeSabre	20
Infiniti Q45	413	Chevrolet Lumina	21
Honda Prelude	329	Oldsmobile Achieva	23
Ford Mustang (conv.)	305	Oldsmobile 88	23

Bumpers

The main purpose of the bumper is to protect your car in low-speed collisions. Despite this intention, most of us have been victims of a $200 to $400 repair bill resulting from a seemingly minor impact. Since most bumpers offered little or no damage protection in low-speed crashes, the federal government *used* to require that auto makers equip cars with bumpers capable of withstanding up to 5-mph crashes with no damage. Unfortunately, this is no longer the case.

In the early eighties, while under pressure from car companies, the government rolled back the requirement that bumpers protect cars in collisions up to 5-mph. Now, car companies only build bumpers to protect cars in 2.5-mph collisions—about the speed at which we walk. This rollback has cost consumers millions of dollars in increased insurance premiums and repair costs. While the rollback satisfied car companies, most car owners were unhappy.

To let consumers know that today's bumpers offer widely varying amounts of protection in 5-mph collisions, each year the Insurance Institute for Highway Safety tests bumpers to see how well they prevent damage. Thankfully, some automobile manufacturers are betting that consumers still want better bumpers on at least some of their models. For example, in a 5-mph front test, the Ford Contour withstood $1056 worth of damage while the Lincoln Continental withstood only $16 worth of damage.

These results are rather startling when you consider that the sole purpose of a bumper is to protect a car from damage in low-speed collisions. Only about one-third of the cars tested to date have bumpers which actually prevented damage in front and rear 5-mph collisions. As the Institute's figures show, there is no correlation between the price of the car and how well the bumper worked.

Unfortunately, we can't simply look at a bumper and determine how good it will be at doing its job—protecting a car from inevitable bumps. The solution to this problem is quite simple—simply require car makers to tell the consumer the highest speed at which their car could be crashed with no damage to the car. Three states—California, Hawaii, and New York—have passed laws requiring car companies to disclose in the showroom, in various formats, the expected performance of the bumper on the car. These laws are currently being challenged by the car companies and we won't see them implemented for some time.

Following are the results of the IIHS bumper crash tests, listed from the best to the worst performers. We have included some of the cars which we believe will have similiar bumpers in 1998. *Note:* If the bumpers have changed at all since the time it was tested, the result could be drastically different. This should, however, give you a good basis for comparison. When available, additional information is on each car's page.

Bumper Bashing—Some Damage Repair Costs in 5-mph Crash Tests

Car (Year)	Front Crash	Rear Crash	Total Cost
Best			
Saab 900 (1994)	$0	$0	$0
Lincoln Continental (1997)	$0	$16	$16
Mazda Millenia (1995)	$75	$311	$386
Nissan Quest (1997)	$408	$0	$408
Dodge Caravan (1995)	$83	$332	$415
Worst			
Ford Aerostar (1997)	$851	$1142	$1993
Mazda MPV (1997)	$764	$1211	$1975
Toyota Previa (1997)	$674	$917	$1591
Mercedes E Class (1997)	$372	$1066	$1438
Ford Contour (1995)	$406	$650	$1056

TIRES

For most of us, buying tires has become an infrequent task. The reason—most cars now come with radial tires, which last much longer than the bias and bias-belted tires of the past. However, when we do get around to buying tires, making an informed purchase is not easy. The tire has to perform more functions simultaneously than any other part of the car (steering, bearing the load, cushioning the ride, and stopping). And not only is the tire the hardest-working item on the car, but there are nearly 1,800 tire lines to choose from. With only a few major tire manufacturers selling all those tires, the difference in many tires may only be the brand name.

Because it is so difficult to compare tires, it is easy to understand why many consumers mistakenly use price and brand name to determine quality. One company's definition of "first line" or "premium" may be entirely different from another's. But there is help. The U.S. government now requires tires to be rated according to their safety and expected mileage.

A little-known system grades tires on their *treadwear*, *traction*, and *heat resistance*. The grades are printed on the sidewall and are also attached to the tire on a paper label. In addition, every dealer can provide you with the grades of the tires he or she sells.

Treadwear: The treadwear grade gives you an idea of the mileage you can expect from a tire. It is shown in numbers—300, 310, 320, 330, and so forth. A tire graded 400 should give you 33 percent more mileage than one graded 300. In order to *estimate* the expected actual mileage, multiply the treadwear grade by 200. Under average conditions a tire graded 300 should last 60,000 miles. Because driving habits vary considerably, use the treadwear as a *relative* basis of comparison rather than an absolute predictor of mileage. Tire wear is affected by regional differences in the level of abrasive material used in road surfaces.

Traction: Traction grades of A, B, and C describe the tire's ability to stop on wet surfaces. Tires graded A will stop on a wet road in a shorter distance than tires graded B or C. Tires rated C have poor traction. If you drive frequently on wet roads, buy a tire with a higher traction grade.

Heat Resistance: Heat resistance is also graded A, B, and C. This grading is important because hot-running tires can result in blowouts or tread separation. An A rating means the tire will run cooler than one rated B or C, and it is less likely to fail if driven over long distances at highway speeds. In addition, tires that run cooler tend to be more fuel efficient. If you do a lot of high speed driving, a high heat resistance grade is best.

Speed Ratings: All passenger car tires meet government standards up to 85 mph. Some tires are tested at higher speeds because certain cars require tires that perform at higher speeds. Consult your owner's manual for the right speed rating for your car. See the tire size code: (For example, P215/60 SR15). The 'S' indicates the tire is tested for speeds up to 112 mph. Other letters include: "T" for up to 118 mph; "H" for up to 130 mph; "V" for up to 149 mph; "Z" for over 149 mph.

The tables at the end of this section give you a list of the highest rated tires on the market. For a complete listing of all the tires on the market, you can call the Auto Safety Hotline toll free, at 800-424-9393 or 800-424-9153 (TTY). (In Washington, DC, the number is 202-366-7800.)

In This Chapter...

Tires: Getting the Best Price

There are few consumer products on the market today as price competitive as tires. While this situation provides a buyer's market, it does require some price shopping.

The price of a tire is based on its size, and tires come in as many as nine sizes. For example, the list price of the same Goodyear Arriva tire can range from $74.20 to $134.35, depending on its size. Some manufacturers do not provide list prices, leaving the appropriate markup to the individual retailer. Even when list prices are provided, dealers rarely use them. Instead, they offer tires at what is called an "everyday low price," which can range from 10 to 25 percent below list.

The following tips can help you get the best buy.

1 Check to see which manufacturer makes the least expensive "off brand." Only twelve manufacturers produce the over 1,800 types of tires sold in the U.S. So you can save money and still get high quality.

2 Remember, generally the wider the tire, the higher the price.

3 Don't forget to inquire about balancing and mounting costs when comparing tire prices. In some stores, the extra charges for balancing, mounting and valve stems can add up to more than $25. Other stores may offer them as a customer service at little or no cost. That good buy in the newspaper may turn into a poor value when coupled with these extra costs. Also, compare warranties; they do vary from company to company.

4 Never pay list price for a tire. A good rule of thumb is to pay at least 30 to 40 percent off the suggested list price.

5 Use the treadwear grade the same way you would the "unit price" in a supermarket. It is the best way to ensure that you are getting the best tire value. The tire with the lowest cost per grade point is the best value. For example, if tire A costs $100 and has a treadwear grade of 300, and tire B costs $80 and has a treadwear grade of 200:

Tire A:
$100÷300 = $.33 per point

Tire B:
$80÷200 = $.40 per point

Since 33 cents is less than 40 cents, tire A is the better buy even though its initial cost is more.

New Tire Registration

You may be missing out on free or low-cost replacement tires or, worse, driving on potentially hazardous ones, if you don't fill out the tire registration form when you buy tires. The law once required all tire sellers to submit buyers' names automatically to the manufacturer, so the company could contact them if the tires were ever recalled. While this is still mandatory for tire dealers and distributors owned by tire manufacturers, it is not required of independent tire dealers. A recent government study found that 70 percent of independent tire dealers had not registered a single tire purchase. Ask for the tire registration card when you buy tires, and remember to fill it out and send it in. This information will allow the company to notify you if the tire is ever recalled.

Do Tires Affect Fuel Economy?

Yes, a tire's *rolling resistance* affects its fuel economy. In the past, fuel efficiency (low rolling resistance) was traded off with traction. Tires with good traction had lower fuel economy. Michelin has introduced a new rubber compound that doesn't sacrifice traction for fuel economy. In order to give consumers better information and to encourage the widespread use of this new compound, we have asked that the government change its heat resistance grade to a fuel efficiency rating.

Tire Grades

America's Top-Rated Tires

Brand Name	Model	Description	Grades			Expected Mileage		
			Trac.	Heat	Tred.	High	Medium	Low
Vogue	P225/	60R1697S	A	B	660	198,000	132,000	99,000
Vogue	P205/	75R1495S	A	B	580	174,000	116,000	87,000
Vogue	P225/	75R15102S	A	B	580	174,000	116,000	87,000
Vogue	P225/	75R15102S	A	B	580	174,000	116,000	87,000
Vogue	P225/	75R15103S	A	B	580	174,000	116,000	87,000
Vogue	P215/	70R1597S	A	B	580	174,000	116,000	87,000
Vogue	P215/	65R1595S	A	B	580	174,000	116,000	87,000
Vogue	P205/	75R1597S	A	B	580	174,000	116,000	87,000
Vogue	P205/	70R1595S	A	B	580	174,000	116,000	87,000
Big-O	Legacy 60/65/70 SR	All	A	B	560	168,000	112,000	84,000
CO-OP	Golden Mark 60/65/70	All	A	B	560	168,000	112,000	84,000
Concorde	Touring 9,000	All	A	B	560	168,000	112,000	84,000
Cooper	Grand Classic STE (SR)	All	A	B	560	168,000	112,000	84,000
Cordovan	Grand Prix Touring	All	A	B	560	168,000	112,000	84,000
Dean	Touring Edition SR	All	A	B	560	168,000	112,000	84,000
El Dorado	Legend	All	A	B	560	168,000	112,000	84,000
Falls	Mark VII (SR)	All	A	B	560	168,000	112,000	84,000
Kelly	Aqua Tour	All	A	B	560	168,000	112,000	84,000
Lee	Ultra Touring GT	All	A	B	560	168,000	112,000	84,000
Multi-Mile	Grand Am Touring ST	All	A	B	560	168,000	112,000	84,000
Sigma	Supreme Touring ST	All	A	B	560	168,000	112,000	84,000
Starfire	Constellation	All	A	B	560	168,000	112,000	84,000
Winston	Signature (C)	All	A	B	560	168,000	112,000	84,000
Dayton	Daytona Premium GT	All	A	B	540	162,000	108,000	81,000
Dunlop	Elite 65	15&16	A	B	540	162,000	108,000	81,000
Falken	FK315	All	A	B	540	162,000	108,000	81,000
Hankook	Mileage Plus	All	A	B	540	162,000	108,000	81,000
Ohtsu	HS311	All	A	B	540	162,000	108,000	81,000
Toyo	800+ 65	All	A	B	540	162,000	108,000	81,000
Toyo	800+ 70, 75	15	A	B	540	162,000	108,000	81,000
Toyo	800+ 60	15&16	A	B	540	162,000	108,000	81,000
Vogue	P215/	75R15100S	A	B	540	162,000	108,000	81,000
American	Gold 6,000 70&75 SR	15	A	B	520	156,000	104,000	78,000
Cavalier	Revelation 70/75	15	A	B	520	156,000	104,000	78,000
Centennial	Interceptor	15&16	A	B	520	156,000	104,000	78,000
Dunlop	Elite 65	14	A	B	520	156,000	104,000	78,000
Michelin	XH4	14&15	A	B	520	156,000	104,000	78,000
Pirelli	P400 Aquamile	All	A	B	520	156,000	104,000	78,000
Remington	Touring	15&16	A	B	520	156,000	104,000	78,000
Riken	Classic MR-60	15	A	B	520	156,000	104,000	78,000
Toyo	800+ 70	175/70R14	B	B	520	156,000	104,000	78,000
Toyo	800+ 75,70,60	14	A	B	520	156,000	104,000	78,000
Atlas	Pinnacle TE70	13	A	B	500	15,0000	1,00000	75,000
Atlas	Pinnacle TE70	14&15	A	B	500	15,0000	1,00000	75,000
Centennial	Interceptor	14	A	B	500	15,0000	1,00000	75,000
Cordovan	Grand Prix Trng LXE	75 SR	A	B	500	15,0000	1,00000	75,000
Dayton	Touring 70/75S	All	A	B	500	15,0000	1,00000	75,000
Duralon	IV Plus	All	A	B	500	15,0000	1,00000	75,000
Gillette	Kodiak LE	All	A	B	500	15,0000	1,00000	75,000
Multi-Mile	Grand Am Touring LSS	75 (SR)	A	B	500	15,0000	1,00000	75,000
Peerless	Permasteel LE	All	A	B	500	15,0000	1,00000	75,000
Remington	Touring	14	A	B	500	15,0000	1,00000	75,000
Sumitomo	SC890 75	15	A	B	500	15,0000	1,00000	75,000
Toyo	800+ 75	235/75RL15	A	B	500	15,0000	1,00000	75,000
CO-OP	Golden Mark 75	All	A	B	480	144,000	96,000	72,000
Cooper	Lifeliner II (SR/TR)	All	A	B	480	144,000	96,000	72,000
Cordovan	Classic	All	A	B	480	144,000	96,000	72,000
Cordovan	Grand Prix SE70	All	A	B	480	144,000	96,000	72,000
Dean	Cheetah Touring 70GT	SR All	A	B	480	144,000	96,000	72,000

Brand Name	Model	Description	Grades			Expected Mileage		
			Trac.	Heat	Tred.	High	Medium	Low
Dean	Quasar	All	A	B	480	144,000	96,000	72,000
Goodyear	Aquatred II	All Others	A	B	480	144,000	96,000	72,000
Hallmark	Pretige PWR4	All Others	A	B	480	144,000	96,000	72,000
Hallmark	Prestige PWR4	235/75R15	A	C	480	144,000	96,000	72,000
Hercules	Ultra Plus	All	A	B	480	144,000	96,000	72,000
Kelly	Navigator 800S	235/75R15	A	C	480	144,000	96,000	72,000
Kelly	Navigator 800S	All Others	A	B	480	144,000	96,000	72,000
Michelin	XH4	13	A	B	480	144,000	96,000	72,000
Monarch	Ultra Trak A/S	235/75R15	A	C	480	144,000	96,000	72,000
Monarch	Ultra Trak A/S	All Others	A	B	480	144,000	96,000	72,000
Multi-Mile	Grand Am STE	All Except	A	B	480	144,000	96,000	72,000
Multi-Mile	Grand Am G/T 70 RWL	All	A	B	480	144,000	96,000	72,000
Multi-Mile	Grand Am STE	XL	A	C	480	144,000	96,000	72,000
Multi-Mile	Grand Am STE	70&65 SR	A	B	480	144,000	96,000	72,000
Pacemark	Premium A/S P235/	75415 XL	A	C	480	144,000	96,000	72,000
Pacemark	Premium A/S	All	A	B	480	144,000	96,000	72,000
Republic	Weather King	All	A	B	480	144,000	96,000	72,000
Sigma	Supreme SE	All	A	B	480	144,000	96,000	72,000
Sigma	Grand Sport 70 RWL	All	A	B	480	144,000	96,000	72,000
Sigma	Supreme STE	XL	A	C	480	144,000	96,000	72,000
Sigma	Supreme STE	All Except	A	B	480	144,000	96,000	72,000
Star	Imperial	235/75R15	A	C	480	144,000	96,000	72,000
Star	Imperial PSR	All Others	A	B	480	144,000	96,000	72,000
Starfire	Spectrum LXR	All	A	B	480	144,000	96,000	72,000
Vanderbilt	Turbo Tech tour A/S	All	A	B	480	144,000	96,000	72,000
American	Gold 6,000 70&75 SR	14	A	B	460	138,000	92,000	69,000
Brigadier	Touring Pro 70/75	15	A	B	460	138,000	92,000	69,000
Brigadier	Touring Pro 65	P205/65R15	A	B	460	138,000	92,000	69,000
Cavalier	Revelation 70/75	14	A	B	460	138,000	92,000	69,000
Cavalier	SRX 70	14&15	A	B	460	138,000	92,000	69,000
Centennial	Interceptor	13	A	B	460	138,000	92,000	69,000
Continental	Contact A/S CS-24	15	A	B	460	138,000	92,000	69,000
Dayton	Quadra LTE	All	A	B	460	138,000	92,000	69,000
General	Ameri Tech St P215	P225/75SR15	A	B	460	138,000	92,000	69,000
General	Ameri Tech ST 70	15	A	B	460	138,000	92,000	69,000
General	GS	All	A	B	460	138,000	92,000	69,000
General	Ameri Tech 4 75	15	A	B	460	138,000	92,000	69,000
Goodyear	Aquatred II	13	A	B	460	138,000	92,000	69,000
Kleber	CPR700S P195-	P235/70R15	A	B	460	138,000	92,000	69,000
Kleber	CPR700S	P215/70R14	A	B	460	138,000	92,000	69,000
Kleber	CP751,701	14	A	B	460	138,000	92,000	69,000
Kumho	782	All	A	B	460	138,000	92,000	69,000
Mont. Ward	Ventura	All Others	A	B	460	138,000	92,000	69,000
Pirelli	P100	All	A	B	460	138,000	92,000	69,000
Remington	Touring	13	A	B	460	138,000	92,000	69,000
Reynolds	Touring Plus 65	P205/65R15	A	B	460	138,000	92,000	69,000
Reynolds	Touring Plus 70/75	15	A	B	460	138,000	92,000	69,000
Riken	Classic MR-GT P225/	70R15	A	B	460	138,000	92,000	69,000
Riken	Classic MR-GT P235/	70R15	A	B	460	138,000	92,000	69,000
Riken	Classic MR-GT P235/	70R15	A	B	460	138,000	92,000	69,000
Riken	Classic MR-GT P215/	70R14	A	B	460	138,000	92,000	69,000
Road King	Grenadier LTE	All	A	B	460	138,000	92,000	69,000
Sears	Aquahandler	All Other	A	B	460	138,000	92,000	69,000
Sears	Aquahandler	13	A	B	460	138,000	92,000	69,000
Sonic	Sentinel 70/75	15	A	B	460	138,000	92,000	69,000
Sonic	Sentinel 65	P205/65R15	A	B	460	138,000	92,000	69,000
Touring Supreme	SE 70/75 Series	15	A	B	460	138,000	92,000	69,000
Touring Supreme	SE 65 Series	P205/65R15	A	B	460	138,000	92,000	69,000
Toyo	800+	13	A	B	460	138,000	92,000	69,000
Toyo	800+ 80	All	A	B	460	138,000	92,000	69,000

COMPLAINTS

Americans spend billions of dollars on motor vehicle repairs every year. While many of those repairs are satisfactory, there are times when getting your vehicle fixed can be a very difficult process. In fact, vehicle defects and repairs are the number one cause of consumer complaints in the U.S., according to the Federal Trade Commission.

This chapter is designed to help you resolve your complaint, whether it's for a new vehicle still under warranty or for one you've had for years. In addition, we offer a guide to arbitration, the names and addresses of consumer groups, federal agencies and the manufacturers themselves. Finally, we tell you how to take the important step of registering your complaint with the U.S. Department of Transportation.

No matter what your complaint, keep accurate records. Copies of the following items are indispensable in helping to resolve your problems:

☑ your service invoices

☑ bills you have paid

☑ letters you have written to the manufacturer or the repair facility owner

☑ written repair estimates from your independent mechanic.

Resolving Complaints : If you are having trouble, here are some basic steps to help you resolve your problem:

1 First, return your vehicle to the repair facility that did the work. Bring a written list of the problems and make sure that you keep a copy of the list. Give the repair facility a reasonable opportunity to examine your vehicle and attempt to fix it. Speak directly to the service manager (not to the service writer who wrote up your repair order), and ask him or her to test drive the vehicle with you so that you can point out the problem.

2 If that doesn't resolve the problem, take the vehicle to a diagnostic center for an independent examination. This may cost $45 to $60. Get a written statement defining the problem and outlining how it may be fixed. Give your repair shop a copy. If your vehicle is under warranty, do not allow any warranty repair by an independent mechanic; you may not be reimbursed by the manufacturer.

3 If your repair shop does not respond to the independent assessment, present your problem to a mediation panel. These panels hear both sides of the story and try to come to a resolution.

If the problem is with a new vehicle dealer, or if you feel that the manufacturer is responsible, you may be able to use one of the manufacturer's mediation programs discussed on pg. 78.

If the problem is solely with an independent dealer, a local Better Business Bureau (BBB) may be able to mediate your complaint. It may also offer an arbitration hearing. In any case, the BBB should enter your complaint into its files on that establishment.

When contacting any mediation program, determine how long the process takes, who makes the final decision, whether you are bound by that decision, and whether the program handles all problems or only warranty complaints.

4 If there are no mediation programs in your area, contact private consumer groups, local government agencies, or your local "action line"

In This Chapter...

newspaper columnist, newspaper editor, or radio or TV broadcaster. A phone call or letter from them may persuade a repair facility to take action. Send a copy of your letter to the repair shop.

5 One of your last resorts is to bring a law suit against the dealer, manufacturer, or repair facility in small claims court. The fee for filing such an action is usually small, and you generally act as your own attorney, saving attorney's fees. There is a monetary limit on the amount you can claim, which varies from state to state. Your local consumer affairs office, state attorney general's office, or the clerk of the court can tell you how to file such a suit.

6 Finally, talk with an attorney. It's best to select an attorney who is familiar with handling automotive problems. If you don't know of one, call the lawyer referral service listed in the telephone directory (or see box) and ask for the names of attorneys who deal with automobile problems. If you can't afford an attorney, contact the Legal Aid Society.

Warranty Complaints: If your vehicle is under warranty or you are having problems with a factory-authorized dealership, here are some special guidelines:

Have the warranty available to show the dealer. Make sure you call the problem to the dealer's attention before the end of the warranty period.

If you are still unsatisfied after giving the dealer a reasonable opportunity to fix your vehicle, contact the manufacturer's representative (also called the zone representative) in your area. This person can authorize the dealer to make repairs or take other steps to resolve the dispute. Your dealer will have your zone representative's name and telephone number. Explain the problem and ask for a meeting and a personal inspection of your vehicle.

If you can't get satisfaction from the zone representative, call or write the manufacturer's owner relations department. Your owner's manual contains this phone number and address. In each case, as you move up the chain, indicate the steps you have already taken.

Your next option is to present your problem to a complaint-handling panel or to the arbitration program in which the manufacturer of your vehicle participates. See page 77 for additional information.

If you complain of a problem during the warranty period, you have a right to have the problem fixed even after the warranty runs out. If your warranty has not been honored, you may be able to "revoke acceptance," which means that you return the vehicle to the dealer. If you are successful, you may be entitled to a replacement vehicle, or to a full refund of the purchase price and reimbursement of legal fees under the Magnuson-Moss Warranty Act. Or, if you are covered by one of the state Lemon Laws (see page 85), you may be able to return the vehicle and receive a refund or replacement from the manufacturer.

Legal Aid

If you need legal assistance with your repair problem, the Center for Auto Safety has a list of lawyers who specialize in helping consumers with auto repair problems. For the names of some attorneys in your area, send a stamped, self-addressed envelope to: Center for Auto Safety, 2001 S Street, NW, Washington, DC 20009-1160.

In addition, the Center has published *The Lemon Book,* a detailed, 368-page guide to resolving automobile complaints. The book is available for $16.50 directly from the Center.

Attorneys Take Note: For information on litigation assistance provided by the Center for Auto Safety, including The Lemon Law Litigation Manual, please contact the Center for Auto Safety at the above address.

Auto Safety Hotline

One of the most valuable but often unused services of the government is the Auto Safety Hotline. By calling the Hotline to report safety problems, your particular concern or problem will become part of the National Highway Traffic Safety Administration's (NHTSA) complaint database. This complaint program is extraordinarily important to government decision makers who often take action based on this information. In addition, it provides consumer groups, like the Center for Auto Safety, with the evidence they need to force the government to act. Unless government engineers or safety advocates have evidence of a wide-scale problem, little can be done to get the manufacturers to correct the defect.

Few government services have the potential to do as much for the consumer as this complaint database, so we encourage you to voice your concerns to the government.

Your letter can be used as the basis of safety defect investigations and recall campaigns. When you file a complaint, be sure to indicate that your name and address can be made public. Without names and addresses, it is more difficult for consumer groups to uncover safety defects.

Hotline Complaints: When you call the Hotline to report a safety problem, you will be mailed a questionnaire asking for information that the agency's technical staff will need to evaluate the problem. This information also gives the government an indication of which vehicles are causing consumers the most problems.

You can also use this questionnaire to report defects in tires and child safety seats. In fact, we strongly encourage you to report problems with child safety seats. Now that they are required by law in all fifty states, we have noticed that numerous design and safety problems have surfaced. If the government knows about these problems, they will be more likely to take action so that modifications are made to these lifesaving devices.

After you complete and return the questionnaire, the following things will happen:

1. A copy will go to NHTSA's safety defect investigators.
2. A copy will be sent to the manufacturer of the car or equipment, with a request for help in resolving the problem.
3. You will be notified that your questionnaire has been received.
4. Your problem will be recorded in the complaint database which we use to provide you with complaint ratings.

Hotline Services: Hotline operators can also provide information on recalls. If you want recall information on a particular automobile, simply tell the Hotline operator the make, model, and year of the car, or the type of equipment involved. You will receive any recall information that NHTSA has about that car or item. This information can be very important if you are not sure whether your car has ever been recalled. If you want a printed copy of the recall information, it will be mailed within twenty-four hours at no charge.

If you have other car-related problems, the Hotline operators can refer you to the appropriate federal, state, and local government agencies. If you need information about federal safety standards and regulations, you'll be referred to the appropriate experts.

You may call the Hotline day or night, seven days a week. If you call when no operators are available, a recorded message will ask you to leave your name and address and a description of the information you want. The appropriate materials will be mailed to you.

Complaints and Safety Information

Auto Safety Hotline
800-424-9393
(in Washington, DC: 202-366-0123)
TTY for hearing impaired:
800-424-9153
(in Washington, DC: 202-366-7800)

The toll-free Auto Safety Hotline can provide information on recalls, record information about safety problems, and refer you to the appropriate government experts on other vehicle related problems. You can even have recall information mailed to you within 24 hours of your call at no charge.

Arbitration

An increasingly popular method of resolving automobile repair problems is through arbitration. This procedure requires that both parties present their cases to an arbitrator or panel that makes a decision based on the merits of the complaint. You can seek repairs, reimbursement of expenses, or a refund or replacement for your car through arbitration.

In theory, arbitration can be an effective means of resolving disputes. It is somewhat informal, relatively speedy, and you do not need a lawyer to present your case. Plus, you avoid the time and expense of going to court.

Almost all manufacturers now offer some form of arbitration, usually for problems that arise during the warranty period. Some companies run their own and others subscribe to programs run by groups like the Better Business Bureau or the National Center for Dispute Settlement. Your owner's manual will identify which programs you can use. Also, contact your state attorney general to find out what programs your state offers.

How it works: Upon receiving your complaint, the arbitration program will attempt to mediate a resolution between you and the manufacturer or dealer. If you are not satisfied with the proposed solution, you have the right to have your case heard at an arbitration hearing.

These hearings vary among the programs. In the BBB program, each party presents its case in person to a volunteer arbitrator. Other programs decide your case based on written submissions from both you and the manufacturer.

If an arbitration program is incorporated into your warranty, you may have to use that program before filing a legal claim. Federal law requires that arbitration programs incorporated into a warranty be nonbinding on the consumer. So, if you do not like the result, you can seek other remedies.

Arbitration programs have different eligibility requirements, so be sure you are eligible for the program you are considering.

Let the Federal Trade Commission, the Center for Auto Safety (their addresses are on pages 81 and 82), and your state attorney general (c/o your state capitol) know of your experience with arbitration. It is particularly important to contact these offices if you have a complaint about how your case was handled.

Ford Dispute Settlement Board: Each case is considered by a four-person panel that includes one dealer. In most cases, no oral presentations are given, although the customer may request to give one. Only cases under warranty are reviewed. For information, call 800-392-3673.

Chrysler Customer Arbitration Board: The National Center for Dispute Settlement (NCDS) handles cases in some states. Otherwise, the Customer Arbitration Board will handle the dispute. In both programs, decisions will be based on written submissions by each party. Customers who live in AR, KY, MN, and OH and in states where complaints are handled by NCDS have the right to request oral presentation. The NCDS board consists of a local consumer advocate, an independent, A.S.E. certified technical representative, and a representative from the general public. The Consumer Arbitration Board is a panel whose members have many years of experience in consumer affairs and/or automotive service. Both boards will only hear cases under warranty. For information, call 800-992-1997.

Better Business Bureau (BBB) Arbitration Programs (Auto Line): The BBB always tries to mediate a dispute before recommending arbitration. About 12% of the disputes it handles actually go to arbitration. The arbitrators are selected at random and an impartial technical expert can be present if requested. The consumer can object if conflict exists.

Arbitrators are volunteers from the local community and are not always automobile experts. This can both help and harm your case. As a result, it is important to be well prepared when participating in the BBB program. If you're not, the potential exists for the dealer or manufacturer to appear as the "expert" on automobiles. For more information, contact your local BBB or 800-955-5100.

Automobile Consumer Action Program: AUTOCAP was established by the National Automobile Dealers Association (NADA) to assist consumers in resolving auto sales or service disputes with dealers and manufacturers. The program is sponsored on a voluntary basis by state and local dealer associations. Currently, most AUTOCAPs do not operate under the FTC guidelines required for warranty cases. For more information and the name of your local panel, contact: AUTOCAP, 8400 Westpark Drive, McLean, Virginia 22102; 703-821-7144.

Arbitration Tips: Arbitration is designed to be easier and less intimidating than going to court. However, the process can still be nerve-racking, especially if you've never been through it before. Here are some tips to help make the process simple and straightforward:

1. Before deciding to go to arbitration, get a written description of how the program works and make sure you understand the details. If you have any questions, contact the local representatives of the program. Remember, the manufacturer or dealer probably has more experience with this process than you do.
2. Make sure the final decision is nonbinding on you. If the decision is binding, you give up your right to appeal.
3. Determine whether the program allows you to appear at the hearing. If not, make sure your written statement is complete and contains all the appropriate receipts and documentation. If you think of something that you want considered after you have sent in your material, send it immediately and specifically request that the additional information be included.
4. Make sure the program follows the required procedures. If the arbitration program is incorporated into the car's warranty, for example, the panel must make a decision on your case within 40 days of receiving your complaint.
5. Contact the manufacturer's zone manager and request copies of any technical service bulletins that apply to your car. (See "Secret Warranties" on page 61 for a description of technical service bulletins and how to get them.) Service bulletins may help you prove that your car is defective.
6. Well before the hearing, ask the program representative to send you copies of all material submitted by the other party. You may want to respond to this information.
7. Make sure all your documents are in chronological order, and include a brief outline of the events. Submit copies of all material associated with your problem and a copy of your warranty.
8. Even though you may be very angry about the situation, try to present your case in a calm, logical manner.
9. If you are asking for a refund or a replacement for your car in accordance with your state's Lemon Law, do not assume that the arbitrator is completely familiar with the law. Be prepared to explain how it entitles you to your request.
10. In most programs, you have to reject the decision in order to go to court to pursue other action. If you accept the decision, you may limit your rights to pursue further action. You will, however, have additional claims if the manufacturer or dealer does not properly follow through on the decision or if your car breaks down again.

TIP

State-Run Arbitration

State-run arbitration programs are often more fair to consumers than national programs. The following states have set up programs (or guidelines) which are far better than their national counterparts. If you live in one of these areas, contact your attorney general's office (in care of your state capitol) for information. If your state is not listed below, you should still contact your state attorney general's office for advice on arbitration.

Connecticut	Hawaii	New Hampshire	Texas
Florida	Maine	New Jersey	Vermont
Georgia	Massachusetts	New York	Washington

Complaint Index

Thanks to the efforts of the Center for Auto Safety, we are able to provide you with the vehicle complaints on file with the National Highway Traffic Safety Administration (NHTSA). Each year, thousands of Americans call the government to register complaints about their vehicles. The federal government collects this information but has never released it to the public.

The complaint index is the result of our analysis of these complaints. It is based on a ratio of the number of complaints for each vehicle to the sales of that vehicle. In order to predict the expected complaint performance of the 1998 models, we have examined the complaint history of that car's *series*. The term *series* refers to the fact that when a manufacturer introduces a new model, that vehicle remains essentially unchanged, on average, for 4-6 years. For example, the Pontiac Bonneville was introduced in 1992 and remains essentially the same car for 1998. As such, we have compiled the complaint experience for that series in order to give you some additional information to use in deciding which car to buy. For those vehicles just introduced in 1997 or 1998, we do not yet have enough data to develop a complaint index.

The following table presents the complaint indexes for the best and worst 1998 models. Higher index numbers mean the vehicle generated a greater number of complaints. Lower numbers indicate fewer complaints. After calculating the indexes, we compared the results among all 1998 vehicles.

1998 Complaint Ratings

The Best

Vehicle	Index
Isuzu Oasis	0
Acura RL	325
Infiniti I30	480
Suzuki Swift	523
Audi A4	679
Acura TL	840
Honda Odyssey	865
Lexus LS400	879
Lexus SC300/400	906
Toyota Paseo	934
Toyota Celica	987
Mazda Miata	992
Plymouth Breeze	1171
Oldsmobile Achieva	1180
Merc-Benz E-Class	1230
Acura Integra	1368
Mazda Millenia	1369
Nissan Maxima	1369
Pontiac Bonneville	1379
BMW Z3	1380
Toyota Tercel	1481
Suzuki Esteem	1483
Pontiac Grand Am	1527
Buick LeSabre	1535

The Worst

Vehicle	Index
Chevrolet Lumina	8847
Chrysler T&C	8543
Dodge Caravan	8445
Chrysler Sebring	8262
Chrysler Cirrus	6990
Mitsubishi Eclipse	6935
Saab 900	6407
Plymouth Voyager	6268
Dodge/Ply. Neon	5871
Dodge Avenger	5784
Eagle Talon	5301
Chevrolet Metro	5145
Ford Windstar	4934
Chrysler LHS	4291
Dodge Stratus	4224
Eagle Vision	4088
Nissan 240SX	3889
Hyundai Accent	3800
Mitsubishi Galant	3667
Hyundai Elantra	3519
Hyundai Sonata	3504
Chevrolet Corvette	3355
Saab 9000	3306
Ford Crown Victoria	3274

Center for Auto Safety

Every year automobile manufacturers spend millions of dollars making their voices heard in government decision making. For example, General Motors and Ford have large staffs in Detroit and Washington that work solely to influence government activity. But who looks out for the consumer?

For over twenty-five years, the nonprofit Center for Auto Safety (CAS) has told the consumer's story to government agencies, to Congress and to the courts. Its efforts focus on all consumers rather than only those with individual complaints.

CAS was established in 1970 by Ralph Nader and Consumers Union. As consumer concerns about auto safety issues expanded, so did the work of CAS. It became an independent group in 1972, and the original staff of two has grown to fourteen attorneys and researchers. CAS' activities include:

Initiating Safety Recalls: CAS analyzes over 50,000 consumer complaints each year. By following problems as they develop, CAS requests government investigations and recalls of defective vehicles. CAS was responsible for the Ford Pinto faulty gas tank recall, the Firestone 500 steel-belted radial tire recall, and the record recall of over 3 million Evenflo One Step child seats.

Representing the Consumer in Washington: CAS follows the activities of federal agencies and Congress to ensure that they carry out their responsibilities to the American taxpayer. CAS brings a consumer's point of view to vehicle safety policies and rule-making. Since 1970, CAS has submitted more than 500 petitions and comments on federal safety standards.

One major effort in this area has been the successful fight for adoption of automatic crash protection in passenger cars. These systems are a more effective and less intrusive alternative to crash protection than mandatory safety belt laws or belts that must be buckled in order to start the car.

In 1992, the Center for Auto Safety uncovered a fire defect that dwarfed the highly publicized flammability of the Ford Pinto. It had to do with the side-saddle gas tanks on full size 1973-87 GM pickups and 1988-90 crew cabs that tend to explode on impact. Over 1,600 people have been killed in fire crashes involving these trucks. After mounting a national campaign to warn consumers to steer clear of these GM fire hazards, the U.S. Department of Transportation (DOT) granted CAS' petition and conducted one of its biggest defect investigations in history. The result—GM was asked to recall its pickups. GM, sadly, denied this request.

Thanks to a petition originally filed by CAS, NHTSA adopted a new registration system to better enable manufacturer notification to parents with defective child seats. This will enable more parents to find out about potentially hazardous safety seats.

Exposing Secret Warranties: CAS played a prominent role in the disclosure of secret warranties, "policy adjustments," as they are called by manufacturers. These occur when an auto maker agrees to pay for repair of certain defects beyond the warranty period but refuses to notify consumers. (See "Secret Warranties" on page 61.)

Improving Rust Warranties: Rust and corrosion cost American car owners up to $14 billion annually. CAS has been successful in its efforts to get domestic and foreign auto companies to lengthen their all-important corrosion warranties.

Lemon Laws: CAS' work on Lemon Laws aided in the enactment of state laws which make it easier to return a defective new automobile and get money back.

Tire Ratings: After a suspension between 1982-84, consumers have reliable treadwear ratings to help them get the most miles for their dollar. CAS' lawsuit overturned DOT's revocation of this valuable new tire information program.

Initiating Legal Action: When CAS has exhausted other means of obtaining relief for consumer problems, it will initiate legal action. For example, in 1978 when the Department of Energy attempted to raise the price of gasoline 4 cents per gallon without notice or comment, CAS succeeded in stopping this illegal move through a lawsuit, thus saving consumers $2 billion for the six month period that the action was delayed.

A CAS lawsuit against the Environmental Protection Agency (EPA) in 1985 forced the EPA to recall polluting cars, rather than let companies promise to make cleaner cars in the future. As part of the settlement, GM (which was responsible for the polluting cars) funded a $7 million methanol bus demonstration program in New York City.

Publications: CAS has many publications on automobiles, motor homes, recreational vehicles, and fuel economy, including a number of free information packets. For each of the packets listed below, or for a complete description of all of CAS' publications, send a separate stamped, self-addressed, business-sized envelope with 55¢ postage to the address below. Unless otherwise noted, the packets listed below cover all known major problems since 1985 for the models indicated and explain what to do about them. Requests for information should include make, model, and year of vehicle (with VIN number), as well as type of problem you are experiencing. (Allow 2 weeks for delivery.)

Audi
BMW
Cadillac
Chrys. Paint/Water Leaks
Chrys. Ultradrive Trans.
Chrys. Aries Reliant/K-Cars
Chrys. Cirrus/Stratus/Neon
Chrys. LHS/Intrepid/Concorde
Chrys. Minivan
Chrys. Pickups/Big Vans
Ford Aerostar
Ford Auto. Trans.: Taurus/Sable/ Continental
Ford Bronco II/Explorer/Ranger
Ford Cr. Vic./Gr. Marquis/ Thunderbird/Cougar/Lincolns
Ford Escort/Lynx/Tracer
Ford F-Series Trucks
Ford Taurus/Sable
Ford Tempo/Topaz
Ford Mustang/Probe
Ford Paint
GM All Geo's/LeMans/Sprint/ Nova
GM Saturn
GM Auto. Trans.: FWD
GM Auto. Trans.: RWD
GM Beretta/Corsica
GM Cut. Supr./Gr. Prix/Lumina/ Regal
GM Celebrity/6000/Century/Cut. Ciera & Cruiser
GM Camaro/Firebird
GM Achieva/Calais/Gr. Am/Skylark/Somerset Regal
GM Roadmaster/Caprice
GM Cavalier/Cimarron/Firenza/ Skyhawk/Sunbird/Sunfire/J2000
GM 98/Electra & Park Ave.
GM 88/LeSabre/Bonneville
GM Power Steering FWD
GM C/K Pickup/Suburban/Tahoe/ Yukon/Blazer/Jimmy
GM S-Series/Blazer/Jimmy/ Sonoma
GM Big Vans/Astro/Safari/APVs
GM Pontiac Fiero
GM Paint
Honda/Acura
Hyundai
Jeep–all models
Infinti
Isuzu
Mazda Cars, Mazda Trucks
Mercedes
Mitsubishi
Nissan Cars, Nissan Vans/Trucks
Renault/Eagle
Saab
Subaru
Toyota
Volkswagen
Volvo

CAS Website: CAS has a website (www.essential.org/cas) to provide information to consumers and to organize consumer campaigns against auto companies on safety defects. All of the above consumer packages are on CAS' website. Consumers with lemons and safety defects can file electronic complaints with CAS and get referred to lemon lawyers. The best consumer campaigns are on stalling Fords (1983-95 Fords with defective ignition modules that cause stalling on the highways) and GM firebombs (1973-82 GM pickups with side saddle gas tanks that explode on impact).

Help CAS help you: CAS depends on the public for its support. Annual consumer membership is $20. All contributions to this non-profit organization are tax-deductible. Annual membership includes a quarterly newsletter called "LEMON TIMES." To join, send a check to: Center for Auto Safety, 2001 S Street, NW, Washington, DC 20009-1160.

Lemon Aid

The Center for Auto Safety has published *The Lemon Book*, a detailed, 368 page guide to resolving automobile complaints. Co-authored by Ralph Nader and CAS Executive Director, Clarence Ditlow, this handbook is designed to help car buyers avoid lemons and tells you what to do if you wind up with one. To obtain this valuable book, send $16.50 to the Center for Auto Safety, 2001 S St., NW, Washington, DC 20009-1160. CAS is a non-profit consumer group supported, in part, by the sales of its publications.

Consumer Groups and Government

Here are the names of additional consumer groups which you may find helpful:

Advocates for Highway and Auto Safety
750 First Street, NE, Suite 901
Washington, DC 20002
(202) 408-1711
Focus: An alliance of consumer, health and safety groups, and insurance companies.

Consumer Action San Francisco
116 New Montgomery St., #233
San Francisco, CA 94105
(415) 777-9635
Focus: General problems of California residents.

Consumers for Auto Reliability and Safety
1500 W. El Camino Ave, #333
Sacramento, CA 95833-1945
(916) 759-9440
Focus: Auto safety, airbags, and lemon laws.

Consumers Education and Protective Association
6048 Ogontz Avenue
Philadelphia, PA 19141
(215) 424-1441
Focus: Pickets on behalf of members to resolve auto purchase and repair problems.

SafetyBelt Safe, U.S.A.
P.O. Box 553
Altadena, CA 91003
(800) 745-SAFE or
(310) 222-6860
Focus: Provides excellent information and training on child safety seats and safety belt usage.

Several federal agencies conduct automobile-related programs. Listed below is each agency with a description of the type of work it performs as well as the address and phone number for its headquarters in Washington, DC. Useful web sites are also listed.

National Highway Traffic Safety Administration
400 7th Street, SW, NOA-40
Washington, DC 20590
(202) 366-9550
www.nhtsa.dot.gov

NHTSA issues safety and fuel economy standards for new motor vehicles; investigates safety defects and enforces recall of defective vehicles and equipment; conducts research and demonstration programs on vehicle safety, fuel economy, driver safety, and automobile inspection and repair; provides grants for state highway safety programs in areas such as police traffic services, driver education and licensing, emergency medical services, pedestrian safety, and alcohol abuse.

Environmental Protection Agency
401 M Street, SW
Washington, DC 20460
(202) 260-2090
www.epa.gov

EPA is responsible for the control and abatement of air, noise, and toxic substance pollution. This includes setting and enforcing air and noise emission standards for motor vehicles and measuring fuel economy in new vehicles (EPA Fuel Economy Guide).

Federal Trade Commission
PA Avenue & 6th Street, NW
Washington, DC 20580
(202) 326-2000
www.ftc.gov

FTC regulates advertising and credit practices, marketing abuses, and professional services and ensures that products are properly labeled (as in fuel economy ratings). The commission covers unfair or deceptive trade practices in motor vehicle sales and repairs, as well as in non-safety defects.

Federal Highway Administration
400 7th Street, SW,
Room 3401, HHS1
Washington, DC 20590
(202) 366-1153

FHA develops standards to ensure highways are constructed to reduce occurrence and severity of accidents.

Department of Justice
Consumer Litigation
Civil Division
1331 Pennsylvania Avenue
National Place Bldg., Suite 950N
Washington, DC 20004
(202) 514-6786

The Department of Justice enforces the federal law that requires manufacturers to label new automobiles and forbids removal or alteration of labels before delivery to consumers. Labels must contain the make, model, vehicle identification number, dealer's name, suggested base price, manufacturer option costs, and manufacturer's suggested retail price.

Automobile Manufacturers

Acura Automobile Division
Mr. Richard B. Thomas
Exec. V. P. and General Manager
1919 Torrance Blvd.
Torrance, CA 90501-2746
(310) 783-2000/(310) 783-3900 (fax)

BMW of North America, Inc.
Mr. Victor H. Doolan
President
300 Chestnut Ridge Road
Woodcliff Lake, NJ 07675
(201) 307-4000/(201) 307-4003 (fax)

Chrysler Corporation
Mr. Robert Eaton
Chairman and CEO
1000 Chrysler Drive
Auburn Hills, MI 48326-2766
(810) 512-9300

Ford Motor Company
Mr. Alex Trotman
Chairman and CEO
The American Road
Dearborn, MI 48121
(313) 322-3000/(313) 446-9475 (fax)

General Motors Corporation
Mr. John F. Smith, Jr.
CEO and Chairman
3044 W. Grand Blvd.
Detroit, MI 48202
(313) 556-5000/(313) 556-5108 (fax)

American Honda Motor Co.
Mr. K. Amemiya
President
1919 Torrance Blvd.
Torrance, CA 90501-2746
(310) 783-2000/(310) 783-3900 (fax)

Hyundai Motor America
Mr. M.H. Juhn
President and CEO
10550 Talbert Avenue
Fountain Valley, CA 92728
(714) 965-3939/(714) 965-3816 (fax)

American Isuzu Motors Inc.
Mr. Yoshito Mochizuki
President
2300 Pellissier Place
Whittier, CA 90601
(562) 699-0500/(562) 692-7135 (fax)

Kia Motors America, Inc.
Mr. W.K. Kim
President and CEO
P.O. Box 52410
Irvine, CA 92619-2410
(714) 470-7000/(714) 470-2801 (fax)

Land Rover of America
Mr. Charles R. Hughes
President
4371 Parliament Place, P.O. Box 1503
Lanham, MD 20706
(301) 731-9040/(301) 731-9054 (fax)

Mazda Motor of America, Inc.
Mr. Richard Beattle
President and CEO
7755 Irvine Center Dr.
Irvine, CA 92718
(714) 727-1990/(714) 727-6529 (fax)

Mercedes-Benz of N.A.
Mr. Michael Jackson
President
1 Mercedes Drive
Montvale, NJ 07645-0350
(201) 573-0600/(201) 573-0117 (fax)

Mitsubishi Motor Sales
Mr. Takashi Sonobe
President
6400 Katella Ave.
Cypress, CA 90630-0064
(714) 372-6000/(714) 373-1019 (fax)

Nissan Motor Corp. U.S.A.
Mr. Robert Thomas
President and CEO
P.O. Box 191
Gardena, CA 90248-0191
(310) 532-3111/(310) 719-3343 (fax)

Saab Cars USA, Inc.
Mr. Joel Manby
President and CEO
4405-A International Drive
Norcross, GA 30093
(770) 279-0100/(770) 279-6499 (fax)

Subaru of America, Inc.
Mr. Yasuo Fujiki
Chairman and CEO
P.O. Box 6000
Cherry Hill, NJ 08034-6000
(609) 488-8500/(609) 488-0485 (fax)

American Suzuki Motor Corp.
Mr. Masao Nagura
President
3251 Imperial Hwy., P.O. Box 1100
Brea, CA 92822-1100
(714) 996-7040/(714) 524-2512 (fax)

Toyota Motor Sales, U.S.A., Inc.
Mr. Yoshio Ishizaka
President and CEO
19001 S. Western Avenue
Torrance, CA 90509
(310) 618-4000/(310) 618-7800 (fax)

Volkswagen of America, Inc.
Mr. Clive Warrilow
President
3800 Hamlin Road
Auburn Hills, MI 48326
(810) 340-5000/(810) 340-4643 (fax)

Volvo Cars of North America
Mr. Helge Alten
President and CEO
7 Volvo Drive
Rockleigh, NJ 07647
(201) 767-4710/(201) 784-4535 (fax)

Lemon Laws

Sometimes, despite our best efforts, we buy a vehicle that just doesn't work right. There may be little problem after little problem, or perhaps one big problem that never seems to be fixed. Because of the bad taste that such vehicles leave in the mouths of consumers who buy them, these vehicles are known as "lemons."

In the past, it's been difficult to obtain a refund or replacement if a vehicle was a lemon. The burden of proof was left to the consumer. Because it is hard to define exactly what constitutes a lemon, many lemon owners were unable to win a case against a manufacturer. However, as of 1993, all states have passed "Lemon Laws." Although there are some important state-to-state variations, all of the laws have similarities: They establish a period of coverage, usually one year from delivery or the written warranty period, whichever is shorter; they may require some form of noncourt arbitration; and most importantly they define a lemon. In most states a lemon is a new car, truck, or van that has been taken back to the shop at least four times for the same repair, or is out of service for a total of 30 days during the covered period.

This time does not mean consecutive days. In some states the total time must be for the same repair; in others, it can be based on different repair problems.

Be sure to keep careful records of your repairs since some states now require only one of the three or four repairs to be within the specified time period.

Specific information about laws in your state can be obtained from your state attorney general's office (c/o your state capitol) or your local consumer protection office. The following table offers a general description of the Lemon Law in your state and what you need to do to set it in motion (*Notification/Trigger*). An **L** indicates that the law covers leased vehicles and we indicate where state-run arbitration programs are available. State-run programs are the best type of arbitration.

Alabama	**Qualification:** 3 unsuccessful repairs or 30 calendar days out of service within shorter of 24 months or 24,000 miles, provided 1 repair attempt or 1 day out of service is within shorter of 1 year or 12,000 miles. **Notification/Trigger:** Certified mail notice to manufacturer, who has 14 calendar days to make final repair.
Alaska	**Qualification:** 3 unsuccessful repairs or 30 business days out of service within shorter of 1 year or warranty. **Notification/Trigger**: Certified mail notice to manufacturer and dealer, or agent within 60 days after expiration of warranty or 1 year. Consumer must demand refund or replacement to be delivered within 60 days after mailing the notice. Final repair attempt within 30 days of receipt of notice.
Arizona	**Qualification:** 4 unsuccessful repairs or 30 calendar days out of service within shorter of 2 years or 24,000 miles. **Notification/Trigger:** Written notice to manufacturer and opportunity to repair.
Arkansas	**Qualification:** 3 unsuccessful repairs, or 1 unsuccessful repair of a problem likely to cause death or serious bodily injury within longer of 24 months or 24,000 miles. **Notification/ Trigger:** Certified or registered mail notice to manufacturer. Manufacturer has 10 days to notify consumer of repair facility. Facility has 10 days to repair.
California	**Qualification:** 4 unsuccessful repairs or 30 calendar days out of service within shorter of 1 year or 12,000 miles. **Notification/Trigger:** Written notice to manufacturer and delivery of car to repair facility for repair attempt within 30 days. *State has certified guidelines for arbitration.* **L**
Colorado	**Qualification:** 4 unsuccessful repairs or 30 business days out of service within shorter of 1 year or warranty. **Notification/Trigger:** Prior certified mail notice for each defect occurrence and opportunity to repair.
Conn.	**Qualification:** 4 unsuccessful repairs or 30 calendar days out of service within shorter of 1 year or warranty. **Notification/Trigger:** Report to manufacturer, agent or dealer. Written notice to manufacturer only if required in owner's manual or warranty. *State-run arbitration program is available.* **L**

State	Provisions
Delaware	**Qualification:** 4 unsuccessful repairs or 30 calendar days out of service within shorter of 1 year or warranty. **Notification/Trigger:** Written notice to manufacturer and opportunity to repair. **L**
D. C.	**Qualification:** 4 unsuccessful repairs or 30 calendar days out of service or 1 unsuccessful repair of a safety-related defect, within shorter of 2 years or 18,000 miles. **Notification/ Trigger:** Report of each defect occurrence to manufacturer, agent or dealer. *District-run arbitration program is available.* Note: Enforcement by D.C. is suspended until October 1, 1998. **L**
Florida	**Qualification:** 3 unsuccessful repairs or **15** calendar days out of service within shorter of 12 months or 12,000 miles. **Notification/Trigger:** Written notice by certified or express mail to manufacturer who has **10** calendar days for final repair attempt after delivery to designated dealer. *State-run arbitration program is available.* **L**
Georgia*	**Qualification:** 3 unsuccessful repair attempts or 30 calendar days out of service within shorter of 24,000 miles or 24 months, with 1 repair or 15 days out of service within shorter of 1 year or 12,000 miles; or one unsuccessful repair of a serious safety defect in the braking or steering system within shorter of 1 year or 12,000 miles. **Notification/Trigger:** Certified mail notice return receipt requested. Manufacturer has 7 days to notify consumer of repair facility. Facility has 14 days to repair. *State-run arbitration program is available.* **L**
Hawaii	**Qualification:** 3 unsuccessful repairs, or 1 unsuccessful repair of a nonconformity likely to cause death or serious bodily injury, or out of service within shorter of 2 years or 24,000 miles. **Notification/Trigger:** Written notice to manufacturer and opportunity to repair. *State-run arbitration program is available.* **L**
Idaho	**Qualification:** 4 repair attempts or 30 business days out of service within shorter of 12 months or 12,000 miles. **Notification/Trigger:** Written notice to manufacturer or dealer.
Illinois*	**Qualification:** 4 unsuccessful repairs or 30 business days out of service within shorter of 1 year or 12,000 miles. **Notification/Trigger:** Written notice to manufacturer and opportunity to repair.
Indiana	**Qualification:** 4 unsuccessful repairs or 30 business days out of service within the shorter of 18 months or 18,000 miles. **Notification/Trigger:** Written notice to manufacturer only if required in warranty. **L**
Iowa	**Qualification:** 3 unsuccessful repairs, or 1 unsuccessful repair of a nonconformity likely to cause death or serious bodily injury, or 20 calendar days out of service within shorter of 2 years or 24,000 miles. **Notification/Trigger:** Written notice to manufacturer and final opportunity to repair within 10 calendar days of receipt of notice. *State has certified guidelines for arbitration.* **L**
Kansas	**Qualification:** 4 unsuccessful repairs of the same problem or 30 calendar days out of service or 10 total repairs of any problem within shorter of 1 year or warranty. **Notification/Trigger:** Actual notice to manufacturer.
Kentucky	**Qualification:** 4 unsuccessful repairs or 30 calendar days out of service within shorter of 1 year or 12,000 miles. **Notification/Trigger:** Written notice to manufacturer.
Louisiana	**Qualification:** 4 unsuccessful repairs or 30 calendar days out of service within shorter of 1 year or warranty. **Notification/Trigger:** Report to manufacturer or dealer. **L**
Maine	**Qualification:** 3 unsuccessful repairs (when at least 2 times the same agent attempted the repair) or 15 business days out of service within shorter of 2 years or 18,000 miles. **Notification/Trigger:** Written notice to manufacturer or dealer only if required in warranty or owner's manual. Manufacturer has 7 business days after receipt for final repair attempt. *State-run arbitration program is available.* **L**
Maryland	**Qualification:** 4 unsuccessful repairs, 30 calendar days out of service or 1 unsuccessful repair of braking or steering system within shorter of 15 months or 15,000 miles. **Notification/ Trigger:** Certified mail notice, return receipt requested to manu. or factory branch and opportunity to repair within 30 calendar days of receipt of notice. **L**
Mass.	**Qualification:** 3 unsuccessful repairs or 15 business days out of service within shorter of 1 year or 15,000 miles. **Notification/Trigger:** Notice to manufacturer or dealer who has 7 business days to attempt a final repair. *State-run arbitration program is available.*

*Warning: Consumers who seek a refund or replacement under the lemon law may lose other important legal rights in regards to the dealer and manufacturer.

State	Requirements
Michigan	**Qualification:** 4 unsuccessful repairs or 30 calendar days out of service within shorter of 1 year or warranty. **Notification/Trigger:** Certified mail notice, return receipt requested, to manufacturer who has 5 business days to repair after delivery.
Minn.	**Qualification:** 4 unsuccessful repairs or 30 business days out of service or 1 unsuccessful repair of total braking or steering loss likely to cause death or serious bodily injury within shorter of 2 years or warranty. **Notification/Trigger:** At least one written notice to manufacturer, agent or dealer and opportunity to repair. **L**
Miss.	**Qualification:** 3 unsuccessful repairs or 15 business days out of service within shorter of 1 year or warranty. **Notification/Trigger:** Written notice to manufacturer who has 10 business days to repair after delivery to designated dealer.
Missouri	**Qualification:** 4 unsuccessful repairs or 30 business days out of service within shorter of 1 year or warranty. **Notification/Trigger:** Written notice to manufacturer who has 10 calendar days to repair after delivery to designated dealer.
Montana	**Qualification:** 4 unsuccessful repairs or 30 business days out of service after notice within shorter of 2 years or 18,000 miles. **Notification/Trigger:** Written notice to manufacturer and opportunity to repair. *State-run arbitration program is available.*
Nebraska	**Qualification:** 4 unsuccessful repairs or 40 calendar days out of service within shorter of 1 year or warranty. **Notification/Trigger:** Certified mail notice to manufacturer and opportunity to repair.
Nevada	**Qualification:** 4 unsuccessful repairs or 30 calendar days out of service within shorter of 1 year or warranty. **Notification/Trigger:** Written notice to manufacturer.
N. H.	**Qualification:** 3 unsuccessful repairs by same dealer or 30 business days out of service within warranty. **Notification/Trigger:** Report to manufacturer, distributor, agent or dealer (on forms provided by manufacturer) and final opportunity to repair before arbitration. *State-run arbitration program is available.* **L**
N. J.	**Qualification:** 3 unsuccessful repairs or 20 calendar days out of service within shorter of 2 years or 18,000 miles. **Notification/Trigger:** Certified mail notice, written notice to manufacturer who has 15 days to repair. *State-run arbitration program is available.* **L**
N. M.	**Qualification:** 4 unsuccessful repairs or 30 business days within shorter of 1 year or warranty. **Notification/Trigger:** Written notice to manufacturer, agent or dealer and opportunity to repair.
N. Y.	**Qualification:** 4 unsuccessful repairs or 30 calendar days out of service within shorter of 2 years or 18,000 miles. **Notification/Trigger:** Certified notice to manufacturer, agent or dealer. *State-run arbitration program is available.* **L**
N. C.	**Qualification:** 4 unsuccessful repairs within the shorter of 24 months, 24,000 miles or warranty or 20 business days out of service during any 12 month period of the warranty. **Notification/Trigger:** Written notice to manufacturer and opportunity to repair within 15 calendar days of receipt only if required in warranty or owner's manual. **L**
N. D.	**Qualification:** 3 unsuccessful repairs or 30 business days out of service within shorter of 1 year or warranty. **Notification/Trigger:** Direct written notice and opportunity to repair to manufacturer. *(Manufacturer's informal arbitration process serves as a prerequisite to consumer refund of replacement.)* **L**
Ohio	**Qualification:** 3 unsuccessful repairs of same nonconformity, 30 calendar days out of service, 8 total repairs of any problem, or 1 unsuccessful repair of problem likely to cause death or serious bodily injury within shorter of 1 year or 18,000 miles. **Notification/Trigger:** Report to manufacturer, its agent or dealer.
Okla.	**Qualification:** 4 unsuccessful repairs or 45 calendar days out of service within shorter of 1 year or warranty. **Notification/Trigger:** Written notice to manufacturer and opportunity to repair.
Oregon	**Qualification:** 4 unsuccessful repairs or 30 business days out of service within shorter of 1 year or 12,000 miles. **Notification/Trigger:** Direct written notice to manufacturer and opportunity to repair. **L**

Penn.	**Qualification:** 3 unsuccessful repairs or 30 calendar days out of service within shorter of 1 year, 12,000 miles, or warranty. **Notification/Trigger:** Delivery to authorized service and repair facility. If delivery impossible, written notice to manufacturer or its repair facility obligates them to pay for delivery.
R. I.	**Qualification:** 4 unsuccessful repairs or 30 calendar days out of service within shorter of 1 year or 15,000 miles. **Notification/Trigger:** Report to dealer or manufacturer who has 7 days for final repair opportunity. *(Manufacturer's informal arbitration process serves as a prerequisite to consumer refund of replacement.)* **L**
S. C.	**Qualification:** 3 unsuccessful repairs or 30 calendar days out of service within shorter of 1 year or 12,000 miles. **Notification/Trigger:** Written notice to manufacturer by certified mail and opportunity to repair only if manufacturer informed consumer of such at time of sale. Manufacturer has 10 days to notify consumer of repair facility. Facility has 10 days to repair. *State-run arbitration program is available.* **L**
S. D.	**Qualification:** 4 unsuccessful repairs, at least 1 of which occurred during the shorter of 1 year or 12,000 miles, or 30 calendar days out of service during the shorter of 24 months or 24,000 miles. **Notification/Trigger:** Certified mail notice to manufacturer and final opportunity to repair. Manufacturer has 7 calendar days to notify consumer of repair facility. Facility has 14 days to repair. *(Manufacturer's informal arbitration process serves as a prerequisite to consumer refund or replacement.)*
Tenn.	**Qualification:** 4 unsuccessful repairs or 30 calendar days out of service within shorter of 1 year or warranty. **Notification/Trigger:** Certified mail notice to manufacturer and final opportunity to repair within 10 calendar days. **L**
Texas	**Qualification:** 4 unsuccessful repairs when 2 occurred within shorter of 1 year or 12,000 miles, and other 2 occur within shorter of 1 year or 12,000 miles from date of 2nd repair attempt; or 2 unsuccessful repairs of a serious safety defect when 1 occurred within shorter of 1 year or 12,000 miles and other occurred within shorter of 1 year or 12,000 miles from date of 1st repair; or 30 calendar days out of service within shorter of 2 years or 24,000 miles and at least 2 attempts were made within shorter of 1 year or 12,000 miles. **Notification/Trigger:** Written notice to manufacturer. *State-run arbitration program is available.* **L**
Utah	**Qualification:** 4 unsuccessful repairs or 30 business days out of service within shorter of 1 year or warranty. **Notification/Trigger:** Report to manufacturer, agent or dealer. **L**
Vermont	**Qualification:** 3 unsuccessful repairs when at least 1st repair was within warranty, or 30 calendar days within warranty. **Notification/Trigger:** Written notice to manufacturer (on provided forms) after 3rd repair attempt, or 30 days. Arbitration must be held within 45 days after notice, during which time manufacturer has 1 final repair. *State-run arbitration program is available.* **L**
Virginia	**Qualification:** 3 unsuccessful repairs, or 1 repair attempt of a serious safety defect, or 30 calendar days out of service within 18 months. **Notification/Trigger:** Written notice to manufacturer. If 3 unsuccessful repairs or 30 days already exhausted before notice, manufacturer has 1 more repair attempt not to exceed 15 days.
Wash.	**Qualification:** 4 unsuccessful repairs, 30 calendar days out of service (15 during warranty period), or 2 repairs of serious safety defects, first reported within shorter of the warranty or 24 months or 24,000 miles. One repair attempt and 15 of the 30 days must fall within manufacturer's express warranty of at least 1 year or 12,000 miles. **Notification/Trigger:** Written notice to manufacturer. *State-run arbitration program is available.* **L** *Note: Consumer should receive replacement or refund within 40 calendar days of request.*
W. V.	**Qualification:** 3 unsuccessful repairs or 30 calendar days out of service or 1 unsuccessful repair of problem likely to cause death or serious bodily injury within shorter of 1 year or warranty. **Notification/Trigger:** Prior written notice to manufacturer and at least one opportunity to repair.
Wisc.	**Qualification:** 4 unsuccessful repairs or 30 calendar days out of service within shorter of 1 year or warranty. **Notification/Trigger:** Report to manufacturer or dealer. **L** *Note: Consumer should receive replacement or refund within 30 calendar days after offer to return title.*
Wyoming	**Qualification:** 3 unsuccessful repairs or 30 business days out of service within 1 year. **Notification/Trigger:** Direct written notice to manufacturer and opportunity to repair.

Showroom Strategies

Buying a car means matching wits with a seasoned professional. But if you know what to expect, you'll have a much better chance of getting a really good deal! This chapter offers practical advice on buying a car, tips on getting the best price and financing, information on buying vs. leasing, and tips on avoiding lemons. We'll also take a peek at some options for the future that will increase driving safety.

For most of us, the auto showroom can be an intimidating environment. We're matching wits with professional negotiators over a very complex product. Being prepared is the best way to turn a potentially intimidating showroom experience into a profitable one. Here's some advice on handling what you'll find in the showroom.

Beware of silence. Silence is often used to intimidate, so be prepared for long periods of time when the salesperson is "talking with the manager." This tactic is designed to make you want to "just get the negotiation over with." Instead of becoming a victim, do something that indicates you are serious about looking elsewhere. Bring the classified section of the newspaper and begin circling other cars or review brochures from other manufacturers. By sending the message that you have other options, you increase your bargaining power and speed up the process.

Don't fall in love with a car. Never look too interested in any particular car. Advise family members who go with you against being too enthusiastic about any one car. *Tip:* Beat the dealers at their own game—bring along a friend who tells you that the price is "too much compared to the *other* deal."

Keep your wallet in your pocket. Don't leave a deposit, even if it's refundable. You'll feel pressure to rush your shopping, and you'll have to return and face the salesperson again before you are ready.

Shop at the end of the month. Salespeople anxious to meet sales goals are more willing to negotiate a lower price at this time.

In This Chapter...

Buy last year's model. The majority of new cars are the same as the previous year, with minor cosmetic changes. You can save considerably by buying in early fall when dealers are clearing space for "new" models. The important trade-off you make using this technique is that the car maker may have added air bags or anti-lock brakes to an otherwise unchanged vehicle.

Buying from stock. You can often get a better deal on a car that the dealer has on the lot. However, these cars usually have expensive options you may not want or need. Do not hesitate to ask the dealer to remove an option (and its accompanying charge) or sell you the car without charging for the option. The longer the car sits there, the more interest the dealer pays on the car, which increases the dealer's incentive to sell.

Ordering a car. Domestic cars can be ordered from the manufacturer. Simply offering a fixed amount over invoice may be attractive because it's a sure sale and the dealership has not invested in the car. All the salesperson has to do is take your order.

If you do order a car, make sure when it arrives that it includes only the options you requested. Don't fall for the trick where the dealer offers you unordered options at a "special price," because it was their mistake. If you didn't order the option, don't pay for it.

Don't trade in. Although it is more work, you can usually do better by selling your old car yourself than by trading it in. To determine what you'll gain by selling the car yourself, check the NADA "Blue Book" at your credit union or library. The difference between the trade-in price (what the dealer will give you) and the retail price (what you typically can sell it for) is your extra payment for selling the car yourself.

If you do decide to trade your car in at the dealership, *keep the buying and selling separate*. First, negotiate the best price for your new car, then find out how much the dealer will give you for your old car. Keeping the two deals separate ensures that you know what you're paying for your new car and simplifies the entire transaction.

Question everything the dealer writes down. Nothing is etched in stone. Because things are written down, we tend not to question them. This is wrong—always assume that anything written down is negotiable.

Test drive without the salesperson. When you test drive a car, go alone and take a good long test drive. If a dealership will not let you take a car without a salesperson, go to another dealership. Test driving without the distraction of a salesperson is a necessity when trying out a new car. See page 54 for tips on test driving.

Avoiding Lemons

One way to avoid the sour taste of a lemon after you've bought your car is to protect yourself *before* you sign on the dotted line. These tips will help you avoid problems down the road.

1 **Avoid new models.** Any new car in its very first year of production often turns out to have a lot of defects. Sometimes the manufacturer isn't able to remedy the defects until the second, third, or even fourth year of production. If the manufacturer has not worked out problems by the third model year, the car will likely be a lemon forever.

2 **Avoid the first cars off the line.** Most companies close down their assembly lines every year to make annual style changes. In addition to adding hundreds of dollars to the price of a new car, these changes can introduce new defects. It can take a few months to iron out these bugs. Ask the dealer when the vehicle you are interested in was manufactured, or look on the metal tag found on the inside of the driver-side door frame to find the date of manufacture.

3 **Avoid delicate options.** Delicate options have the highest frequency-of-repair records. Power seats, power windows, power antennas, and special roofs are nice conveniences—until they break down. Of all the items on the vehicles, they tend to be the most expensive to repair.

4 **Inspect the dealer's checklist.** Request a copy of the dealer's pre-delivery service and adjustment checklist (also called a "make-ready list") at the time your new vehicle is delivered. Write the request directly on the new vehicle order. This request informs the dealer that you are aware of the dealer's responsibility to check your new car for defects.

5 **Examine the car on delivery.** Most of us are very excited when it comes time to take the vehicle home. This is the time where a few minutes of careful inspection can save hours of aggravation later. Carefully look over the body for any damage, check for the spare tire and jack equipment, make sure all electrical items work, and make sure all the hubcaps and body molding are on. You may want to take a short test drive. Finally, make sure you have the owner's manual, warranty forms, and all the legal documents.

Getting the Best Price

One of the most difficult aspects of buying a new car is getting the best price. Most of us are at a disadvantage negotiating because we don't know how much the car actually cost the dealer. The difference between what the dealer paid and the sticker price represents the negotiable amount.

Until recently, the key to getting the best price was finding out the dealer cost. Many shoppers now ask to see the factory invoice, so some dealers promote their cars by offering to sell at only $49 or $99 over invoice. This sounds like a good deal, but these cars often have options you may not want and most invoice prices do not reveal the extra, hidden profit to the dealer.

Now that most savvy consumers know to check the so-called "dealer invoice," the industry has camouflaged this number. Special incentives, rebates, and kickbacks can account for $500 to $2,000 worth of extra profit to a dealer selling a car at "dealer invoice." The non-profit Center for the Study of Services recently discovered that in 37 percent of cases when dealers are forced to bid against each other for the sale, they offered the buyer a price below the "dealer invoice"—an unlikely event if the dealer was actually losing money. The bottom line is that "dealer invoice" doesn't mean anything anymore.

Because the rules have changed, we believe that most consumers are ill-advised to try and negotiate with a dealer. Introducing competition is the best way to get the lowest price on a new car. What this means is that you have to convince 3 or 4 dealers that you are, in fact, prepared to buy a car; that you have decided on the make, model, and features; and that your decision now rests solely on which dealer will give you the best price. You can try to do this by phone, but often dealers will not give you the best price, or will quote you a price over the phone that they will not honor later. Instead, you should try to do this in person. As anyone knows who has ventured into an auto showroom simply to get the best price, the process can be lengthy and arduous. Nevertheless, if you can convice the dealer that you are serious and are willing to take the time to go to a number of dealers, it will pay off. Otherwise, we suggest you use the CarBargains service listed on the next page.

If you find a big savings at a dealership far from your home, call a local dealer with the price. They may very well match it. If not, pick up the car from the distant dealer, knowing your trip has saved you hundreds of dollars. You can still bring it to your local dealer for warranty work and repairs. Here are some other showroom strategies:

Beware of misleading advertising. New car ads are meant to get you into the showroom. They usually promise low prices, big rebates, high trade-in, and spotless integrity—don't be deceived. Advertised prices are rarely the true selling price. They usually exclude transportation charges, service fees, or document fees. And always look out for the asterisk, both in advertisements and on invoices. It can be a signal that the advertiser has something to hide.

Don't talk price until you're ready to buy. On your first few trips to the showroom, simply look over the cars, decide what options you want, and do your test driving.

Shop the corporate twins. Page 18 contains a list of corporate twins—nearly identical cars that carry different name plates. Check the price and options of the twins of the car you like. A higher priced twin may have more options, so it may be a better deal than the lower priced car without the options you want.

Watch out for dealer preparation overcharges. Before paying the dealer to clean your car, make sure that preparation is not included in the basic price. The price sticker will state: "Manufacturer's suggested retail price of this model includes dealer preparation."

If you must negotiate . . . negotiate up from the "invoice" price rather than down from the sticker price. Simply make an offer close to or at the "invoice" price. If the sales person says that your offer is too low to make a profit, ask to see the factory invoice.

The 180-Degree Turn

If you try to negotiate a car purchase, remember that you have the most important weapon in the bargaining process: *the 180-degree turn*. Be prepared to walk away from a deal, even at the risk of losing the "very best deal" your salesperson has ever offered, and you will be in the best position to get a genuine "best deal." Remember: dealerships need you, the buyer, to survive.

Price Shopping Service

Even with the information that we provide you in this chapter of *The Car Book*, most of us will *not* be well prepared to negotiate a good price for the cars we are considering. In fact, as we indicated on the previous page, we don't believe that you can negotiate the best price with *a* dealer. The key to getting the best price is to get the dealers to compete with each other. This page describes a new and easy way to find the best price by actually getting the dealers to compete.

CarBargains is a service of the non-profit Center for the Study of Services, a Washington, DC, consumer group, set up to provide comparative price information for many products and services.

CarBargains will "shop" the dealerships in your area and obtain at least five price quotes for the make and model of the car that you want to buy. The dealers who submit quotes know that they are competing with other area dealerships and have agreed to honor the prices that they submit. It is important to note that CarBargains is not an auto broker or "car buying" service; they have no affiliation with dealers.

Here's how the service works:

1. You provide CarBargains with the make, model, and style of car you wish to buy (Ford Taurus GL, for example) by phone or mail.

2. Within two weeks, CarBargains will send you dealer quote sheets from at least 5 local dealers who have bid against one another to sell you that car. The offer is actually a commitment to a dollar amount above (or below) "factory invoice cost" for that model.

You will also receive a printout with the exact dealer cost for the car and each available option. Included in the information will be the name of the sales manager responsible for honoring the quote.

3. Use the factory invoice cost printout to add up the invoice cost for the base car and the options you want and then determine which dealer offers the best price using the dealer quote sheets. Contact the sales manager of that dealership and arrange to purchase the car.

If a car with the options you want is not available on the dealer's lot, you can have the dealer order the car from the factory or, in some cases, from another dealer at the agreed price.

When you receive your quotes, you will also get some suggestions on low-cost sources of financing and a valuation of your used car (trade-in).

The price for this service may seem expensive, but when you consider the savings that will result by having dealers bid against each other, as well as the time and effort of trying to get these bids yourself, we believe it's a great value. First of all, the dealers know they have a bona fide buyer (you've paid $165 for the service) and they know they are bidding against 5–7 of their competitors.

To obtain CarBargains' competitive price quotes, send a check for $165 to CarBargains, 733 15th St., NW, Suite 820CB, Washington, DC 20005. Include your complete mailing address, phone number (in case of questions), and the exact make, model, and year of the car you want to buy. You should receive your bids within 2-3 weeks. For faster service, call them at 800-475-7283. They will accept Visa or Mastercard on phone orders.

Auto Brokers

While CarBargains is a non-profit organization created to help you find the best price for the car you want to purchase, auto brokers are typically in the business to make money. As such, what ever price you end up paying for the car will include additional profit for the broker. While many brokers are legitimately trying to get their customers the best price, others have developed special relationships with certain dealers and may not do much shopping for you. As a consumer, it is difficult to tell which are which. If you use a broker, make sure the contract to purchase the car is with the dealer, not the broker. In addition, it is best to pay the broker *after* the service is rendered, not before. There have been cases where the auto broker makes certain promises, takes your money, and you never hear from him or her again. If CarBargains is not for you, then we suggest you consider using a buying service associated with your credit union or auto club, which can arrange for the purchase of a car at some fixed price over "dealer invoice."

Depreciation

Over the past 20 years, new vehicle depreciation costs have steadily increased. A recent study conducted by Runzheimer International shows that depreciation and interest now account for slightly over 50 percent of the costs of owning and operating a vehicle. This number is up from 41 percent in 1976. On the other hand, the relative cost of gasoline has dropped by half, from 35 percent to 17 percent of every dollar spent on the average car. Other costs, including insurance, maintenance, and tires, have remained at relatively steady shares of the automotive dollar.

The high cost of depreciation is largely due to skyrocketing new car prices. While there is no reliable method of predicting retained value, your best bet is to purchase a popular new car. Chances are that it will also be popular as a used car.

Most new cars are traded in within four years and are then available on the used car market. The priciest used cars may not necessarily be the highest quality. Supply and demand, as well as appearance, are extremely important factors in determining used car prices.

1993 Cars with the Best and Worst Resale Value

The following table indicates which of the 100 top-selling '93 cars held their value the best and which did not.

The Best				The Worst			
Model	1993 Price	1997 Price	Retained Value	Model	1993 Price	1997 Price	Retained Value
Mazda 323/Protégé	$7,449	$6,300	85%	Mercury Gr. Marquis	$22,082	$10,425	47%
Suzuki Swift	$7,299	$5,675	78%	Dodge Dynasty	$15,430	$7,275	47%
Mazda Miata	$15,300	$11,925	78%	Cadillac Seville	$36,990	$17,250	47%
Honda Civic	$10,350	$8,050	78%	Cadillac Fleetwood	$33,990	$16,100	47%
Geo Prizm	$9,995	$7,550	76%	Audi 100/200	$30,400	$14,375	47%
Acura Integra	$14,835	$11,325	76%	Mercury Sable	$17,480	$7,975	46%
VW Golf/Jetta	$11,600	$8,725	75%	Infiniti Q45	$45,400	$20,800	46%
Volvo 850	$24,100	$18,150	75%	Cadillac DeVille	$32,990	$14,700	45%
Toyota Previa	$18,498	$13,625	74%	Lincoln Mark VIII	$36,640	$15,125	41%
Subaru Loyale	$10,349	$7,650	74%	Lincoln Town Car	$34,190	$13,950	41%
Nissan Sentra	$8,415	$6,450	74%	Ford Crown Victoria	$20,563	$8,375	41%
Mercury Villager	$16,504	$12,250	74%	Lincoln Continental	$33,328	$12,225	37%

Prices based on the *N.A.D.A. Official Used Car Guide*, July 1997.

Financing

You've done your test drive, researched prices, studied crash tests, determined the options you want, and haggled to get the best price. Now you have to decide how to pay for the car.

If you have the cash, *pay for the car right away*. You avoid finance charges, you won't have a large debt haunting over you and the full value of the car is yours. You can then make the monthly payments to yourself to save up for your next car.

However, most of us cannot afford to pay cash for a car, which leaves two options: financing or leasing. While leasing *seems* more affordable, financing will actually cost you less. When you finance a car, you own it after you finish your payments. At the end of a lease, you have nothing. We don't recommend leasing, but if you want more information, see page 96.

Here are some tips when financing your car:

Shop around for interest rates. Most banks and credit unions will knock off at least a quarter of a percent for their customers. Have these quotes handy when you talk financing with the dealer.

The higher your down payment, the less you'll have to finance. This will not only reduce your overall interest charges, but often qualifies you for a lower interest rate. Down payments are typically 10-20% of the final price.

Avoid long car loans. The monthly payments are lower, but you'll pay far more in overall interest charges. For example, a two year, $15,000 loan at 9% will cost you $1,446.51 in interest; the same amount at five years will cost you $3,682.52 — over twice as much!

Check out manufacturer promotional rates — the 2.9-3.9% rates you see advertised. These low rates are usually only valid on 2-3 year loans.

Read everything you are asked to sign and ask questions about anything you don't fully understand.

Make sure that an extended warranty has *not* been added to the purchase price. Dealers will sometimes add this cost without informing the consumer. Extended warranties are generally a bad value. See the "Warranties" chapter for more information.

GAP Insurance: GAP insurance covers the difference between what you owe on a car and its actual value, should the car be "totaled" or stolen. If you finance or lease through a dealer, he or she will likely suggest you purchase GAP insurance, which can cost up to $500. If you think this situation is likely, then your financing plan is probably too long.

Whether you need GAP or not, be wary of how dealers try to sell GAP. Dealers may insist the only way to give you financing is if you purchase GAP insurance — this is untrue. When negotiating finance

Don't Be Tongue-Tied

Beware of high pressure phrases like "I've talked to the manager and this is really the best we can do...as it is, we're losing money on this deal." It is rare that this is true. Dealers are in the business to make money and most do very well. Don't tolerate a take it or leave it attitude. Simply repeat that you will only buy when you see the deal you want and that you don't appreciate the dealer pressuring you. Threaten to leave if the dealer continues to pressure you to buy today.

Don't let the dealer answer your questions with a question. For instance, if you ask, "Can I get air conditioning with this car?" And the salesperson answers, "If I get you air conditioning in this car, will you buy today?" This response tries to force you to decide to buy before you are ready. Ask the dealer to just answer your question and that you'll buy when you're ready. Remember, its the dealer's job to answer questions, not yours.

If you are having a difficult time getting what you want, ask the dealer: "Why won't you let me buy a car today?" Most salespeople will be thrown off by this phrase as they are often too busy trying to use it on you. If they respond in frustration, "OK, what do you want?" then you can say straightforward answers to simple questions.

Make sure you get a price, don't settle for: "If you're shopping price, go to the other dealers first and then come back." This technique insures that they don't have to truly negotiate. Your best response is: "I only plan to come back if your price is the lowest, so that's what I need today, your lowest price."

terms, be sure to ask if GAP insurance has been added to the cost, as the dealer may not tell you.

Credit Unions vs. Banks: Credit unions generally charge fewer and lower fees and offer better rates than banks. In addition, credit unions offer counseling services where consumers can find pricing information on cars or compare monthly payments for financing. You can join a credit union either through your employer, an organization or club, or if you have a relative who is part of a credit union.

Low Rate or Cash Back? Sometimes auto manufacturers offer a choice of below market financing or cash back. The following table will tell you if it is better to take the lower rate or the cash back rebate. For example, say you want to finance $18,000. Your credit union or bank offers you 8.5% for an auto loan and the dealer offers either a 6% loan or a $1,500 rebate. Which is better? Find your bank or credit union's rate (8.5%) and the dealer's low rate (6%) on the table. Find where the two intersect on the table and you will find the difference per thousand dollars between the two interest rates (47). When you multiply this number (47) by the number of thousands you're financing (18 for $18,000), you get $846. Since the dealer's $1,500 rebate is more than the breakeven $846, taking your bank's rate (8.5%) and the rebate is a better deal than the dealer's low rate (6%). If the answer had been more than $1,500, then the dealer's rate would have been the better deal. An asterisk (*) means that the bank or credit union's rate is the better deal.

TIP: Destination Charges

There once was a time when you could go directly to the factory and buy a car, saving yourself a few hundred dollars in destination and freight charges. Today, destination charges are a non-negotiable part of buying a new car, no matter where you purchase it. They are, however, an important factor when comparing prices. You'll find the destination charges on the price sticker attached to the vehicle. According to automakers, destination charges are the cost of shipping a vehicle from its "final assembly point" to the dealership. The cost of shipping other components for final assembly is sometimes also added.

But, the following table illustrates that there is little correlation between destination charges and where the cars are assembled:

Vehicle	Destination Charge	Assembly Country	Parts from N. America
Acura Integra	$435	Japan	5%
BMW 318i	$570	U.S./Germany	5%
Cadillac DeVille	$665	U.S.	95%
Chevrolet Lumina	$550	Canada	95%

Based on data from Automotive News 1997 Market Data Book.

Rebate vs. Low Rates (Four Year Loan)

Multiply the number that intersects your dealer's rate with the rate from your credit union or bank by the number of thousands you are financing. If the result is less than the rebate, take the rebate; if it is above the rebate, go for the dealer financing.

Bank/ C.U. Rate	Dealer Rate 2%	3%	4%	5%	6%	7%	8%
7.0	94	76	57	38	19	*	*
7.5	103	85	66	48	29	10	*
8.0	111	93	75	57	38	19	*
8.5	120	102	84	66	47	28	10
9.0	128	111	93	75	56	38	19
9.5	136	119	101	83	65	47	28

Based on data from *Everybody's Money*, a publication of the Credit Union National Association.

Leasing vs. Buying

As car prices continue to rise, many car buyers are being seduced by the heavily advertised low monthly lease payments. Don't be deceived—in general, leasing costs more than buying outright or financing. When you pay cash or finance a car, you own an asset; leasing leaves you with nothing except all the headaches and responsibilities of ownership with none of the benefits. In addition, leased cars are often not covered by lemon laws. When you lease you pay a monthly fee for a predetermined time in exchange for the use of a car. However, you also pay for maintenance, insurance and repairs as if you owned the car. Finally, when it comes time to turn in the car, it has to be in top shape — otherwise, you'll have to pay for repairs or body work.

If you are considering a lease, here are some leasing terms you need to know and some tips to get you through the process:

Capitalized Cost is the price of the car if you were to purchase it. Negotiate this as if you were buying the cars. **Capitalized Cost Reduction** is your down payment.

Know the make and model of the vehicle you want. Tell the agent exactly how you want the car equipped. You don't have to pay for options you don't request. Decide in advance how long you will keep the car.

Find out the price of the options on which the lease is based. Typically, they will be full retail price. Their cost can be negotiated (albeit with some difficultly) before you settle on the monthly payment.

Find out how much you are required to pay at delivery. Most leases require at least the first month's payment. Others have a security deposit, registration fees, or other "hidden" costs. When shopping around, make sure price quotes include security deposit and taxes—sales tax, monthly use tax, or gross receipt tax. Ask how the length of the lease affects your monthly cost.

Find out the annual mileage limit. Don't accept a contract with a lower limit than you need. Most standard contracts allow 15,000 to 18,000 miles per year. If you go under the allowance one year, you can go over it the next. Watch out for **Excess Mileage fees**. If you go over, you'll get charged per mile.

Avoid "capitalized cost reduction" or "equity leases." Here the lessor offers to lower the monthly payment by asking you for more money up front — in other words, a down payment.

Ask about early termination. Between 30 and 40 percent of two year leases are terminated early, and 40–60 percent of four-year leases terminate early—this means expensive early termination fees. If you terminate the lease before it is up, what are the financial penalties? Typically, they are very high, so watch out. Ask the dealer *exactly* what you would owe at the end of each year if you wanted out of the lease. Remember, if your car is stolen, the lease will typically be terminated. While your insurance should cover the value of the car, you still may owe additional amounts per your lease contract.

Avoid maintenance contracts. Getting work done privately is cheaper in the long run—and don't forget, this is a new car with a standard warranty.

Arrange for your own insurance. By shopping around, you can generally find less expensive insurance than what's offered by the lessor.

Ask how quickly you can expect delivery. If your agent can't deliver in a reasonable time, maybe he or she can't meet the price quoted.

Retain your option to buy the car at the end of the lease at a predetermined price. The price should equal the residual value; if it is more, then the lessor is trying to make an additional profit. Regardless of how the end-of-lease value is determined, if you want the car make an offer based on the current "Blue

Leasewise

Why haggle when you can let someone else do it for you. *Leasewise*, a new service from the Center for the Study of Services, makes dealers bid for your lease. First, they get leasing bids from dealers on the vehicles you're interest in. Next, you'll receive a detailed report with all the bids, the dealer and invoice cost of the vehicle, and a complete explanation of the various bids. Then, you can lease from the lowest bidder or use the report as leverage with another dealer. The service costs $290. For more information, call 800-475-7283.

Book" value of the car at the end of the lease.

Residual Value is the value of your car at the end of the lease.

Find out how the lease price was figured. Lease prices are generally based on the manufacturer's suggested retail price, less the predetermined residual value. The best values are cars with a high expected residual value. To protect themselves, lessors tend to underestimate residual value, but you can do little about this estimate.

Make sure options like a sunroof or stereo are added to the Capitalized Cost. When you purchase dealer-added options, be sure they add the full cost of the option to the Capitalized Cost so that you only pay for the depreciated value of the option, not the full cost.

Send away for Driving A Bargain. This handy brochure from the Consumer Federation of America is guaranteed to keep the cost of leasing down. Send a self-addressed stamped envelope to: Driving a Bargain, Box 12099, Washington, DC 20005.

Here's what First National Lease Systems' Automotive Lease Guide estimates the residual values for a few 1998 cars will be after four years:

Cadillac DeVille	38%
Dodge Caravan SE	43%
Ford Taurus LX	38%
Honda Accord DX sdn.	52%
Infiniti Q45	44%
Lexus LS400	46%
Lincoln Mark VIII	38%
Mazda Miata	45%
Mercury Tracer GS sdn.	39%
Nissan Quest XE	40%
Plymouth Neon sdn.	37%
Toyota Camry LE sdn.	52%

Financing vs. Leasing

The following table compares the typical costs of leasing vs. buying the same car over a three and six years. Your actual costs may vary, but you can use this format to compare the cars you are considering. Our example assumes the residual value to be about 54% after three years and 36% after six years.

	Lease	Finance
3 Years		
MSRP	$22,000.00	$22,000.00
Purchase Cost of Car	$20,000.00	$20,000.00
Down Payment		$2,000.00
Monthly Payment	$359.49	$364.98
Total Payments	$12,941.64	$13,139.11[1]
Amount left on loan		$7,758.62
Less value of vehicle		$11,017.90
Overall Cost, first 3 years	$12,941.64	$11,879.83
6 Years		
MSRP	$22,000.00	$22,000.00
Cost of Car	$40,000.00[2]	$20,000.00
Down Payment		$2,000.00
Monthly Payment	$359.49	$364.98
Total Payment	$25,883.28	$21,898.51[3]
Less value of vehicle		$8,000.00
Overall Cost, 6 years	$25,883.28	$15,898.51

[1]First 3 years of 5 year loan with 8% annual percentage rate.
[2]Two 3-year leases.
[3]5 year loan with 8% annual percentage rate, no monthly payments in 6th year.

Options: The Future of Safety

Many car manufacturers claim that cars are safe enough today since airbags, anti-lock brakes and traction control are becoming standard features. The fact is there's lots more that can be done. We continue to pay high prices in personal injury and insurance premiums for accidents that could be less serious if manufacturers would market more advanced safety features.

While these features may increase the car costs, those increases would be minor in relation to the dramatic reduction in the risk of injuries in crashes. Unfortunately, car makers are slow to offer us new technology. Following are a few options that will dramatically increase driving safety—if manufacturers choose to offer them.

Radar Brakes: Using radar to detect objects in front of you, a warning sounds for the need to brake. It could perhaps be used to automatically apply the brakes when a driver falls asleep.

Side Airbags: The newest automatic crash protection technology has found its way into a handful of 1998 models, and one day may become the standard. These airbags ignite out of doors and out of the back of the front seat to protect the driver and passenger in crashes from all directions as well as rollovers.

Air Pads: Air pads are double layers of plastic with multiple compartments which look like ordinary trim in the uninflated condition. When the crash sensors for the airbags detect a crash, the air pads inflate out a few inches over all hard surfaces, such as the area over the windshield.

Glass-Plastic Glazing: This adds a layer of thin, strong, transparent plastic on the inside surface of all windows. When the glass breaks, the plastic layer holds the pieces of glass away from the occupants and provides a "safety net" to reduce the chance of ejection.

Night Vision Enhancement: This device will see through fog, rain, and darkness to provide an image of any obstacles or problems in the road. Infared light cameras project a visible image of what is ahead on a screen located on the car's instrument panel. The system could also detect, through a heat-seeking infrared system, someone lurking in a darkened parking lot.

Navigation Computer: With the use of global-positioning satellites, these on-board computers would eliminate the need for road maps. They could provide instructions on how to get to particular locations, such as hospitals, airports, restaurants and hotels, as well as warn of traffic and construction delays. GM, Volvo and Acura have begun experimenting with these systems in their cars. Using much the same technology, Lincoln's RESCU (Remote Emergency Satellite Cellular Unit) will send a distress signal for help to either a tow truck or an ambulance, depending on which signal you send.

Smart Airbags: Several auto makers are devloping smart airbag systems which will differentiate between an adult, a child, a rear-facing child seat or an empty seat, using various heat, ultrasonic sound wave and infrared sensors. Not only will they save lives, smart airbags will prevent the passenger side airbag from deploying when the passenger seat is empty—saving thousands in repair costs.

Black Box Monitor: This device would detect whether the driver is driving drunk or irresponsibly. By monitoring the car's behavior and noting irregular actions, it will shut the car down.

Intelligent Brakes: These brakes sense and compensate for over- or under-steering.

Crash Recorder: This would record airbag performance in the event of an accident. (Introduced in 1995 Saturns.)

Toyota's Drowsy Driving Warning Sytem: By monitoring the steering and pulse of the driver, this innovation checks the driver to verify alertness. Once it detects drowsiness, the system will warn the driver with lights and sound to wake up, then shake the seat, and finally automatically stop the car.

Self-Dimming Mirrors: A gel-like material placed between two glass sheets darkens and lightens to reduce the headlight glare from mirrors while driving at night.

Inflatable Curtain: Volvo is developing an inflatable curtain, which deploys like an airbag, to provide increased protection against head injuries during side impact collisions. The curtain covers the sides of the car's interior, cushioning the heads of all the occupants.

RATINGS

This chapter provides an overview of the most important features of the new 1998 cars. In this section of *The Car Book,* you can see on each "car page" all the ingredients you need to make a smart choice. In addition to some descriptive text and a photo, the page contains six important information boxes:

THE DESCRIPTION

The vast majority of information in *The Car Book* is purely objective—we research and present the facts so that you can make an informed choice among the models that fit your taste and pocketbook. For the third year we are adding, among other new features, some background details. Specifically, for every car we include some general information to help you round out the hard facts. Much of the information in this section is subjective and you may not share our opinion. Nevertheless, like the photo which gives you a general idea of what the car looks like, the description will give you a snapshot of some of the features we think are worth noting and which may not show up in the statistics.

GENERAL INFORMATION

This is additional information you may want to consider when buying a new car.

Where made: Here we tell you where the car was assembled and where its parts were manufactured. If more than one country is listed, the first is where the majority of parts originate or where the vehicle was assembled.

Year of Production: We generally recommend against buying a car during its first model year of production. Each year the model is made, the production process is usually improved and there are fewer minor design defects. Therefore, the longer a car has been made, the less likely you are to be plagued with manufacturing and design defects. On the other hand, the newer a car is, the more likely it is to have the latest in engineering.

Parking Index: Using the car's length, wheelbase and turning circle, we have calculated how easy it will be to maneuver this car in tight spots. This rating of *very easy* to *very hard* is an indicator of how much difficulty you may have parking. If you regularly parallel park, or find yourself maneuvering in and out of tight spaces, this can be an important factor in the car you choose.

Bumpers: Here we indicate the damage-resistance of the car's bumpers. *Weak* bumpers meet only the basic government requirements at 2.5-mph. *Strong* bumpers are just as damage-resistant at 5-mph. This information may not be available for some minivans.

Theft Rating: This rating is given by the Insurance Institute for Highway Safety. It predicts the likelihood of the car being stolen or broken into based on its past history. If no information appears, it means that the car is too new to have a rating.

Corporate Twins: Often a car company will make numerous models on the same platform. This is a list of this car's twins.

Drive: This tells if the car comes with front, rear or four wheel drive, or if you have a choice.

In This Chapter...

PRICES

This box contains sample price information. When available, we list the base and the most luxurious version of the car. The difference is often substantial. Usually the more expensive versions have fancy trim, larger engines and lots of automatic equipment. The least expensive versions usually have manual transmission and few extra features. In addition, some manufacturers try to sell popular options as part of a package.

This information provides an idea of the price range and the expected dealer markup. Be prepared for higher retail prices when you get to the showroom. Manufacturers like to load their cars with factory options, and dealers like to add their own items such as fabric protection and paint sealant. Remember, prices and dealer costs can change during the year. Use these figures for general reference and comparisons, not as a precise indication of exactly how much the car you are interested in will cost. See page 92 for a new buying service designed to ensure that you get the very best price.

RATINGS

These are ratings in eight important categories, as well as an overall comparative rating. We have adopted the Olympic rating system with "10" being the best.

Comparative Rating: This is the "bottom line." Using a combination of all of the ratings, this tells how this car stacks up against the other '98's on a scale of 1 to 10. Due to the importance of crash tests, cars with no crash test results as of our publication date cannot be given an overall rating. More recent results may be available from the Auto Safety Hotline at 800-424-9393.

Crash Test Performance: This rating compares the 1998 models against all crash test results to date. We give the best performers a 10 and the worst a 1. Remember to compare crash test results relative to other cars in the same size class. For details, see the "safety" chapter.

Safety Features: This is an evaluation of how much extra safety is built into the car. We give credit for airbags, ABS, daytime running lights, belt height adjustors and pretensioners, and built-in child safety seats. For details, see the "safety" chapter.

Fuel Economy: Here we compare the EPA mileage ratings of each car. The gas misers get a 10 and the guzzlers get a 1. For more information, see the "fuel economy" chapter.

PM Cost: Each manufacturer suggests a preventive maintenance schedule designed to keep the car in good shape and to protect your rights under the warranty. Those with the lowest PM costs get a 10 and the highest a 1. See the "maintenance" chapter for the actual costs and more information.

Repair Cost: It is virtually impossible to predict exactly what any new car will cost you in repairs. As such, we take nine typical repairs that you are likely to experience *after* your warranty expires and compare those costs among this year's models. Those with the lowest cost get a 10 and the highest a 1. For details, see the "maintenance" chapter.

Warranty: This is an overall assessment of the car's warranty when compared to all 1998 warranties. We give the highest rated warranties a 10 and the lowest a 1. See the "warranty" chapter for details.

Complaints: This is where you'll find how your car stacks up against hundreds of others on the road, based on the U.S. government complaint data. If the car has not been around long enough to have developed a complaint history, it is given a 5. The least complained about cars get a 10 and the most problematic, a 1. See the "complaints" chapter for details.

Insurance Cost: Insurance companies have rated most of the cars on the road to determine how they plan to charge for insurance. Here, you'll find whether you can expect a discount or a surcharge for what we expect to be the most popular model. If the car is likely to receive neither, we label it *regular*. Those receiving a discount get a 10, any cars with a surcharge get a 1; any with neither get a 5.

SAFETY

For most of us, safety is a critical consideration in buying a new car. This box will tell you, at a glance, whether or not the car has the safety features you care about.

Frontal Crash Test: Here's where we tell you if the frontal crash test was either *very good, good, average, poor,* or *very poor.*

Side Crash Test: We've also included the car's performance in side crash tests. Here we indicate whether the side crash test was *very good, good, average, poor,* or *very poor.*

Airbag: Here's where you'll find out which occupants benefit from this invaluable safety feature, including side airbags, and who is left unprotected.

Anti-lock Brakes: Find out if this model has the two- or four-wheel anti-lock brakes, and whether you'll have to pay extra for it.

Daytime Running Lights: Daytime runnings lights reduce your chances of being in a crash by up to 40 percent by increasing the visibility of your vehicle. Here we indicate whether daytime running lights are *standard*, *optional* or *none.*

Belt Adjustors: People often don't wear safety belts because they are uncomfortable. In fact, a belt's effectiveness is due, in part, to how well it fits your body. In order to make sure shoulder belts fit properly (squarely across the front of your chest) some manufacturers have installed height adjustable seat belt adjusters. Availability is indicated for either the front and back seat occupants, just the front seat occupants, or neither.

Built-in Child Safety Seats: Some manufacturers are offering "built-in" child safety seats which reduces the chances that your child rides unprotected.

Pretensioners: This valuable safety feature improves the seat belt's effectiveness at protecting occupants in a crash. During the collision, the seat belt not only locks, but automatically retracts to keep passengers from further harm. Availability is indicated for both front occupants, unless otherwise noted.

SPECIFICATIONS

Here are the "nuts and bolts." In this box we have listed seven key specifications which enable you to evaluate how best that car meets your particular needs. We provide the information for what we expect to be the most popular model.

Fuel Economy: This is the EPA-rated fuel economy for city and highway driving measured in miles per gallon. Most models have a number of fuel economy ratings because of different engine and transmission options. For more individual ratings, see the "fuel economy" chapter.

Driving Range: Given the car's expected fuel economy and gas tank size, this gives an idea of how far you can go on a full tank.

Seating: This figure represents the maximum number of seating positions equipped with safety belts. When more than one number is listed (for example, 5/6/7) it means that different models have different seat configurations.

Length: This is the overall length of the car from bumper to bumper.

Head/Leg Room: This tells how roomy the front seat is.

Interior Space: This tells how roomy the car is. For minivans, see cargo space.

Cargo Space: This gives you the cubic feet available for cargo. For minivans, it is the back of the two front seats to the rear of the vehicle. In cars, it's the trunk space.

COMPETITION

Here we tell you how the car stacks up with its competition. Use this information to compare the overall rating of similar cars and broaden your choice of new car possibilities. This may help you select a more economical or better performing car than the one you were originally considering. We've added page references so you can easily check out the competition. This list is only a guideline, not an all-inclusive list of every possible alternative.

Acura CL

Large

The newest addition to the Acura family is a two-door, U.S.-designed and produced replacement for the Legend called the CL. Its 4-door sibling is the RL and, with minor exceptions, is no different. For '98, the CL gets a new grill and aluminum wheels. The CL comes standard with dual airbags and a-sheel ABS.

You have a choice of two engines. For '98, a new 2.3-liter, 4-cylinder engine is standard, which produces 150 hp. The optional 3.0-liter V-6 provides more power at the cost of fuel economy. Like other Acura's, the CL offers a smooth, comfortable ride. Other standard features include a keyless entry system and a theft deterrent system. The CL should be competitive in a crowded luxury coupe market. No government crash tests scheduled for next year.

General Information

WHERE MADE	U.S.
YEAR OF PRODUCTION	Second
PARKING INDEX	Hard
BUMPERS	Strong
THEFT RATING	
TWINS	
DRIVE	Front

Prices**

Model	Retail	Mkup
CL man.	22,100	15%
CL auto.	22,910	15%

**1998 prices not available at press time. Prices based on 1997 data.

The Ratings

	POOR / GOOD
COMPARATIVE RATING*	
FRONTAL CRASH TEST	
SAFETY FEATURES	
FUEL ECONOMY	
PM COST	
REPAIR COST	
WARRANTY	
COMPLAINTS	
INSURANCE COST	

Safety

FRONTAL CRASH TEST	No government results
SIDE CRASH TEST	No government results
AIRBAGS	Dual Only
ANTI-LOCK BRAKES	4-wheel
DAY. RUNNING LIGHTS	None
BELT ADJUSTORS	None
BUILT-IN CHILD SEAT	None
PRETENSIONERS	None

Specifications

FUEL ECONOMY (cty/hwy)	23/29	Average
DRIVING RANGE (miles)	447	Long
SEATING	5	
LENGTH (in.)	190.0	Long
HEAD/LEG ROOM (in.)	37.4/42.9	Cramped
INTERIOR SPACE (cu. ft.)	84.7	Vry. Cramped
CARGO SPACE (cu. ft.)	12.0	Small

Specifications may vary.

Competition

	POOR / GOOD	Pg.
Acura CL		**102**
Audi A4		106
Lexus ES300		162
Saab 900		205

*Due to the importance of crash tests, cars with no results as of publication date cannot be given an overall rating.

Acura Integra

Compact

This Honda Civic-based hatchback continues to be the least expensive Acura. For 1998, the Integra receives new front and rear end styling plus new wheels. Dual airbags are still standard; ABS is optional.

The standard engine, a 1.8-liter, on the base RS and mid-level LS delivers over 140 hp, more than enough for this fairly light car. The GS-R gets a 170-hp VTEC version of the 1.8-liter and doesn't lose a bit in fuel economy. The 5-speed is responsive and the handling ranks among the best for small cars. The Integra emphasizes sportiness rather than luxury. Front seats, driver's controls, and instruments are fine, but the rear seat is definitely not for adults on long trips. If you're in the market for a sports car, the Integra should be on your list of test drives.

The Ratings

	POOR — GOOD
COMPARATIVE RATING	□□□□□■□□□□
FRONTAL CRASH TEST	□□□□□■□□□□
SAFETY FEATURES	□□□□■□□□□□
FUEL ECONOMY	□□□□□■□□□□
PM COST	■□□□□□□□□□
REPAIR COST	□□■□□□□□□□
WARRANTY	□□□□□■□□□□
COMPLAINTS	□□□□□□□■□□
INSURANCE COST	□□□□■□□□□□

Safety

FRONTAL CRASH TEST	Average
SIDE CRASH TEST	No government results
AIRBAGS	Dual Only
ANTI-LOCK BRAKES	4-wheel (optional)
DAY. RUNNING LIGHTS	None
BELT ADJUSTORS	Front
BUILT-IN CHILD SEAT	None
PRETENSIONERS	None

General Information

WHERE MADE	Japan
YEAR OF PRODUCTION	Fifth
PARKING INDEX	Easy
BUMPERS	Strong
THEFT RATING	Very High
TWINS	
DRIVE	Front

Specifications

FUEL ECONOMY (cty/hwy)	25/31	Average
DRIVING RANGE (miles)	370	Very Short
SEATING	5	
LENGTH (in.)	178.1	Short
HEAD/LEG ROOM (in.)	38.9/42.2	Average
INTERIOR SPACE (cu. ft.)	83.2	Vry. Cramped
CARGO SPACE (cu. ft.)	11.0	Very Small

Specifications may vary.

Prices**

Model	Retail	Mkup
Integra RS 3dr.	16,100	14%
Integra LS 3dr.	18,850	14%
Integra LS 4dr.	19,650	14%

Competition

	POOR — GOOD	Pg.
Acura Integra	□□□□□■□□□□	**103**
Eagle Talon	□■□□□□□□□□	139
Mazda Miata	□□□■□□□□□□	170
Mitsubishi Eclipse	□□■□□□□□□□	183

**1998 prices not available at press time. Prices based on 1997 data.

Acura RL

Large

The RL is Acura's third generation replacement for its former luxury flagship, the Legend. Of all Acura models, the RL is the most luxurious. It is built on the same wheelbase and track width as the previous Legend; however, major improvements have been made in ride and comfort. The RL comes standard with dual airbags and 4-wheel ABS.

Oddly enough, the new V6 found in the RL, a 3.5-liter, is actually less powerful than the old 3.2-liter V6 found in the Legend. Acura engineers sacrificed hp for torque and the new engine feels more like a V8 than a V6. For '98, check out the new sport package which offers a VTEC engine and better handling. Noise, vibration and harshness are all improved due to increased insulation and a beefed-up suspension.

The Ratings	POOR → GOOD
COMPARATIVE RATING*	
FRONTAL CRASH TEST	
SAFETY FEATURES	
FUEL ECONOMY	
PM COST	
REPAIR COST	
WARRANTY	
COMPLAINTS	
INSURANCE COST	

Safety	
FRONTAL CRASH TEST	No government results
SIDE CRASH TEST	No government results
AIRBAGS	Dual Only
ANTI-LOCK BRAKES	4-wheel
DAY. RUNNING LIGHTS	None
BELT ADJUSTORS	Front
BUILT-IN CHILD SEAT	None
PRETENSIONERS	Standard

General Information	
WHERE MADE	Japan
YEAR OF PRODUCTION	Third
PARKING INDEX	Average
BUMPERS	Strong
THEFT RATING	
TWINS	
DRIVE	Front

Specifications		
FUEL ECONOMY (cty/hwy)	19/25	Poor
DRIVING RANGE (miles)	396	Short
SEATING	5	
LENGTH (in.)	195.1	Long
HEAD/LEG ROOM (in.)	38.8/42.1	Average
INTERIOR SPACE (cu. ft.)	96.5	Average
CARGO SPACE (cu. ft.)	14.0	Average

Specifications may vary.

Prices**

Model	Retail	Mkup
RL	41,000	17%

Competition

	POOR → GOOD	Pg.
Acura RL		**104**
BMW 3 Series		106
Infiniti I30		158
Merc.-Benz C-Class		174

**1998 prices not available at press time. Prices based on 1997 data.

*Due to the importance of crash tests, cars with no results as of publication date cannot be given an overall rating.

Acura TL

Large

The Acura TL continues into 1998 unchanged. The TL stands for "Touring Luxury" and Acura is hoping to attract Lexus ES300 buyers. The TL comes standard with dual airbags and 4-wheel ABS; traction control is a great option.

You'll find two models, the 3.2TL or the 2.5TL. Like other Acuras, the 3.2 and 2.5 stand for engine sizes and both engines should provide plenty of power. However, more power from the 3.2 hurts gas mileage. Its speed-sensitive power steering is responsive and light. There are few options to choose from, so be prepared for a high base price. With good crash test results, the TL has a conservative look and the spacious interior and smooth ride are what you expect from a luxury car. Don't miss test driving the highly rated TL.

The Ratings

	POOR — GOOD
COMPARATIVE RATING	
FRONTAL CRASH TEST	
SAFETY FEATURES	
FUEL ECONOMY	
PM COST	
REPAIR COST	
WARRANTY	
COMPLAINTS	
INSURANCE COST	

Safety

FRONTAL CRASH TEST	Good
SIDE CRASH TEST	No government results
AIRBAGS	Dual Only
ANTI-LOCK BRAKES	4-wheel
DAY. RUNNING LIGHTS	None
BELT ADJUSTORS	Front
BUILT-IN CHILD SEAT	None
PRETENSIONERS	None

General Information

WHERE MADE	Japan
YEAR OF PRODUCTION	Third
PARKING INDEX	Average
BUMPERS	Strong
THEFT RATING	Very High
TWINS	
DRIVE	Front

Specifications

FUEL ECONOMY (cty/hwy)	20/25	Poor
DRIVING RANGE (miles)	396	Short
SEATING	5	
LENGTH (in.)	191.5	Long
HEAD/LEG ROOM (in.)	37.5/43.7	Average
INTERIOR SPACE (cu. ft.)	94.7	Average
CARGO SPACE (cu. ft.)	14.1	Average

Specifications may vary.

Prices**

Model	Retail	Mkup
TL 2.5	28,450	14%
TL 3.2	32,950	14%

Competition

	POOR — GOOD	Pg.
Acura TL		**105**
BMW 3 Series		193
Lexus ES300		162
Merc.-Benz C-Class		174

**1998 prices not available at press time. Prices based on 1997 data.

Audi A4

Intermediate

The A4 enters 1998 with few changes, except for a new wagon version called the Avant. Previously the 90, the A4 is basically a lower priced version of the Audi A6. ABS, dual airbags, and side airbags are all standard.

The base engine, a 1.8-liter four cylinder turbo, will provide ample power, but if you are looking for more power, go for the optional 2.8 liter V6. The A4 is available with either front-wheel drive or all-wheel drive, called Quattro, which improves overall handling and traction on slick roads. The A4 has a large trunk and cabin and is well equipped to handle 4 passengers. Preventive maintenance costs are minimal; Audi covers the preventive maintenance costs for the first 50,000 miles. Also, the warranty is tops. If you're shopping for a luxury car, the A4 is hard to beat and the new Avant wagon is an attractive addition.

The Ratings

	POOR → GOOD
COMPARATIVE RATING	□□□□□□□□□■
FRONTAL CRASH TEST	□□□□□□□□■□
SAFETY FEATURES	□□□□□□■□□□
FUEL ECONOMY	□□□□□■□□□□
PM COST	□□□□□□□□□■
REPAIR COST	□□□■□□□□□□
WARRANTY	□□□□□□□□■□
COMPLAINTS	□□□□□□□□□■
INSURANCE COST	□□□□■□□□□□

Safety

FRONTAL CRASH TEST	Very Good
SIDE CRASH TEST	No government results
AIRBAGS	Dual & Side
ANTI-LOCK BRAKES	4-wheel
DAY. RUNNING LIGHTS	None
BELT ADJUSTORS	Front
BUILT-IN CHILD SEAT	None
PRETENSIONERS	Standard

General Information

WHERE MADE	Germany
YEAR OF PRODUCTION	Third
PARKING INDEX	Average
BUMPERS	Strong
THEFT RATING	
TWINS	
DRIVE	Front

Specifications

FUEL ECONOMY (cty/hwy)	23/32	Average
DRIVING RANGE (miles)	459	Long
SEATING	5	
LENGTH (in.)	178.0	Short
HEAD/LEG ROOM (in.)	38.1/41.3	Cramped
INTERIOR SPACE (cu. ft.)	87.7	Cramped
CARGO SPACE (cu. ft.)	14.0	Average

Specifications may vary.

Prices

Model	Retail	Mkup
A4 1.8	23,790	14%
A4 2.8	28,390	14%
A4 Avant	30,465	14%

Competition

	POOR → GOOD	Pg.
Audi A4	□□□□□□□□□■	**106**
BMW 3 Series	□□□□□□□□□■	108
Lexus ES300	□□□□□□□□■□	162
Saab 900	□■□□□□□□□□	205

Audi A6

Large

The all-new A6 is essentially a stretched out A4. The roofline was lowered slightly to give the A6 a sportier, coupe look — a performance car disguised as a luxury sedan. Expect a wagon to join the sedan in the spring. Dual airbags, side airbags and ABS are standard.

A new standard 2.8-liter, V6 engine that gives out 200 hp comes with an improved cylinder design. The suspension is improved and there is an all-wheel drive option. Expect preventive maintenance costs to be low as Audi covers the preventive maintenance costs for the first 50,000 miles. Additionally, Audi's warranty is the best in the industry. No frontal or side crash tests are available and only time will tell about reliability, but Audi's reputation for quality makes the A6 a safe choice.

The Ratings

	POOR — GOOD
COMPARATIVE RATING*	□□□□□□□□□□
FRONTAL CRASH TEST	□□□□□□□□□□
SAFETY FEATURES	□□□□□□■□□□
FUEL ECONOMY	□□□■□□□□□□
PM COST	□□□□□□□□□■
REPAIR COST	□□■□□□□□□□
WARRANTY	□□□□□□□□■□
COMPLAINTS	□□□□■□□□□□
INSURANCE COST	□□□□■□□□□□

Safety

FRONTAL CRASH TEST	No government results
SIDE CRASH TEST	No government results
AIRBAGS	Dual & Side
ANTI-LOCK BRAKES	4-wheel
DAY. RUNNING LIGHTS	None
BELT ADJUSTORS	Front
BUILT-IN CHILD SEAT	None
PRETENSIONERS	Standard

General Information

WHERE MADE	Germany
YEAR OF PRODUCTION	First
PARKING INDEX	Hard
BUMPERS	Strong
THEFT RATING	
TWINS	
DRIVE	Front

Specifications

FUEL ECONOMY (cty/hwy)	17/28	Poor
DRIVING RANGE (miles)	426	Average
SEATING	5	
LENGTH (in.)	192.0	Long
HEAD/LEG ROOM (in.)	39.3/41.3	Average
INTERIOR SPACE (cu. ft.)	108.3	Very Roomy
CARGO SPACE (cu. ft.)	17.2	Large

Specifications may vary.

Prices

Model	Retail	Mkup
A6	33,750	14%

Competition

	POOR — GOOD	Pg.
Audi A6	□□□□□□□□□□	**107**
BMW 3 Series	□□□□□□□□□■	108
Infiniti I30	□□□□□□□□□■	158
Saab 9000	□□□□■□□□□□	206

*Due to the importance of crash tests, cars with no results as of publication date cannot be given an overall rating.

BMW 3 Series

Compact

BMW's entry level 3 Series continues into 1998 unchanged. BMW says big changes are in store for 1999. In the meantime, if you're looking for selection, the 3 Series has eight variations of sedan, coupe, and convertible. Great safety features this year include standard front side airbags (optional for the base 318ti) and standard adjustable rear head rests. Dual airbags and 4-wheel ABS are standard, as well.

The 1.8-liter engine on the base level 318 is strong enough. The 2.5-liter on the 323 is better, but less fuel efficient. Front seats offer excellent comfort on long trips; however, the back seat is a squeeze for adults. Controls are excellent. The 3 Series is expensive to own, but did perform well in frontal crash tests. Look over all the possible variations carefully as there's lots to choose from. The 3 Series is well worth a test drive.

The Ratings

	POOR — GOOD
COMPARATIVE RATING	
FRONTAL CRASH TEST	
SAFETY FEATURES	
FUEL ECONOMY	
PM COST	
REPAIR COST	
WARRANTY	
COMPLAINTS	
INSURANCE COST	

Safety

FRONTAL CRASH TEST	Good
SIDE CRASH TEST	No government results
AIRBAGS	Dual/Opt. Side
ANTI-LOCK BRAKES	4-wheel
DAY. RUNNING LIGHTS	None
BELT ADJUSTORS	Front
BUILT-IN CHILD SEAT	None
PRETENSIONERS	Standard

General Information

WHERE MADE	Germany
YEAR OF PRODUCTION	Seventh
PARKING INDEX	Easy
BUMPERS	Weak
THEFT RATING	Very High
TWINS	
DRIVE	Rear

Specifications

FUEL ECONOMY (cty/hwy)	23/32	Average
DRIVING RANGE (miles)	459	Long
SEATING	4	
LENGTH (in.)	174.5	Short
HEAD/LEG ROOM (in.)	38.1/41.1	Vry. Cramped
INTERIOR SPACE (cu. ft.)	85.7	Cramped
CARGO SPACE (cu. ft.)	10.3	Very Small

Specifications may vary.

Prices

Model	Retail	Mkup
318ti Coupe 3-Door	21,960	11%
318i Sedan	26,720	14%
328i Sedan	33,670	15%
328i Conv.	33,770	14%

Competition

	POOR — GOOD	Pg.
BMW 3 Series		**108**
Audi A4		106
Lexus ES300		162
Merc.-Benz C-Class		174

BMW 5 Series

Large

Last year, BMW redesigned the 5 Series to be roomier and more luxurious and they continue this year with safety features leading the way. The 5 Series comes with dual airbags, side airbags up front, and a head-level side airbag that inflates next to passengers' heads for protection during rollover collisions. If six standard airbags aren't enough, you can get two more optional side airbags for rear passengers. 4-wheel ABS and traction control are also standard.

The 528 comes with a powerful 2.8-liter, inline 6 engine. A whopping 4.4-liter V8 engine is available on the 540 with a six speed transmission. A stiffer suspension and 17 inch tires highlight a sport package for the 5 Series sedans. While expensive to repair (not to mention purchase!), BMW gets high marks for safety.

The Ratings

	POOR → GOOD (1–10)
COMPARATIVE RATING*	□□□□□□□□□□
FRONTAL CRASH TEST	□□□□□□□□□□
SAFETY FEATURES	□□□□□□■□□□
FUEL ECONOMY	□□□■□□□□□□
PM COST	□□□□□□□□□■
REPAIR COST	□□■□□□□□□□
WARRANTY	□□□□□□□■□□
COMPLAINTS	□□□□■□□□□□
INSURANCE COST	□□□□■□□□□□

Safety

FRONTAL CRASH TEST	No government results
SIDE CRASH TEST	No government results
AIRBAGS	Dual & Side
ANTI-LOCK BRAKES	4-wheel
DAY. RUNNING LIGHTS	None
BELT ADJUSTORS	Front
BUILT-IN CHILD SEAT	None
PRETENSIONERS	Standard

General Information

WHERE MADE	Germany
YEAR OF PRODUCTION	Second
PARKING INDEX	Average
BUMPERS	Weak
THEFT RATING	
TWINS	
DRIVE	Rear

Specifications

FUEL ECONOMY (cty/hwy)	18/26	Poor
DRIVING RANGE (miles)	407	Short
SEATING	4	
LENGTH (in.)	188.0	Average
HEAD/LEG ROOM (in.)	38.7/41.7	Cramped
INTERIOR SPACE (cu. ft.)	92.5	Cramped
CARGO SPACE (cu. ft.)	11.1	Very Small

Specifications may vary.

Prices

Model	Retail	Mkup
528i	39,470	13%
540i auto.	51,070	14%
540i man.	53,870	14%

Competition

	POOR → GOOD (1–10)	Pg.
BMW 5 Series	□□□□□□□□□□	**109**
Infiniti I30	□□□□□□□□□■	158
Lexus ES300	□□□□□□□□■□	162
Merc.-Benz C-Class	□□□□□□□■□□	174

*Due to the importance of crash tests, cars with no results as of publication date cannot be given an overall rating.

BMW Z3

Compact

The Z3, based on the 3 Series platform, continues to turn heads for 1998 after a splashy debut last year, which included an appearance in a James Bond film. Standard safety features include dual airbags, seat belt pretensioners, traction control, and 4-wheel ABS

Engine choices are better this year. You can get a 1.9-liter, 4-cylinder engine with 138 hp, but most will want the bigger 2.8-liter, 6-cylinder engine which offers 189 hp. Better yet, new for 1998, an M roadster version of the Z3 will come with 17 inch wheels and a must-have 3.2-liter, 240 hp engine. The interior offers bins for small luggage, but don't expect to bring much along with you. Noise levels should be tolerable and controls easy to use. With its long-nosed, short-tailed appearance, the Z3 is the 90's version of the traditional sports car.

The Ratings

	POOR □□□ GOOD
COMPARATIVE RATING *	□□□□□□□□□□
FRONTAL CRASH TEST	□□□□□□□□□□
SAFETY FEATURES	□□□□□□■□□□
FUEL ECONOMY	□□□□□■□□□□
PM COST	□□□□□□□□□■
REPAIR COST	□□■□□□□□□□
WARRANTY	□□□□□□□■□□
COMPLAINTS	□□□□□□□■□□
INSURANCE COST	□□□□■□□□□□

Safety

FRONTAL CRASH TEST	No government results
SIDE CRASH TEST	No government results
AIRBAGS	Dual Only
ANTI-LOCK BRAKES	4-wheel
DAY. RUNNING LIGHTS	None
BELT ADJUSTORS	Front
BUILT-IN CHILD SEAT	None
PRETENSIONERS	Standard

General Information

WHERE MADE	Germany/U.S.
YEAR OF PRODUCTION	Third
PARKING INDEX	Very Easy
BUMPERS	Weak
THEFT RATING	
TWINS	
DRIVE	Front

Specifications

FUEL ECONOMY (cty/hwy)	23/32	Average
DRIVING RANGE (miles)	378	Short
SEATING	2	
LENGTH (in.)	158.5	Very Short
HEAD/LEG ROOM (in.)	37.6/41.8	Cramped
INTERIOR SPACE (cu. ft.)	47.0	Vry. Cramped
CARGO SPACE (cu. ft.)	5.0	Very Small

Specifications may vary.

Prices

Model	Retail	Mkup
Z3 1.9	29,995	14%
Z3 2.8	36,470	14%

Competition

	POOR □□□ GOOD	Pg.
BMW Z3	□□□□□□□□□□	**110**
Acura Integra	□□□□□■□□□□	103
Mazda Miata	□□□■□□□□□□	170
Mitsubishi Eclipse	□□■□□□□□□□	183

*Due to the importance of crash tests, cars with no results as of publication date cannot be given an overall rating.

Buick Century

Intermediate

The Buick Century received a much-needed makeover last year and it remains unchanged for 1998. This Century is a great improvement over past versions. Its platform is shared by the just introduced Oldsmobile Intrigue and the Pontiac Grand Prix. Smoother and sleeker on the outside, this six passenger car is 5.4 inches longer than the previous version plus more attention was paid to interior comfort. Dual airbags, 4-wheel ABS and daytime running lamps are standard.

Powering the new Century is a 3.1-liter V6 engine with 160 hp. There are two trim levels: Custom and Limited. A "can't miss" option for parents is the new built-in child seat. Ride and handling are improved by a new rear suspension. Scheduled to be crash tested next year, we expect the Century to continue to perform well.

The Ratings

	POOR … GOOD
COMPARATIVE RATING	□□□□□□■□□□
FRONTAL CRASH TEST*	□□□□□□■□□□
SAFETY FEATURES	□□□□□□□■□□
FUEL ECONOMY	□□□□■□□□□□
PM COST	□□□□□■□□□□
REPAIR COST	□□□□□□□□□■
WARRANTY	□■□□□□□□□□
COMPLAINTS	□□□□■□□□□□
INSURANCE COST	□□□□□□□□□■

Safety

FRONTAL CRASH TEST	Good
SIDE CRASH TEST	No government results
AIRBAGS	Dual Only
ANTI-LOCK BRAKES	4-wheel
DAY. RUNNING LIGHTS	Standard
BELT ADJUSTORS	Front/Rear
BUILT-IN CHILD SEAT	Optional
PRETENSIONERS	None

General Information

WHERE MADE	Canada/U.S.
YEAR OF PRODUCTION	Second
PARKING INDEX	Hard
BUMPERS	Strong
THEFT RATING	
TWINS	Regal, Intrigue, Gr. Prix
DRIVE	Front

Specifications

FUEL ECONOMY (cty/hwy)	20/29	Average
DRIVING RANGE (miles)	425	Average
SEATING	6	
LENGTH (in.)	194.6	Long
HEAD/LEG ROOM (in.)	39.3/42.4	Roomy
INTERIOR SPACE (cu. ft.)	118.5	Very Roomy
CARGO SPACE (cu. ft.)	16.7	Large

Specifications may vary.

Prices

Model	Retail	Mkup
Century Custom	18,215	7%
Century Limited	19,575	7%

Competition

	POOR … GOOD	Pg.
Buick Century	□□□□□□■□□□	**111**
Ford Contour	□□□□□□■□□□	141
Mazda Millenia	□□□□□□■□□□	171
Pontiac Grand Prix	□□□□□■□□□□	202

*A version of this vehicle is scheduled to be tested later this year. Results are expected to be similar.

Buick LeSabre

Large

For many years, Buick has been attracting consumers with conservative automobiles and the 1998 LeSabre is no exception. Redesigned last year, the LeSabre comes in two trim levels: Limited or Custom Sedan. An improved transmission and GM's Onstar roadside assistance system was added for '98. Dual airbags, 4-wheel ABS and daytime running lamps are standard.

Buick offers only one engine with the LeSabre, a 3.8-liter V6 engine that can deliver up to 30 mpg on the highway. Like its twin, the Oldsmobile 88, the LeSabre emphasizes a soft ride. For crisper handling, order LeSabre's Gran Touring package. Interior room is spacious, especially in back. There are many new options like delayed locking which helps prevent lock-outs.

The Ratings

	POOR — GOOD
COMPARATIVE RATING	
FRONTAL CRASH TEST*	
SAFETY FEATURES	
FUEL ECONOMY	
PM COST	
REPAIR COST	
WARRANTY	
COMPLAINTS	
INSURANCE COST	

Safety

FRONTAL CRASH TEST	Good
SIDE CRASH TEST	No government results
AIRBAGS	Dual Only
ANTI-LOCK BRAKES	4-wheel
DAY. RUNNING LIGHTS	Standard
BELT ADJUSTORS	Front/Rear
BUILT-IN CHILD SEAT	None
PRETENSIONERS	None

General Information

WHERE MADE	U.S./Canada
YEAR OF PRODUCTION	Seventh
PARKING INDEX	Hard
BUMPERS	Strong
THEFT RATING	Very Low
TWINS	Olds 88, Pont. Bonneville
DRIVE	Front

Specifications

FUEL ECONOMY (cty/hwy)	19/30	Average
DRIVING RANGE (miles)	450	Long
SEATING	6	
LENGTH (in.)	200.8	Very Long
HEAD/LEG ROOM (in.)	38.8/42.6	Average
INTERIOR SPACE (cu. ft.)	125.5	Very Roomy
CARGO SPACE (cu. ft.)	18.0	Large

Specifications may vary.

Prices

Model	Retail	Mkup
LeSabre Custom	22,465	9%
LeSabre Limited	25,790	9%

Competition

	POOR — GOOD	Pg.
Buick LeSabre		**112**
Ford Taurus		145
Olds Achieva		192
Toyota Camry		214

*A version of this vehicle is scheduled to be tested later this year. Results are expected to be similar.

Buick Park Avenue

Large

Last year, Buick redesigned half of its six car lineup including the Park Avenue. Their goal was to provide a smooth ride without sacrificing comfort and handling. Now a twin of the Riviera and the Olds Aurora, the Park Avenue is aimed at car buyers looking for an affordable luxury car. Virtually unchanged for '98, the Park Avenue comes standard with dual airbags, seat belt adjustors in both front and back, and 4-wheel ABS.

There are two engines choices available for 1998, both are 3.8-liter V-6's. The standard engine delivers a respectable 19/28 mpg while the turbo charged version sacrifices fuel economy slightly, delivering 18/27 mpg. Standard features include keyless entry and delayed locking. The revised Park Avenue should continue to be a best-seller for Buick.

The Ratings	POOR ... GOOD
COMPARATIVE RATING	□□■□□□□□□□
FRONTAL CRASH TEST	□□□□■□□□□□
SAFETY FEATURES	□□□□□□■□□□
FUEL ECONOMY	□□□□■□□□□□
PM COST	□□□□□■□□□□
REPAIR COST	□□□□□□□■□□
WARRANTY	□■□□□□□□□□
COMPLAINTS	□□□□■□□□□□
INSURANCE COST	□□□□□□□□□■

Safety	
FRONTAL CRASH TEST	Average
SIDE CRASH TEST	No government results
AIRBAGS	Dual Only
ANTI-LOCK BRAKES	4-wheel
DAY. RUNNING LIGHTS	Standard
BELT ADJUSTORS	Front/Rear
BUILT-IN CHILD SEAT	None
PRETENSIONERS	None

General Information	
WHERE MADE	U.S./Canada
YEAR OF PRODUCTION	Second
PARKING INDEX	Hard
BUMPERS	Strong
THEFT RATING	
TWINS	Riviera, Seville, Aurora
DRIVE	Front

Specifications		
FUEL ECONOMY (cty/hwy)	19/28	Average
DRIVING RANGE (miles)	444	Long
SEATING	6	
LENGTH (in.)	206.8	Very Long
HEAD/LEG ROOM (in.)	39.8/42.4	Roomy
INTERIOR SPACE (cu. ft.)	130.3	Very Roomy
CARGO SPACE (cu. ft.)	19.1	Large

Specifications may vary.

Prices

Model	Retail	Mkup
Park Avenue	30,675	11%
Park Avenue Ultra	35,550	10%

Competition

	POOR ... GOOD	Pg.
Buick Park Avenue	□□■□□□□□□□	**113**
Chevrolet Lumina	□□□■□□□□□□	123
Ford Crown Victoria	□□□□■□□□□□	142
Toyota Avalon	□□□□■□□□□□	213

Buick Regal

Intermediate

An all-new Regal was introduced last year as a 1997½ model. It now shares a platform with the Century, Olds Intrigue, and Pontiac Grand Prix. Standard safety features include dual airbags, 4-wheel ABS, belt adjustors for front and rear occupants, and daytime running lamps.

The Regal comes in two trim levels: RS and GS. The RS gets a 3.80-liter, V6 engine, while the GS comes with a 240 hp, supercharged version of the V6. With a slightly longer wheelbase, there is a bit more interior room and trunk space than last year's version. Buick engineers designed the Regal to be the smoothest and quietest running sedan they make. With good ratings for maintenance costs and crash tests, the Regal is worth considering.

The Ratings

	POOR → GOOD
COMPARATIVE RATING	□□□□□■□□□□
FRONTAL CRASH TEST*	□□□□□□■□□□
SAFETY FEATURES	□□□□□□■□□□
FUEL ECONOMY	□□□□■□□□□□
PM COST	□□□□□■□□□□
REPAIR COST	□□□□□□■□□□
WARRANTY	□■□□□□□□□□
COMPLAINTS	□□□□■□□□□□
INSURANCE COST	□□□□□□□□□■

Safety

FRONTAL CRASH TEST	Good
SIDE CRASH TEST	No government results
AIRBAGS	Dual Only
ANTI-LOCK BRAKES	4-wheel
DAY. RUNNING LIGHTS	Standard
BELT ADJUSTORS	Front/Rear
BUILT-IN CHILD SEAT	None
PRETENSIONERS	None

General Information

WHERE MADE	Canada/U.S.
YEAR OF PRODUCTION	Second
PARKING INDEX	Hard
BUMPERS	Strong
THEFT RATING	
TWINS	Century, Intrigue, Gr. Prix
DRIVE	Front

Specifications

FUEL ECONOMY (cty/hwy)	19/30	Average
DRIVING RANGE (miles)	425	Average
SEATING	5	
LENGTH (in.)	196.2	Long
HEAD/LEG ROOM (in.)	39.3/42.4	Roomy
INTERIOR SPACE (cu. ft.)	118.5	Very Roomy
CARGO SPACE (cu. ft.)	16.7	Large

Specifications may vary.

Prices

Model	Retail	Mkup
Regal LS	20,945	9%
Regal GS	23,690	9%

Competition

	POOR → GOOD	Pg.
Buick Regal	□□□□□■□□□□	**114**
Ford Contour	□□□□□□■□□□	141
Hyundai Sonata	□□■□□□□□□□	156
Volkswagen Golf	□□□□□□□■□□	220

*A version of this vehicle is scheduled to be tested later this year. Results are expected to be similar.

Buick Riviera

Large

The Riviera, Buick's sleek luxury sports coupe, is designed to grab your eye with its unique style. Its twins include the Park Avenue, Cadillac Seville, and Olds Aurora—all big, American cars. For 1998, the Riviera gets a new engine, a better transmission, and a bigger fuel tank. Dual airbags and ABS are standard.

At over 17 feet and almost two tons, the Riviera is big, especially for a coupe. The new, and only, engine is a supercharged, 3.8-liter V8 engine that produces 240 hp. The seats are very comfortable with ample interior room and interior noise is very low. Improvements were made to the steering and suspension for better highway steering. New options for the front passenger include lumbar support and heated seats.

The Ratings	POOR — GOOD
COMPARATIVE RATING	
FRONTAL CRASH TEST	
SAFETY FEATURES	
FUEL ECONOMY	
PM COST	
REPAIR COST	
WARRANTY	
COMPLAINTS	
INSURANCE COST	

Safety	
FRONTAL CRASH TEST	Average
SIDE CRASH TEST	No government results
AIRBAGS	Dual Only
ANTI-LOCK BRAKES	4-wheel
DAY. RUNNING LIGHTS	Standard
BELT ADJUSTORS	Front/Rear
BUILT-IN CHILD SEAT	None
PRETENSIONERS	None

General Information	
WHERE MADE	U.S./Canada
YEAR OF PRODUCTION	Fourth
PARKING INDEX	Hard
BUMPERS	Strong
THEFT RATING	Very Low
TWINS	Park Ave., Seville, Aurora
DRIVE	Front

Specifications		
FUEL ECONOMY (cty/hwy)	18/27	Poor
DRIVING RANGE (miles)	426	Average
SEATING	5	
LENGTH (in.)	207.2	Very Long
HEAD/LEG ROOM (in.)	38.2/42.6	Average
INTERIOR SPACE (cu. ft.)	116.9	Very Roomy
CARGO SPACE (cu. ft.)	17.4	Large

Specifications may vary.

Prices

Model	Retail	Mkup
Riviera	32,500	11%

Competition

	POOR — GOOD	Pg.
Buick Riviera		**115**
Infiniti I30		158
Lexus ES300		162
Merc.-Benz C-Class		174

Cadillac Catera

Intermediate

This is not your grandfather's Caddy. The Catera, which was introduced last year, is designed to appeal to buyers younger than the typical Cadillac owner. However, sales have been slow and Cadillac hasn't been able to tap into the baby boomer market as it had hoped. The Catera's competitors are the Mercedes C-Class and the BMW 3 Series. Standard features include dual airbags and 4-wheel ABS.

If you look for the usual Northstar engine under the hood, you'll find, instead, a 3.0-liter V6. Interior comfort and ride are what you have come to expect from a Cadillac—excellent with little noise. Up front, the controls are nicely designed. A nice addition for 1998 is a shoulder-lap belt for the center passenger in the rear. Unfortunately, no government crash tests results are available.

General Information

WHERE MADE	Germany
YEAR OF PRODUCTION	Second
PARKING INDEX	Easy
BUMPERS	Weak
THEFT RATING	
TWINS	
DRIVE	Rear

Prices

Model	Retail	Mkup
Catera (cloth)	29,995	5%
Catera (leather)	33,160	8%

The Ratings

	POOR — GOOD
COMPARATIVE RATING*	
FRONTAL CRASH TEST	
SAFETY FEATURES	
FUEL ECONOMY	
PM COST	
REPAIR COST	
WARRANTY	
COMPLAINTS	
INSURANCE COST	

Safety

FRONTAL CRASH TEST	No government results
SIDE CRASH TEST	No government results
AIRBAGS	Dual Only
ANTI-LOCK BRAKES	4-wheel
DAY. RUNNING LIGHTS	Standard
BELT ADJUSTORS	Front
BUILT-IN CHILD SEAT	None
PRETENSIONERS	Standard

Specifications

FUEL ECONOMY (cty/hwy)	18/25	Poor
DRIVING RANGE (miles)	396	Short
SEATING	5	
LENGTH (in.)	194.0	Long
HEAD/LEG ROOM (in.)	38.7/42.2	Average
INTERIOR SPACE (cu. ft.)	98.2	Average
CARGO SPACE (cu. ft.)	14.5	Average

Specifications may vary.

Competition

	POOR — GOOD	Pg.
Cadillac Catera		**116**
Audi A4		106
BMW 3 Series		108
Merc.-Benz C-Class		174

*Due to the importance of crash tests, cars with no results as of publication date cannot be given an overall rating.

Cadillac DeVille

Large

The DeVille comes off a redesign last year unchanged for 1998. The changes last year for this five-passenger sedan included a new interior and a restyled exterior along with changes under the hood which improved its handling. The DeVille comes standard with dual airbags, 4-wheel ABS, traction control and even side airbags, too.

Like most other big GM cars, the DeVille emphasizes a soft, quiet ride and lots of room for six adults. The standard Northstar engine provides plenty of horsepower. Speed-sensitive steering and a new chassis control system which includes road texture detection help improve traction and control. Not only does the DeVille perform excellently in frontal crash tests, but it also performed well in the new side crash tests.

The Ratings

	POOR — GOOD
COMPARATIVE RATING	
FRONTAL CRASH TEST	
SAFETY FEATURES	
FUEL ECONOMY	
PM COST	
REPAIR COST	
WARRANTY	
COMPLAINTS	
INSURANCE COST	

Safety

FRONTAL CRASH TEST	Very Good
SIDE CRASH TEST	Very Good
AIRBAGS	Dual & Side
ANTI-LOCK BRAKES	4-wheel
DAY. RUNNING LIGHTS	Standard
BELT ADJUSTORS	Front
BUILT-IN CHILD SEAT	None
PRETENSIONERS	None

General Information

WHERE MADE	U.S./Canada
YEAR OF PRODUCTION	Sixth
PARKING INDEX	Very Hard
BUMPERS	Weak
THEFT RATING	Very Low
TWINS	
DRIVE	Front

Specifications

FUEL ECONOMY (cty/hwy)	17/26	Poor
DRIVING RANGE (miles)	440	Average
SEATING	6	
LENGTH (in.)	209.8	Very Long
HEAD/LEG ROOM (in.)	38.5/42.6	Average
INTERIOR SPACE (cu. ft.)	116.8	Very Roomy
CARGO SPACE (cu. ft.)	20.0	Very Large

Specifications may vary.

Prices

Model	Retail	Mkup
DeVille	37,695	9%
DeVille d'Elegance	41,295	9%
DeVille Concours	42,295	9%

Competition

	POOR — GOOD	Pg.
Cadillac DeVille		**117**
Acura TL		105
Lincoln Mark VIII		167
Toyota Avalon		213

Cadillac Eldorado

Large

For 1998, the Eldorado is unchanged and showing its age. Performance and comfort are what Cadillac aims for in both the base level Eldorado and the upscale Touring Coupe. The Eldorado comes standard with 4-wheel ABS, daytime running lamps, traction control, and dual airbags.

As with other large Cadillacs, the signature Northstar V8 comes standard with the base model Eldorado. The Touring Coupe comes with an even more powerful, 300 hp engine. Both of these sacrifice fuel economy for performance. The front seat is as comfortable and roomy, but the rear seat is cramped and inaccessible like on other sports coupes. The Eldorado is plagued by a high theft rate, expensive repair costs, and unavailable crash test results.

The Ratings

	POOR … GOOD
COMPARATIVE RATING*	□□□□□□□□□□
FRONTAL CRASH TEST	□□□□□□□□□□
SAFETY FEATURES	□□□□□■□□□□
FUEL ECONOMY	□□□■□□□□□□
PM COST	□□□□□□□□■□
REPAIR COST	■□□□□□□□□□
WARRANTY	□□□□□□■□□□
COMPLAINTS	□□□□■□□□□□
INSURANCE COST	□□□□□□□□□■

Safety

FRONTAL CRASH TEST	No government results
SIDE CRASH TEST	No government results
AIRBAGS	Dual Only
ANTI-LOCK BRAKES	4-wheel
DAY. RUNNING LIGHTS	Standard
BELT ADJUSTORS	None
BUILT-IN CHILD SEAT	None
PRETENSIONERS	None

General Information

WHERE MADE	U.S./Canada
YEAR OF PRODUCTION	Seventh
PARKING INDEX	Hard
BUMPERS	Weak
THEFT RATING	Very High
TWINS	
DRIVE	Front

Specifications

FUEL ECONOMY (cty/hwy)	17/26	Poor
DRIVING RANGE (miles)	440	Average
SEATING	5	
LENGTH (in.)	200.6	Very Long
HEAD/LEG ROOM (in.)	37.8/42.6	Cramped
INTERIOR SPACE (cu. ft.)	100.2	Roomy
CARGO SPACE (cu. ft.)	15.3	Average

Specifications may vary.

Prices

Model	Retail	Mkup
Eldorado	38,495	9%
Eldorado Touring	42,695	9%

Competition

	POOR … GOOD	Pg.
Cadillac Eldorado	□□□□□□□□□□	**118**
Acura TL	□□□□□□□□■□	105
Lincoln Mark VIII	□□□□□□□■□□	167
Toyota Avalon	□□□□■□□□□□	213

*Due to the importance of crash tests, cars with no results as of publication date cannot be given an overall rating.

Cadillac Seville

Large

While the '98 Seville may not look significantly different from the '97, Cadillac is hoping its redesign this year will prove that the Seville is a contender in a highly competitive luxury sedan market. The Seville is built off the same platform as the Buick Park Avenue, Buick Riviera, and Olds Aurora. In fact, the new Seville will spearhead Cadillac's entry into the European markets. Side airbags have been added as a standard safety feature along with dual airbags, traction control, and 4-wheel ABS.

The SLS trim level comes with a 4.6-liter, V8 engine with 275 hp. The STS comes with a more powerful V8. Ride and handling are improved and there is more interior room. Trunk space and fuel tank both increased in volume. The STS also comes with adaptive seats up front, which self-adjust to the passenger's shape.

The Ratings

	POOR ... GOOD
COMPARATIVE RATING	□□□□■□□□□□
FRONTAL CRASH TEST	□□□□■□□□□□
SAFETY FEATURES	□□□□□□■□□□
FUEL ECONOMY	□□□■□□□□□□
PM COST	□□□□□□□□■□
REPAIR COST	■□□□□□□□□□
WARRANTY	□□□□□□■□□□
COMPLAINTS	□□□□■□□□□□
INSURANCE COST	□□□□□□□□□■

Safety

FRONTAL CRASH TEST	Average
SIDE CRASH TEST	No government results
AIRBAGS	Dual & Side
ANTI-LOCK BRAKES	4-wheel
DAY. RUNNING LIGHTS	Standard
BELT ADJUSTORS	Front
BUILT-IN CHILD SEAT	None
PRETENSIONERS	Standard

General Information

WHERE MADE	U.S./Canada
YEAR OF PRODUCTION	First
PARKING INDEX	Hard
BUMPERS	Weak
THEFT RATING	
TWINS	Park Ave., Riviera, Aurora
DRIVE	Front

Specifications

FUEL ECONOMY (cty/hwy)	17/26	Poor
DRIVING RANGE (miles)	407	Short
SEATING	5	
LENGTH (in.)	201.0	Very Long
HEAD/LEG ROOM (in.)	38.1/42.5	Average
INTERIOR SPACE (cu. ft.)	120.5	Very Roomy
CARGO SPACE (cu. ft.)	15.7	Large

Specifications may vary.

Prices**

Model	Retail	Mkup
Seville SLS	40,660	16%
Seville STS	45,660	16%

Competition

	POOR ... GOOD	Pg.
Cadillac Seville	□□□□■□□□□□	**119**
Acura TL	□□□□□□□□■□	105
Lincoln Mark VIII	□□□□□□□■□□	167
Nissan Maxima	□□□■□□□□□□	188

**1998 prices not available at press time. Prices based on 1997 data.

Chevrolet Astro

Minivan

The Astro continues into 1998 unchanged. Like its twin, the Safari, the Astro is a basic van which is used primarily for hauling and towing. It offers one of the largest cargo and towing capacities in the van market. Standard features include dual airbags, 4-wheel ABS and daytime running lamps. A built-in child safety seat is optional and highly recommended.

The standard 4.3-liter, V6 engine with automatic transmission provides plenty of power, but sloppy handling. Fuel economy is fairly dismal, as well. You can choose between rear-wheel drive or all-wheel drive. The seats are comfortable enough, but make sure there is enough leg room. If you are looking to carry cargo, this is a good bet. But if you are looking for a people-mover, the Astro is easily outclassed by its younger minivan competitors.

The Ratings	POOR ... GOOD
COMPARATIVE RATING	□■□□□□□□□□
FRONTAL CRASH TEST	□□□■□□□□□□
SAFETY FEATURES	□□□□□□■□□□
FUEL ECONOMY	□□■□□□□□□□
PM COST	□□□□□□□■□□
REPAIR COST	□□□□□□■□□□
WARRANTY	□■□□□□□□□□
COMPLAINTS	□□□□□■□□□□
INSURANCE COST	□□□□□□□□□■

Safety	
FRONTAL CRASH TEST	Poor
SIDE CRASH TEST	No government results
AIRBAGS	Dual Only
ANTI-LOCK BRAKES	4-wheel
DAY. RUNNING LIGHTS	Standard
BELT ADJUSTORS	Rear
BUILT-IN CHILD SEAT	Optional
PRETENSIONERS	None

General Information	
WHERE MADE	U.S.
YEAR OF PRODUCTION	Fourteenth
PARKING INDEX	Hard
BUMPERS	Strong
THEFT RATING	Very Low
TWINS	GMC Safari
DRIVE	Rear

Specifications		
FUEL ECONOMY (cty/hwy)	16/21	Poor
DRIVING RANGE (miles)	475	Long
SEATING	8	
LENGTH (in.)	189.8	Long
HEAD/LEG ROOM (in.)	39.2/41.6	Average
INTERIOR SPACE (cu. ft.)		
CARGO SPACE (cu. ft.)	170.4	Very Large

Specifications may vary.

Prices		
Model	**Retail**	**Mkup**
Astro	20,074	11%
Astro awd	22,374	11%

Competition	POOR ... GOOD	Pg.
Chevrolet Astro	□■□□□□□□□□	**120**
Ford Windstar	□■□□□□□□□□	146
Dodge Caravan	□□■□□□□□□□	135
Mazda MPV	■□□□□□□□□□	172

Chevrolet Camaro

Intermediate

For 1998, the Camaro sports a restyled front end that includes new composite headlamps to improve nighttime visibility. 4-wheel ABS is standard on all models. Standard dual airbags and daytime running lamps, plus optional traction control are also available. A new sport appearance package gets you bigger wheels and extensions for the front fascia and rear spoiler.

If you are looking for a car with lots of power, the Camaro is a good choice. The standard engine is a 3.8-liter V6 with 200 hp. If you need even more power, the Z28 models have a 5.7-liter V8 that is slightly less economical. The standard manual transmission is more fuel efficient than the optional automatic. The Camaro is roomy up front, but the rear seat is almost too small for even young children. Of course, this is no family car!

The Ratings

	POOR — GOOD
COMPARATIVE RATING	
FRONTAL CRASH TEST	
SAFETY FEATURES	
FUEL ECONOMY	
PM COST	
REPAIR COST	
WARRANTY	
COMPLAINTS	
INSURANCE COST	

Safety

FRONTAL CRASH TEST	Very Good
SIDE CRASH TEST	Good
AIRBAGS	Dual Only
ANTI-LOCK BRAKES	4-wheel
DAY. RUNNING LIGHTS	Standard
BELT ADJUSTORS	Front
BUILT-IN CHILD SEAT	None
PRETENSIONERS	None

General Information

WHERE MADE	Canada
YEAR OF PRODUCTION	Sixth
PARKING INDEX	Hard
BUMPERS	Strong
THEFT RATING	Average
TWINS	Pontiac Firebird
DRIVE	Rear

Specifications

FUEL ECONOMY (cty/hwy)	18/27	Poor
DRIVING RANGE (miles)	357	Very Short
SEATING	4	
LENGTH (in.)	193.5	Long
HEAD/LEG ROOM (in.)	37.2/42.9	Cramped
INTERIOR SPACE (cu. ft.)	82.0	Vry. Cramped
CARGO SPACE (cu. ft.)	13.0	Small

Specifications may vary.

Prices

Model	Retail	Mkup
Camaro	16,625	9%
Camaro Z28	20,470	9%
Camaro Convertible	22,125	9%
Camaro Z28 Convertible	27,450	9%

Competition

	POOR — GOOD	Pg.
Chevrolet Camaro		**121**
Ford Mustang		144
Nissan 240SX		186
Pontiac Firebird		200

Chevrolet Cavalier

Compact

One of the most popular vehicles for 1997, the Cavalier remains unchanged for 1998. It comes with a long list of standard safety features including dual airbags, 4-wheel ABS, and daytime running lamps. Traction control is optional. While the Cavalier has good frontal crash test scores, the coupe performed poorly on side crash tests.

For 1998, the models to choose from include a base coupe and sedan, RS coupe, LS sedan, plus the Z24 coupe and convertible. The standard 2.2-liter engine delivers good power; a more powerful 2.4-liter engine is optional on the base sedan and coupe, standard on the LS and Z24 models. Ride is good on smooth roads, but highway driving can be noisy. The Cavalier easily holds its own against its competitors: the Escort, Neon and Saturn. A poor side crash test performance keeps the Cavalier from being a Best Bet.

The Ratings

	POOR ← → GOOD
COMPARATIVE RATING	□□□□□□□■□□
FRONTAL CRASH TEST*	□□□□□□■□□□
SAFETY FEATURES	□□□□□■□□□□
FUEL ECONOMY	□□□□□□■□□□
PM COST	□□□□□□■□□□
REPAIR COST	□□□□□■□□□□
WARRANTY	□■□□□□□□□□
COMPLAINTS	□□□□□■□□□□
INSURANCE COST	□□□□□□□□□■

Safety

FRONTAL CRASH TEST	Good
SIDE CRASH TEST	Very Poor
AIRBAGS	Dual Only
ANTI-LOCK BRAKES	4-wheel
DAY. RUNNING LIGHTS	Standard
BELT ADJUSTORS	Front (sedan only)
BUILT-IN CHILD SEAT	None
PRETENSIONERS	None

General Information

WHERE MADE	U.S./Mexico
YEAR OF PRODUCTION	Fourth
PARKING INDEX	Easy
BUMPERS	Strong
THEFT RATING	Very Low
TWINS	Pontiac Sunfire
DRIVE	Front

Specifications

FUEL ECONOMY (cty/hwy)	25/37	Good
DRIVING RANGE (miles)	471	Long
SEATING	5	
LENGTH (in.)	180.7	Short
HEAD/LEG ROOM (in.)	38.9/42.3	Average
INTERIOR SPACE (cu. ft.)	92.0	Cramped
CARGO SPACE (cu. ft.)	13.6	Average

Specifications may vary.

Prices

Model	Retail	Mkup
Cavalier 2dr.	11,610	7%
Cavalier 4dr.	11,810	7%
Cavalier LS 4dr.	14,250	7%
Cavalier Z24 2dr.	15,710	7%

Competition

	POOR ← → GOOD	Pg.
Chevrolet Cavalier	□□□□□□□■□□	**122**
Dodge/Plym. Neon	■□□□□□□□□□	137
Ford Escort	□□□■□□□□□□	143
Honda Civic	□□□□□□■□□□	150

*A version of this vehicle is scheduled to be tested later this year. Results are expected to be similar.

Chevrolet Lumina

Large

This steady seller for Chevrolet competes well in the crowded intermediate market. Little has changed for 1998. Of note however, the Lumina now comes with the optional Onstar system, which is a 24-hour roadside assistance system operated from the car's cellular phone. Dual airbags are standard and 4-wheel ABS is optional on the base sedan, standard on all other models. Chevy also revised the daytime running lamps to increase their longevity.

The standard 3.1-liter provides adequate power, but a new, more powerful 3.8-liter, V6 engine is available for the LTZ. The LTZ package also comes with an improved sport suspension. Ride is good and controls are logically designed. Optional child safety seats are a great safety feature. Unfortunately, the Lumina is hurt by a high number of complaints.

The Ratings

	POOR ... GOOD
COMPARATIVE RATING	□□□■□□□□□□
FRONTAL CRASH TEST*	□□□□□□□□■□
SAFETY FEATURES	□□□□□□■□□□
FUEL ECONOMY	□□□□■□□□□□
PM COST	□□□□□■□□□□
REPAIR COST	□□□□□□□□■□
WARRANTY	□■□□□□□□□□
COMPLAINTS	■□□□□□□□□□
INSURANCE COST	□□□□□□□□□■

Safety

FRONTAL CRASH TEST	Very Good
SIDE CRASH TEST	Good
AIRBAGS	Dual Only
ANTI-LOCK BRAKES	4-wheel (optional)
DAY. RUNNING LIGHTS	Standard
BELT ADJUSTORS	Front
BUILT-IN CHILD SEAT	Optional
PRETENSIONERS	None

General Information

WHERE MADE	Canada
YEAR OF PRODUCTION	Fourth
PARKING INDEX	Average
BUMPERS	Strong
THEFT RATING	Very Low
TWINS	Chevy Monte Carlo
DRIVE	Front

Specifications

FUEL ECONOMY (cty/hwy)	20/29	Average
DRIVING RANGE (miles)	415	Average
SEATING	6	
LENGTH (in.)	200.9	Very Long
HEAD/LEG ROOM (in.)	38.4/42.4	Average
INTERIOR SPACE (cu. ft.)	100.5	Roomy
CARGO SPACE (cu. ft.)	15.5	Average

Specifications may vary.

Prices

Model	Retail	Mkup
Lumina	17,245	9%
Lumina LS	19,245	9%
Lumina LTZ	19,745	9%

Competition

	POOR ... GOOD	Pg.
Chevrolet Lumina	□□□■□□□□□□	**123**
Buick Park Avenue	□□■□□□□□□□	113
Nissan Maxima	□□□□■□□□□□	188
Toyota Avalon	□□□□■□□□□□	213

*A version of this vehicle is scheduled to be tested later this year. Results are expected to be similar.

Chevrolet Malibu

Large

Now in its sophomore year, the Malibu is Chevy's challenge to the best-selling Taurus, Camry and Accord trio. You can choose between the base model or the fancier LS; both come standard with dual airbags, 4-wheel ABS and daytime running lamps. On the LS, leather seats have been added to the list of options along with power seats for the driver.

Chevrolet has equipped this new car with its powerful 2.4-liter, 4-cylinder engine which can deliver 150 hp. Optional on the base and standard on the LS is a 3.1-liter, V6 engine. You'll find good interior room, nice handling and owner-friendly features such as 100,000 mile coolant and platinum-tip spark plugs. The Malibu performed well on frontal crash tests, but did not fare as well on side crash tests.

The Ratings

	POOR — GOOD
COMPARATIVE RATING	
FRONTAL CRASH TEST	
SAFETY FEATURES	
FUEL ECONOMY	
PM COST	
REPAIR COST	
WARRANTY	
COMPLAINTS	
INSURANCE COST	

Safety

FRONTAL CRASH TEST	Good
SIDE CRASH TEST	Poor
AIRBAGS	Dual Only
ANTI-LOCK BRAKES	4-wheel
DAY. RUNNING LIGHTS	Standard
BELT ADJUSTORS	Front/Rear
BUILT-IN CHILD SEAT	None
PRETENSIONERS	None

General Information

WHERE MADE	U.S.
YEAR OF PRODUCTION	Second
PARKING INDEX	Average
BUMPERS	Strong
THEFT RATING	
TWINS	Oldsmobile Cutlass
DRIVE	Front

Specifications

FUEL ECONOMY (cty/hwy)	23/32	Average
DRIVING RANGE (miles)	420	Average
SEATING	5	
LENGTH (in.)	190.4	Long
HEAD/LEG ROOM (in.)	39.4/41.9	Average
INTERIOR SPACE (cu. ft.)	115.6	Very Roomy
CARGO SPACE (cu. ft.)	17.0	Large

Specifications may vary.

Prices

Model	Retail	Mkup
Malibu	15,670	9%
Malibu LS	18,470	9%

Competition

	POOR — GOOD	Pg.
Chevrolet Malibu		**124**
Buick Regal		114
Ford Taurus		145
Pontiac Grand Am		201

Chevrolet Metro

Subcompact

Are American cars now as good as Asian imports? Chevrolet thinks so. For 1998, the Geo nameplate has been dropped and the Metro is now marketed as a Chevrolet. Not much is different besides the name, though the front and rear have been slightly restyled. 4-wheel ABS is optional, daytime running lamps and dual airbags are standard.

A coupe is the only base model available; the LSi models come in coupe and sedan. The base coupe's 1.0-liter engine puts out a puny 55 hp, but leads the industry in fuel efficiency with an astonishing 44/49 mpg. The 1.3-liter engine, standard on the LSi models, now uses multiport fuel injection, upping hp from 70 to 79. Interior space is cramped and trunk space is skimpy. With a price tag under $10,000, the Metro is as basic as transportation gets.

The Ratings

	POOR — GOOD
COMPARATIVE RATING	■□□□□□□□□□
FRONTAL CRASH TEST	□□□□□□■□□□
SAFETY FEATURES	□□□□□■□□□□
FUEL ECONOMY	□□□□□□□□□■
PM COST	□□□■□□□□□□
REPAIR COST	□■□□□□□□□□
WARRANTY	□■□□□□□□□□
COMPLAINTS	□■□□□□□□□□
INSURANCE COST	■□□□□□□□□□

Safety

FRONTAL CRASH TEST	Good
SIDE CRASH TEST	No government results
AIRBAGS	Dual Only
ANTI-LOCK BRAKES	4-wheel (optional)
DAY. RUNNING LIGHTS	Standard
BELT ADJUSTORS	None
BUILT-IN CHILD SEAT	None
PRETENSIONERS	None

General Information

WHERE MADE	Canada
YEAR OF PRODUCTION	Fourth
PARKING INDEX	Very Easy
BUMPERS	Weak
THEFT RATING	Very Low
TWINS	Suzuki Swift
DRIVE	Front

Specifications

FUEL ECONOMY (cty/hwy)	44/49	Very Good
DRIVING RANGE (miles)	498	Very Long
SEATING	4	
LENGTH (in.)	149.4	Very Short
HEAD/LEG ROOM (in.)	39.1/42.5	Average
INTERIOR SPACE (cu. ft.)	85.8	Cramped
CARGO SPACE (cu. ft.)	8.4	Very Small

Specifications may vary.

Prices

Model	Retail	Mkup
Metro 3dr.	8,655	6%
Metro LSi 3 dr	9,455	7%
Metro LSi 4dr.	10,055	7%

Competition

	POOR — GOOD	Pg.
Chevrolet Metro	■□□□□□□□□□	**125**
Ford Escort	□□□■□□□□□□	143
Hyundai Accent	□□□□□□■□□□	154
Toyota Tercel	□□□□□□■□□□	219

Chevrolet Monte Carlo

Large

Like the Malibu, the Monte Carlo name is a carryover from the '70s and '80s. The Monte Carlo model carries over into 1998 virtually unchanged. This year, the optional Onstar roadside assistance system is available and the Monte Carlo comes with two trim levels, an LS or Z34. Dual airbags, 4-wheel ABS, belt adjustors for front and rear occupants, and daytime running lamps are both standard.

The standard engine is a 3.1-liter V6 that produces 160 hp. The Z34 receives a new 3.8-liter V6 that delivers more power with no decrease in fuel economy. A high performance suspension also comes with the Z34. Other features include 100,000 mile spark plugs and 150,000 mile coolant. Essentially a two-door version of the popular Lumina, the Monte Carlo offers many options so choose carefully.

The Ratings

	POOR → GOOD
COMPARATIVE RATING	□□■□□□□□□□
FRONTAL CRASH TEST	□□□□□□■□□□
SAFETY FEATURES	□□□□□□■□□□
FUEL ECONOMY	□□□□■□□□□□
PM COST	□□□□□■□□□□
REPAIR COST	□□□□□□□■□□
WARRANTY	□■□□□□□□□□
COMPLAINTS	□□□■□□□□□□
INSURANCE COST	□□□□■□□□□□

Safety

FRONTAL CRASH TEST	Good
SIDE CRASH TEST	No government results
AIRBAGS	Dual Only
ANTI-LOCK BRAKES	4-wheel
DAY. RUNNING LIGHTS	Standard
BELT ADJUSTORS	Front/Rear
BUILT-IN CHILD SEAT	None
PRETENSIONERS	None

General Information

WHERE MADE	Canada
YEAR OF PRODUCTION	Fourth
PARKING INDEX	Average
BUMPERS	Strong
THEFT RATING	Very Low
TWINS	Chevy Lumina
DRIVE	Front

Specifications

FUEL ECONOMY (cty/hwy)	20/29	Average
DRIVING RANGE (miles)	415	Average
SEATING	6	
LENGTH (in.)	200.7	Very Long
HEAD/LEG ROOM (in.)	37.9/42.4	Cramped
INTERIOR SPACE (cu. ft.)	96.1	Average
CARGO SPACE (cu. ft.)	15.5	Average

Specifications may vary.

Prices

Model	Retail	Mkup
Monte Carlo LS	17,795	9%
Monte Carlo Z34	20,295	9%

Competition

	POOR → GOOD	Pg.
Chev. Monte Carlo	□□■□□□□□□□	**126**
Buick Park Avenue	□□■□□□□□□□	113
Nissan Maxima	□□□□■□□□□□	188
Toyota Avalon	□□□□■□□□□□	213

Chevrolet Prizm

Compact

For 1998, the Prizm is all-new with new engines, a new exterior and interior, new safety features, and a new name. Gone is Geo, the new Prizm is now a Chevrolet. Available in a base and up-level LSi model, this redesigned sedan gets high marks for safety as it comes standard with dual airbags, day-time running lamps and rear shoulder belts. Safety options include 4-wheel ABS and side airbags, which are a must.

The new 1.8-liter, dual overhead cam engine weighs less than the old engine and is more powerful. Inside, the seats are comfortable and firm, but the rear is a bit tight. Built off the same assembly line as the Toyota Corolla, the Prizm cost much less than its more popular twin, offering Toyota's top quality craftsmanship along with highly sought after safety features like side airbags for a low price.

The Ratings	POOR ... GOOD
COMPARATIVE RATING*	
FRONTAL CRASH TEST	
SAFETY FEATURES	
FUEL ECONOMY	
PM COST	
REPAIR COST	
WARRANTY	
COMPLAINTS	
INSURANCE COST	

Safety	
FRONTAL CRASH TEST	No government results
SIDE CRASH TEST	No government results
AIRBAGS	Dual/Opt. Side
ANTI-LOCK BRAKES	4-wheel
DAY. RUNNING LIGHTS	Standard
BELT ADJUSTORS	Front/Rear
BUILT-IN CHILD SEAT	Optional
PRETENSIONERS	Standard

General Information	
WHERE MADE	U.S./Canada
YEAR OF PRODUCTION	First
PARKING INDEX	Easy
BUMPERS	Strong
THEFT RATING	
TWINS	Toyota Corolla
DRIVE	Front

Specifications		
FUEL ECONOMY (cty/hwy)	31/37	Good
DRIVING RANGE (miles)	449	Long
SEATING	5	
LENGTH (in.)	174.2	Short
HEAD/LEG ROOM (in.)	39.3/42.5	Roomy
INTERIOR SPACE (cu. ft.)	100.1	Roomy
CARGO SPACE (cu. ft.)	12.1	Small

Specifications may vary.

Prices**

Model	Retail	Mkup
Prizm	12,840	8%
Prizm LSi	13,485	8%

Competition	POOR ... GOOD	Pg.
Chevrolet Prizm		**127**
Ford Escort		143
Mitsubishi Galant		184
Saturn SL/S		208

**1998 prices not available at press time. Prices based on 1997 data.

*Due to the importance of crash tests, cars with no results as of publication date cannot be given an overall rating.

Chevrolet Venture

Minivan

In an effort to catch up with the highly successful Chrysler minivans, GM introduced the Chevy Venture last year. The Venture was designed with 'global' thinking as both US and European engineers designed this contemporary minivan. Like the Caravan, the Venture has sliding doors on both sides. For 1998, you'll find standard dual airbags, 4-wheel ABS and daytime running lamps.

You have only one engine choice, a 3.4-liter V6. The interior is spacious, allowing this minivan to carry some of the largest loads in the industry. You have a choice between standard or extended length versions and the options list is quite long. Seating for seven is comfortable and removal of the seats is relatively easy. The Venture performed well in recent crash tests which should make it a viable alternative to the Chrysler minivans.

The Ratings

	POOR → GOOD
COMPARATIVE RATING	□□□■□□□□□□
FRONTAL CRASH TEST*	□□□□□□■□□□
SAFETY FEATURES	□□□□□□■□□□
FUEL ECONOMY	□□□■□□□□□□
PM COST	□□□□□□□■□□
REPAIR COST	□□□□□□■□□□
WARRANTY	□■□□□□□□□□
COMPLAINTS	□□□□■□□□□□
INSURANCE COST	□□□□■□□□□□

Safety

FRONTAL CRASH TEST	Good
SIDE CRASH TEST	No government results
AIRBAGS	Dual Only
ANTI-LOCK BRAKES	4-wheel
DAY. RUNNING LIGHTS	Standard
BELT ADJUSTORS	Rear
BUILT-IN CHILD SEAT	Optional
PRETENSIONERS	None

General Information

WHERE MADE	U.S.
YEAR OF PRODUCTION	Second
PARKING INDEX	Average
BUMPERS	Strong
THEFT RATING	
TWINS	Silhouette, Trans Sport
DRIVE	Front

Specifications

FUEL ECONOMY (cty/hwy)	18/25	Poor
DRIVING RANGE (miles)	440	Average
SEATING	7	
LENGTH (in.)	186.9	Average
HEAD/LEG ROOM (in.)	39.9/36.9	Vry. Cramped
INTERIOR SPACE (cu. ft.)		
CARGO SPACE (cu. ft.)	126.6	Very Large

Specifications may vary.

Prices

Model	Retail	Mkup
Venture 3dr.	20,249	11%
Venture 4dr.	21,429	11%
Venture Extended 3dr.	21,669	11%
Venture Extended 4dr.	22,259	11%

Competition

	POOR → GOOD	Pg.
Chevrolet Venture	□□□■□□□□□□	**128**
Dodge Caravan	□□■□□□□□□□	135
Honda Odyssey	□□□□□□■□□□	152
Nissan Quest	□□□□□■□□□□	189

*A version of this vehicle is scheduled to be tested later this year. Results are expected to be similar.

Chrysler Cirrus

Intermediate

The Cirrus changes little for 1998 with only minor improvements. Consider the Cirrus the top trim level of its two siblings, the Stratus and Breeze. To simplify sales and marketing, the LX model was dropped. Only the LXi model is available, but it comes fully loaded with lots of standard features including leather seats and power everything. Dual airbags and ABS also come standard.

The Cirrus comes with a 2.5-liter V6 engine, the only engine available. Chrysler's innovative cab-forward design increases interior room, similar to their bigger LH cousins. The Cirrus fared only average in recent government side crash tests; frontal test results are unavailable. Additionally, the Cirrus has a high number of complaints and the warranty isn't much better, either. All good reasons to shop elsewhere.

The Ratings

	POOR → GOOD
COMPARATIVE RATING*	□□□□□□□□□□
FRONTAL CRASH TEST	□□□□□□□□□□
SAFETY FEATURES	□□□□□■□□□□
FUEL ECONOMY	□□□□■□□□□□
PM COST	□□□□□□■□□□
REPAIR COST	□□□□□□□□■□
WARRANTY	□■□□□□□□□□
COMPLAINTS	■□□□□□□□□□
INSURANCE COST	□□□□■□□□□□

Safety

FRONTAL CRASH TEST	No government results
SIDE CRASH TEST	Average
AIRBAGS	Dual Only
ANTI-LOCK BRAKES	4-wheel
DAY. RUNNING LIGHTS	None
BELT ADJUSTORS	Front
BUILT-IN CHILD SEAT	None
PRETENSIONERS	None

General Information

WHERE MADE	U.S.
YEAR OF PRODUCTION	Fourth
PARKING INDEX	Average
BUMPERS	Weak
THEFT RATING	Low
TWINS	Stratus, Breeze
DRIVE	Front

Specifications

FUEL ECONOMY (cty/hwy)	20/30	Average
DRIVING RANGE (miles)	400	Short
SEATING	5	
LENGTH (in.)	187.0	Average
HEAD/LEG ROOM (in.)	38.1/42.3	Cramped
INTERIOR SPACE (cu. ft.)	95.5	Average
CARGO SPACE (cu. ft.)	15.7	Large

Specifications may vary.

Prices

Model	Retail	Mkup
Cirrus LXi	19,460	9%

Competition

	POOR → GOOD	Pg.
Chrysler Cirrus	□□□□□□□□□□	**129**
Buick LeSabre	□□□□□□□□■□	112
Mercury Sable	□□□□□□□■□□	179
Pontiac Grand Am	□□□□□□□■□□	201

*Due to the importance of crash tests, cars with no results as of publication date cannot be given an overall rating.

Chrysler Concorde

Intermediate

Chrysler has redesigned the Concorde, along with its twin, the Intrepid, into an aggressive round shape with a stylish, new front and rear end, while maintaining the cab-forward design inside. Dual airbags and belt adjustors up front are standard but you still have to pay extra for ABS.

Two trim levels are available. The LX gets a 2.7-liter, V6 engine that puts out 200 hp. The LXi comes with a larger 3.2-liter, V6 with 20 more hp than the base engine. Both engines are all aluminum with improved performance and better fuel economy than last year's engines. Head and leg room is ample and there is even more room in the trunk. Chrysler expects the new Concorde to be a hot seller. Too bad the government won't be crash testing it next year.

The Ratings

	POOR ... GOOD
COMPARATIVE RATING*	□□□□□□□□□□
FRONTAL CRASH TEST	□□□□□□□□□□
SAFETY FEATURES	□□□□■□□□□□
FUEL ECONOMY	□□□□□■□□□□
PM COST	□□□□□□■□□□
REPAIR COST	□□□□□□□□■□
WARRANTY	□■□□□□□□□□
COMPLAINTS	□□□□■□□□□□
INSURANCE COST	□□□□■□□□□□

Safety

FRONTAL CRASH TEST	No government results
SIDE CRASH TEST	No government results
AIRBAGS	Dual Only
ANTI-LOCK BRAKES	4-wheel (optional)
DAY. RUNNING LIGHTS	None
BELT ADJUSTORS	Front
BUILT-IN CHILD SEAT	None
PRETENSIONERS	None

General Information

WHERE MADE	Canada
YEAR OF PRODUCTION	First
PARKING INDEX	Hard
BUMPERS	Strong
THEFT RATING	
TWINS	Dodge Intrepid
DRIVE	Front

Specifications

FUEL ECONOMY (cty/hwy)	21/30	Average
DRIVING RANGE (miles)	442	Average
SEATING	5/6	
LENGTH (in.)	209.1	Very Long
HEAD/LEG ROOM (in.)	38.3/42.2	Average
INTERIOR SPACE (cu. ft.)	107.6	Very Roomy
CARGO SPACE (cu. ft.)	18.7	Large

Specifications may vary.

Prices**

Model	Retail	Mkup
Concorde LX	20,435	9%

Competition

	POOR ... GOOD	Pg.
Chrysler Concorde	□□□□□□□□□□	**130**
Buick Park Avenue	□□■□□□□□□□	113
Ford Crown Victoria	□□□□■□□□□□	142
Nissan Maxima	□□□■□□□□□□	188

**1998 prices not available at press time. Prices based on 1997 data.

*Due to the importance of crash tests, cars with no results as of publication date cannot be given an overall rating.

Chrysler LHS

Large

An all-new LHS will be introduced in 1998 as a 1999 model. Unfortunately, information on this all-new model was unavailable at press time. So, the photo and data shown are based on the outgoing model.

Most anything you'll want comes standard on the outgoing LHS including dual airbags and ABS with the only options being a sunroof and a CD-player. The 3.5-liter V6 is powerful and should deliver average gas mileage for such a large car. Thanks to the touring suspension that comes standard, the handling is as precise as any other car this size. Like the LH sedans, the LHS has excellent interior space due to the cab-forward design. Controls are nicely placed and passengers will ride in comfort with plenty of room in the back seat.

The Ratings

	POOR — GOOD
COMPARATIVE RATING	□■□□□□□□□□
FRONTAL CRASH TEST	□□□□□□■□□□
SAFETY FEATURES	□□□□□■□□□□
FUEL ECONOMY	□□□■□□□□□□
PM COST	□□□□□□■□□□
REPAIR COST	□□□□□□□□■□
WARRANTY	□■□□□□□□□□
COMPLAINTS	□□■□□□□□□□
INSURANCE COST	□□□□□□□□□■

Safety

FRONTAL CRASH TEST	Good
SIDE CRASH TEST	No government results
AIRBAGS	Dual Only
ANTI-LOCK BRAKES	4-wheel
DAY. RUNNING LIGHTS	None
BELT ADJUSTORS	Front
BUILT-IN CHILD SEAT	None
PRETENSIONERS	None

General Information

WHERE MADE	Canada
YEAR OF PRODUCTION	Fifth
PARKING INDEX	Hard
BUMPERS	Weak
THEFT RATING	Average
TWINS	
DRIVE	Front

Specifications

FUEL ECONOMY (cty/hwy)	17/26	Poor
DRIVING RANGE (miles)	396	Short
SEATING	5/6	
LENGTH (in.)	207.4	Very Long
HEAD/LEG ROOM (in.)	38.3/42.4	Average
INTERIOR SPACE (cu. ft.)	108.0	Very Roomy
CARGO SPACE (cu. ft.)	18.0	Large

Specifications may vary.

Prices**

Model	Retail	Mkup
LHS	30,255	

Competition

	POOR — GOOD	Pg.
Chrysler LHS	□■□□□□□□□□	**131**
Chevrolet Lumina	□□□■□□□□□□	123
Ford CrownVictoria	□□□□■□□□□□	142
Nissan Maxima	□□□■□□□□□□	188

**1998 prices not available at press time. Prices based on 1997 data.

Chrysler Sebring

Compact

Three years after its introduction, the Sebring's stylish front end still turns heads. No changes have been made for 1998 other than a few new color choices like Caffe Latte. This aggressive looking coupe is both sporty and practical and it competes well with other sports coupes. Dual airbags are standard, but you'll have to pay extra for ABS.

The standard 2-liter, 4-cylinder engine on the LX trim level will probably not satisfy the drivers Chrysler is hoping to reach; the optional 2.5-liter V6 on the uplevel LXi is slightly more peppy. Interior room is better than most competitors, and rear-seat occupants will find lots of comfort. Please note that the convertible Sebring JT is not the same car as the hard-top Sebring; it is based on the Cirrus. Despite a great frontal crash test score, the Sebring's warranty and complaint rating keep it from Best Bet status.

The Ratings

	POOR — GOOD
COMPARATIVE RATING	
FRONTAL CRASH TEST	
SAFETY FEATURES	
FUEL ECONOMY	
PM COST	
REPAIR COST	
WARRANTY	
COMPLAINTS	
INSURANCE COST	

Safety

FRONTAL CRASH TEST	Very Good
SIDE CRASH TEST	No government results
AIRBAGS	Dual Only
ANTI-LOCK BRAKES	4-wheel (optional)
DAY. RUNNING LIGHTS	None
BELT ADJUSTORS	None
BUILT-IN CHILD SEAT	None
PRETENSIONERS	None

General Information

WHERE MADE	U.S.
YEAR OF PRODUCTION	Fourth
PARKING INDEX	Hard
BUMPERS	Strong
THEFT RATING	Very High
TWINS	Dodge Avenger
DRIVE	Front

Specifications

FUEL ECONOMY (cty/hwy)	22/31	Average
DRIVING RANGE (miles)	456	Long
SEATING	5	
LENGTH (in.)	190.9	Long
HEAD/LEG ROOM (in.)	39.1/43.3	Roomy
INTERIOR SPACE (cu. ft.)	91.0	Cramped
CARGO SPACE (cu. ft.)	13.1	Small

Specifications may vary.

Prices

Model	Retail	Mkup
Sebring LX	16,840	9%
Sebring LXi	20,775	9%

Competition

	POOR — GOOD	Pg.
Chrysler Sebring		**132**
Buick Regal		114
Oldsmobile Achieva		192
Subaru Legacy		210

Chrysler Town and Country

Minivan

An upscale model of the Grand Caravan/Voyager, the Town and Country offers luxuries like leather seats, which are converting luxury sedan buyers into minivan owners. For the extra money, you get lots of power equipment. Changes for '98 include a minor restyling of the front end and improved headlamps. Dual airbags and ABS are standard; optional built-in child seats are a must for any parents, but not available with leather seats.

The Town and Country offers a 3.3-liter V6 to go with the standard automatic overdrive, but its gas mileage is among the lowest for minivans. You may want to opt for the new optional 3.8-liter V6 that comes with all-wheel drive. If you want a firmer suspension, check out the trailer-towing package. The ride is comfortable on smooth roads. A high number of complaints overshadows an otherwise popular minivan.

The Ratings	POOR — GOOD
COMPARATIVE RATING	
FRONTAL CRASH TEST*	
SAFETY FEATURES	
FUEL ECONOMY	
PM COST	
REPAIR COST	
WARRANTY	
COMPLAINTS	
INSURANCE COST	

Safety	
FRONTAL CRASH TEST	Good
SIDE CRASH TEST	No government results
AIRBAGS	Dual Only
ANTI-LOCK BRAKES	4-wheel
DAY. RUNNING LIGHTS	None
BELT ADJUSTORS	Front/Rear
BUILT-IN CHILD SEAT	Optional (two)
PRETENSIONERS	None

General Information	
WHERE MADE	U.S.
YEAR OF PRODUCTION	Third
PARKING INDEX	Hard
BUMPERS	Strong
THEFT RATING	Average
TWINS	Gr. Caravan, Gr. Voyager
DRIVE	Front

Specifications		
FUEL ECONOMY (cty/hwy)	17/24	Poor
DRIVING RANGE (miles)	420	Average
SEATING	7	
LENGTH (in.)	199.7	Long
HEAD/LEG ROOM (in.)	39.8/40.6	Cramped
INTERIOR SPACE (cu. ft.)		
CARGO SPACE (cu. ft.)	162.9	Very Large

Specifications may vary.

Prices

Model	Retail	Mkup
Town and Country SX	26,860	11%
Town and Country LX	27,135	10%
Town and Country LXi	31,720	11%
Town and Country LX awd	34,095	11%

Competition

	POOR — GOOD	Pg.
Chrys. T&C		**133**
Ford Windstar		146
Honda Odyssey		152
Olds Silhouette		196

*A version of this vehicle is scheduled to be tested later this year. Results are expected to be similar.

Dodge Avenger

Compact

The Avenger, twin of the Chrysler Sebring, is a stylish coupe first introduced in 1995. No changes have been made for 1998. Sporty and practical, the Avenger gets a new sport package that comes with bigger wheels and a spoiler. Dual airbags are standard, but you'll have to pay extra for ABS.

The standard 2-liter, 4-cylinder engine on the base and ES models is barely adequate. Most buyers will probably want the optional 2.5-liter V6 which is more powerful but fuel economy will suffer. Interior room is better than most competitors, and rear-seat occupants will find lots of comfort. While an excellent performer in frontal crash tests, the Avenger suffers from a high number of complaints and a poor warranty — both hurt its overall score.

The Ratings	POOR GOOD
COMPARATIVE RATING	
FRONTAL CRASH TEST	
SAFETY FEATURES	
FUEL ECONOMY	
PM COST	
REPAIR COST	
WARRANTY	
COMPLAINTS	
INSURANCE COST	

Safety	
FRONTAL CRASH TEST	Very Good
SIDE CRASH TEST	No government results
AIRBAGS	Dual Only
ANTI-LOCK BRAKES	4-wheel (optional)
DAY. RUNNING LIGHTS	None
BELT ADJUSTORS	None
BUILT-IN CHILD SEAT	None
PRETENSIONERS	None

General Information	
WHERE MADE	U.S.
YEAR OF PRODUCTION	Fourth
PARKING INDEX	Hard
BUMPERS	Strong
THEFT RATING	Very Low
TWINS	Chrys. Sebring
DRIVE	Front

Specifications		
FUEL ECONOMY (cty/hwy)	22/32	Average
DRIVING RANGE (miles)	456	Long
SEATING	5	
LENGTH (in.)	190.2	Long
HEAD/LEG ROOM (in.)	39.1/43.3	Roomy
INTERIOR SPACE (cu. ft.)	90.7	Cramped
CARGO SPACE (cu. ft.)	13.1	Small

Specifications may vary.

Prices

Model	Retail	Mkup
Avenger	14,930	9%
Avenger ES	17,310	9%

Competition

	POOR GOOD	Pg.
Dodge Avenger		**134**
Buick Regal		114
Olds Achieva		192
Pontiac Grand Am		201

Dodge Caravan

Minivan

The #1 selling minivan in America receives few changes for 1998. After a redesign in '96, the Caravan remains the standard by which all other minivans are compared to. Dual airbags are standard as is 4-wheel ABS. The Caravan also meets 1999 side impact standards for trucks, 4x4s and vans early.

The standard 4-cylinder engine is really not adequate—go for one of the three V6 engines to get more power with only a small sacrifice in fuel efficiency. Order the heavy duty suspension or "sport handling group" for improved cornering. The longer wheelbase and length of the Grand Caravan translates into more cargo room. The built-in child restraints are a great option. Comfort is good for seven and the seats are easy to remove. However, be cautious as the Caravan has a poor complaint rating.

The Ratings

	POOR — GOOD
COMPARATIVE RATING	□□■□□□□□□□
FRONTAL CRASH TEST*	□□□□□□□■□□
SAFETY FEATURES	□□□□□□■□□□
FUEL ECONOMY	□□□■□□□□□□
PM COST	□□□□□□□□■□
REPAIR COST	□□□□□□□□■□
WARRANTY	□■□□□□□□□□
COMPLAINTS	■□□□□□□□□□
INSURANCE COST	□□□□□□□□□■

Safety

FRONTAL CRASH TEST	Good
SIDE CRASH TEST	No government results
AIRBAGS	Dual Only
ANTI-LOCK BRAKES	4-wheel
DAY. RUNNING LIGHTS	None
BELT ADJUSTORS	Front/Rear
BUILT-IN CHILD SEAT	Optional (two)
PRETENSIONERS	None

General Information

WHERE MADE	U.S./Canada
YEAR OF PRODUCTION	Third
PARKING INDEX	Average
BUMPERS	Strong
THEFT RATING	Very Low
TWINS	Voyager, Town & Country
DRIVE	Front

Specifications

FUEL ECONOMY (cty/hwy)	20/25	Poor
DRIVING RANGE (miles)	460	Long
SEATING	7	
LENGTH (in.)	186.3	Average
HEAD/LEG ROOM (in.)	39.8/40.6	Cramped
INTERIOR SPACE (cu. ft.)		
CARGO SPACE (cu. ft.)	142.9	Very Large

Specifications may vary.

Prices

Model	Retail	Mkup
Caravan	17,415	10%
Grand Caravan	20,125	10%
Caravan SE	21,290	11%
Grand Caravan SE	22,285	11%

Competition

	POOR — GOOD	Pg.
Dodge Caravan	□□■□□□□□□□	**135**
Ford Windstar	□■□□□□□□□□	146
Honda Odyssey	□□□□□□■□□□	152
Mercury Villager	□□■□□□□□□□	181

*A version of this vehicle is scheduled to be tested later this year. Results are expected to be similar.

Dodge Intrepid

Intermediate

For '98, the Intrepid, along with its twin the Concorde, gets a new aggressive round shape with a stylish, new front end, while maintaining the cab-forward design inside. Chrysler is looking to set a new standard with this latest redesign. Dual airbags are standard but you still have to pay extra for ABS.

Two trim levels are available. The base gets a 2.7-liter, V6 engine. The ES trim level comes with a larger 3.2-liter, V6 with 20 more hp than the base engine. Both engines are all aluminum with improved performance and better fuel economy than last year's engines. Also, the ES's engine comes with the Autostick, a stick/automatic combo, which is growing in popularity. Head and leg room and trunk space are ample. Expect the new Intrepid to garner much interest. Too bad the government won't be crash testing it next year.

The Ratings

	POOR — GOOD
COMPARATIVE RATING*	□□□□□□□□□□
FRONTAL CRASH TEST	□□□□□□□□□□
SAFETY FEATURES	□□□□■□□□□□
FUEL ECONOMY	□□□□□■□□□□
PM COST	□□□□□□■□□□
REPAIR COST	□□□□□□□□□■
WARRANTY	□■□□□□□□□□
COMPLAINTS	□□□□■□□□□□
INSURANCE COST	□□□□■□□□□□

Safety

FRONTAL CRASH TEST	No government results
SIDE CRASH TEST	No government results
AIRBAGS	Dual Only
ANTI-LOCK BRAKES	4-wheel (optional)
DAY. RUNNING LIGHTS	None
BELT ADJUSTORS	Front
BUILT-IN CHILD SEAT	None
PRETENSIONERS	None

General Information

WHERE MADE	Canada
YEAR OF PRODUCTION	First
PARKING INDEX	Hard
BUMPERS	Strong
THEFT RATING	Very Low
TWINS	Chrys. Concorde
DRIVE	Front

Specifications

FUEL ECONOMY (cty/hwy)	21/30	Average
DRIVING RANGE (miles)	442	Average
SEATING	5	
LENGTH (in.)	203.7	Very Long
HEAD/LEG ROOM (in.)	38.3/42.2	Average
INTERIOR SPACE (cu. ft.)	104.5	Roomy
CARGO SPACE (cu. ft.)	18.4	Large

Specifications may vary.

Prices**

Model	Retail	Mkup
Intrepid	19,445	9%
Intrepid ES	22,910	10%

Competition

	POOR — GOOD	Pg.
Dodge Intrepid	□□□□□□□□□□	**136**
Buick Park Avenue	□□■□□□□□□□	113
Chevrolet Lumina	□□□■□□□□□□	123
Toyota Avalon	□□□□■□□□□□	213

**1998 prices not available at press time. Prices based on 1997 data.

*Due to the importance of crash tests, cars with no results as of publication date cannot be given an overall rating.

Dodge/Plymouth Neon

Subcompact

The Neon is trying to take over the title of cutest subcompact, formerly held by the VW Beetle (which, incidentally, VW is bringing back in late 1998). The Neon benefits from its cab-forward design, which provides excellent interior space for a small car. Dual airbags are standard; ABS is optional.

The single-cam version of the 2-liter engine provides adequate power, but the dual-cam version has even more zing. Not only is it longer than its competitors, the Neon is also taller, resulting in more head room. Choose the sedan with options, or get the "sport" coupe package with dual cams and a firmer suspension. A built-in child restraint is an excellent option. The Neon is an affordable compact which faces tough competition in competitors like the Honda Civic, Chevrolet Cavalier and Ford Escort.

The Ratings

	POOR → GOOD
COMPARATIVE RATING	■□□□□□□□□□
FRONTAL CRASH TEST*	□□□□□■□□□□
SAFETY FEATURES	□□□□□■□□□□
FUEL ECONOMY	□□□□□□□■□□
PM COST	□□□□□□■□□□
REPAIR COST	□□□□□□□□□■
WARRANTY	□■□□□□□□□□
COMPLAINTS	□■□□□□□□□□
INSURANCE COST	■□□□□□□□□□

Safety

FRONTAL CRASH TEST	Average
SIDE CRASH TEST	No government results
AIRBAGS	Dual Only
ANTI-LOCK BRAKES	4-wheel (optional)
DAY. RUNNING LIGHTS	None
BELT ADJUSTORS	None
BUILT-IN CHILD SEAT	Optional
PRETENSIONERS	None

General Information

WHERE MADE	U.S./Mexico
YEAR OF PRODUCTION	Fourth
PARKING INDEX	Easy
BUMPERS	Strong
THEFT RATING	Average
TWINS	
DRIVE	Front

Specifications

FUEL ECONOMY (cty/hwy)	29/39	Good
DRIVING RANGE (miles)	425	Average
SEATING	5	
LENGTH (in.)	171.8	Very Short
HEAD/LEG ROOM (in.)	39.6/42.5	Roomy
INTERIOR SPACE (cu. ft.)	89.9	Cramped
CARGO SPACE (cu. ft.)	11.8	Small

Specifications may vary.

Prices

Model	Retail	Mkup
Neon 2dr	10,900	6%
Neon 4dr	11,355	10%
Neon Highline 2dr	11,155	8%
Neon Highline 4dr	11,355	8%

Competition

	POOR → GOOD	Pg.
Dodge/Plym. Neon	■□□□□□□□□□	**137**
Chevrolet Cavalier	□□□□□□□■□□	122
Ford Escort	□□□■□□□□□□	143
Honda Civic	□□□□□□■□□□	150

*A version of this vehicle is scheduled to be tested later this year. Results are expected to be similar.

Dodge Stratus

Intermediate

The Stratus, along with its close twins, the Cirrus and Breeze, carryover into 1998 with little changes. Besides new colors and fabrics, other changes include minor improvements to reduce road noise, ride and the optional 4-wheel ABS system. Dual airbags are standard. A built-in child seat makes a nice option for parents.

The base model and ES trim level come standard with the 2.0-liter engine with a manual transmission. A 2.4-liter engine is optional, but you'll want to try out the optional 2.5-liter V6 engine with the AutoStick, a combination stick and automatic. The cab-forward design gives passenger ample interior space. The Stratus scored well in term of maintenance costs, but a low complaint rating and a poor warranty prevent it from being a top pick.

The Ratings	POOR — GOOD
COMPARATIVE RATING*	□□□□□□□□□□
FRONTAL CRASH TEST	□□□□□□□□□□
SAFETY FEATURES	□□□□□■□□□□
FUEL ECONOMY	□□□□□□□■□□
PM COST	□□□□□□■□□□
REPAIR COST	□□□□□□□□□■
WARRANTY	□■□□□□□□□□
COMPLAINTS	□□■□□□□□□□
INSURANCE COST	□□□□■□□□□□

Safety	
FRONTAL CRASH TEST	No government results
SIDE CRASH TEST	Average
AIRBAGS	Dual Only
ANTI-LOCK BRAKES	4-wheel (optional)
DAY. RUNNING LIGHTS	None
BELT ADJUSTORS	None
BUILT-IN CHILD SEAT	Optional
PRETENSIONERS	None

General Information	
WHERE MADE	U.S.
YEAR OF PRODUCTION	Fourth
PARKING INDEX	Average
BUMPERS	Weak
THEFT RATING	Very Low
TWINS	Cirrus, Breeze
DRIVE	Front

Specifications		
FUEL ECONOMY (cty/hwy)	26/37	Good
DRIVING RANGE (miles)	512	Very Long
SEATING	5	
LENGTH (in.)	186.0	Average
HEAD/LEG ROOM (in.)	38.1/42.3	Cramped
INTERIOR SPACE (cu. ft.)	95.5	Average
CARGO SPACE (cu. ft.)	15.7	Large

Specifications may vary.

Prices

Model	Retail	Mkup
Stratus	14,840	9%
Stratus ES	17,665	7%

Competition	POOR — GOOD	Pg.
Dodge Stratus	□□□□□□□□□□	**138**
Buick LeSabre	□□□□□□□□■□	112
Oldsmobile Achieva	□□□□□□□□□■	192
Pontiac Grand Am	□□□□□□□■□□	201

*Due to the importance of crash tests, cars with no results as of publication date cannot be given an overall rating.

Eagle Talon

Compact

A twin of the Mitsubishi Eclipse, the Talon enters 1998 unchanged. Chrysler is considering dropping the Eagle nameplate due to low profits so the future of the Talon is uncertain. Available in four trim levels: Base, ESi, TSi and TSi AWD (all-wheel drive), the Talon received a new front fascia, a new sleeker side panel and a redesigned control panel last year. It has standard dual airbags, but you will still have to pay extra for ABS.

The base and ESi models come with a more-than-adequate 2-liter engine. However, the turbo version found on the up-level TSi is much more powerful and just as efficient. All-wheel drive is an attractive option, but is only available on the pricier TSi. The Talon competes poorly with other sports cars considering its poor complaint rating.

The Ratings

	POOR — GOOD
COMPARATIVE RATING	
FRONTAL CRASH TEST	
SAFETY FEATURES	
FUEL ECONOMY	
PM COST	
REPAIR COST	
WARRANTY	
COMPLAINTS	
INSURANCE COST	

Safety

FRONTAL CRASH TEST	Good
SIDE CRASH TEST	No government results
AIRBAGS	Dual Only
ANTI-LOCK BRAKES	4-wheel (optional)
DAY. RUNNING LIGHTS	None
BELT ADJUSTORS	None
BUILT-IN CHILD SEAT	None
PRETENSIONERS	None

General Information

WHERE MADE	U.S.
YEAR OF PRODUCTION	Fourth
PARKING INDEX	Average
BUMPERS	Strong
THEFT RATING	Average
TWINS	Mitsubishi Eclipse
DRIVE	Front

Specifications

FUEL ECONOMY (cty/hwy)	22/33	Average
DRIVING RANGE (miles)	473	Long
SEATING	4	
LENGTH (in.)	174.9	Short
HEAD/LEG ROOM (in.)	37.9/43.3	Average
INTERIOR SPACE (cu. ft.)	79.0	Vry. Cramped
CARGO SPACE (cu. ft.)	15.0	Average

Specifications may vary.

Prices

Model	Retail	Mkup
Talon	14,505	8%
Talon ESi	15,275	8%
Talon TSi	18,460	8%
Talon TSi awd	20,715	8%

Competition

	POOR — GOOD	Pg.
Eagle Talon		**139**
Acura Integra		103
Mazda Miata		170
Mitsubishi Eclipse		183

*A version of this vehicle is scheduled to be tested later this year. Results are expected to be similar.

Eagle Vision

The Eagle Vision will be reintroduced in 1998 as a 1999 model, though the future of the Eagle nameplate is uncertain. No information was available before press time, so the photo and data are for the outgoing model.

The outgoing Vision's cab-forward design makes it very roomy inside. Although you'll have to pay extra for ABS on the base ESi model, dual airbags are standard. The AutoStick transmission is an excellent feature and worth just test driving. The 3.5-liter V6 is quite powerful. The base ESi and the up-level TSi are well-equipped, and the "touring" suspension on both provide a nice compromise between ride and handling. The TSi's optional "performance handling" suspension may make the ride a bit too firm. The Vision offers large-car comfort and safety in a mid-sized package.

General Information

WHERE MADE	Canada
YEAR OF PRODUCTION	Sixth
PARKING INDEX	Hard
BUMPERS	Strong
THEFT RATING	Very Low
TWINS	
DRIVE	Front

Prices**

Model	Retail	Mkup
Vision ESi	20,305	9%
Vision Tsi	24,485	9%

**1998 prices not available at press time. Prices based on 1997 data.

The Ratings

	POOR □□□□□□□□□□ GOOD
COMPARATIVE RATING*	□□□□□□□□□□
FRONTAL CRASH TEST	□□□□□□□□□□
SAFETY FEATURES	□□□□■□□□□□
FUEL ECONOMY	□□□■□□□□□□
PM COST	□□□□□□■□□□
REPAIR COST	□□□□□□□□□■
WARRANTY	□■□□□□□□□□
COMPLAINTS	□□■□□□□□□□
INSURANCE COST	□□□□□□□□□■

Safety

FRONTAL CRASH TEST	No government results
SIDE CRASH TEST	No government results
AIRBAGS	Dual Only
ANTI-LOCK BRAKES	4-wheel (optional)
DAY. RUNNING LIGHTS	None
BELT ADJUSTORS	None
BUILT-IN CHILD SEAT	None
PRETENSIONERS	None

Specifications

FUEL ECONOMY (cty/hwy)	19/27	Poor
DRIVING RANGE (miles)	414	Average
SEATING	5	
LENGTH (in.)	201.6	Very Long
HEAD/LEG ROOM (in.)	38.4/42.4	Average
INTERIOR SPACE (cu. ft.)	105.0	Roomy
CARGO SPACE (cu. ft.)	17.0	Large

Specifications may vary.

Competition

	POOR □□□□□□□□□□ GOOD	Pg.
Eagle Vision	□□□□□□□□□□	**140**
Buick Park Avenue	□□■□□□□□□□	113
Chevrolet Lumina	□□□■□□□□□□	123
Nissan Maxima	□□□■□□□□□□	188

*Due to the importance of crash tests, cars with no results as of publication date cannot be given an overall rating.

Ford Contour

Compact

The Contour, along with its twin the Mercury Mystique, are the U.S. versions of Ford's new "world car," which is called the Mondeo in Europe. For 1998, Ford tweaked this sedan's engines to improve performance, but no other major changes occurred. Dual airbags are standard, but you'll have to pay extra for ABS.

The spare base GL trim level was dropped, so you can choose between the LX, which comes with more features standard, or the sportier SE. The LX's 2.0-liter engine is adequate, but you may want the SE's much more powerful 2.5-liter V6 that is very quiet and peppy. An optional child seat is an attractive feature for parents. The Contour performed fairly well on frontal crash tests, excellently on side. However, complaint problems hurt an otherwise good car.

The Ratings

	POOR ... GOOD
COMPARATIVE RATING	□□□□□□■□□□
FRONTAL CRASH TEST*	□□□□□□□■□□
SAFETY FEATURES	□□□□□■□□□□
FUEL ECONOMY	□□□□□□■□□□
PM COST	□□□□□□□■□□
REPAIR COST	□□□□□□□■□□
WARRANTY	□■□□□□□□□□
COMPLAINTS	□□□■□□□□□□
INSURANCE COST	□□□□■□□□□□

Safety

FRONTAL CRASH TEST	Good
SIDE CRASH TEST	Very Good
AIRBAGS	Dual Only
ANTI-LOCK BRAKES	4-wheel (optional)
DAY. RUNNING LIGHTS	None
BELT ADJUSTORS	Front
BUILT-IN CHILD SEAT	Optional
PRETENSIONERS	None

General Information

WHERE MADE	U.S./Canada/Mexico
YEAR OF PRODUCTION	Fourth
PARKING INDEX	Average
BUMPERS	Strong
THEFT RATING	Very Low
TWINS	Mercury Mystique
DRIVE	Front

Specifications

FUEL ECONOMY (cty/hwy)	24/35	Good
DRIVING RANGE (miles)	435	Average
SEATING	5	
LENGTH (in.)	184.6	Average
HEAD/LEG ROOM (in.)	39.0/42.4	Average
INTERIOR SPACE (cu. ft.)	90.2	Cramped
CARGO SPACE (cu. ft.)	13.9	Average

Specifications may vary.

Prices

Model	Retail	Mkup
Contour LX	14,460	7%
Contour SE	15,785	9%

Competition

	POOR ... GOOD	Pg.
Ford Contour	□□□□□□■□□□	**141**
Buick Century	□□□□□□■□□□	111
Hyundai Sonata	□□■□□□□□□□	156
Pontiac Grand Prix	□□□□□■□□□□	202

*A version of this vehicle is scheduled to be tested later this year. Results are expected to be similar.

Ford Crown Victoria

Large

The Crown Victoria, and its twin the Grand Marquis, are big, rear-wheel drive cars from another era. They both received a facelift for 1998. The exterior is more contemporary and the suspension, tires and brakes were improved. Dual airbags, seat belt adjustors for the front passengers and ABS are standard. Traction control is also optional. Photo is the '97 model.

The 4.6-liter V8 is powerful. The base-level model comes with plenty of equipment, but to get some of the more choice options, you have to move up to the LX. A handling and performance package increases engine's hp by 20. An anti-theft system has been added as a standard feature, but it performed excellently on both frontal and side government crash tests. Ford's improvements make the Crown Victoria worth looking at.

The Ratings

	POOR — GOOD
COMPARATIVE RATING	
FRONTAL CRASH TEST*	
SAFETY FEATURES	
FUEL ECONOMY	
PM COST	
REPAIR COST	
WARRANTY	
COMPLAINTS	
INSURANCE COST	

Safety

FRONTAL CRASH TEST	Very Good
SIDE CRASH TEST	Very Good
AIRBAGS	Dual Only
ANTI-LOCK BRAKES	4-wheel
DAY. RUNNING LIGHTS	None
BELT ADJUSTORS	Front
BUILT-IN CHILD SEAT	None
PRETENSIONERS	None

General Information

WHERE MADE	Canada
YEAR OF PRODUCTION	Seventh
PARKING INDEX	Very Hard
BUMPERS	Strong
THEFT RATING	Very Low
TWINS	Town Car, Gr. Marq.
DRIVE	Rear

Specifications

FUEL ECONOMY (cty/hwy)	17/25	Poor
DRIVING RANGE (miles)	399	Short
SEATING	6	
LENGTH (in.)	212.0	Very Long
HEAD/LEG ROOM (in.)	33.4/42.5	Vry. Cramped
INTERIOR SPACE (cu. ft.)	111.4	Very Roomy
CARGO SPACE (cu. ft.)	20.6	Very Large

Specifications may vary.

Prices**

Model	Retail	Mkup
Crown Victoria	21,575	7%
Crown Victoria LX	23,295	7%

Competition

	POOR — GOOD	Pg.
Ford Cr. Victoria		**142**
Buick Park Avenue		113
Chevrolet Lumina		123
Nissan Maxima		188

**1998 prices not available at press time. Prices based on 1997 data.

*A version of this vehicle is scheduled to be tested later this year. Results are expected to be similar.

Ford Escort

Subcompact

In an attempt to add excitement to the Escort's mom-and-pop image, a ZX2 coupe was added to the lineup for 1998. Ford calls it the 'coolest Ford since the original Mustang.' The new coupe comes in a base 'Cool' version and a well-equipped 'Hot' version. The sedan and wagon, available in a base LX or uplevel SE, carryover unchanged. Dual airbags are standard, ABS is optional.

The sedan and wagon come standard with a 2-liter, 110 hp engine that is much improved from previous versions. The ZX2 gets a peppier Zetec 2-liter, 130 hp engine. The trunk is roomy, especially with the fold down rear seat. Seating for four is good, tight for three in the back. Merely an average performer on frontal and side crash tests, the Escort is a good, economical choice, which is not so boring anymore with the new, spicier ZX2 coupe.

The Ratings

	POOR → GOOD
COMPARATIVE RATING	□□□■□□□□□□
FRONTAL CRASH TEST*	□□□□■□□□□□
SAFETY FEATURES	□□□□□■□□□□
FUEL ECONOMY	□□□□□□□■□□
PM COST	□□□□□□□■□□
REPAIR COST	□□□□□□□□□■
WARRANTY	□■□□□□□□□□
COMPLAINTS	□□□□■□□□□□
INSURANCE COST	■□□□□□□□□□

Safety

FRONTAL CRASH TEST	Average
SIDE CRASH TEST	Average
AIRBAGS	Dual Only
ANTI-LOCK BRAKES	4-wheel (optional)
DAY. RUNNING LIGHTS	None
BELT ADJUSTORS	Front
BUILT-IN CHILD SEAT	Optional
PRETENSIONERS	None

General Information

WHERE MADE	U.S./Canada/Mexico
YEAR OF PRODUCTION	Second
PARKING INDEX	Very Easy
BUMPERS	Strong
THEFT RATING	
TWINS	Mercury Tracer
DRIVE	Front

Specifications

FUEL ECONOMY (cty/hwy)	28/37	Good
DRIVING RANGE (miles)	419	Average
SEATING	5	
LENGTH (in.)	174.7	Short
HEAD/LEG ROOM (in.)	39.0/42.5	Average
INTERIOR SPACE (cu. ft.)	87.2	Cramped
CARGO SPACE (cu. ft.)	12.8	Small

Specifications may vary.

Prices

Model	Retail	Mkup
Escort LX 4dr	11,280	7%
Escort ZX2 Cool Coupe 2dr	12,580	7%
Escort SE 4dr	12,580	7%
Escort ZX2 Hot Coupe 2dr	13,895	7%

Competition

	POOR → GOOD	Pg.
Ford Escort	□□□■□□□□□□	**143**
Chevrolet Cavalier	□□□□□□□■□□	122
Dodge/Plym. Neon	■□□□□□□□□□	137
Honda Civic	□□□□□□■□□□	150

*A version of this vehicle is scheduled to be tested later this year. Results are expected to be similar.

Ford Mustang

Intermediate

One of Ford's bread-and-butter cars, the 1998 Mustang is a great sports/performance car with a surprisingly affordable price tag—Ford has added more options and lowered pricing for '98. Coupes and convertibles are available in base, sporty GT or limited-production Cobra models. All models have dual airbags and ABS.

A 3.8-liter, 150 hp V6 comes standard and should provide ample power for most drivers. However, you can choose between two 4.6-liter V8 engines; they are smaller than the V8 engines of the past, but deliver the same amount of horses with smoother shifts. With steering and suspension improvements, handling should be better than on the older models. The Mustang has a high theft rate, which is no surprise—it's a highly desirable sports car.

The Ratings

	POOR — GOOD
COMPARATIVE RATING	
FRONTAL CRASH TEST*	
SAFETY FEATURES	
FUEL ECONOMY	
PM COST	
REPAIR COST	
WARRANTY	
COMPLAINTS	
INSURANCE COST	

Safety

FRONTAL CRASH TEST**	Good
SIDE CRASH TEST	No government results
AIRBAGS	Dual Only
ANTI-LOCK BRAKES	4-wheel
DAY. RUNNING LIGHTS	None
BELT ADJUSTORS	None
BUILT-IN CHILD SEAT	None
PRETENSIONERS	None

General Information

WHERE MADE	U.S./Canada
YEAR OF PRODUCTION	Fifth
PARKING INDEX	Hard
BUMPERS	Strong
THEFT RATING	Very High
TWINS	
DRIVE	Rear

Specifications

FUEL ECONOMY (cty/hwy)	20/30	Average
DRIVING RANGE (miles)	393	Short
SEATING	4	
LENGTH (in.)	181.5	Short
HEAD/LEG ROOM (in.)	38.2/42.6	Average
INTERIOR SPACE (cu. ft.)	93.9	Average
CARGO SPACE (cu. ft.)	10.9	Very Small

Specifications may vary.

Prices

Model	Retail	Mkup
Mustang	15,970	9%
Mustang GT	19,970	10%
Mustang Convertible	20,470	10%
Mustang Cobra Convertible	28,430	10%

Competition

	POOR — GOOD	Pg.
Ford Mustang		**144**
Chevrolet Camaro		121
Nissan 240SX		186
Pontiac Firebird		200

*A version of this vehicle is scheduled to be tested later this year. Results are expected to be similar.
**Data for coupe; frontal crash test for conv. is Very Good for an overall rating of 5.

Ford Taurus

Intermediate

The Taurus has a lineage of revolutionary car design and the current incarnation is no exception. A longer wheelbase make this car very spacious inside and oval-shaped headlights and dash give it a fresh, unique look. For '98, minor cosmetic changes were implemented to the exterior and the powertrains were improved. All come standard with dual airbags, but ABS is optional.

A standard 3-liter V6 engine should provide ample power, although you can opt for the same sized engine with more horses. The SHO comes with many features that are optional on the base models as well as a 3.4-liter V8 which will really make the car move. The Taurus remains a fine choice, despite tough competitors like the best-selling Toyota Camry or the newly redesigned Honda Accord.

The Ratings

	POOR … GOOD
COMPARATIVE RATING	□□□□□□■□□□
FRONTAL CRASH TEST*	□□□□□□□□■□
SAFETY FEATURES	□□□□□■□□□□
FUEL ECONOMY	□□□□■□□□□□
PM COST	□□□□□□□■□□
REPAIR COST	□□□□□■□□□□
WARRANTY	□■□□□□□□□□
COMPLAINTS	□□□□■□□□□□
INSURANCE COST	□□□□■□□□□□

Safety

FRONTAL CRASH TEST	Very Good
SIDE CRASH TEST	Good
AIRBAGS	Dual Only
ANTI-LOCK BRAKES	4-wheel (optional)
DAY. RUNNING LIGHTS	None
BELT ADJUSTORS	Front
BUILT-IN CHILD SEAT	Optional
PRETENSIONERS	None

General Information

WHERE MADE	U.S./Canada
YEAR OF PRODUCTION	Third
PARKING INDEX	Hard
BUMPERS	Strong
THEFT RATING	Very Low
TWINS	Mercury Sable
DRIVE	Front

Specifications

FUEL ECONOMY (cty/hwy)	20/28	Average
DRIVING RANGE (miles)	384	Short
SEATING	5	
LENGTH (in.)	197.5	Long
HEAD/LEG ROOM (in.)	39.2/42.2	Average
INTERIOR SPACE (cu. ft.)	101.0	Roomy
CARGO SPACE (cu. ft.)	15.8	Large

Specifications may vary.

Prices

Model	Retail	Mkup
Taurus LX	18,245	8%
Taurus SE	19,445	9%
Taurus SE Wagon	21,105	10%

Competition

	POOR … GOOD	Pg.
Ford Taurus	□□□□□□■□□□	**145**
Buick LeSabre	□□□□□□□□■□	112
Oldsmobile Intrigue	□□□■□□□□□□	195
Toyota Camry	□■□□□□□□□□	214

*A version of this vehicle is scheduled to be tested later this year. Results are expected to be similar.

Minivan

Chrysler's fourth sliding door has haunted Ford Windstar engineers for the past year. Sometime in the future, the Windstar may get it, but not for 1998. Instead, the driver's side door was increased in length to provide easier access to the rear seat. The Windstar offers great optional built-in child restraints; dual airbags and 4-wheel ABS are both standard. The Windstar also meets 1999 side impact protection standards early.

The base GL comes standard with the same 3-liter V6 also available on the Aerostar and Ranger. A 3.8-liter V6 is optional on the GL and standard on the LX, which provides much more power. The interior is very roomy. The Windstar continues to perform phenomenally on frontal government crash tests, but a high number of complaints casts doubts on its reliability.

The Ratings

	POOR — GOOD
COMPARATIVE RATING	
FRONTAL CRASH TEST*	
SAFETY FEATURES	
FUEL ECONOMY	
PM COST	
REPAIR COST	
WARRANTY	
COMPLAINTS	
INSURANCE COST	

Safety

FRONTAL CRASH TEST	Very Good
SIDE CRASH TEST	No government results
AIRBAGS	Dual Only
ANTI-LOCK BRAKES	4-wheel
DAY. RUNNING LIGHTS	None
BELT ADJUSTORS	Front
BUILT-IN CHILD SEAT	Optional
PRETENSIONERS	None

General Information

WHERE MADE	Canada/U.S.
YEAR OF PRODUCTION	Fourth
PARKING INDEX	Very Hard
BUMPERS	Strong
THEFT RATING	Very Low
TWINS	
DRIVE	Front

Specifications

FUEL ECONOMY (cty/hwy)	18/25	Poor
DRIVING RANGE (miles)	440	Average
SEATING	7	
LENGTH (in.)	201.2	Very Long
HEAD/LEG ROOM (in.)	39.3/40.7	Cramped
INTERIOR SPACE (cu. ft.)		
CARGO SPACE (cu. ft.)	152.6	Very Large

Specifications may vary.

Prices

Model	Retail	Mkup
Windstar GL	20,960	12%
Windstar LX	26,205	12%
Windstar Limited	29,505	13%

Competition

	POOR — GOOD	Pg.
Ford Windstar		**146**
Dodge Caravan		135
Isuzu Oasis		160
Nissan Quest		189

*A version of this vehicle is scheduled to be tested later this year. Results are expected to be similar.

GM EV1

Subcompact

The first of its kind, the EV1's introduction last year was only the beginning. Other electric vehicles are becoming available. The EV1 is an actual car, not a glorified golf cart, and comes standard with dual airbags, traction control, ABS, daytime running lights and self-sealing tires with a tire pressure monitoring system. Marketed through Saturn, you'll find the EV1 available for lease in southern California and Arizona.

The EV1 runs on lead-acid batteries, which take up to 8 hours to recharge for a driving range of 70-90 miles. Acceleration is good but drains the juice faster. The interior is sparse and spacious. The typical engine purr is replaced by a high pitched whining during acceleration. While only good for people with short commutes or quick trips, the EV1 continues to be a great start to a promising technology.

The Ratings

	POOR ... GOOD
COMPARATIVE RATING*	□□□□□□□□□□
FRONTAL CRASH TEST	□□□□□□□□□□
SAFETY FEATURES	□□□□□■□□□□
FUEL ECONOMY	□□□□□□□□□□
PM COST	□□□□□□□□□□
REPAIR COST	□□□□□□□□□□
WARRANTY	□□□□□□□□□□
COMPLAINTS	□□□□■□□□□□
INSURANCE COST	□□□□□□□□□□

Safety

FRONTAL CRASH TEST	No government results
SIDE CRASH TEST	No government results
AIRBAGS	Dual Only
ANTI-LOCK BRAKES	4-wheel
DAY. RUNNING LIGHTS	Standard
BELT ADJUSTORS	Front
BUILT-IN CHILD SEAT	None
PRETENSIONERS	None

General Information

WHERE MADE	U.S.
YEAR OF PRODUCTION	Second
PARKING INDEX	Very Easy
BUMPERS	Weak
THEFT RATING	
TWINS	
DRIVE	Front

Specifications

FUEL ECONOMY (cty/hwy)		
DRIVING RANGE (miles)	70-90	Very Short
SEATING	2	
LENGTH (in.)	169.7	Very Short
HEAD/LEG ROOM (in.)	37.6/42.6	Cramped
INTERIOR SPACE (cu. ft.)	50.4	Vry. Cramped
CARGO SPACE (cu. ft.)	9.7	Very Small

Specifications may vary.

Prices

Model	Retail	Mkup
EV1	33,995	
Monthly payment is about $480-549.		

Competition

	POOR ... GOOD	Pg.
GM EV1	□□□□□□□□□□	**147**
Honda EV Plus	□□□□□□□□□□	151
Chevrolet Metro	■□□□□□□□□□	125
Toyota Tercel	□□□□□□■□□□	219

*Due to the importance of crash tests, cars with no results as of publication date cannot be given an overall rating.

GMC Safari

Minivan

The Safari continues into 1998 unchanged. Like its twin, the Astro, the Safari is a basic van which is used primarily for hauling and towing. It offers one of the largest cargo and towing capacities in the van market. Standard features include dual airbags, 4-wheel ABS and daytime running lamps. A child safety seat is optional and highly recommended for parents.

The standard 4.3-liter, V6 engine with automatic transmission provides plenty of power, but sloppy handling. Fuel economy is fairly dismal, as well. You can choose between rear-wheel drive or all-wheel drive. The seats are comfortable enough, but make sure there is enough leg room. Consider the Safari if you're looking to move cargo; if not, check out the Odyssey/Oasis, the all-new Sienna, based on the popular Camry, or one of the GM minivans.

The Ratings

	POOR — GOOD
COMPARATIVE RATING	
FRONTAL CRASH TEST	
SAFETY FEATURES	
FUEL ECONOMY	
PM COST	
REPAIR COST	
WARRANTY	
COMPLAINTS	
INSURANCE COST	

Safety

FRONTAL CRASH TEST	Poor
SIDE CRASH TEST	No government results
AIRBAGS	Dual Only
ANTI-LOCK BRAKES	4-wheel
DAY. RUNNING LIGHTS	Standard
BELT ADJUSTORS	Front
BUILT-IN CHILD SEAT	Optional (two)
PRETENSIONERS	None

General Information

WHERE MADE	U.S./Canada
YEAR OF PRODUCTION	Fourteenth
PARKING INDEX	Hard
BUMPERS	Strong
THEFT RATING	Very Low
TWINS	Chevy Astro
DRIVE	Rear/AWD

Specifications

FUEL ECONOMY (cty/hwy)	16/21	Poor
DRIVING RANGE (miles)	475	Long
SEATING	8	
LENGTH (in.)	189.8	Long
HEAD/LEG ROOM (in.)	39.1/41.6	Average
INTERIOR SPACE (cu. ft.)		
CARGO SPACE (cu. ft.)	170.4	Very Large

Specifications may vary.

Prices

Model	Retail	Mkup
Safari	20,183	11%
Safari awd	22,438	11%

Competition

	POOR — GOOD	Pg.
GMC Safari		**148**
Chevrolet Astro		120
Ford Windstar		146
Pontiac Trans Sport		204

Honda Accord

Intermediate

The redesigned Accord is poised to take over the #1 best-seller in America. Its latest makeover is its most dramatic in its 22 year history. Changes were made to structure, engine, suspension, interior, exterior—nothing was untouched. The '98 Accord has more interior room and trunk space, has a smoother transmission, and gets a more distinctively styled coupe. More importantly, the base model's price remains unchanged, there are minor increases for mid-levels, and the top trim level *decreased* in price by up to $900! Dual airbags are standard, ABS is optional.

The new standard engine on the base DX is a 2.3-liter engine which cranks out 135 hp. The LX and EX get the peppier version of the same engine with 150 hp. But, many will want the optional VTEC V6 engine. The Accord is scheduled to be crash tested next year, so stay tuned.

The Ratings

	POOR — GOOD
COMPARATIVE RATING*	
FRONTAL CRASH TEST	
SAFETY FEATURES	
FUEL ECONOMY	
PM COST	
REPAIR COST	
WARRANTY	
COMPLAINTS	
INSURANCE COST	

Safety

FRONTAL CRASH TEST	No government results
SIDE CRASH TEST	No government results
AIRBAGS	Dual Only
ANTI-LOCK BRAKES	4-wheel (optional)
DAY. RUNNING LIGHTS	None
BELT ADJUSTORS	Front
BUILT-IN CHILD SEAT	None
PRETENSIONERS	None

General Information

WHERE MADE	U.S.
YEAR OF PRODUCTION	First
PARKING INDEX	Average
BUMPERS	Strong
THEFT RATING	
TWINS	
DRIVE	Front

Specifications

FUEL ECONOMY (cty/hwy)	25/31	Average
DRIVING RANGE (miles)	479	Very Long
SEATING	5	
LENGTH (in.)	188.8	Average
HEAD/LEG ROOM (in.)	40.0/42.1	Roomy
INTERIOR SPACE (cu. ft.)	101.7	Roomy
CARGO SPACE (cu. ft.)	14.1	Average

Specifications may vary.

Prices

Model	Retail	Mkup
Accord DX 4dr.	15,100	13%
Accord LX 2dr.	18,290	13%
Accord LX 4dr.	18,290	13%
Accord LX 2dr. V6	21,550	13%

Competition

	POOR — GOOD	Pg.
Honda Accord		**149**
Chevrolet Malibu		124
Ford Taurus		145
Toyota Camry		214

*Due to the importance of crash tests, cars with no results as of publication date cannot be given an overall rating.

Honda Civic

Subcompact

Little needed to be changed to the Civic for 1998—it remains the epitome of style and reliability. As before, you can buy a coupe with trim levels DX, HX, and EX; a sedan with trim levels DX, LX and EX; or a hatchback with trim levels, CX or DX. Dual airbags are standard and ABS is standard on the EX sedan, but remains optional on all other models.

The base engine is a 1.6-liter 4-cylinder which delivers 106 hp, and you can upgrade to more powerful engines with 115 or 127 hp on higher trim levels. The ride is characterized by responsive handling and a smooth suspension. Interior space increased with last year's reworking, especially in back. The Civic performed excellently in frontal crash tests, but only average in side tests. Against competitors like Cavalier, Escort and Neon, the Civic holds its own.

The Ratings

	POOR — GOOD
COMPARATIVE RATING	
FRONTAL CRASH TEST*	
SAFETY FEATURES	
FUEL ECONOMY	
PM COST	
REPAIR COST	
WARRANTY	
COMPLAINTS	
INSURANCE COST	

Safety

FRONTAL CRASH TEST	Very Good
SIDE CRASH TEST	Average
AIRBAGS	Dual Only
ANTI-LOCK BRAKES	4-wheel (optional)
DAY. RUNNING LIGHTS	None
BELT ADJUSTORS	Front
BUILT-IN CHILD SEAT	None
PRETENSIONERS	None

General Information

WHERE MADE	U.S./Canada/Japan
YEAR OF PRODUCTION	Third
PARKING INDEX	Very Easy
BUMPERS	Strong
THEFT RATING	Average
TWINS	
DRIVE	Front

Specifications

FUEL ECONOMY (cty/hwy)	33/38	Very Good
DRIVING RANGE (miles)	428	Average
SEATING	5	
LENGTH (in.)	175.1	Short
HEAD/LEG ROOM (in.)	39.8/42.7	Roomy
INTERIOR SPACE (cu. ft.)	89.8	Cramped
CARGO SPACE (cu. ft.)	11.9	Small

Specifications may vary.

Prices

Model	Retail	Mkup
Civic CX 3-dr man.	10,650	7%
Civic DX 2dr man.	12,580	11%
Civic DX 4dr auto.	13,535	11%
Civic EX 4dr auto.	17,280	11%

Competition

	POOR — GOOD	Pg.
Honda Civic		**150**
Chevrolet Cavalier		122
Dodge/Ply. Neon		137
Ford Escort		143

*A version of this vehicle is scheduled to be tested later this year. Results are expected to be similar.

Honda EV Plus

Subcompact

Joining the EV1, Honda's EV Plus may prove to be the better electric car option for 1998. Available only for lease, the EV Plus is being marketed through a few dealers in Los Angeles and Sacramento, CA. It comes with power everything and a keyless entry and security system. Dual airbags and ABS are standard.

The nickel-metal hydride batteries will allow you an estimated 100 miles before recharging. And recharging will take about 8 hours. Seating is generous with plenty of room for four. The interior is more attractively designed than the sparse EV1. One nice feature is the climate control system, which you can turn on and off by remote before you get in. Like the EV1, the EV Plus is another promising look at a futuristic technology.

The Ratings

	POOR — GOOD
COMPARATIVE RATING*	□□□□□□□□□□
FRONTAL CRASH TEST	□□□□□□□□□□
SAFETY FEATURES	□□□□□■□□□□
FUEL ECONOMY	□□□□□□□□□□
PM COST	□□□□□□□□□□
REPAIR COST	□□□□□□□□□□
WARRANTY	□□□□□□□□□□
COMPLAINTS	□□□□■□□□□□
INSURANCE COST	□□□□□□□□□□

Safety

FRONTAL CRASH TEST	No government results
SIDE CRASH TEST	No government results
AIRBAGS	Dual Only
ANTI-LOCK BRAKES	4-wheel
DAY. RUNNING LIGHTS	None
BELT ADJUSTORS	None
BUILT-IN CHILD SEAT	None
PRETENSIONERS	None

General Information

WHERE MADE	Japan
YEAR OF PRODUCTION	First
PARKING INDEX	Easy
BUMPERS	
THEFT RATING	
TWINS	
DRIVE	Front

Specifications

FUEL ECONOMY (cty/hwy)		
DRIVING RANGE (miles)	100	Very Short
SEATING	4	
LENGTH (in.)	159.3	Very Short
HEAD/LEG ROOM (in.)	39.6/41.9	Average
INTERIOR SPACE (cu. ft.)	90.0	Cramped
CARGO SPACE (cu. ft.)	12.0	Small

Specifications may vary.

Prices

Model	Retail	Mkup
EV Plus	53,999	
Monthly payment is about $499.		

Competition

	POOR — GOOD	Pg.
Honda EV Plus	□□□□□□□□□□	**151**
GM EV1	□□□□□□□□□□	147
Chevrolet Metro	■□□□□□□□□□	125
Toyota Tercel	□□□□□□■□□□	219

*Due to the importance of crash tests, cars with no results as of publication date cannot be given an overall rating.

Honda Odyssey

Minivan

The Odyssey, and its twin the Isuzu Oasis, differs from most other minivans in many respects. It is lower and narrower, which makes it easier to maneuver. It also has two sedan-type doors for access to the rear seats. Dual airbags and ABS are standard.

The Odyssey gets a new 2.3-liter, 150 hp engine for 1998. More powerful and smoother than its predecessor, the new 2.3-liter is the same engine that is found on the all-new Accord. The middle bench seat doesn't come out, and the rear seat, which cleverly folds into the floor of the cargo bay, doesn't quite become flush with the floor, making the loading surface uneven. As a result, cargo space is not quite as generous as the competition. A fine crash test performer with excellent complaint ratings, the Odyssey is worth looking at if a traditional minivan is too big.

The Ratings

	POOR … GOOD
COMPARATIVE RATING	
FRONTAL CRASH TEST	
SAFETY FEATURES	
FUEL ECONOMY	
PM COST	
REPAIR COST	
WARRANTY	
COMPLAINTS	
INSURANCE COST	

Safety

FRONTAL CRASH TEST	Good
SIDE CRASH TEST	No government results
AIRBAGS	Dual Only
ANTI-LOCK BRAKES	4-wheel
DAY. RUNNING LIGHTS	None
BELT ADJUSTORS	Front
BUILT-IN CHILD SEAT	None
PRETENSIONERS	None

General Information

WHERE MADE	Japan
YEAR OF PRODUCTION	Fourth
PARKING INDEX	Average
BUMPERS	Strong
THEFT RATING	Very Low
TWINS	Isuzu Oasis
DRIVE	Front

Specifications

FUEL ECONOMY (cty/hwy)	20/24	Poor
DRIVING RANGE (miles)	378	Short
SEATING	7	
LENGTH (in.)	187.6	Average
HEAD/LEG ROOM (in.)	40.1/40.7	Average
INTERIOR SPACE (cu. ft.)		
CARGO SPACE (cu. ft.)	102.5	Very Large

Specifications may vary.

Prices**

Model	Retail	Mkup
Odyssey LX	23,560	13%
Odyssey EX	25,550	13%

Competition

	POOR … GOOD	Pg.
Honda Odyssey		**152**
Dodge Caravan		135
Ford Windstar		146
Nissan Quest		189

**1998 prices not available at press time. Prices based on 1997 data.

Honda Prelude

Compact

A mix between luxury and performance, the Prelude was redesigned last year and changes little for 1998. The redesign included more interior room, upgrades to the engines, and new exterior styling. Dual airbags, front belt adjustors and ABS are standard.

The only engine sold with the new Prelude will be a 2.2-liter 4-cylinder engine which will be capable of producing 150 hp, which is plenty to power this compact car. Expect the ride to be firm, yet comfortable and provide the driver and passengers with the feel of a sports car. Controls are conventional and a larger trunk will make road trips more comfortable. Test driving the Prelude is a must for sports car enthusiasts, despite Honda's lousy warranty. Unfortunately, the government has no plans to crash test the Prelude next year.

The Ratings

	POOR … GOOD
COMPARATIVE RATING*	□□□□□□□□□□
FRONTAL CRASH TEST	□□□□□□□□□□
SAFETY FEATURES	□□□□□■□□□□
FUEL ECONOMY	□□□□■□□□□□
PM COST	□□■□□□□□□□
REPAIR COST	□□□■□□□□□□
WARRANTY	■□□□□□□□□□
COMPLAINTS	□□□□■□□□□□
INSURANCE COST	□□□□□□□□□■

Safety

FRONTAL CRASH TEST	No government results
SIDE CRASH TEST	No government results
AIRBAGS	Dual Only
ANTI-LOCK BRAKES	4-wheel
DAY. RUNNING LIGHTS	None
BELT ADJUSTORS	Front
BUILT-IN CHILD SEAT	None
PRETENSIONERS	None

General Information

WHERE MADE	Japan
YEAR OF PRODUCTION	Second
PARKING INDEX	Easy
BUMPERS	Strong
THEFT RATING	
TWINS	
DRIVE	Front

Specifications

FUEL ECONOMY (cty/hwy)	22/27	Average
DRIVING RANGE (miles)	398	Short
SEATING	4	
LENGTH (in.)	178.0	Short
HEAD/LEG ROOM (in.)	37.9/43.0	Average
INTERIOR SPACE (cu. ft.)	77.5	Vry. Cramped
CARGO SPACE (cu. ft.)	8.7	Very Small

Specifications may vary.

Prices**

Model	Retail	Mkup
Prelude	23,200	13%
Prelude Type SH	25,700	13%

Competition

	POOR … GOOD	Pg.
Honda Prelude	□□□□□□□□□□	**153**
Acura Integra	□□□□□■□□□□	103
Eagle Talon	□■□□□□□□□□	139
Mazda Miata	□□□■□□□□□□	170

**1998 prices not available at press time. Prices based on 1997 data.

*Due to the importance of crash tests, cars with no results as of publication date cannot be given an overall rating.

Hyundai Accent

Subcompact

The Accent gets a new front and rear end for 1998. Available in a hatchback or sedan, the front-wheel drive Accent is much improved over its predecessor, the Hyundai Excel, and it should give competitors like the Tercel a few worries. The Accent comes with dual airbags and ABS is available.

The 1.5-liter 4-cylinder engine that comes on all Accents is adequate for this light car and is fuel efficient. Although front seat occupants will be comfortable, passengers in the rear will feel cramped; choose the 4-door for more room. The Accent is just as powerful as the Toyota Tercel, but it's not quite as fuel efficient or roomy as the Geo Metro and Suzuki Swift. Not outstanding in any one category, the Accent is a decent subcompact which offers a little bit of everything.

The Ratings

	POOR — GOOD
COMPARATIVE RATING	
FRONTAL CRASH TEST	
SAFETY FEATURES	
FUEL ECONOMY	
PM COST	
REPAIR COST	
WARRANTY	
COMPLAINTS	
INSURANCE COST	

Safety

FRONTAL CRASH TEST	Average
SIDE CRASH TEST	No government results
AIRBAGS	Dual Only
ANTI-LOCK BRAKES	4-wheel (optional)
DAY. RUNNING LIGHTS	None
BELT ADJUSTORS	Front
BUILT-IN CHILD SEAT	None
PRETENSIONERS	None

General Information

WHERE MADE	Korea
YEAR OF PRODUCTION	Fourth
PARKING INDEX	Very Easy
BUMPERS	Strong
THEFT RATING	Very Low
TWINS	
DRIVE	Front

Specifications

FUEL ECONOMY (cty/hwy)	28/36	Good
DRIVING RANGE (miles)	381	Short
SEATING	5	
LENGTH (in.)	162.1	Very Short
HEAD/LEG ROOM (in.)	38.7/42.6	Average
INTERIOR SPACE (cu. ft.)	88.0	Cramped
CARGO SPACE (cu. ft.)	10.7	Very Small

Specifications may vary.

Prices**

Model	Retail	Mkup
Accent Coupe L	8,599	10%
Accent Coupe GS man.	9,399	10%
Accent Sedan GL	9,799	10%

Competition

	POOR — GOOD	Pg.
Hyundai Accent		**154**
Chevrolet Metro		125
Ford Escort		143
Toyota Tercel		219

**1998 prices not available at press time. Prices based on 1997 data.

Hyundai Elantra

Compact

Unchanged for 1998, the Hyundai Elantra is a subcompact that gives you a lot for your money. You will find standard dual airbags which should help improve the average crash test rating. Unfortunately, you still have to pay extra for ABS.

The only engine offered will be a 1.8-liter 4 cylinder, not especially powerful but good enough to move this subcompact. The front seats are comfortable, but adults will feel cramped in the back. Handling was improved last year with a sturdier front and rear sub-frames. Ride and comfort are good in this small car and, with refined insulation, it should be relatively quiet. Available in both a sedan and wagon, the Elantra comes with plenty options to choose from. Of course, the low prices are what you expect from Hyundai and the Elantra is no exception.

The Ratings

	POOR → GOOD
COMPARATIVE RATING	5 of 10
FRONTAL CRASH TEST*	5 of 10
SAFETY FEATURES	5 of 10
FUEL ECONOMY	6 of 10
PM COST	10 of 10
REPAIR COST	10 of 10
WARRANTY	4 of 10
COMPLAINTS	3 of 10
INSURANCE COST	10 of 10

Safety

FRONTAL CRASH TEST	Average
SIDE CRASH TEST	No government results
AIRBAGS	Dual Only
ANTI-LOCK BRAKES	4-wheel (optional)
DAY. RUNNING LIGHTS	None
BELT ADJUSTORS	Front
BUILT-IN CHILD SEAT	None
PRETENSIONERS	None

General Information

WHERE MADE	Korea
YEAR OF PRODUCTION	Third
PARKING INDEX	Very Easy
BUMPERS	Strong
THEFT RATING	
TWINS	
DRIVE	Front

Specifications

FUEL ECONOMY (cty/hwy)	24/32	Average
DRIVING RANGE (miles)	406	Short
SEATING	5	
LENGTH (in.)	174.0	Short
HEAD/LEG ROOM (in.)	38.6/43.2	Roomy
INTERIOR SPACE (cu. ft.)	93.6	Average
CARGO SPACE (cu. ft.)	11.4	Small

Specifications may vary.

Prices**

Model	Retail	Mkup
Elantra	11,899	11%
Elantra Watgon	11,899	11%
Elantra GLS	12,549	11%

Competition

	POOR → GOOD	Pg.
Hyundai Elantra	5 of 10	**155**
Chevrolet Cavalier	8 of 10	122
Dodge/Plym. Neon	1 of 10	137
Subaru Impreza	9 of 10	209

**1998 prices not available at press time. Prices based on 1997 data.

*A version of this vehicle is scheduled to be tested later this year. Results are expected to be similar.

Hyundai Sonata

Intermediate

Refined both inside and out last year, the Sonata is Hyundai's attempt to break into the tough mid-size market with competitors like the best-selling Camry, the all-new Accord, and the Taurus. The wheelbase on the Sonata is slightly longer than most other intermediate cars, resulting in a little more leg room inside and the refined interior helps make the ride more comfortable. ABS will cost extra, but dual airbags are standard.

The base comes with an adequately powered 2-liter engine. The 3-liter that is standard on the GLS gives more horsepower. With added insulation, the Sonata should do a good job at keeping the road noise down. The Sonata has a low sticker price and low repairs costs. However, its frontal crash test results are merely average and, on side crash tests, the Sonata performed fairly poorly.

The Ratings

	POOR — GOOD
COMPARATIVE RATING	
FRONTAL CRASH TEST	
SAFETY FEATURES	
FUEL ECONOMY	
PM COST	
REPAIR COST	
WARRANTY	
COMPLAINTS	
INSURANCE COST	

Safety

FRONTAL CRASH TEST	Average
SIDE CRASH TEST	Very Poor
AIRBAGS	Dual Only
ANTI-LOCK BRAKES	4-wheel (optional)
DAY. RUNNING LIGHTS	None
BELT ADJUSTORS	Front
BUILT-IN CHILD SEAT	None
PRETENSIONERS	None

General Information

WHERE MADE	Korea
YEAR OF PRODUCTION	Fourth
PARKING INDEX	Easy
BUMPERS	Strong
THEFT RATING	Average
TWINS	
DRIVE	Front

Specifications

FUEL ECONOMY (cty/hwy)	21/28	Average
DRIVING RANGE (miles)	430	Average
SEATING	5	
LENGTH (in.)	185.0	Average
HEAD/LEG ROOM (in.)	38.5/43.3	Roomy
INTERIOR SPACE (cu. ft.)	101.3	Roomy
CARGO SPACE (cu. ft.)	13.2	Small

Specifications may vary.

Prices**

Model	Retail	Mkup
Sonata	14,749	12%
Sonata GL	16,349	12%
Sonata GLS	18,549	12%

Competition

	POOR — GOOD	Pg.
Hyundai Sonata		156
Buick Regal		114
Ford Contour		141
Pontiac Grand Prix		202

**1998 prices not available at press time. Prices based on 1997 data.

Hyundai Tiburon

Compact

Hyundai's newest car continues in 1998 with no changes. The Tiburon closely resembles the exterior styling of the Toyota Celica and the interior designs of the Mitsubishi Eclipse and Ford Probe. This is no surprise since the Tiburon is Hyundai's challenge to more established coupes like the Celica and Probe. Dual airbags are standard; ABS is optional.

Powering this all-new coupe will be a pair of engines, a 1.8-liter and a 2.0-liter which produce 130 and 138 horsepower, respectively. Surprising for a Hyundai, the suspension was tuned by engineers at Porsche. Expect the ride to be good on smooth roads; get onto something bumpy and you won't have much fun. The controls are well placed and easy to read. With a low price, the Tiburon is an attractive alternative to competitors.

The Ratings	POOR ... GOOD
COMPARATIVE RATING*	
FRONTAL CRASH TEST	
SAFETY FEATURES	
FUEL ECONOMY	
PM COST	
REPAIR COST	
WARRANTY	
COMPLAINTS	
INSURANCE COST	

Safety	
FRONTAL CRASH TEST	No government results
SIDE CRASH TEST	No government results
AIRBAGS	Dual Only
ANTI-LOCK BRAKES	4-wheel (optional)
DAY. RUNNING LIGHTS	None
BELT ADJUSTORS	Front
BUILT-IN CHILD SEAT	None
PRETENSIONERS	None

General Information	
WHERE MADE	Korea
YEAR OF PRODUCTION	Second
PARKING INDEX	Easy
BUMPERS	Strong
THEFT RATING	
TWINS	
DRIVE	Front

Specifications		
FUEL ECONOMY (cty/hwy)	22/30	Average
DRIVING RANGE (miles)	377	Short
SEATING	5	
LENGTH (in.)	170.9	Very Short
HEAD/LEG ROOM (in.)	38.0/43.1	Average
INTERIOR SPACE (cu. ft.)	80.0	Vry. Cramped
CARGO SPACE (cu. ft.)	12.8	Small

Specifications may vary.

Prices**

Model	Retail	Mkup
Tiburon	13,499	10%
Tiburon FX	14,899	10%

Competition

	POOR ... GOOD	Pg.
Hyundai Tiburon		**157**
Acura Integra		103
Eagle Talon		139
Mazda Miata		170

**1998 prices not available at press time. Prices based on 1997 data.

*Due to the importance of crash tests, cars with no results as of publication date cannot be given an overall rating.

Infiniti I30

Large

Infiniti has dropped the J30 for '98, leaving the I30 as the entry level model. Essentially an upscale Nissan Maxima, the I30 has minor changes like restyled headlamps for 1998. Dual airbags and 4-wheel ABS are standard. Side airbags are a welcome addition for 1998.

Like the Maxima, the I30 is powered by a 3.0-liter V6 engine, which is powerful enough to please most people. Fuel economy for this heavy car will be slightly lower than the Maxima, but still competitive with other mid-sized luxury cars. With a very rigid body shell, driver and passengers will move in comfort; the controls and gauges are easy to read and use. If you can live without the name-plate, consider a fully-loaded Maxima and save a couple thousand dollars.

The Ratings

	POOR — GOOD
COMPARATIVE RATING	□□□□□□□□□■
FRONTAL CRASH TEST	□□□□□■□□□□
SAFETY FEATURES	□□□□□■□□□□
FUEL ECONOMY	□□□□■□□□□□
PM COST	□□□□□■□□□□
REPAIR COST	■□□□□□□□□□
WARRANTY	□□□□□□□□■□
COMPLAINTS	□□□□□□□□□■
INSURANCE COST	□□□□■□□□□□

Safety

FRONTAL CRASH TEST	Average
SIDE CRASH TEST	Good
AIRBAGS	Dual/Opt. Side
ANTI-LOCK BRAKES	4-wheel
DAY. RUNNING LIGHTS	None
BELT ADJUSTORS	Front
BUILT-IN CHILD SEAT	None
PRETENSIONERS	None

General Information

WHERE MADE	Japan
YEAR OF PRODUCTION	Third
PARKING INDEX	Easy
BUMPERS	Strong
THEFT RATING	High
TWINS	Nissan Maxima
DRIVE	Front

Specifications

FUEL ECONOMY (cty/hwy)	21/28	Average
DRIVING RANGE (miles)	463	Long
SEATING	5	
LENGTH (in.)	189.6	Average
HEAD/LEG ROOM (in.)	40.1/43.9	Very Roomy
INTERIOR SPACE (cu. ft.)	99.6	Roomy
CARGO SPACE (cu. ft.)	14.1	Average

Specifications may vary.

Prices

Model	Retail	Mkup
I30	28,900	13%
I30 Touring man.	31,500	14%
I30 Touring auto.	32,500	14%

Competition

	POOR — GOOD	Pg.
Infiniti I30	□□□□□□□□□■	**158**
Audi A4	□□□□□□□□□■	106
BMW 3-Series	□□□□□□□□□■	108
Merc.-Benz C-Class	□□□□□□□■□□	174

Infiniti Q45

Large

The Q45, Infiniti's flagship sedan, first debuted in 1989 with a very aggressive ad campaign and an equally aggressively styled car. Since then, the Q45 has evolved into a quiet, luxury sedan. After a revision last year, the Q45 enters '98 with little change. However, performance is still its strong point. Dual airbags, 4-wheel ABS, pretensioners, and side airbags lead the list of safety features.

Tipping the scales at almost 3,900 pounds, Infiniti needed to find an engine powerful enough to move the Q45, so they chose a 4.1 liter V8 which produces over 260 horsepower. Plushness and comfort are what you would expect from the top of the luxury line and ride will be as smooth as silk, though not bouncy or floaty like other large cars. This conservative luxury sedan is among the best.

The Ratings	POOR → GOOD
COMPARATIVE RATING*	□□□□□□□□□□
FRONTAL CRASH TEST	□□□□□□□□□□
SAFETY FEATURES	□□□□□□■□□□
FUEL ECONOMY	□□□■□□□□□□
PM COST	□□□□□■□□□□
REPAIR COST	■□□□□□□□□□
WARRANTY	□□□□□□□□■□
COMPLAINTS	□□□□■□□□□□
INSURANCE COST	□□□□□□□□□■

Safety	
FRONTAL CRASH TEST	No government results
SIDE CRASH TEST	No government results
AIRBAGS	Dual & Side
ANTI-LOCK BRAKES	4-wheel
DAY. RUNNING LIGHTS	None
BELT ADJUSTORS	Front
BUILT-IN CHILD SEAT	None
PRETENSIONERS	Standard

General Information	
WHERE MADE	Japan
YEAR OF PRODUCTION	Second
PARKING INDEX	Average
BUMPERS	Strong
THEFT RATING	
TWINS	
DRIVE	Rear

Specifications		
FUEL ECONOMY (cty/hwy)	18/23	Poor
DRIVING RANGE (miles)	449	Long
SEATING	5	
LENGTH (in.)	199.6	Long
HEAD/LEG ROOM (in.)	37.6/43.6	Average
INTERIOR SPACE (cu. ft.)	97.4	Average
CARGO SPACE (cu. ft.)	12.6	Small

Specifications may vary.

Prices**

Model	Retail	Mkup
Q45	47,900	19%
Q45	49,900	19%

Competition

	POOR → GOOD	Pg.
Infiniti Q45	□□□□□□□□□□	**159**
Acura TL	□□□□□□□□■□	105
Cadillac DeVille	□□□□□□□□□■	117
Lexus ES300	□□□□□□□□■□	162

**1998 prices not available at press time. Prices based on 1997 data.

*Due to the importance of crash tests, cars with no results as of publication date cannot be given an overall rating.

The Oasis, and its twin the Honda Odyssey, are unchanged for 1998. Like the Odyssey, the Oasis is designed to be more like a car than a minivan. With a wide stance and low ground clearance, the Oasis drives much like a car and also has conventional doors instead of a sliding door like the rest of its minivan competition. Dual airbags and ABS are standard.

The power comes from a new 2.3-liter 4-cylinder engine which is more powerful than last year's engine. The middle seat in the Oasis does not come out, and the rear seat cleverly folds into the floor, but not quite flush, making the loading surface uneven. Good crash tests and a low number of complaints make the Oasis one of the top rated minivans for this year, especially if you're looking for something smaller than the typical minivan.

The Ratings

	POOR — GOOD
COMPARATIVE RATING	
FRONTAL CRASH TEST	
SAFETY FEATURES	
FUEL ECONOMY	
PM COST	
REPAIR COST	
WARRANTY	
COMPLAINTS	
INSURANCE COST	

Safety

FRONTAL CRASH TEST	Good
SIDE CRASH TEST	No government results
AIRBAGS	Dual Only
ANTI-LOCK BRAKES	4-wheel
DAY. RUNNING LIGHTS	None
BELT ADJUSTORS	Front
BUILT-IN CHILD SEAT	None
PRETENSIONERS	None

General Information

WHERE MADE	Japan
YEAR OF PRODUCTION	Third
PARKING INDEX	Average
BUMPERS	Strong
THEFT RATING	
TWINS	Honda Odyssey
DRIVE	Front

Specifications

FUEL ECONOMY (cty/hwy)	21/26	Average
DRIVING RANGE (miles)	413	Average
SEATING	7	
LENGTH (in.)	187.2	Average
HEAD/LEG ROOM (in.)	40.1/40.7	Average
INTERIOR SPACE (cu. ft.)		
CARGO SPACE (cu. ft.)	93.5	Very Large

Specifications may vary.

Prices**

Model	Retail	Mkup
Oasis S	23,730	14%
Oasis LS	25,990	14%

Competition

	POOR — GOOD	Pg.
Isuzu Oasis		**160**
Chevrolet Venture		128
Dodge Caravan		135
Ford Windstar		146

**1998 prices not available at press time. Prices based on 1997 data.

Kia Sephia

Subcompact

For 1998, the Sephia has been redesigned with larger dimensions and a new engine. No information was available at press time, so the photo and data are for the outgoing model.

The outgoing '97 Sephia comes standard with dual airbags and optional ABS. To power the Sephia, Kia has equipped it with an impressive 1.8-liter, 4-cylinder engine, which produces 122 hp. The Sephia comes in several trim levels: RS, LS, and GS—but is available only as a sedan, unlike its competitors. The styling is similar to the old Mazda 323, which is no surprise as Mazda is a part-owner of Kia. The Sephia is a major player in the small sedan market due to its attractive price tag. As of this writing, Kia's parent company in Korea is undergoing bankruptcy proceedings which may not bode well for Kia.

The Ratings

	POOR □□□□□□□□□□ GOOD
COMPARATIVE RATING*	□□□□□□□□□□
FRONTAL CRASH TEST	□□□□□□□□□□
SAFETY FEATURES	□□□□■□□□□□
FUEL ECONOMY	□□□□□□■□□□
PM COST	□□□□□□■□□□
REPAIR COST	□□□■□□□□□□
WARRANTY	□□□□■□□□□□
COMPLAINTS	□□□□■□□□□□
INSURANCE COST	□□□□■□□□□□

Safety

FRONTAL CRASH TEST	No government results
SIDE CRASH TEST	No government results
AIRBAGS	Dual Only
ANTI-LOCK BRAKES	4-wheel (optional)
DAY. RUNNING LIGHTS	None
BELT ADJUSTORS	Front
BUILT-IN CHILD SEAT	None
PRETENSIONERS	None

General Information

WHERE MADE	Korea/Japan
YEAR OF PRODUCTION	First
PARKING INDEX	Very Easy
BUMPERS	Strong
THEFT RATING	
TWINS	
DRIVE	Front

Specifications

FUEL ECONOMY (cty/hwy)	28/34	Good
DRIVING RANGE (miles)	394	Short
SEATING	5	
LENGTH (in.)	171.7	Very Short
HEAD/LEG ROOM (in.)	38.2/42.9	Average
INTERIOR SPACE (cu. ft.)	93.0	Average
CARGO SPACE (cu. ft.)	11.0	Very Small

Specifications may vary.

Prices**

Model	Retail	Mkup
Sephia RS	9,795	11%
Sephia LS	10,895	12%

Competition

	POOR □□□□□□□□□□ GOOD	Pg.
Kia Sephia	□□□□□□□□□□	**161**
Chevrolet Cavalier	□□□□□□■□□□	122
Ford Escort	□□□■□□□□□□	143
Honda Civic	□□□□□□■□□□	150

**1998 prices not available at press time. Prices based on 1997 data.

*Due to the importance of crash tests, cars with no results as of publication date cannot be given an overall rating.

Lexus ES300

Large

The Lexus ES300 enters 1998 with no changes. Based on the wildly popular Toyota Camry, the ES300 was equally hot because Lexus had trouble meeting demand last year. Dual airbags and 4-wheel ABS are standard. The addition of standard side airbags for '98 is a welcome safety feature.

The standard engine for the ES300, shared with the Camry and Avalon, is a 3.0 liter V6 which produces 200 horsepower. Head and leg room were increased, making the cabin more comfortable. Noise and vibration are kept to a minimum and handling is responsive. Unlike the Camry, the ES does not have a fold-down rear seat. The ES300 is a solid, affordable luxury sedan, but if you can live without the nameplate, a fully-loaded Camry will be just as good and costs less, too.

The Ratings

	POOR — GOOD
COMPARATIVE RATING	
FRONTAL CRASH TEST*	
SAFETY FEATURES	
FUEL ECONOMY	
PM COST	
REPAIR COST	
WARRANTY	
COMPLAINTS	
INSURANCE COST	

Safety

FRONTAL CRASH TEST	Good
SIDE CRASH TEST	Good
AIRBAGS	Dual & Side
ANTI-LOCK BRAKES	4-wheel
DAY. RUNNING LIGHTS	None
BELT ADJUSTORS	Front
BUILT-IN CHILD SEAT	None
PRETENSIONERS	Standard

General Information

WHERE MADE	Japan/U.S.
YEAR OF PRODUCTION	Second
PARKING INDEX	Average
BUMPERS	Weak
THEFT RATING	
TWINS	Toyota Camry
DRIVE	Front

Specifications

FUEL ECONOMY (cty/hwy)	19/25	Poor
DRIVING RANGE (miles)	407	Short
SEATING	5	
LENGTH (in.)	190.2	Long
HEAD/LEG ROOM (in.)	38.0/43.5	Average
INTERIOR SPACE (cu. ft.)	92.1	Cramped
CARGO SPACE (cu. ft.)	13.0	Small

Specifications may vary.

Prices

Model	Retail	Mkup
ES300	30,790	15%

Competition

	POOR — GOOD	Pg.
Lexus ES300		**162**
BMW 3-Series		108
Infiniti I30		158
Saab 9000		206

*A version of this vehicle is scheduled to be tested later this year. Results are expected to be similar.

Lexus GS300/400

Large

Fully revised for 1998, Lexus is hoping the GS sedans will become the new definitive luxury sports cars. Hoping to take on the BMW 5 Series and Mercedes-Benz E-Class, the GS sedans have been improved with bigger engines, a better suspension, and a more aggressive exterior design. Dual airbags, side airbags, pretensioners, traction control and 4-wheel ABS are all standard.

The GS300 gets a 3.0-liter engine that cranks out 225 hp. Most sports car enthusiasts will want to bigger 4.0-liter V8 engine on the GS400. An increased wheelbase allows for more interior room and a bigger trunk. On the GS sedans, 13 onboard computers are linked through a local-area network that lets you customize electronic features like interior lights. The GS300/400 represent the best of high tech luxury, but it'll cost you.

The Ratings

	POOR — GOOD
COMPARATIVE RATING*	
FRONTAL CRASH TEST	
SAFETY FEATURES	7 of 10
FUEL ECONOMY	4 of 10
PM COST	6 of 10
REPAIR COST	4 of 10
WARRANTY	8 of 10
COMPLAINTS	5 of 10
INSURANCE COST	5 of 10

Safety

FRONTAL CRASH TEST	No government results
SIDE CRASH TEST	No government results
AIRBAGS	Dual & Side
ANTI-LOCK BRAKES	4-wheel
DAY. RUNNING LIGHTS	None
BELT ADJUSTORS	Front/Rear
BUILT-IN CHILD SEAT	None
PRETENSIONERS	Standard

General Information

WHERE MADE	Japan
YEAR OF PRODUCTION	First
PARKING INDEX	Average
BUMPERS	Strong
THEFT RATING	
TWINS	
DRIVE	Rear

Specifications

FUEL ECONOMY (cty/hwy)	20/25	Poor
DRIVING RANGE (miles)	455	Long
SEATING	5	
LENGTH (in.)	189.0	Average
HEAD/LEG ROOM (in.)	39.2/44.5	Very Roomy
INTERIOR SPACE (cu. ft.)	100.0	Roomy
CARGO SPACE (cu. ft.)	14.8	Average

Specifications may vary.

Prices

Model	Retail	Mkup
GS300	36,800	16%
GS400	44,800	16%

Competition

	POOR — GOOD	Pg.
Lexus GS300/400		**163**
Acura TL	9 of 10	105
Cadillac DeVille	10 of 10	117
Merc.-Benz C-Class	8 of 10	174

*Due to the importance of crash tests, cars with no results as of publication date cannot be given an overall rating.

Lexus LS400

Large

The LS400, Lexus's flagship sedan, continues into 1998 with minor changes. The front and rear end received a minor restyling and the headlamps have been upgraded. Dual airbags and 4-wheel ABS are standard. Standard side airbags were added last year.

The engine that powers this large car is a 4.0-liter V8, shared by the GS400, making the LS400 one of the quickest luxury cars around. Fuel economy in the city, though certainly not great, is surprising for a car in this size class. You'll find a very smooth ride and an extremely roomy rear seat. But, trunk space is rather small when compared to other large cars. For '98, the anti-theft system received minor improvements, as well. With all its standard features and its powerful engine, the LS400 is worth the money if you can afford it.

The Ratings

	POOR — GOOD
COMPARATIVE RATING*	□□□□□□□□□□
FRONTAL CRASH TEST	□□□□□□□□□□
SAFETY FEATURES	□□□□□□■□□□
FUEL ECONOMY	□□□■□□□□□□
PM COST	□□□□□■□□□□
REPAIR COST	□■□□□□□□□□
WARRANTY	□□□□□□□■□□
COMPLAINTS	□□□□□□□□□■
INSURANCE COST	■□□□□□□□□□

Safety

FRONTAL CRASH TEST	No government results
SIDE CRASH TEST	No government results
AIRBAGS	Dual/Side
ANTI-LOCK BRAKES	4-wheel
DAY. RUNNING LIGHTS	None
BELT ADJUSTORS	Front
BUILT-IN CHILD SEAT	None
PRETENSIONERS	Standard

General Information

WHERE MADE	Japan
YEAR OF PRODUCTION	Fourth
PARKING INDEX	Average
BUMPERS	Weak
THEFT RATING	Very High
TWINS	
DRIVE	Rear

Specifications

FUEL ECONOMY (cty/hwy)	19/25	Poor
DRIVING RANGE (miles)	495	Very Long
SEATING	5	
LENGTH (in.)	196.7	Long
HEAD/LEG ROOM (in.)	38.9/43.7	Roomy
INTERIOR SPACE (cu. ft.)	102.0	Roomy
CARGO SPACE (cu. ft.)	13.9	Average

Specifications may vary.

Prices

Model	Retail	Mkup
LS400	52,900	18%

Competition

	POOR — GOOD	Pg.
Lexus LS400	□□□□□□□□□□	**164**
Acura TL	□□□□□□□□■□	105
Cadillac DeVille	□□□□□□□□□■	117
Merc.-Benz C-Class	□□□□□□□■□□	174

*Due to the importance of crash tests, cars with no results as of publication date cannot be given an overall rating.

Lexus SC300/400

Large

These two luxuriously-equipped coupes differ only in standard engines and luxury appointments; many items standard on the more expensive SC400 will cost extra on the SC300. For 1998, neither of these coupes received any major changes. All SC models have dual airbags and ABS. Inexplicably, side airbags aren't even an option for this class of car.

The SC300 shares a powerful 3-liter 6-cylinder engine with the GS300. For about $7,500 more, you can step up to the SC400, with the 4-liter V8, from the big Lexus LS400 and the all-new GS400. Be sure to get traction control. Handling is excellent, and ride is comfortably firm. The front seats are close to ideal for people of the right size, but check them out before you buy. Back seat is for kids only, and the trunk is skimpy. The instrument panel and controls are well designed.

The Ratings

	POOR ... GOOD
COMPARATIVE RATING*	□□□□□□□□□□
FRONTAL CRASH TEST	□□□□□□□□□□
SAFETY FEATURES	□□□□□■□□□□
FUEL ECONOMY	□□□■□□□□□□
PM COST	□□□□□■□□□□
REPAIR COST	□□■□□□□□□□
WARRANTY	□□□□□□□■□□
COMPLAINTS	□□□□□□□□■□
INSURANCE COST	■□□□□□□□□□

Safety

FRONTAL CRASH TEST	No government results
SIDE CRASH TEST	No government results
AIRBAGS	Dual Only
ANTI-LOCK BRAKES	4-wheel
DAY. RUNNING LIGHTS	None
BELT ADJUSTORS	None
BUILT-IN CHILD SEAT	None
PRETENSIONERS	Standard

General Information

WHERE MADE	Japan
YEAR OF PRODUCTION	Seventh
PARKING INDEX	Average
BUMPERS	Strong
THEFT RATING	Very High
TWINS	
DRIVE	Rear

Specifications

FUEL ECONOMY (cty/hwy)	19/24	Poor
DRIVING RANGE (miles)	453	Long
SEATING	5	
LENGTH (in.)	192.5	Long
HEAD/LEG ROOM (in.)	38.3/44.1	Roomy
INTERIOR SPACE (cu. ft.)	75.4	Vry. Cramped
CARGO SPACE (cu. ft.)	9.3	Very Small

Specifications may vary.

Prices

Model	Retail	Mkup
SC300	40,900	15%
SC400	52,700	16%

Competition

	POOR ... GOOD	Pg.
Lexus SC300/400	□□□□□□□□□□	**165**
Acura TL	□□□□□□□□■□	105
Lincoln Mark VIII	□□□□□□□■□□	167
Toyota Avalon	□□□□■□□□□□	213

*Due to the importance of crash tests, cars with no results as of publication date cannot be given an overall rating.

Lincoln Continental

Large

The Continental, a front-wheel drive sedan, received major revisions for 1998 including a brand new, more aerodynamic exterior and a revised engine. The front and rear ends are smoother and more rounded. Dual airbags and 4-wheel ABS are standard.

The new engine is a 4.6-liter V8 engine which provides plenty of power. There is plenty of interior space in this living room on wheels. The Continental's mufflers were upgraded to be quieter and, as for the ride, you can get an optional suspension system that lets you select from three different ride settings. Inside, you can get front and rear bench seats to seat up to six people, but most buyers opt for the two single bucket seats up front. No government crash tests are scheduled for next year.

The Ratings

	POOR — GOOD
COMPARATIVE RATING*	
FRONTAL CRASH TEST	
SAFETY FEATURES	
FUEL ECONOMY	
PM COST	
REPAIR COST	
WARRANTY	
COMPLAINTS	
INSURANCE COST	

Safety

FRONTAL CRASH TEST	No government results
SIDE CRASH TEST	No government results
AIRBAGS	Dual Only
ANTI-LOCK BRAKES	4-wheel
DAY. RUNNING LIGHTS	None
BELT ADJUSTORS	Front
BUILT-IN CHILD SEAT	None
PRETENSIONERS	None

General Information

WHERE MADE	U.S./Canada
YEAR OF PRODUCTION	First
PARKING INDEX	Very Hard
BUMPERS	Strong
THEFT RATING	
TWINS	
DRIVE	Front

Specifications

FUEL ECONOMY (cty/hwy)	17/25	Poor
DRIVING RANGE (miles)	420	Average
SEATING	6	
LENGTH (in.)	207.0	Very Long
HEAD/LEG ROOM (in.)	39.2/41.9	Average
INTERIOR SPACE (cu. ft.)	101.5	Roomy
CARGO SPACE (cu. ft.)	18.9	Large

Specifications may vary.

Prices

Model	Retail	Mkup
Continental	37,830	6%

Competition

	POOR — GOOD	Pg.
Lincoln Continental		**166**
Acura TL		105
Cadillac DeVille		117
Toyota Avalon		213

*Due to the importance of crash tests, cars with no results as of publication date cannot be given an overall rating.

Lincoln Mark VIII

Large

The Lincoln Mark VIII stands alone this year due to the discontinuation of its twins, the Ford Thunderbird and Mercury Cougar. The Mark VIII got a minor facelift last year and continues into 1998 unchanged. It has a distinctive styling, inside and out, and a slightly better ride than its former twins. Be sure to check out its full-width neon taillight system. Dual airbags and ABS are standard, and traction control is optional.

This two-ton car comes in only one well-equipped version, though you can add about $4,000 worth of options to the sticker price. The modular 4.6-liter V8 engine is smooth and quite powerful. The ride is outstanding on smooth roads. There's room for four, but the rear seat is tight. A top notch crash test performer, the Mark VIII is worth a test drive.

The Ratings

	POOR — GOOD
COMPARATIVE RATING	
FRONTAL CRASH TEST	
SAFETY FEATURES	
FUEL ECONOMY	
PM COST	
REPAIR COST	
WARRANTY	
COMPLAINTS	
INSURANCE COST	

Safety

FRONTAL CRASH TEST	Very Good
SIDE CRASH TEST	No government results
AIRBAGS	Dual Only
ANTI-LOCK BRAKES	4-wheel
DAY. RUNNING LIGHTS	None
BELT ADJUSTORS	None
BUILT-IN CHILD SEAT	None
PRETENSIONERS	None

General Information

WHERE MADE	U.S./Canada
YEAR OF PRODUCTION	Sixth
PARKING INDEX	Hard
BUMPERS	Strong
THEFT RATING	Average
TWINS	Mercury Cougar
DRIVE	Rear

Specifications

FUEL ECONOMY (cty/hwy)	18/26	Poor
DRIVING RANGE (miles)	396	Short
SEATING	5	
LENGTH (in.)	207.2	Very Long
HEAD/LEG ROOM (in.)	38.1/42.6	Average
INTERIOR SPACE (cu. ft.)	97.3	Average
CARGO SPACE (cu. ft.)	14.4	Average

Specifications may vary.

Prices

Model	Retail	Mkup
Mark VIII	37,830	10%
Mark VIII LSC	39,320	10%

Competition

	POOR — GOOD	Pg.
Lincoln Mark VIII		**167**
Acura TL		105
Chev. Monte Carlo		126
Infiniti I30		158

Lincoln Town Car

Large

The Town Car, along with its twins the Ford Crown Vic and the Mercury Grand Marquis, gets totally restyled for 1998. The largest of the three Lincoln cars, the Town Car is one of the few rear wheel drive cars still sold in the U.S. Conservative and huge, the Town Car's average buyer is 67 years young. While exterior changes appear minor, the improvements inside were numerous including a new suspension. Dual airbags and 4-wheel ABS are standard.

The engine is still the same 4.6-liter V8 found on previous versions of the Town Car. It produces 200 hp and is more than adequate to powering this over 4,000 lbs, six passenger sedan. The interior space was decreased but you won't notice it. The trunk space also decreased, as well, but the Town Car is still a competitive choice.

The Ratings

	POOR — GOOD
COMPARATIVE RATING*	
FRONTAL CRASH TEST	
SAFETY FEATURES	
FUEL ECONOMY	
PM COST	
REPAIR COST	
WARRANTY	
COMPLAINTS	
INSURANCE COST	

Safety

FRONTAL CRASH TEST	No government results
SIDE CRASH TEST	No government results
AIRBAGS	Dual Only
ANTI-LOCK BRAKES	4-wheel
DAY. RUNNING LIGHTS	None
BELT ADJUSTORS	Front
BUILT-IN CHILD SEAT	None
PRETENSIONERS	None

General Information

WHERE MADE	Canada
YEAR OF PRODUCTION	First
PARKING INDEX	Very Hard
BUMPERS	Strong
THEFT RATING	
TWINS	Crown Vic, Gr. Marquis
DRIVE	Rear

Specifications

FUEL ECONOMY (cty/hwy)	17/25	Poor
DRIVING RANGE (miles)	420	Average
SEATING	6	
LENGTH (in.)	215.3	Very Long
HEAD/LEG ROOM (in.)	39.2/42.6	Roomy
INTERIOR SPACE (cu. ft.)	133.0	Very Roomy
CARGO SPACE (cu. ft.)	20.6	Very Large

Specifications may vary.

Prices**

Model	Retail	Mkup
Town Car	37,950	13%
Town Car Signature	40,310	13%
Town Car Cartier	43,870	13%

Competition

	POOR — GOOD	Pg.
Lincoln Town Car		**168**
Acura TL		105
Cadillac DeVille		117
Toyota Avalon		213

**1998 prices not available at press time. Prices based on 1997 data.

*Due to the importance of crash tests, cars with no results as of publication date cannot be given an overall rating.

Mazda 626

Compact

The Mazda 626 is all-new for 1998. No new information was available at press time, so the data is for the outgoing 1997 model. However, the redesigned '98 model is pictured and '98 pricing is listed below.

The 626 is Mazda's alternative to the Accord and Camry. Over the past few years, it has done fairly well against stiff competition. On the 1997 model, dual airbags are standard, but you'll pay extra for ABS. The base 2.2-liter, 4-cylinder engine is adequate and reasonably economical. For more power, consider the 2.5-liter V6, available on the LX and ES. However, the bigger V6 does require premium gas and gets worse mileage. Room, comfort and trunk space are good for four. With more room up front and a smaller price tag, the 1997 626 competes fairly well against the more popular competition.

The Ratings

	POOR ... GOOD
COMPARATIVE RATING*	□□□□□□□□□□
FRONTAL CRASH TEST	□□□□□□□□□□
SAFETY FEATURES	□□□□■□□□□□
FUEL ECONOMY	□□□□□□■□□□
PM COST	□□□■□□□□□□
REPAIR COST	□□□□□□□■□□
WARRANTY	□■□□□□□□□□
COMPLAINTS	□□□□■□□□□□
INSURANCE COST	□□□□■□□□□□

Safety

FRONTAL CRASH TEST	No government results
SIDE CRASH TEST	No government results
AIRBAGS	Dual Only
ANTI-LOCK BRAKES	4-wheel (optional)
DAY. RUNNING LIGHTS	None
BELT ADJUSTORS	Front
BUILT-IN CHILD SEAT	None
PRETENSIONERS	None

General Information

WHERE MADE	Japan
YEAR OF PRODUCTION	First
PARKING INDEX	Easy
BUMPERS	Strong
THEFT RATING	
TWINS	
DRIVE	Front

Specifications

FUEL ECONOMY (cty/hwy)	26/34	Good
DRIVING RANGE (miles)	477	Very Long
SEATING	5	
LENGTH (in.)	184.4	Average
HEAD/LEG ROOM (in.)	39.2/43.5	Roomy
INTERIOR SPACE (cu. ft.)	97.2	Average
CARGO SPACE (cu. ft.)	13.8	Average

Specifications may vary.

Prices

Model	Retail	Mkup
626 DX	15,695	8%
626 LX	17,895	11%
626 ES V6	23,995	12%

Competition

	POOR ... GOOD	Pg.
Mazda 626	□□□□□□□□□□	**169**
Buick LeSabre	□□□□□□□□■□	112
Ford Taurus	□□□□□□■□□□	145
Oldsmobile Cutlass	□□□□□■□□□□	194

*Due to the importance of crash tests, cars with no results as of publication date cannot be given an overall rating.

Mazda Miata

Subcompact

Now a decade old, Mazda has hinted at some changes in store for the Miata in the near future, perhaps as soon as mid-year 1998. For now, the Miata continues into 1998 unchanged. Not much has changed since the original 1989 models; however, dual airbags are now standard, and ABS is an expensive option.

The 1.8-liter, 4-cylinder powering this small car should provide enough acceleration for most drivers. Brakes are good, even better with ABS. Controls and displays are sensibly designed. Fuel economy is just average and could be much better with only 2,200 pounds to haul. You won't get a soft, quiet ride, a spacious interior, or much of a trunk in a Miata, but you aren't be buying it for any of those reasons either. You'll get crisp, responsive handling, a peppy engine, and a car that will turn heads with the top down.

The Ratings

	POOR — GOOD
COMPARATIVE RATING	
FRONTAL CRASH TEST	
SAFETY FEATURES	
FUEL ECONOMY	
PM COST	
REPAIR COST	
WARRANTY	
COMPLAINTS	
INSURANCE COST	

Safety

FRONTAL CRASH TEST	Average
SIDE CRASH TEST	No government results
AIRBAGS	Dual Only
ANTI-LOCK BRAKES	4-wheel (optional)
DAY. RUNNING LIGHTS	None
BELT ADJUSTORS	None
BUILT-IN CHILD SEAT	None
PRETENSIONERS	None

General Information

WHERE MADE	Japan
YEAR OF PRODUCTION	Ninth
PARKING INDEX	Very Easy
BUMPERS	Weak
THEFT RATING	Average
TWINS	
DRIVE	Rear

Specifications

FUEL ECONOMY (cty/hwy)	23/29	Average
DRIVING RANGE (miles)	330	Very Short
SEATING	2	
LENGTH (in.)	155.4	Very Short
HEAD/LEG ROOM (in.)	37.1/42.7	Cramped
INTERIOR SPACE (cu. ft.)		
CARGO SPACE (cu. ft.)	3.6	Very Small

Specifications may vary.

Prices**

Model	Retail	Mkup
Miata	19,125	11%

Competition

	POOR — GOOD	Pg.
Mazda Miata		**170**
Acura Integra		103
Eagle Talon		139
Mitsubishi Eclipse		183

**1998 prices not available at press time. Prices based on 1997 data.

Mazda Millenia

Intermediate

For 1998, the Millenia receives no changes. After the demise of the 929, Mazda is betting the Millenia will be a winner in the competitive intermediate market. Dual airbags, belt adjustors for front occupants and ABS are standard.

The standard 2.5-liter V6 found on the base model is more than adequate; however, the Millenia S comes with the more powerful and responsive supercharged 2.3-liter V6. The base engine runs on regular fuel, while the S version requires premium fuel which will increase your operating costs. This front wheel drive sedan is slightly smaller than the old 929, though it still should be quite comfortable for 4 passengers, 5 in a pinch. A well designed car with good crash test scores, the Millenia deserves a close look in spite of its high maintenance costs.

The Ratings

	POOR — GOOD
COMPARATIVE RATING	
FRONTAL CRASH TEST	
SAFETY FEATURES	
FUEL ECONOMY	
PM COST	
REPAIR COST	
WARRANTY	
COMPLAINTS	
INSURANCE COST	

Safety

FRONTAL CRASH TEST	Very Good
SIDE CRASH TEST	No government results
AIRBAGS	Dual Only
ANTI-LOCK BRAKES	4-wheel
DAY. RUNNING LIGHTS	None
BELT ADJUSTORS	Front
BUILT-IN CHILD SEAT	None
PRETENSIONERS	None

General Information

WHERE MADE	Japan
YEAR OF PRODUCTION	Fourth
PARKING INDEX	Average
BUMPERS	Weak
THEFT RATING	Very High
TWINS	
DRIVE	Front

Specifications

FUEL ECONOMY (cty/hwy)	20/27	Average
DRIVING RANGE (miles)	432	Average
SEATING	5	
LENGTH (in.)	189.8	Long
HEAD/LEG ROOM (in.)	39.3/43.3	Roomy
INTERIOR SPACE (cu. ft.)	93.8	Average
CARGO SPACE (cu. ft.)	13.3	Small

Specifications may vary.

Prices

Model	Retail	Mkup
Millenia	28,995	13%
Millenia S	36,595	16%

Competition

	POOR — GOOD	Pg.
Mazda Millenia		**171**
BMW 3-Series		108
Merc.-Benz C-Class		174
Oldsmobile Aurora		193

Mazda MPV

Minivan

The Mazda MPV, or multi-purpose passenger vehicle, enters 1998 with few changes. With the Toyota Previa and Ford Aerostar gone, the MPV is one of the few remaining rear wheel drive minivans, although it looks more like a sport utility than a minivan. Dual airbags and 4-wheel ABS are standard.

The engine is a 2.0-liter V6 engine that gives out 155 hp. There are plenty of options to choose from, among which are the choice of four captain's chairs or a bench seat which will raise the seating to eight. Fuel economy is poor; it gets even worse if you choose the optional 4-wheel drive. Brakes, handling and ride are inferior to most minivans. Like the Honda minivan, the MPV comes with swing-out sedan style side doors. Despite good crash tests, the MPV is still outclassed by its competitors.

The Ratings

	POOR — GOOD
COMPARATIVE RATING	
FRONTAL CRASH TEST	
SAFETY FEATURES	
FUEL ECONOMY	
PM COST	
REPAIR COST	
WARRANTY	
COMPLAINTS	
INSURANCE COST	

Safety

FRONTAL CRASH TEST	Very Good
SIDE CRASH TEST	No government results
AIRBAGS	Dual Only
ANTI-LOCK BRAKES	4-wheel
DAY. RUNNING LIGHTS	None
BELT ADJUSTORS	None
BUILT-IN CHILD SEAT	None
PRETENSIONERS	None

General Information

WHERE MADE	Japan
YEAR OF PRODUCTION	Tenth
PARKING INDEX	Average
BUMPERS	Weak
THEFT RATING	
TWINS	
DRIVE	Rear/All

Specifications

FUEL ECONOMY (cty/hwy)	16/21	Poor
DRIVING RANGE (miles)	372	Short
SEATING	7/8	
LENGTH (in.)	183.5	Short
HEAD/LEG ROOM (in.)	40.0/40.4	Cramped
INTERIOR SPACE (cu. ft.)		
CARGO SPACE (cu. ft.)	42.1	Very Large

Specifications may vary.

Prices

Model	Retail	Mkup
MPV LX 2wd	23,095	11%
MPV LX 4wd	26,895	11%
MPV ES 4wd	28,895	11%

Competition

	POOR — GOOD	Pg.
Mazda MPV		**172**
Dodge Caravan		135
Isuzu Oasis		160
Pontiac Trans Sport		204

Mazda Protégé

Subcompact

The Protégé, unchanged for 1998, offers more room inside than you might expect from a subcompact car. The Protégé was the replacement for the 323 and its larger size has produced a better riding car. Dual airbags are standard, and ABS can be found on higher models.

The Protégé comes only in a sedan model with three trim levels. DX and LX models come standard with a 1.5-liter 4-cylinder engine that is relatively weak, although quite fuel efficient. The fancier ES comes with a 1.8-liter engine—more powerful, but less fuel efficient. The Protégé faces tough competition in a crowded subcompact market with the Honda Civic and Nissan Sentra and also with its American competitors, the Dodge/Plymouth Neon and Chevrolet Cavalier.

The Ratings

	POOR ... GOOD (position 1–10)
COMPARATIVE RATING*	
FRONTAL CRASH TEST	
SAFETY FEATURES	5
FUEL ECONOMY	8
PM COST	4
REPAIR COST	5
WARRANTY	2
COMPLAINTS	4
INSURANCE COST	1

Safety

FRONTAL CRASH TEST	No government results
SIDE CRASH TEST	No government results
AIRBAGS	Dual Only
ANTI-LOCK BRAKES	4-wheel (optional)
DAY. RUNNING LIGHTS	None
BELT ADJUSTORS	Front
BUILT-IN CHILD SEAT	None
PRETENSIONERS	None

General Information

WHERE MADE	Japan
YEAR OF PRODUCTION	Fourth
PARKING INDEX	Easy
BUMPERS	Strong
THEFT RATING	Very Low
TWINS	
DRIVE	Front

Specifications

FUEL ECONOMY (cty/hwy)	30/37	Good
DRIVING RANGE (miles)	493	Very Long
SEATING	5	
LENGTH (in.)	174.8	Short
HEAD/LEG ROOM (in.)	39.2/42.2	Average
INTERIOR SPACE (cu. ft.)	95.5	Average
CARGO SPACE (cu. ft.)	13.1	Small

Specifications may vary.

Prices

Model	Retail	Mkup
Protege DX	12,145	6%
Protege LX	13,545	8%
Protege ES	15,295	10%
Protege ES	15,295	10%

Competition

	POOR ... GOOD (position 1–10)	Pg.
Mazda Protege		**173**
Chevrolet Cavalier	8	122
Ford Escort	4	143
Honda Civic	7	150

*Due to the importance of crash tests, cars with no results as of publication date cannot be given an overall rating.

Mercedes-Benz C-Class

Intermediate

A new grille and headlamps highlight the minor changes for the 1998 C-Class. Though its styling resembles the larger S-class sedans, the C-class replaced the 190E as the smallest Mercedes sedan you can buy. Dual airbags, side airbags and ABS are standard.

The C-class is available with a 2.3-liter 4-cylinder engine (C230), a 2.8-liter 6-cylinder engine (C280), or a new 3.6-liter V6 engine (C360). Steering may not be quite as responsive as with a BMW 3-Series, but it should be close. Front seats are firm but very comfortable. The rear seat has more room than the 190's, so four adults will be more comfortable. Notable features include a unique brake system which shortens braking distances and a special child seat system that will detect a special child seat and deactivate the passenger-side airbag.

The Ratings

	POOR — GOOD
COMPARATIVE RATING	
FRONTAL CRASH TEST*	
SAFETY FEATURES	
FUEL ECONOMY	
PM COST	
REPAIR COST	
WARRANTY	
COMPLAINTS	
INSURANCE COST	

Safety

FRONTAL CRASH TEST	Good
SIDE CRASH TEST	No government results
AIRBAGS	Dual & Side
ANTI-LOCK BRAKES	4-wheel
DAY. RUNNING LIGHTS	None
BELT ADJUSTORS	Front/Rear
BUILT-IN CHILD SEAT	None
PRETENSIONERS	Standard

General Information

WHERE MADE	Germany
YEAR OF PRODUCTION	Fifth
PARKING INDEX	Easy
BUMPERS	Weak
THEFT RATING	Very High
TWINS	
DRIVE	Rear

Specifications

FUEL ECONOMY (cty/hwy)	23/30	Average
DRIVING RANGE (miles)	443	Long
SEATING	5	
LENGTH (in.)	177.4	Short
HEAD/LEG ROOM (in.)	37.2/41.5	Vry. Cramped
INTERIOR SPACE (cu. ft.)	88.0	Cramped
CARGO SPACE (cu. ft.)	12.9	Small

Specifications may vary.

Prices

Model	Retail	Mkup
C230	30,450	15%
C280	35,400	15%

Competition

	POOR — GOOD	Pg.
Merc.-Benz C-Class		174
Audi A4		106
BMW 3-Series		108
Oldsmobile Aurora		193

*A version of this vehicle is scheduled to be tested later this year. Results are expected to be similar.

Mercedes-Benz E-Class

Large

The E-Class has received critical acclaim since its introduction and sales of this $40,000 car have been high. No major changes for 1998. The E-Class has a distinctive styling with oval headlamps and a molded hood. Dual airbags, side airbags and ABS are standard.

With Mercedes' new nomenclature, the E stands for the mid-level size, and the numbers stand for the engine size. Available engines include a 3-liter diesel (E300), a new 3.2-liter V6 (E320), and a new 4.3-liter V8 (E430). Front seats are firm, yet relaxing on long drives; the rear seat is nearly as good. Notable features include a unique brake system which shortens braking distances and a special child seat system that will detect a special child seat and deactivate the passenger-side airbag.

The Ratings

	POOR — GOOD
COMPARATIVE RATING*	
FRONTAL CRASH TEST	
SAFETY FEATURES	
FUEL ECONOMY	
PM COST	
REPAIR COST	
WARRANTY	
COMPLAINTS	
INSURANCE COST	

Safety

FRONTAL CRASH TEST	No government results
SIDE CRASH TEST	No government results
AIRBAGS	Dual & Side
ANTI-LOCK BRAKES	4-wheel
DAY. RUNNING LIGHTS	None
BELT ADJUSTORS	Front/Rear
BUILT-IN CHILD SEAT	None
PRETENSIONERS	Standard

General Information

WHERE MADE	Germany
YEAR OF PRODUCTION	Third
PARKING INDEX	Average
BUMPERS	Weak
THEFT RATING	
TWINS	
DRIVE	Rear

Specifications

FUEL ECONOMY (cty/hwy)	21/29	Average
DRIVING RANGE (miles)	528	Very Long
SEATING	5	
LENGTH (in.)	189.4	Average
HEAD/LEG ROOM (in.)	37.6/41.3	Vry. Cramped
INTERIOR SPACE (cu. ft.)	95.0	Average
CARGO SPACE (cu. ft.)	15.3	Average

Specifications may vary.

Prices

Model	Retail	Mkup
E300	41,800	15%
E320	45,500	15%

Competition

	POOR — GOOD	Pg.
Merc.-Benz E-Class		**175**
Acura TL		105
Cadillac DeVille		117
Infiniti I30		158

*Due to the importance of crash tests, cars with no results as of publication date cannot be given an overall rating.

Mercury Cougar

Large

For 1998, the Cougar remains unchanged. A brand new Cougar, completely rebuilt from the ground up, will be introduced later this year as a 1999 model. The data and photo are from the outgoing 1997 model.

On the outgoing model, dual airbags are standard, but you'll have to pay extra for ABS. The Cougar comes in one model, the XR7, which has just about everything you need. Engine choices are a 3.8-liter V6 and a 4.6-liter V8 with much more power. The Cougar's long wheelbase leads to a smooth ride and handling is average for a car this large. There are no optional suspensions to give you a more high-performance ride. Inside, there's room for four and plenty of luggage space.

The Ratings

	POOR — GOOD
COMPARATIVE RATING	
FRONTAL CRASH TEST	
SAFETY FEATURES	
FUEL ECONOMY	
PM COST	
REPAIR COST	
WARRANTY	
COMPLAINTS	
INSURANCE COST	

Safety

FRONTAL CRASH TEST	Very Good
SIDE CRASH TEST	No government results
AIRBAGS	Dual Only
ANTI-LOCK BRAKES	4-wheel (optional)
DAY. RUNNING LIGHTS	None
BELT ADJUSTORS	None
BUILT-IN CHILD SEAT	None
PRETENSIONERS	None

General Information

WHERE MADE	U.S.
YEAR OF PRODUCTION	Tenth
PARKING INDEX	Average
BUMPERS	Strong
THEFT RATING	Low
TWINS	Lincoln Mark VIII
DRIVE	Rear

Specifications

FUEL ECONOMY (cty/hwy)	18/26	Poor
DRIVING RANGE (miles)	396	Short
SEATING	5	
LENGTH (in.)	199.9	Long
HEAD/LEG ROOM (in.)	38.1/42.5	Average
INTERIOR SPACE (cu. ft.)	102.0	Roomy
CARGO SPACE (cu. ft.)	15.0	Average

Specifications may vary.

Prices**

Model	Retail	Mkup
Cougar XR7	18,340	9%

Competition

	POOR — GOOD	Pg.
Mercury Cougar		**176**
Buick Riviera		115
Chev. Monte Carlo		126
Chrysler Sebring		132

**1998 prices not available at press time. Prices based on 1997 data.

Mercury Grand Marquis

Large

Based on the same chassis as the Ford Crown Victoria and the Lincoln Town Car, the Grand Marquis gets a revision for 1998. The new Grand Marquis should please Mercury traditionalists looking for a fluid, smooth ride. You'll find a new front and rear end, a new suspension system, bigger brakes and bigger tires. You still have to pay extra for ABS, but dual airbags are standard. Optional traction control is welcome addition.

The 4.6-liter V8 is responsive and powerful, but has predictably poor gas mileage for a car this size. While the Grand Marquis isn't quite as difficult to handle as some other big American sedans, it will benefit from the improvements to the suspension. There's plenty of room for six and their luggage.

The Ratings

	POOR □□□□□□□□ GOOD
COMPARATIVE RATING	□□□□□■□□□□
FRONTAL CRASH TEST*	□□□□□□□□□■
SAFETY FEATURES	□□□□■□□□□□
FUEL ECONOMY	□□□■□□□□□□
PM COST	□□□□□■□□□□
REPAIR COST	□□□□□■□□□□
WARRANTY	□■□□□□□□□□
COMPLAINTS	□□□■□□□□□□
INSURANCE COST	□□□□□□□□□■

Safety

FRONTAL CRASH TEST	Very Good
SIDE CRASH TEST	Very Good
AIRBAGS	Dual Only
ANTI-LOCK BRAKES	4-wheel (optional)
DAY. RUNNING LIGHTS	None
BELT ADJUSTORS	Front
BUILT-IN CHILD SEAT	None
PRETENSIONERS	None

General Information

WHERE MADE	Canada
YEAR OF PRODUCTION	Seventh
PARKING INDEX	Very Hard
BUMPERS	Strong
THEFT RATING	Low
TWINS	Crown Vic, Town Car
DRIVE	Rear

Specifications

FUEL ECONOMY (cty/hwy)	17/25	Poor
DRIVING RANGE (miles)	399	Short
SEATING	6	
LENGTH (in.)	212.0	Very Long
HEAD/LEG ROOM (in.)	39.4/42.5	Roomy
INTERIOR SPACE (cu. ft.)	112.0	Very Roomy
CARGO SPACE (cu. ft.)	20.6	Very Large

Specifications may vary.

Prices

Model	Retail	Mkup
Grand Marquis GS	23,100	7%
Grand Marquis LS	24,520	7%

Competition

	POOR □□□□□□□□ GOOD	Pg.
Merc. Gr. Marquis	□□□□□■□□□□	**177**
Buick Park Avenue	□□■□□□□□□□	113
Chevrolet Lumina	□□□■□□□□□□	123
Toyota Avalon	□□□□■□□□□□	213

*A version of this vehicle is scheduled to be tested later this year. Results are expected to be similar.

Mercury Mystique

Compact

For 1998, the Mystique comes with few changes other than a revised front grille. Other minor improvements include upgrades to the suspension and steering. Teamed with its twin, the Ford Contour, the Mystique has been attracting many buyers because of its ride and solid mid-size car features. Dual airbags are standard, but you'll have to pay extra for ABS and traction control.

The Mystique is about 6 inches longer than its predecessor, the Topaz, and front seat passengers are the biggest beneficiaries of the extra room. Both the base GS and the up-level LS come standard with a 2-liter engine that is only adequate. A more powerful 2.5-liter V6 with a tighter suspension system is optional. With good frontal and side crash test results, the Mystique is a good choice.

The Ratings

	POOR — GOOD
COMPARATIVE RATING	□□□□□□■□□□
FRONTAL CRASH TEST*	□□□□□□□■□□
SAFETY FEATURES	□□□□□■□□□□
FUEL ECONOMY	□□□□□□■□□□
PM COST	□□□□□□■□□□
REPAIR COST	□□□□□□□■□□
WARRANTY	□■□□□□□□□□
COMPLAINTS	□□□□■□□□□□
INSURANCE COST	□□□□■□□□□□

Safety

FRONTAL CRASH TEST	Good
SIDE CRASH TEST	Very Good
AIRBAGS	Dual Only
ANTI-LOCK BRAKES	4-wheel (optional)
DAY. RUNNING LIGHTS	None
BELT ADJUSTORS	Front
BUILT-IN CHILD SEAT	Optional
PRETENSIONERS	None

General Information

WHERE MADE	U.S./Canada/Mexico
YEAR OF PRODUCTION	Fourth
PARKING INDEX	Average
BUMPERS	Strong
THEFT RATING	Very Low
TWINS	Ford Contour
DRIVE	Front

Specifications

FUEL ECONOMY (cty/hwy)	24/35	Good
DRIVING RANGE (miles)	435	Average
SEATING	5	
LENGTH (in.)	184.8	Average
HEAD/LEG ROOM (in.)	39.0/42.4	Average
INTERIOR SPACE (cu. ft.)	89.6	Cramped
CARGO SPACE (cu. ft.)	13.9	Average

Specifications may vary.

Prices

Model	Retail	Mkup
Mystique GS	16,235	9%
Mystique LS	17,645	10%

Competition

	POOR — GOOD	Pg.
Mercury Mystique	□□□□□□■□□□	**178**
Buick Century	□□□□□□■□□□	111
Hyundai Sonata	□□■□□□□□□□	156
Pontiac Grand Prix	□□□□□■□□□□	202

*A version of this vehicle is scheduled to be tested later this year. Results are expected to be similar.

Mercury Sable

Intermediate

The Sable, twin to Ford's bread and butter Taurus, continues into 1998 with only minor revisions. Unlike the Taurus, the Sable does not sell nearly as well, but it is geared towards the upscale buyer—the luxury line of the Taurus. It has many more standard features. Dual airbags are standard and ABS is optional.

Like its headlights, the interior takes the shape of an ovoid which allows for easy-to-use controls and dash. The standard engine, a 3-liter V6, is quite powerful and delivers decent gas millage. For more power and slightly lower gas mileage, you can select the bigger version of the same engine. A stiff structure improves handling over the past Sables. There is plenty of room for 4 adults and you can even squeeze in 5 or 6 if needed. The optional child seat on the wagon is a must for parents.

The Ratings

	POOR → GOOD
COMPARATIVE RATING	□□□□□□□■□□
FRONTAL CRASH TEST*	□□□□□□□□■□
SAFETY FEATURES	□□□□□■□□□□
FUEL ECONOMY	□□□□■□□□□□
PM COST	□□□□□□□■□□
REPAIR COST	□□□□□■□□□□
WARRANTY	□■□□□□□□□□
COMPLAINTS	□□□□■□□□□□
INSURANCE COST	□□□□□□□□□■

Safety

FRONTAL CRASH TEST	Very Good
SIDE CRASH TEST	Good
AIRBAGS	Dual Only
ANTI-LOCK BRAKES	4-wheel (optional)
DAY. RUNNING LIGHTS	None
BELT ADJUSTORS	Front
BUILT-IN CHILD SEAT	Optional (wgn only)
PRETENSIONERS	None

General Information

WHERE MADE	U.S./Canada
YEAR OF PRODUCTION	Third
PARKING INDEX	Hard
BUMPERS	Strong
THEFT RATING	Very Low
TWINS	Ford Taurus
DRIVE	Front

Specifications

FUEL ECONOMY (cty/hwy)	20/28	Average
DRIVING RANGE (miles)	384	Short
SEATING	5	
LENGTH (in.)	199.7	Long
HEAD/LEG ROOM (in.)	39.4/42.2	Average
INTERIOR SPACE (cu. ft.)	101.8	Roomy
CARGO SPACE (cu. ft.)	16.0	Large

Specifications may vary.

Prices

Model	Retail	Mkup
Sable GS	19,445	9%
Sable LS	20,445	10%
Sable LS Wagon	22,285	10%

Competition

	POOR → GOOD	Pg.
Mercury Sable	□□□□□□□■□□	**179**
Buick LeSabre	□□□□□□□□■□	112
Oldsmobile Intrigue	□□□■□□□□□□	195
Toyota Camry	□■□□□□□□□□	214

*A version of this vehicle is scheduled to be tested later this year. Results are expected to be similar.

Mercury Tracer

Subcompact

Revised last year with its sibling the Escort, the Tracer receives no changes for 1998. Last year's revision provided a much rounder exterior and promises to be a better seller and, more importantly, a better car. Like other Mercurys, the Tracer is aimed at a more upscale car buyer unlike its Ford twin. The Tracer comes with standard dual airbags, however, and ABS is only optional.

The 2.0-liter, 4-cylinder engine has been refined and should produce quick accelerations and smooth shifts. As is expected in a small car, fuel economy should be good. Ride is comfortable, but don't expect a bump free drive. Noise levels are good under average acceleration, anything more than average and you may have to turn up the radio. The Tracer is an upscale sedan for a low price.

The Ratings

	POOR — GOOD
COMPARATIVE RATING	□□□□□■□□□□
FRONTAL CRASH TEST*	□□□□■□□□□□
SAFETY FEATURES	□□□□□■□□□□
FUEL ECONOMY	□□□□□□□■□□
PM COST	□□□□□□□■□□
REPAIR COST	□□□□□□□□□■
WARRANTY	□■□□□□□□□□
COMPLAINTS	□□□□■□□□□□
INSURANCE COST	□□□□■□□□□□

Safety

FRONTAL CRASH TEST	Average
SIDE CRASH TEST	Average
AIRBAGS	Dual Only
ANTI-LOCK BRAKES	4-wheel (optional)
DAY. RUNNING LIGHTS	None
BELT ADJUSTORS	Front
BUILT-IN CHILD SEAT	Optional
PRETENSIONERS	None

General Information

WHERE MADE	U.S./Canada/Mexico
YEAR OF PRODUCTION	Second
PARKING INDEX	Very Easy
BUMPERS	Strong
THEFT RATING	
TWINS	Ford Escort
DRIVE	Front

Specifications

FUEL ECONOMY (cty/hwy)	28/37	Good
DRIVING RANGE (miles)	422	Average
SEATING	5	
LENGTH (in.)	174.7	Short
HEAD/LEG ROOM (in.)	39.0/42.5	Average
INTERIOR SPACE (cu. ft.)	87.2	Cramped
CARGO SPACE (cu. ft.)	12.8	Small

Specifications may vary.

Prices

Model	Retail	Mkup
Tracer GS	11,355	7%
Tracer LS	12,710	7%
Tracer LS Wagon	14,205	7%

Competition

	POOR — GOOD	Pg.
Mercury Tracer	□□□□□■□□□□	180
Mitsubishi Galant	□□□■□□□□□□	184
Nissan Sentra	□□□□□□□■□□	190
Subaru Impreza	□□□□□□□□■□	209

*A version of this vehicle is scheduled to be tested later this year. Results are expected to be similar.

Mercury Villager

Minivan

The Villager minivan, a twin of the Nissan Quest, is more like a tall car than a minivan. Developed jointly with Nissan and built in Ohio, the Villager is available in three trim levels: base GS, luxury LS, and sport-luxury Nautica. The Villager's resemblance to the Dodge Caravan is no coincidence; Villager designers know who they need to beat. ABS and dual airbags are standard.

The 3.0-liter V6, with automatic overdrive, is acceptably responsive. Go for the towing package if you'll be hauling anything at all. The ride is a bit soft, very much like a regular passenger car's, with standard suspension. Handling is competent, but can be firmed up with the optional handling package. The integrated child seats are excellent options. The middle and rear seats are easy to remove to increase cargo space.

The Ratings

	POOR ... GOOD
COMPARATIVE RATING	□□■□□□□□□□
FRONTAL CRASH TEST	□□□□□□■□□□
SAFETY FEATURES	□□□□□□■□□□
FUEL ECONOMY	□□■□□□□□□□
PM COST	□□□□□□□□■□
REPAIR COST	□□□□■□□□□□
WARRANTY	□■□□□□□□□□
COMPLAINTS	□□□■□□□□□□
INSURANCE COST	□□□□□□□□□■

Safety

FRONTAL CRASH TEST	Good
SIDE CRASH TEST	No government results
AIRBAGS	Dual Only
ANTI-LOCK BRAKES	4-wheel
DAY. RUNNING LIGHTS	None
BELT ADJUSTORS	Front
BUILT-IN CHILD SEAT	Optional (two)
PRETENSIONERS	None

General Information

WHERE MADE	U.S./Canada/Japan
YEAR OF PRODUCTION	Sixth
PARKING INDEX	Hard
BUMPERS	Weak
THEFT RATING	Very Low
TWINS	Nissan Quest
DRIVE	Front

Specifications

FUEL ECONOMY (cty/hwy)	17/23	Poor
DRIVING RANGE (miles)	400	Short
SEATING	7	
LENGTH (in.)	190.2	Long
HEAD/LEG ROOM (in.)	39.4/39.9	Cramped
INTERIOR SPACE (cu. ft.)		
CARGO SPACE (cu. ft.)	126.0	Very Large

Specifications may vary.

Prices

Model	Retail	Mkup
Villager GS	20,705	10%
Villager LS	24,975	11%
Villager Nautica	26,805	11%

Competition

	POOR ... GOOD	Pg.
Mercury Villager	□□■□□□□□□□	**181**
Chevrolet Venture	□□□■□□□□□□	128
Dodge Caravan	□□■□□□□□□□	135
Honda Odyssey	□□□□□□■□□□	152

Mitsubishi Diamante

Large

Mitsubishi redesigned the Diamante last year, giving it a new exterior and refined interior. No major changes are in store for 1998. Previously optional, 4-wheel ABS is now standard along with dual airbags.

There are two trim levels, the base ES and up-level LS. Powering this new Diamante is a refined 3.5-liter V6 engine, which is good enough for this mid-size sedan. As with past Diamante's, the ride should be smooth and comfortable. The increase in length last year allowed for more room inside for passengers. A sixth cupholder was added for '98. Great safety features include an optional fold-down child safety seat and a standard 3-point seatbelt for the middle back seat. With its redesign, the new Diamante is a definite improvement over past versions.

The Ratings

	POOR — GOOD
COMPARATIVE RATING*	
FRONTAL CRASH TEST	
SAFETY FEATURES	
FUEL ECONOMY	
PM COST	
REPAIR COST	
WARRANTY	
COMPLAINTS	
INSURANCE COST	

Safety

FRONTAL CRASH TEST	No government results
SIDE CRASH TEST	No government results
AIRBAGS	Dual Only
ANTI-LOCK BRAKES	4-wheel
DAY. RUNNING LIGHTS	None
BELT ADJUSTORS	Front
BUILT-IN CHILD SEAT	Optional
PRETENSIONERS	Standard

General Information

WHERE MADE	Australia/Japan
YEAR OF PRODUCTION	Second
PARKING INDEX	Average
BUMPERS	Strong
THEFT RATING	
TWINS	
DRIVE	Front

Specifications

FUEL ECONOMY (cty/hwy)	18/26	Poor
DRIVING RANGE (miles)	418	Average
SEATING	5	
LENGTH (in.)	194.1	Long
HEAD/LEG ROOM (in.)	39.4/43.6	Very Roomy
INTERIOR SPACE (cu. ft.)	100.9	Roomy
CARGO SPACE (cu. ft.)	14.2	Average

Specifications may vary.

Prices

Model	Retail	Mkup
Diamante ES	27,650	16%
Diamante LS	33,050	18%

Competition

	POOR — GOOD	Pg.
Mitsu. Diamante		**182**
Chevrolet Lumina		123
Ford Crown Victoria		142
Nissan Maxima		188

*Due to the importance of crash tests, cars with no results as of publication date cannot be given an overall rating.

Mitsubishi Eclipse

Compact

As a twin of the Eagle Talon, a sedan brother of the Mitsubishi Galant, and the coupe cousin of the Chrysler Sebring and Dodge Avenger, its no wonder than the Eclipse looks vaguely familiar. The Eclipse gets no changes for 1998. Dual airbags are standard, but you'll have to pay extra for ABS.

The RS is the stripped-down base model and the GS has a few more bells and whistles, some of which are optional. Both of those models get the standard 2-liter engine, which may not be powerful enough for sports enthusiasts. The up-level GS-T and GSX both get a turbo version that pumps out 50% more power, and the GSX comes with all-wheel drive. The Eclipse does have a back seat, but it's not really meant for adults. A high number of complaints hurts the Eclipse, despite a good crash test performance.

The Ratings

	POOR — GOOD
COMPARATIVE RATING	□□■□□□□□□□
FRONTAL CRASH TEST*	□□□□□□■□□□
SAFETY FEATURES	□□□□■□□□□□
FUEL ECONOMY	□□□□□■□□□□
PM COST	□□□□□□■□□□
REPAIR COST	□□□□□□□■□□
WARRANTY	□□□□■□□□□□
COMPLAINTS	■□□□□□□□□□
INSURANCE COST	□□□□□□□□□■

Safety

FRONTAL CRASH TEST	Good
SIDE CRASH TEST	No government results
AIRBAGS	Dual Only
ANTI-LOCK BRAKES	4-wheel (optional)
DAY. RUNNING LIGHTS	None
BELT ADJUSTORS	Front
BUILT-IN CHILD SEAT	None
PRETENSIONERS	None

General Information

WHERE MADE	U.S./Canada/Japan
YEAR OF PRODUCTION	Fourth
PARKING INDEX	Average
BUMPERS	Strong
THEFT RATING	
TWINS	Eagle Talon
DRIVE	Front

Specifications

FUEL ECONOMY (cty/hwy)	23/33	Average
DRIVING RANGE (miles)	445	Long
SEATING	4	
LENGTH (in.)	172.4	Very Short
HEAD/LEG ROOM (in.)	37.9/43.3	Average
INTERIOR SPACE (cu. ft.)	79.1	Vry. Cramped
CARGO SPACE (cu. ft.)	16.6	Large

Specifications may vary.

Prices

Model	Retail	Mkup
Eclipse RS man.	15,740	20%
Eclipse GS man.	17,880	17%
Eclipse GS-T man.	21,980	19%
Eclipse GSX man.	25,320	27%

Competition

	POOR — GOOD	Pg.
Mitsubishi Eclipse	□□■□□□□□□□	**183**
Acura Integra	□□□□□■□□□□	103
Eagle Talon	□■□□□□□□□□	139
Mazda Miata	□□□■□□□□□□	170

*A version of this vehicle is scheduled to be tested later this year. Results are expected to be similar.

Mitsubishi Galant

Compact

Scheduled for a redesign next year, the Galant receives minor improvements for 1998 like window glass treated to block ultraviolet light. The lineup includes three trim levels, each with specific product features. Dual airbags have greatly improved results in the government's crash test program. ABS will cost you extra on all but the top of the line LS.

The base DE, mid-level ES, and up-level LS all come with the same 2.4-liter 4-cylinder engine, which is powerful but gets lousy mileage. An optional 2.5-liter V6 engine has more power, but will sacrifice even more fuel efficiency. The Galant's ride is on the firm side. The rear seat is somewhat uncomfortable, and the front seat's head and leg room is nothing to brag about. The price of the Galant helps it survive amidst more popular competition.

The Ratings	POOR — GOOD
COMPARATIVE RATING	□□□■□□□□□□
FRONTAL CRASH TEST	□□□□□□■□□□
SAFETY FEATURES	□□□□■□□□□□
FUEL ECONOMY	□□□□□■□□□□
PM COST	□■□□□□□□□□
REPAIR COST	□□□□□□□■□□
WARRANTY	□□□□■□□□□□
COMPLAINTS	□□■□□□□□□□
INSURANCE COST	□□□□□□□□□■

Safety	
FRONTAL CRASH TEST	Good
SIDE CRASH TEST	Poor
AIRBAGS	Dual Only
ANTI-LOCK BRAKES	4-wheel (optional)
DAY. RUNNING LIGHTS	None
BELT ADJUSTORS	Front
BUILT-IN CHILD SEAT	None
PRETENSIONERS	None

General Information	
WHERE MADE	U.S./Canada/Japan
YEAR OF PRODUCTION	Fifth
PARKING INDEX	Easy
BUMPERS	Strong
THEFT RATING	High
TWINS	
DRIVE	Front

Specifications		
FUEL ECONOMY (cty/hwy)	23/30	Average
DRIVING RANGE (miles)	456	Long
SEATING	5	
LENGTH (in.)	187.6	Average
HEAD/LEG ROOM (in.)	39.4/43.3	Roomy
INTERIOR SPACE (cu. ft.)	97.3	Average
CARGO SPACE (cu. ft.)	12.5	Small

Specifications may vary.

Prices

Model	Retail	Mkup
Galant DE man.	15,680	12%
Galant DE auto.	16,550	12%
Galant ES auto.	18,450	14%
Galant LS	25,310	18%

Competition

	POOR — GOOD	Pg.
Mitsubishi Galant	□□□■□□□□□□	**184**
Ford Escort	□□□■□□□□□□	143
Honda Civic	□□□□□□■□□□	150
Subaru Impreza	□□□□□□□□■□	209

Mitsubishi Mirage

Subcompact

The Mirage, Mitsubishi's entry level offering, remains unchanged for 1998 after a major revision last year. You can choose from either a sedan or coupe model with two trim levels. The revised car is longer and taller giving passengers more room inside which should make the ride much more comfortable. All Mirages have dual airbags, but ABS is optional.

The 1.5-liter 4-cylinder engine that comes with the base model Mirage DE is not very powerful, though you'll be pleased with its fuel economy. The 1.8-liter engine on the LS coupes and sedans is much more powerful, but gas mileage suffers dramatically. The Mirage handles crisply, and the interior is fairly comfortable for four people. Ride is decent. The redesign last year is a major improvement over previous models, keeping the Mirage competitive against tough competition.

The Ratings

	POOR — GOOD
COMPARATIVE RATING*	
FRONTAL CRASH TEST	
SAFETY FEATURES	
FUEL ECONOMY	
PM COST	
REPAIR COST	
WARRANTY	
COMPLAINTS	
INSURANCE COST	

Safety

FRONTAL CRASH TEST	No government results
SIDE CRASH TEST	No government results
AIRBAGS	Dual Only
ANTI-LOCK BRAKES	4-wheel (optional)
DAY. RUNNING LIGHTS	None
BELT ADJUSTORS	Front
BUILT-IN CHILD SEAT	None
PRETENSIONERS	None

General Information

WHERE MADE	Japan
YEAR OF PRODUCTION	Second
PARKING INDEX	Very Easy
BUMPERS	Strong
THEFT RATING	
TWINS	
DRIVE	Front

Specifications

FUEL ECONOMY (cty/hwy)	33/40	Very Good
DRIVING RANGE (miles)	488	Very Long
SEATING	5	
LENGTH (in.)	173.6	Very Short
HEAD/LEG ROOM (in.)	39.8/43.0	Roomy
INTERIOR SPACE (cu. ft.)	91.4	Cramped
CARGO SPACE (cu. ft.)	11.5	Small

Specifications may vary.

Prices

Model	Retail	Mkup
Mirage DE 2dr man.	10,830	10%
Mirage DE 4dr auto.	13,070	12%
Mirage LS 2dr. man.	14,330	13%
Mirage LS 4dr auto.	13,980	12%

Competition

	POOR — GOOD	Pg.
Mitsubishi Mirage		**185**
Chevrolet Cavalier		122
Mercury Tracer		180
Saturn SL/SW		208

*Due to the importance of crash tests, cars with no results as of publication date cannot be given an overall rating.

Nissan 240SX

Intermediate

Due for a revision next year, there are doubts whether the 240SX will still be around because of low sales. For 1998, it remains unchanged. The 240SX is less of a sports car than a luxury vehicle and it looks more like a Lexus than a Camaro. Dual airbags are standard, but you'll have to pay extra for ABS.

The 2.4-liter 4-cylinder engine is adequate, but won't please performance-seekers; unfortunately, you do not have another engine choice. The 240 comes in three trim levels: base, SE, or a new LE which will include leather seats. An improved interior should make the 240SX more comfortable to ride in, however, adults in the rear seats will still not be comfortable. The ride is smooth and the handling is good due to the wide stance of the car.

The Ratings

	POOR — GOOD
COMPARATIVE RATING	
FRONTAL CRASH TEST	
SAFETY FEATURES	
FUEL ECONOMY	
PM COST	
REPAIR COST	
WARRANTY	
COMPLAINTS	
INSURANCE COST	

Safety

FRONTAL CRASH TEST	Average
SIDE CRASH TEST	No government results
AIRBAGS	Dual Only
ANTI-LOCK BRAKES	4-wheel (optional)
DAY. RUNNING LIGHTS	None
BELT ADJUSTORS	None
BUILT-IN CHILD SEAT	None
PRETENSIONERS	None

General Information

WHERE MADE	Japan
YEAR OF PRODUCTION	Fourth
PARKING INDEX	Very Easy
BUMPERS	Strong
THEFT RATING	Very High
TWINS	
DRIVE	Rear

Specifications

FUEL ECONOMY (cty/hwy)	22/28	Average
DRIVING RANGE (miles)	430	Average
SEATING	5	
LENGTH (in.)	177.2	Short
HEAD/LEG ROOM (in.)	38.3/42.6	Average
INTERIOR SPACE (cu. ft.)	79.3	Vry. Cramped
CARGO SPACE (cu. ft.)	8.6	Very Small

Specifications may vary.

Prices**

Model	Retail	Mkup
240SX	18,359	12%
240SX SE	21,999	12%
240SX LE	24,449	12%

Competition

	POOR — GOOD	Pg.
Nissan 240SX		**186**
Chevrolet Camaro		121
Ford Mustang		144
Pontiac Firebird		200

**1998 prices not available at press time. Prices based on 1997 data.

Nissan Altima

Intermediate

The all-new Altima headlines Nissan's lineup for 1998. The changes include a new front end, more interior room and a restyled instrument panel. Road noise has also decreased with new sheet metal insulation. Dual airbags are standard, ABS is still optional.

A revised 2.4-liter, 4-cylinder engine powers the new Altima, providing 150 hp. Four trim levels are available with a variety of new options packages. Be sure to look over the options list carefully. A remote keyless entry and security system is standard on the SE and GLE models. Expect the Altima to compete well against tough competitors like the Taurus and Camry. The government will be performing frontal and side crash tests on the Altima later in the model year.

The Ratings

	POOR — GOOD
COMPARATIVE RATING*	
FRONTAL CRASH TEST	
SAFETY FEATURES	
FUEL ECONOMY	
PM COST	
REPAIR COST	
WARRANTY	
COMPLAINTS	
INSURANCE COST	

Safety

FRONTAL CRASH TEST	No government results
SIDE CRASH TEST	No government results
AIRBAGS	Dual Only
ANTI-LOCK BRAKES	4-wheel (optional)
DAY. RUNNING LIGHTS	None
BELT ADJUSTORS	Front
BUILT-IN CHILD SEAT	None
PRETENSIONERS	None

General Information

WHERE MADE	U.S.
YEAR OF PRODUCTION	First
PARKING INDEX	Average
BUMPERS	Strong
THEFT RATING	
TWINS	
DRIVE	Front

Specifications

FUEL ECONOMY (cty/hwy)	24/31	Average
DRIVING RANGE (miles)	445	Long
SEATING	5	
LENGTH (in.)	183.1	Short
HEAD/LEG ROOM (in.)	39.4/42.0	Average
INTERIOR SPACE (cu. ft.)	94.0	Average
CARGO SPACE (cu. ft.)	13.8	Average

Specifications may vary.

Prices

Model	Retail	Mkup
Altima XE man.	14,990	5%
Altima GXE auto.	17,990	10%
Altima SE man.	18,490	11%
Altima GLE	19,890	11%

Competition

	POOR — GOOD	Pg.
Nissan Altima		**187**
Ford Taurus		145
Oldsmobile Cutlass		194
Toyota Camry		214

*Due to the importance of crash tests, cars with no results as of publication date cannot be given an overall rating.

Nissan Maxima

Intermediate

Nissan's flagship, the Maxima, gets no major changes for 1998 after an interior and exterior restyling last year. Dual airbags are standard, and you'll have to pay extra for ABS. Side airbags are a must-have option.

The 3-liter V6 is very powerful and quite fuel efficient. The GXE and GLE trim levels come standard with an automatic transmission, while the SE comes with a five speed manual. The large wheelbase increases interior room, making the front seats quite comfortable and improving the ride. But handling is mediocre. The rear seats will be comfortable for most adults. You'll have the typical Nissan variety of trim levels and option packages, so shop carefully. Adequate crash test results and a good complaint rating make the Maxima worth test driving.

The Ratings

	POOR — GOOD
COMPARATIVE RATING	□□□■□□□□□□
FRONTAL CRASH TEST*	□□□□□■□□□□
SAFETY FEATURES	□□□□□■□□□□
FUEL ECONOMY	□□□□■□□□□□
PM COST	□□□□■□□□□□
REPAIR COST	■□□□□□□□□□
WARRANTY	□□□■□□□□□□
COMPLAINTS	□□□□□□□■□□
INSURANCE COST	□□□□■□□□□□

Safety

FRONTAL CRASH TEST	Average
SIDE CRASH TEST	Good
AIRBAGS	Dual/Opt. Side
ANTI-LOCK BRAKES	4-wheel (optional)
DAY. RUNNING LIGHTS	None
BELT ADJUSTORS	Front
BUILT-IN CHILD SEAT	None
PRETENSIONERS	None

General Information

WHERE MADE	Japan
YEAR OF PRODUCTION	Fourth
PARKING INDEX	Easy
BUMPERS	Strong
THEFT RATING	Very High
TWINS	Infinti I30
DRIVE	Front

Specifications

FUEL ECONOMY (cty/hwy)	22/27	Average
DRIVING RANGE (miles)	463	Long
SEATING	5	
LENGTH (in.)	189.4	Average
HEAD/LEG ROOM (in.)	40.1/43.9	Very Roomy
INTERIOR SPACE (cu. ft.)	99.6	Roomy
CARGO SPACE (cu. ft.)	14.5	Average

Specifications may vary.

Prices

Model	Retail	Mkup
Maxima GXE man.	21,499	10%
Maxima GXE auto.	23,249	12%
Maxima SE man.	23,499	12%
Maxima GLE	26,899	12%

Competition

	POOR — GOOD	Pg.
Nissan Maxima	□□□■□□□□□□	**188**
Chevrolet Lumina	□□□■□□□□□□	123
Merc. Gr. Marquis	□□□□□■□□□□	177
Toyota Avalon	□□□□■□□□□□	213

*A version of this vehicle is scheduled to be tested later this year. Results are expected to be similar.

Nissan Quest

Minivan

There are no changes for the Quest for 1998. Along with its twin, the Mercury Villager, the Quest has about as much interior room as a Dodge Caravan. Dual airbags are standard. 4-wheel ABS is standard on the GXE and GLE, optional on the base SE.

The only available engine is a 3-liter V6, but acceleration and power are good with poor fuel economy. You'll find the ride and handling are good by minivan standards. On the interior, seating is comfortable and the Quest offers integrated child safety seats which are great options for parents. With Nissan's flexible seating system, you should be able to arrange the seating to suit most any purpose. The middle and rear seats are easy to remove to increase cargo space. The Quest is among this year's top minivans.

The Ratings	POOR — GOOD
COMPARATIVE RATING	□□□□□■□□□□
FRONTAL CRASH TEST	□□□□□□■□□□
SAFETY FEATURES	□□□□□■□□□□
FUEL ECONOMY	□□■□□□□□□□
PM COST	□□□□□□□□■□
REPAIR COST	□□□□■□□□□□
WARRANTY	□□□■□□□□□□
COMPLAINTS	□□□□■□□□□□
INSURANCE COST	□□□□□□□□□■

Safety	
FRONTAL CRASH TEST	Good
SIDE CRASH TEST	No government results
AIRBAGS	Dual Only
ANTI-LOCK BRAKES	4-wheel (optional)
DAY. RUNNING LIGHTS	None
BELT ADJUSTORS	Front
BUILT-IN CHILD SEAT	Optional
PRETENSIONERS	None

General Information	
WHERE MADE	U.S.
YEAR OF PRODUCTION	Sixth
PARKING INDEX	Hard
BUMPERS	Strong
THEFT RATING	Very Low
TWINS	Mercury Villager
DRIVE	Front

Specifications		
FUEL ECONOMY (cty/hwy)	17/23	Poor
DRIVING RANGE (miles)	400	Short
SEATING	7	
LENGTH (in.)	189.9	Long
HEAD/LEG ROOM (in.)	39.5/39.9	Cramped
INTERIOR SPACE (cu. ft.)		
CARGO SPACE (cu. ft.)	125.0	Very Large

Specifications may vary.

Prices**

Model	Retail	Mkup
Quest XE	21,249	12%
Quest GXE	26,049	12%

Competition	POOR — GOOD	Pg.
Nissan Quest	□□□□□■□□□□	**189**
Chevrolet Venture	□□□■□□□□□□	128
Dodge Caravan	□□■□□□□□□□	135
Honda Odyssey	□□□□□□■□□□	152

**1998 prices not available at press time. Prices based on 1997 data.

Nissan Sentra

Subcompact

The Sentra's more rounded and contemporary styling has attracted many subcompact buyers since its redesign in 1996. The coupe model was converted into the 200SX and the sedan remained the Sentra. For '98, the front and rear end received some minor restyling. You have five trim levels to choose from: base, XE, GXE, GLE and the new sporty SE. Dual airbags are standard, optional ABS is available only on the GXE, SE, and GLE models.

The 1.6-liter, 4-cylinder engine, standard on all the trim levels except SE, is only adequate, but gets good gas mileage. The SE gets a 2.0-liter, 140 hp engine that provides more power. The Sentra handles and rides better than its predecessors and is good, basic transportation. With good crash test results and an up-to-date look, the Sentra is worth a test drive.

General Information

WHERE MADE	U.S./Mexico
YEAR OF PRODUCTION	Fourth
PARKING INDEX	Easy
BUMPERS	Strong
THEFT RATING	Low
TWINS	
DRIVE	Front

Prices

Model	Retail	Mkup
Sentra	11,499	5%
Sentra XE auto.	14,499	7%
Sentra GXE man.	14,899	10%
Sentra GLE auto.	16,549	10%

The Ratings

	POOR → GOOD
COMPARATIVE RATING	□□□□□□□■□□
FRONTAL CRASH TEST*	□□□□□□□■□□
SAFETY FEATURES	□□□□■□□□□□
FUEL ECONOMY	□□□□□□□□■□
PM COST	□□□□□■□□□□
REPAIR COST	□□□□□■□□□□
WARRANTY	□□□■□□□□□□
COMPLAINTS	□□□□□■□□□□
INSURANCE COST	■□□□□□□□□□

Safety

FRONTAL CRASH TEST	Good
SIDE CRASH TEST	No government results
AIRBAGS	Dual Only
ANTI-LOCK BRAKES	4-wheel (optional)
DAY. RUNNING LIGHTS	None
BELT ADJUSTORS	Front
BUILT-IN CHILD SEAT	None
PRETENSIONERS	None

Specifications

FUEL ECONOMY (cty/hwy)	30/40	Very Good
DRIVING RANGE (miles)	462	Long
SEATING	5	
LENGTH (in.)	171.1	Very Short
HEAD/LEG ROOM (in.)	39.1/42.3	Average
INTERIOR SPACE (cu. ft.)	87.2	Cramped
CARGO SPACE (cu. ft.)	10.7	Very Small

Specifications may vary.

Competition

	POOR → GOOD	Pg.
Nissan Sentra	□□□□□□□■□□	**190**
Chevrolet Cavalier	□□□□□□□■□□	122
Honda Civic	□□□□□□■□□□	150
Saturn SL/SW	□□□□□□□□□■	208

*A version of this vehicle is scheduled to be tested later this year. Results are expected to be similar.

Oldsmobile 88

Large

For 1998, the Oldsmobile 88 remains unchanged. The 88, which shares a platform with the Buick LeSabre and Pontiac Bonneville, used to come in three trim levels, but now only has two: the base and LS. The LSS trim level has becomes its own line (but don't be fooled, it's still based on the 88). Dual airbags and ABS are standard.

The 88's 3.8-liter V6, connected to an automatic overdrive, delivers plenty of smooth power. You no longer have another engine choice as in years past, but this one should do well. The 88's suspension favors a too-soft ride at the expense of handling. However, the optional touring suspension and speed-sensitive steering renders good handling and a comfortable ride. The LSS is slightly smaller and aimed at the import car buyer. The 88, with good crash tests, is worth considering.

The Ratings

	POOR → GOOD
COMPARATIVE RATING	□□□□□□□□■□
FRONTAL CRASH TEST	□□□□□□□■□□
SAFETY FEATURES	□□□□□■□□□□
FUEL ECONOMY	□□□□■□□□□□
PM COST	□□□□□■□□□□
REPAIR COST	□□□□□□■□□□
WARRANTY	□□■□□□□□□□
COMPLAINTS	□□□□□□■□□□
INSURANCE COST	□□□□□□□□□■

Safety

FRONTAL CRASH TEST	Good
SIDE CRASH TEST	No government results
AIRBAGS	Dual Only
ANTI-LOCK BRAKES	4-wheel
DAY. RUNNING LIGHTS	Standard
BELT ADJUSTORS	Front
BUILT-IN CHILD SEAT	None
PRETENSIONERS	None

General Information

WHERE MADE	U.S.
YEAR OF PRODUCTION	Seventh
PARKING INDEX	Hard
BUMPERS	Strong
THEFT RATING	Very Low
TWINS	LeSabre, Bonneville
DRIVE	Front

Specifications

FUEL ECONOMY (cty/hwy)	19/29	Average
DRIVING RANGE (miles)	432	Average
SEATING	5	
LENGTH (in.)	200.4	Very Long
HEAD/LEG ROOM (in.)	38.7/42.5	Average
INTERIOR SPACE (cu. ft.)	106.0	Roomy
CARGO SPACE (cu. ft.)	18.0	Large

Specifications may vary.

Prices

Model	Retail	Mkup
88	22,795	9%
88 LS	24,195	9%

Competition

	POOR → GOOD	Pg.
Oldsmobile 88	□□□□□□□□■□	**191**
Buick LeSabre	□□□□□□□□■□	112
Ford Taurus	□□□□□□■□□□	145
Toyota Camry	□■□□□□□□□□	214

Oldsmobile Achieva

Compact

Industry sources say the Achieva will likely be replaced in mid-1998 by the Alero. As of press time, no information is available on the Alero. Until then, the Achieva will enter 1998 with no major changes. This solid car comes with dual airbags and 4-wheel ABS is standard.

The Achieva is nearly as large as some mid-size cars, but you'll find its back seat cramped for adults. The new standard 2.4-liter 4-cylinder engine is adequate, and the optional 3.1-liter V6 only gives you five more horsepower. At least you don't lose much in fuel economy. Speed-sensitive steering is standard, and the suspension is firm. A very poor performance on government side crash tests prevents the Achieva from being a Best Bet.

The Ratings

	POOR — GOOD
COMPARATIVE RATING	
FRONTAL CRASH TEST	
SAFETY FEATURES	
FUEL ECONOMY	
PM COST	
REPAIR COST	
WARRANTY	
COMPLAINTS	
INSURANCE COST	

Safety

FRONTAL CRASH TEST	Very Good
SIDE CRASH TEST	Very Poor
AIRBAGS	Dual Only
ANTI-LOCK BRAKES	4-wheel
DAY. RUNNING LIGHTS	Standard
BELT ADJUSTORS	None
BUILT-IN CHILD SEAT	None
PRETENSIONERS	None

General Information

WHERE MADE	U.S.
YEAR OF PRODUCTION	Seventh
PARKING INDEX	Easy
BUMPERS	Strong
THEFT RATING	Very Low
TWINS	Pont. Grand Am
DRIVE	Front

Specifications

FUEL ECONOMY (cty/hwy)	22/32	Average
DRIVING RANGE (miles)	410	Average
SEATING	5	
LENGTH (in.)	187.9	Average
HEAD/LEG ROOM (in.)	37.8/43.1	Average
INTERIOR SPACE (cu. ft.)	88.0	Cramped
CARGO SPACE (cu. ft.)	14.0	Average

Specifications may vary.

Prices

Model	Retail	Mkup
Achieva SL	17,815	6%

Competition

	POOR — GOOD	Pg.
Olds Achieva		**192**
Chrysler Sebring		132
Oldsmobile Cutlass		194
Pontiac Grand Am		201

Oldsmobile Aurora

Large

First introduced in 1995, the Aurora enters 1998 with only minor changes. The Aurora represents Oldsmobile's first attempt at updating the styling of their aging cars. The Onstar roadside assistance system is now available as an option. Dual airbags, ABS, traction control, speed-variable power steering, and a host of other items are standard.

The Aurora benefits greatly from a very rigid structure and rides well for a car its size. However, the car wallows in turns which is typical of large cars. The 4-liter V8 is more powerful than most any of its competitors, and its fuel economy, though not notable by any means, holds its own with the competition. Room for five is more than spacious, though not quite as generous as some of the larger domestic cars, and it's priced lower than the smaller imports it targets.

The Ratings

	POOR — GOOD
COMPARATIVE RATING	■□□□□□□□□□
FRONTAL CRASH TEST	□□□□■□□□□□
SAFETY FEATURES	□□□□□■□□□□
FUEL ECONOMY	□□□■□□□□□□
PM COST	□□□□■□□□□□
REPAIR COST	□□□■□□□□□□
WARRANTY	□□□□□□■□□□
COMPLAINTS	□□□□■□□□□□
INSURANCE COST	■□□□□□□□□□

Safety

FRONTAL CRASH TEST	Average
SIDE CRASH TEST	No government results
AIRBAGS	Dual Only
ANTI-LOCK BRAKES	4-wheel
DAY. RUNNING LIGHTS	Standard
BELT ADJUSTORS	Front
BUILT-IN CHILD SEAT	None
PRETENSIONERS	None

General Information

WHERE MADE	U.S./Canada
YEAR OF PRODUCTION	Fourth
PARKING INDEX	Very Hard
BUMPERS	Strong
THEFT RATING	Very Low
TWINS	Park Ave., Riviera, Seville
DRIVE	Front

Specifications

FUEL ECONOMY (cty/hwy)	17/26	Poor
DRIVING RANGE (miles)	440	Average
SEATING	5	
LENGTH (in.)	205.4	Very Long
HEAD/LEG ROOM (in.)	38.4/42.6	Average
INTERIOR SPACE (cu. ft.)	102.0	Roomy
CARGO SPACE (cu. ft.)	16.1	Large

Specifications may vary.

Prices

Model	Retail	Mkup
Aurora	35,960	11%

Competition

	POOR — GOOD	Pg.
Oldsmobile Aurora	■□□□□□□□□□	**193**
Buick Riviera	■□□□□□□□□□	115
Infiniti I30	□□□□□□□□□■	158
Saab 9000	□□□□■□□□□□	206

Oldsmobile Cutlass

Intermediate

Last year, Oldsmobile introduced the new Cutlass, twin of the Chevrolet Malibu, in an effort to attract younger buyers. With sleeker lines and an improved interior, the Cutlass was a nice addition to Oldsmobile's lineup. For 1998, the Cutlass remains unchanged. Dual airbags are standard, ABS is optional.

Powering the new Cutlass will be an improved 3.1 liter V6 engine which should provide good, smooth power. A refined suspension should make the ride more enjoyable and the noise levels should be acceptable. Because of an increased wheelbase, passengers will have more head and leg room, making the refined interior very comfortable. Overall, this should be a very competitive car, except the poor side crash performance is a cause for concern.

The Ratings

	POOR — GOOD
COMPARATIVE RATING	
FRONTAL CRASH TEST	
SAFETY FEATURES	
FUEL ECONOMY	
PM COST	
REPAIR COST	
WARRANTY	
COMPLAINTS	
INSURANCE COST	

Safety

FRONTAL CRASH TEST	Good
SIDE CRASH TEST	Poor
AIRBAGS	Dual Only
ANTI-LOCK BRAKES	4-wheel (optional)
DAY. RUNNING LIGHTS	Standard
BELT ADJUSTORS	Front
BUILT-IN CHILD SEAT	None
PRETENSIONERS	None

General Information

WHERE MADE	U.S.
YEAR OF PRODUCTION	Second
PARKING INDEX	Average
BUMPERS	Strong
THEFT RATING	
TWINS	Chevy Malibu
DRIVE	Front

Specifications

FUEL ECONOMY (cty/hwy)	20/29	Average
DRIVING RANGE (miles)	380	Short
SEATING	5	
LENGTH (in.)	192.0	Long
HEAD/LEG ROOM (in.)	39.4/42.2	Average
INTERIOR SPACE (cu. ft.)	98.0	Average
CARGO SPACE (cu. ft.)	17.0	Large

Specifications may vary.

Prices

Model	Retail	Mkup
Cutlass GL	17,800	9%
Cutlass GLS	19,425	9%

Competition

	POOR — GOOD	Pg.
Olds Cutlass		**194**
Buick LeSabre		112
Mercury Sable		179
Toyota Camry		214

Oldsmobile Intrigue

Intermediate

With the introduction of the 1998 Oldsmobile Intrigue, Olds wants to win over luxury import buyers, who like the Toyota Camry, Honda Accord and Nissan Maxima. A replacement for the geriatric Cutlass Supreme, the Intrigue looks vaguely like the Oldsmobile Aurora, but shares a platform with the Buick Regal and Pontiac Grand Prix. Dual airbags, 4-wheel ABS and traction control all come standard.

You'll find a 3.8-liter V6 engine under the hood, which provides adequate power. Interior space is good, and trunk space is ample. Consider the autobahn package which includes bigger tires, better steering and a higher performance brake system. A good performer on government crash tests, the Intrigue could give import buyers something to consider.

General Information

WHERE MADE	U.S./Canada
YEAR OF PRODUCTION	First
PARKING INDEX	Average
BUMPERS	Strong
THEFT RATING	
TWINS	Century, Regal, Gr. Prix
DRIVE	Front

Prices

Model	Retail	Mkup
Intrigue	20,700	9%
Intrigue GL	22,100	9%

The Ratings

	POOR — GOOD
COMPARATIVE RATING	
FRONTAL CRASH TEST*	
SAFETY FEATURES	
FUEL ECONOMY	
PM COST	
REPAIR COST	
WARRANTY	
COMPLAINTS	
INSURANCE COST	

Safety

FRONTAL CRASH TEST	Good
SIDE CRASH TEST	No government results
AIRBAGS	Dual Only
ANTI-LOCK BRAKES	4-wheel
DAY. RUNNING LIGHTS	Standard
BELT ADJUSTORS	Front
BUILT-IN CHILD SEAT	None
PRETENSIONERS	None

Specifications

FUEL ECONOMY (cty/hwy)	19/30	Average
DRIVING RANGE (miles)	450	Long
SEATING	5	
LENGTH (in.)	195.9	Long
HEAD/LEG ROOM (in.)	39.3/42.4	Roomy
INTERIOR SPACE (cu. ft.)	102.0	Roomy
CARGO SPACE (cu. ft.)	16.0	Large

Specifications may vary.

Competition

	POOR — GOOD	Pg.
Oldsmobile Intrigue		**195**
Chevrolet Lumina		123
Ford Taurus		145
Toyota Camry		214

*A version of this vehicle is scheduled to be tested later this year. Results are expected to be similar.

Oldsmobile Silhouette

Minivan

A new exterior and interior style and the addition of a fourth door last year turned the Silhouette, and its GM minivans twins the Chevrolet Venture and the Pontiac Trans Sport, into an attractive alternative to their chief competitors, the Chrysler minivans. Dual airbags and 4-wheel ABS are standard. Standard side airbags are a great addition for 1998.

There are three models available: the base, GL and GLS. Each comes with an increasingly higher level of standard equipment. This new minivan is powered by a 3.4 liter V6 which should provide good acceleration. There are many different seating arrangements and there are plenty of cup holders. A handy option is the power assist right-side sliding door. Parents should consider the two built-in child seats. The new Silhouette should compete well.

The Ratings

	POOR — GOOD
COMPARATIVE RATING	
FRONTAL CRASH TEST*	
SAFETY FEATURES	
FUEL ECONOMY	
PM COST	
REPAIR COST	
WARRANTY	
COMPLAINTS	
INSURANCE COST	

Safety

FRONTAL CRASH TEST	Good
SIDE CRASH TEST	No government results
AIRBAGS	Dual & Side
ANTI-LOCK BRAKES	4-wheel
DAY. RUNNING LIGHTS	Standard
BELT ADJUSTORS	Front
BUILT-IN CHILD SEAT	Optional (two)
PRETENSIONERS	Standard

General Information

WHERE MADE	U.S./Canada
YEAR OF PRODUCTION	Second
PARKING INDEX	Average
BUMPERS	Weak
THEFT RATING	
TWINS	Venture, Trans Sport
DRIVE	Front

Specifications

FUEL ECONOMY (cty/hwy)	18/25	Poor
DRIVING RANGE (miles)	440	Average
SEATING	7/8	
LENGTH (in.)	187.4	Average
HEAD/LEG ROOM (in.)	39.9/39.9	Cramped
INTERIOR SPACE (cu. ft.)		
CARGO SPACE (cu. ft.)	133.0	Very Large

Specifications may vary.

Prices

Model	Retail	Mkup
Silhouette GL	23,965	11%
Silhouette GS	24,430	11%
Silhouette GLS	27,165	11%

Competition

	POOR — GOOD	Pg.
Olds Silhouette		**196**
Chrys. T & C		133
Mercury Villager		181
Honda Odyssey		152

*A version of this vehicle is scheduled to be tested later this year. Results are expected to be similar.

Plymouth Breeze

Intermediate

The Breeze, along with its close twins, the Chrysler Cirrus and Dodge Stratus, carryover into 1998 with little changes. Essentially a base model to its more upscale twins, the Breeze does get the Espresso package for 1998 which includes wheel covers, accent colors on the front and rear end and a premium audio system. Dual airbags and 4-wheel ABS are standard.

Only one model is available and it comes standard with the 2.0-liter engine with a manual transmission. A 2.4-liter engine is optional and provides more power. The cab-forward design gives passenger ample interior space. The Breeze only performed average on side crash tests and no frontal scores are available. A low price keeps the Breeze competitive and the optional built-in child seat will interest parents.

The Ratings

	POOR □□□□□□□□□□ GOOD
COMPARATIVE RATING*	□□□□□□□□□□
FRONTAL CRASH TEST	□□□□□□□□□□
SAFETY FEATURES	□□□□□□■□□□
FUEL ECONOMY	□□□□□□□■□□
PM COST	□□□□□□■□□□
REPAIR COST	□□□□□□□□■□
WARRANTY	□■□□□□□□□□
COMPLAINTS	□□□□□□□□■□
INSURANCE COST	□□□□■□□□□□

Safety

FRONTAL CRASH TEST	No government results
SIDE CRASH TEST	Average
AIRBAGS	Dual Only
ANTI-LOCK BRAKES	4-wheel
DAY. RUNNING LIGHTS	None
BELT ADJUSTORS	None
BUILT-IN CHILD SEAT	Optional
PRETENSIONERS	None

General Information

WHERE MADE	U.S.
YEAR OF PRODUCTION	Third
PARKING INDEX	Average
BUMPERS	Weak
THEFT RATING	
TWINS	Chrys. Cirrus, Dodge Stratus
DRIVE	Front

Specifications

FUEL ECONOMY (cty/hwy)	26/37	Good
DRIVING RANGE (miles)	512	Very Long
SEATING	5	
LENGTH (in.)	186.7	Average
HEAD/LEG ROOM (in.)	38.1/42.3	Cramped
INTERIOR SPACE (cu. ft.)	96.0	Average
CARGO SPACE (cu. ft.)	16.0	Large

Specifications may vary.

Prices

Model	Retail	Mkup
Breeze	14,675	9%

Competition

	POOR □□□□□□□□□□ GOOD	Pg.
Plymouth Breeze	□□□□□□□□□□	**197**
Buick Regal	□□□□□■□□□□	114
Oldsmobile Achieva	□□□□□□□□□■	192
Pontiac Grand Am	□□□□□□□■□□	201

*Due to the importance of crash tests, cars with no results as of publication date cannot be given an overall rating.

Plymouth Voyager

Minivan

The Voyager, along with the other Chrysler minivans, is leading the pack in sales in a highly competitive minivan market. Safety features include standard dual airbags and a structure that meets 1999 government side impact standards for trucks, vans and 4x4s early. Unfortunately, you have to pay extra for ABS.

You get to choose between four engines: an inadequate 2.5-liter 4-cylinder, an adequate 3-liter V6, or the more powerful 3.3-liter V6. All are equally efficient. Since Grand Voyagers have a longer wheelbase and a body with more room, the 3.3-liter is worth the extra money. Handling improves with the heavy duty suspension, and the ride remains good. The built-in child restraints are an excellent option. Of the three Chrysler minivans, the Voyager is the most affordable.

The Ratings

	POOR → GOOD
COMPARATIVE RATING	□■□□□□□□□□
FRONTAL CRASH TEST*	□□□□□□□■□□
SAFETY FEATURES	□□□□□□■□□□
FUEL ECONOMY	□□□■□□□□□□
PM COST	□□□□□□□□■□
REPAIR COST	□□□□□□□□■□
WARRANTY	□■□□□□□□□□
COMPLAINTS	■□□□□□□□□□
INSURANCE COST	□□□□■□□□□□

Safety

FRONTAL CRASH TEST	Good
SIDE CRASH TEST	No government results
AIRBAGS	Dual Only
ANTI-LOCK BRAKES	4-wheel (optional)
DAY. RUNNING LIGHTS	None
BELT ADJUSTORS	Front/Rear
BUILT-IN CHILD SEAT	Optional (two)
PRETENSIONERS	None

General Information

WHERE MADE	U.S./Canada
YEAR OF PRODUCTION	Third
PARKING INDEX	Average
BUMPERS	Strong
THEFT RATING	Very Low
TWINS	Caravan, T & Country
DRIVE	Front

Specifications

FUEL ECONOMY (cty/hwy)	20/25	Poor
DRIVING RANGE (miles)	460	Long
SEATING	7	
LENGTH (in.)	186.3	Average
HEAD/LEG ROOM (in.)	39.8/40.6	Cramped
INTERIOR SPACE (cu. ft.)		
CARGO SPACE (cu. ft.)	142.9	Very Large

Specifications may vary.

Prices

Model	Retail	Mkup
Voyager	17,415	10%
Grand Voyager	20,125	10%
Voyager SE	21,290	11%
Grand Voyager SE	22,285	10%

Competition

	POOR → GOOD	Pg.
Plymouth Voyager	□■□□□□□□□□	**198**
Chevrolet Venture	□□□■□□□□□□	128
Ford Windstar	□■□□□□□□□□	146
Isuzu Oasis	□□□□□□□□□■	160

*A version of this vehicle is scheduled to be tested later this year. Results are expected to be similar.

Pontiac Bonneville

Large

A roomy full-size sports car is the best description for the Pontiac Bonneville. The base model is the SE, and the SSE is the up-level version. The SLE is a sporty package available on the SE. Traction control is available on the SSE, and a supercharged engine is offered on both the SE and SSE. Dual airbags and ABS are standard; daytime running lamps are a great standard safety feature.

You can easily spend over $25,000 for a Bonneville, so shop wisely. Stick to the base SE with the performance and handling package. The base 3.8-liter V6 is powerful enough; the optional, supercharged V6 only adds a little more power and more repair complexity. Interior room and trunk space is good; the driver's visibility could be better. The Bonneville is a viable alternative to the Japanese luxury sports sedans.

The Ratings

	POOR → GOOD
COMPARATIVE RATING	□□□□□□□□□■
FRONTAL CRASH TEST*	□□□□□□□■□□
SAFETY FEATURES	□□□□□■□□□□
FUEL ECONOMY	□□□□■□□□□□
PM COST	□□□□□■□□□□
REPAIR COST	□□□□□□□■□□
WARRANTY	□■□□□□□□□□
COMPLAINTS	□□□□□□□■□□
INSURANCE COST	□□□□□□□□□■

Safety

FRONTAL CRASH TEST	Good
SIDE CRASH TEST	No government results
AIRBAGS	Dual Only
ANTI-LOCK BRAKES	4-wheel
DAY. RUNNING LIGHTS	Standard
BELT ADJUSTORS	Front
BUILT-IN CHILD SEAT	None
PRETENSIONERS	None

General Information

WHERE MADE	U.S.
YEAR OF PRODUCTION	Seventh
PARKING INDEX	Hard
BUMPERS	Strong
THEFT RATING	Very Low
TWINS	LeSabre, Olds 88
DRIVE	Front

Specifications

FUEL ECONOMY (cty/hwy)	19/28	Average
DRIVING RANGE (miles)	432	Average
SEATING	5	
LENGTH (in.)	200.5	Very Long
HEAD/LEG ROOM (in.)	39.2/42.6	Roomy
INTERIOR SPACE (cu. ft.)	110.0	Very Roomy
CARGO SPACE (cu. ft.)	18.0	Large

Specifications may vary.

Prices

Model	Retail	Mkup
Bonneville SE	22,390	13%
Bonneville SSE	29,390	9%

Competition

	POOR → GOOD	Pg.
Pontiac Bonneville	□□□□□□□□□■	199
BMW 3 Series	□□□□□□□□□■	108
Ford Taurus	□□□□□□■□□□	145
Toyota Camry	□■□□□□□□□□	214

*A version of this vehicle is scheduled to be tested later this year. Results are expected to be similar.

Pontiac Firebird

Intermediate

Like its twin, the Camaro, the Firebird has been a mainstay in the American sports car market for years. For 1998, the Firebird gets a restyling that is sure to turn heads. Unfortunately, '98 model information was unavailable at press time, so we've included data is from the '97 model. However, the Firebird does continues to be a strong crash test performer plus dual airbags is standard; ABS is optional.

The standard 3.8 liter V6 should offer good power and acceleration. The Trans Am comes standard with a 5.7-Liter V8 that is more powerful and only slightly less economical than the standard engine. The ride is firm and the handling is good. Room inside is good for the driver and front seat passenger.

The Ratings

	POOR → GOOD
COMPARATIVE RATING	□■□□□□□□□□
FRONTAL CRASH TEST	□□□□□□□□□■
SAFETY FEATURES	□□□□□■□□□□
FUEL ECONOMY	□□□□■□□□□□
PM COST	□□□□□■□□□□
REPAIR COST	□□□□■□□□□□
WARRANTY	□■□□□□□□□□
COMPLAINTS	□□□■□□□□□□
INSURANCE COST	■□□□□□□□□□

Safety

FRONTAL CRASH TEST	Very Good
SIDE CRASH TEST	Good
AIRBAGS	Dual Only
ANTI-LOCK BRAKES	4-wheel (optional)
DAY. RUNNING LIGHTS	Standard
BELT ADJUSTORS	None
BUILT-IN CHILD SEAT	None
PRETENSIONERS	None

General Information

WHERE MADE	Canada
YEAR OF PRODUCTION	Sixth
PARKING INDEX	Average
BUMPERS	Strong
THEFT RATING	Average
TWINS	Chevy Camaro
DRIVE	Rear

Specifications

FUEL ECONOMY (cty/hwy)	19/30	Average
DRIVING RANGE (miles)	388	Short
SEATING	4	
LENGTH (in.)	195.6	Long
HEAD/LEG ROOM (in.)	37.2/43.0	Cramped
INTERIOR SPACE (cu. ft.)	84.0	Vry. Cramped
CARGO SPACE (cu. ft.)	13.0	Small

Specifications may vary.

Prices

Model	Retail	Mkup
Firebird	18,015	9%
Firebird Convertible	24,305	9%
Firebird Formula	22,865	9%
Firebird Trans Am	25,975	9%

Competition

	POOR → GOOD	Pg.
Pontiac Firebird	□■□□□□□□□□	**200**
Chevrolet Camaro	□■□□□□□□□□	121
Ford Mustang	□□■□□□□□□□	144
Nissan 240SX	■□□□□□□□□□	186

Pontiac Grand Am

Compact

After a redesign two years ago, the Grand Am continues into 1998 unchanged. However, Pontiac has hinted about a redesigned Grand Am coming sometime later in 1998. Dual airbags and daytime running lamps are standard and you can find height adjustable safety belts which should improve comfort and safety.

The standard 2.4-liter Twin Cam engine makes the Grand Am fun to drive, though fuel economy is poor. There are plenty of options including 2 trim levels: SE coupe and sedan, and GT coupe and sedan. Seating is tight when you have three adults in the back seat; two should be comfortable. Ride is good and the Grand Am handles well. Interior noise is acceptable and driver vision is good. The Grand Am competes poorly against stiff competitors due to poor side crash tests.

The Ratings

	POOR ... GOOD
COMPARATIVE RATING	□□□□□□□■□□
FRONTAL CRASH TEST	□□□□□□□□■□
SAFETY FEATURES	□□□□□■□□□□
FUEL ECONOMY	□□□□□■□□□□
PM COST	□□□□□■□□□□
REPAIR COST	□□□□■□□□□□
WARRANTY	□■□□□□□□□□
COMPLAINTS	□□□□□□■□□□
INSURANCE COST	□□□□■□□□□□

Safety

FRONTAL CRASH TEST	Very Good
SIDE CRASH TEST	Very Poor
AIRBAGS	Dual Only
ANTI-LOCK BRAKES	4-wheel (optional)
DAY. RUNNING LIGHTS	Standard
BELT ADJUSTORS	Front
BUILT-IN CHILD SEAT	None
PRETENSIONERS	None

General Information

WHERE MADE	U.S.
YEAR OF PRODUCTION	Seventh
PARKING INDEX	Easy
BUMPERS	Strong
THEFT RATING	Very Low
TWINS	Olds Achieva
DRIVE	Front

Specifications

FUEL ECONOMY (cty/hwy)	23/33	Average
DRIVING RANGE (miles)	426	Average
SEATING	5	
LENGTH (in.)	186.9	Average
HEAD/LEG ROOM (in.)	37.8/43.1	Average
INTERIOR SPACE (cu. ft.)	89.0	Cramped
CARGO SPACE (cu. ft.)	13.0	Small

Specifications may vary.

Prices

Model	Retail	Mkup
Grand Am SE 2dr.	14,874	9%
Grand Am SE 4dr.	15,024	9%
Grand Am GT 2dr.	16,324	9%

Competition

	POOR ... GOOD	Pg.
Pontiac Grand Am	□□□□□□□■□□	**201**
Chev. Monte Carlo	□□■□□□□□□□	126
Ford Taurus	□□□□□□■□□□	145
Toyota Camry	□■□□□□□□□□	214

Pontiac Grand Prix

Intermediate

Last year's revision on the Grand Prix gave car buyer's something totally new. The most obvious changes can be seen on the exterior as Pontiac developed a wide track stance and a low roof line to produce a unique and fast look. The exterior lines are flowing and nicely complement the new front and rear fascias. There are no changes for 1998. The Grand Prix comes with dual airbags and 4-wheel ABS.

The Grand Prix is available in both coupe and sedan body styles with two trim levels: the base SE or the up-level GT. The standard 195 horsepower 3.8 liter V6 engine should deliver more than enough power for this car, though you can choose a supercharged version of the same engine and get 45 more horses. Inside, a new driver control cockpit should improve comfort. The Grand Prix is worth, at least, a test drive.

The Ratings

	POOR → GOOD
COMPARATIVE RATING	□□□□□■□□□□
FRONTAL CRASH TEST*	□□□□□□■□□□
SAFETY FEATURES	□□□□□□■□□□
FUEL ECONOMY	□□□□■□□□□□
PM COST	□□□□□■□□□□
REPAIR COST	□□□□□□■□□□
WARRANTY	□■□□□□□□□□
COMPLAINTS	□□□□■□□□□□
INSURANCE COST	□□□□□□□□□■

Safety

FRONTAL CRASH TEST	Good
SIDE CRASH TEST	No government results
AIRBAGS	Dual Only
ANTI-LOCK BRAKES	4-wheel
DAY. RUNNING LIGHTS	Standard
BELT ADJUSTORS	None
BUILT-IN CHILD SEAT	Optional
PRETENSIONERS	None

General Information

WHERE MADE	U.S.
YEAR OF PRODUCTION	Second
PARKING INDEX	Average
BUMPERS	Strong
THEFT RATING	
TWINS	
DRIVE	Front

Specifications

FUEL ECONOMY (cty/hwy)	20/29	Average
DRIVING RANGE (miles)	450	Long
SEATING	5	
LENGTH (in.)	196.5	Long
HEAD/LEG ROOM (in.)	38.3/42.4	Average
INTERIOR SPACE (cu. ft.)	99.0	Roomy
CARGO SPACE (cu. ft.)	16.0	Large

Specifications may vary.

Prices

Model	Retail	Mkup
Grand Prix SE 4dr.	18,795	9%
Grand Prix GT 2dr.	20,665	9%
Grand Prix GT 4dr.	20,415	9%

Competition

	POOR → GOOD	Pg.
Pontiac Grand Prix	□□□□□■□□□□	**202**
Dodge Avenger	□□□■□□□□□□	134
Ford Taurus	□□□□□□■□□□	145
Toyota Camry	□■□□□□□□□□	214

*A version of this vehicle is scheduled to be tested later this year. Results are expected to be similar.

Pontiac Sunfire

Compact

The Sunfire, twin of the Cavalier, is a good seller with attractive styling. The coupe and convertible models borrowed heavily from the Firebird's design, helping cater to young drivers looking for an affordable, sporty car. Dual airbags and ABS are standard. Standard daytime running lamps and optional traction control are great features.

The SE coupe, sedan and convertible come standard with a 2.2-liter engine that is only adequate. The GT coupe has a 2.4-liter dual cam engine with 25% more power. Ride is good on smooth roads, a little bumpy on anything else. Noise level is better than most competitors. Attractive styling, adequate performance and generous front seat room make the Sunfire a strong choice among inexpensive sports cars. Due to poor side crash tests, we can't recommend the Sunfire.

The Ratings

	POOR — GOOD
COMPARATIVE RATING	□□□□□□□□■□
FRONTAL CRASH TEST*	□□□□□□■□□□
SAFETY FEATURES	□□□□□■□□□□
FUEL ECONOMY	□□□□□□■□□□
PM COST	□□□□□■□□□□
REPAIR COST	□□□□□■□□□□
WARRANTY	□■□□□□□□□□
COMPLAINTS	□□□□□□■□□□
INSURANCE COST	□□□□□□□□□■

Safety

FRONTAL CRASH TEST	Good
SIDE CRASH TEST	Very Poor
AIRBAGS	Dual Only
ANTI-LOCK BRAKES	4-wheel
DAY. RUNNING LIGHTS	Standard
BELT ADJUSTORS	Front (Sdn Only)
BUILT-IN CHILD SEAT	None
PRETENSIONERS	None

General Information

WHERE MADE	U.S.
YEAR OF PRODUCTION	Fourth
PARKING INDEX	Average
BUMPERS	Strong
THEFT RATING	Very Low
TWINS	Chevy Cavalier
DRIVE	Front

Specifications

FUEL ECONOMY (cty/hwy)	25/37	Good
DRIVING RANGE (miles)	471	Long
SEATING	5	
LENGTH (in.)	181.7	Short
HEAD/LEG ROOM (in.)	38.9/42.1	Average
INTERIOR SPACE (cu. ft.)	92.0	Cramped
CARGO SPACE (cu. ft.)	13.0	Small

Specifications may vary.

Prices

Model	Retail	Mkup
Sunfire SE 2dr.	12,495	8%
Sunfire SE 4dr.	12,495	8%
Sunfire GT 2dr.	15,495	8%
Sunfire SE Convertible	19,495	8%

Competition

	POOR — GOOD	Pg.
Pontiac Sunfire	□□□□□□□□■□	**203**
Dodge/Plym. Neon	■□□□□□□□□□	137
Mercury Tracer	□□□□□■□□□□	180
Subaru Impreza	□□□□□□□□■□	209

*A version of this vehicle is scheduled to be tested later this year. Results are expected to be similar.

Pontiac Trans Sport

Minivan

The Trans Sport, twin of the Chevrolet Venture and Oldsmobile Silhouette, received a redesigned exterior and an improved interior last year. Seats are now easier to move and, like the Chrysler minivans, the Trans Sport has a driver's side sliding door. It continues into 1998 unchanged. Dual airbags, side airbags and ABS are standard. Built-in child seats are a good option for parents.

The Trans Sport comes in three versions: regular length with one sliding door, extended length with one sliding door, or extended length with two sliding doors. There are also five seating arrangements with a total capacity of eight. The standard engine is a 3.4 liter V6 which should proved ample power. Many comfort features are available including 17 cup holders! With good crash test results, the Trans Sport is well worth considering.

The Ratings

	POOR ... GOOD
COMPARATIVE RATING	
FRONTAL CRASH TEST*	
SAFETY FEATURES	
FUEL ECONOMY	
PM COST	
REPAIR COST	
WARRANTY	
COMPLAINTS	
INSURANCE COST	

Safety

FRONTAL CRASH TEST	Good
SIDE CRASH TEST	No government results
AIRBAGS	Dual & Side
ANTI-LOCK BRAKES	4-wheel
DAY. RUNNING LIGHTS	Standard
BELT ADJUSTORS	None
BUILT-IN CHILD SEAT	Optional (two)
PRETENSIONERS	Standard

General Information

WHERE MADE	U.S.
YEAR OF PRODUCTION	Second
PARKING INDEX	Average
BUMPERS	Strong
THEFT RATING	
TWINS	Venture, Silhouette
DRIVE	Front

Specifications

FUEL ECONOMY (cty/hwy)	18/25	Poor
DRIVING RANGE (miles)	440	Average
SEATING	7/8	
LENGTH (in.)	187.3	Average
HEAD/LEG ROOM (in.)	39.9/39.9	Cramped
INTERIOR SPACE (cu. ft.)		
CARGO SPACE (cu. ft.)	127.0	Very Large

Specifications may vary.

Prices

Model	Retail	Mkup
Trans Sport SE 3dr.	20,840	11%
Trans Sport SE 4dr.	22,380	11%
Trans Sport SE Extended	23,090	11%

Competition

	POOR ... GOOD	Pg.
Pont. Trans Sport		**204**
Dodge Caravan		135
Ford Windstar		146
Mercury Villager		181

*A version of this vehicle is scheduled to be tested later this year. Results are expected to be similar.

Saab 900

Intermediate

This is the final year for the 900 and there are no changes from last year's model. A new model, called the 9-3, will replace the 900 next year. Dual airbags, front belt adjustors, seat belt pretensioners and ABS are standard, as are daytime running lights.

The 900 S comes with an adequate 2.3-liter 4-cylinder engine, but the SE sedan and convertible come with a more powerful 2.5-liter V6. If you want even more power, choose the turbocharged version of the 4-cylinder available on the SE coupe and convertible. The 900 has room for four, plus plenty of luggage, though adults will be cramped in the rear of the convertible. Handling is responsive, and controls are designed well and easy to use. A dealer-installed integrated child safety seat is an excellent option.

The Ratings

	POOR … GOOD
COMPARATIVE RATING	□■□□□□□□□□
FRONTAL CRASH TEST	□□□□□□□■□□
SAFETY FEATURES	□□□□□□□■□□
FUEL ECONOMY	□□□□■□□□□□
PM COST	□□□□□□□□■□
REPAIR COST	□■□□□□□□□□
WARRANTY	□□□□□□■□□□
COMPLAINTS	■□□□□□□□□□
INSURANCE COST	■□□□□□□□□□

Safety

FRONTAL CRASH TEST	Good
SIDE CRASH TEST	No government results
AIRBAGS	Dual Only
ANTI-LOCK BRAKES	4-wheel
DAY. RUNNING LIGHTS	Standard
BELT ADJUSTORS	Front
BUILT-IN CHILD SEAT	Optional (two)
PRETENSIONERS	Standard

General Information

WHERE MADE	Sweden/Germany
YEAR OF PRODUCTION	Fifth
PARKING INDEX	Easy
BUMPERS	Strong
THEFT RATING	Very Low
TWINS	
DRIVE	Front

Specifications

FUEL ECONOMY (cty/hwy)	22/28	Average
DRIVING RANGE (miles)	450	Long
SEATING	5	
LENGTH (in.)	182.6	Short
HEAD/LEG ROOM (in.)	39.3/42.3	Average
INTERIOR SPACE (cu. ft.)	113.7	Very Roomy
CARGO SPACE (cu. ft.)	24.0	Very Large

Specifications may vary.

Prices

Model	Retail	Mkup
900 S 3dr	24,500	11%
900 S 5dr.	26,955	11%
900 SE 5dr.	31,995	11%
900 S conv. 2dr	36,395	15%

Competition

	POOR … GOOD	Pg.
Saab 900	□■□□□□□□□□	**205**
Audi A4	□□□□□□□□□■	106
BMW 3-Series	□□□□□□□□□■	108
Oldsmobile Aurora	■□□□□□□□□□	193

Saab 9000

Intermediate

Due to be replaced by the 9-5 in mid-1998, Saab's flagship, the 9000, enters the '98 model year with few changes. A strong performer in the government crash test program, the 9000 comes with dual airbags, seat belt adjustors up front, pretensioners and ABS as standard.

The 9000 comes in three trim levels, the CS, CSE and Aero, all of which are hatchbacks. With three engine choices, you will find the right amount of power, but the 2.4-liter base engine is the better choice. Interior room is spacious and comfortable. Standard daytime running lights help make the car more conspicuous and contribute greatly to car safety. Luggage space is generous, and controls and instruments are easy to use. Ride is comfortable for both driver and passengers.

The Ratings

	POOR ... GOOD
COMPARATIVE RATING	□□□□■□□□□□
FRONTAL CRASH TEST	□□□□□□□■□□
SAFETY FEATURES	□□□□□□■□□□
FUEL ECONOMY	□□□□■□□□□□
PM COST	□□□□□□■□□□
REPAIR COST	□■□□□□□□□□
WARRANTY	□□□□□□■□□□
COMPLAINTS	□□■□□□□□□□
INSURANCE COST	□□□□■□□□□□

Safety

FRONTAL CRASH TEST	Good
SIDE CRASH TEST	No government results
AIRBAGS	Dual Only
ANTI-LOCK BRAKES	4-wheel
DAY. RUNNING LIGHTS	Standard
BELT ADJUSTORS	Front
BUILT-IN CHILD SEAT	None
PRETENSIONERS	Standard

General Information

WHERE MADE	Sweden/Germany
YEAR OF PRODUCTION	Thirteenth
PARKING INDEX	Average
BUMPERS	Strong
THEFT RATING	Very Low
TWINS	
DRIVE	Front

Specifications

FUEL ECONOMY (cty/hwy)	21/27	Average
DRIVING RANGE (miles)	418	Average
SEATING	5	
LENGTH (in.)	187.4	Average
HEAD/LEG ROOM (in.)	38.6/41.7	Cramped
INTERIOR SPACE (cu. ft.)	123.0	Very Roomy
CARGO SPACE (cu. ft.)	23.5	Very Large

Specifications may vary.

Prices

Model	Retail	Mkup
9000 CSE man.	38,580	15%
9000 CSE auto.	39,625	15%

Competition

	POOR ... GOOD	Pg.
Saab 9000	□□□□■□□□□□	**206**
Audi A4	□□□□□□□□□■	106
Lexus ES300	□□□□□□□□■□	162
Merc.-Benz C-Class	□□□□□□□■□□	174

Saturn SC

Subcompact

A redesigned sleeker-looking SC was introduced last year with a new exterior which included a new trunk lid and a slightly adjusted headlight configuration to include standard daytime running lamps. For 1998, there are no significant changes. Other safety features include standard dual airbags and optional ABS.

On the interior, the SC looks much like the SL/SW. New interior trim and freshened controls help make you more comfortable. The SC is powered by a 1.9 liter, 4-cylinder engine that delivers 100 horsepower, not tops in this competitive market. Ride should be fairly smooth, though less so on rough roads. Noise levels inside have been reduced to increase comfort. A great product and a pleasant showroom experience are what you'll find at Saturn.

The Ratings

	POOR — GOOD
COMPARATIVE RATING*	
FRONTAL CRASH TEST	
SAFETY FEATURES	
FUEL ECONOMY	
PM COST	
REPAIR COST	
WARRANTY	
COMPLAINTS	
INSURANCE COST	

Safety

FRONTAL CRASH TEST	No government results
SIDE CRASH TEST	No government results
AIRBAGS	Dual Only
ANTI-LOCK BRAKES	4-wheel (optional)
DAY. RUNNING LIGHTS	Standard
BELT ADJUSTORS	Front
BUILT-IN CHILD SEAT	None
PRETENSIONERS	None

General Information

WHERE MADE	U.S./Canada
YEAR OF PRODUCTION	Second
PARKING INDEX	Average
BUMPERS	Strong
THEFT RATING	
TWINS	
DRIVE	Front

Specifications

FUEL ECONOMY (cty/hwy)	28/39	Good
DRIVING RANGE (miles)	411	Average
SEATING	4	
LENGTH (in.)	180.0	Short
HEAD/LEG ROOM (in.)	38.5/42.6	Average
INTERIOR SPACE (cu. ft.)	84.1	Vry. Cramped
CARGO SPACE (cu. ft.)	11.4	Small

Specifications may vary.

Prices

Model	Retail	Mkup
SC1	12,595	15%
SC2	14,855	15%

Competition

	POOR — GOOD	Pg.
Saturn SC		**207**
Dodge/Plym. Neon		137
Ford Escort		143
Honda Civic		150

*Due to the importance of crash tests, cars with no results as of publication date cannot be given an overall rating.

Saturn SL/SW

Subcompact

Saturn's sedan and wagon enter 1998 unchanged. The transmission was improved slightly to make shifting smoother. Saturn's consumer friendly showroom and economical prices have combined for a phenomenal success. The SL and SW come with standard dual airbags and optional ABS.

The dual over-head cam engine available on the SL and the SW is more powerful than the base 4-cylinder model and only reduces fuel efficiency slightly. The raised roofline adds headroom which makes the sedan and wagon more comfortable, although the back seat is still tight for adults. The ride is good on smooth roads. Gauges and controls are well placed and easy to use. Noise level is not the best available in this crowded compact market. This economically priced car fares nicely with tough competition like the Ford Escort, Honda Civic and Chevy Cavalier.

The Ratings	POOR ... GOOD
COMPARATIVE RATING	
FRONTAL CRASH TEST*	
SAFETY FEATURES	
FUEL ECONOMY	
PM COST	
REPAIR COST	
WARRANTY	
COMPLAINTS	
INSURANCE COST	

Safety	
FRONTAL CRASH TEST	Very Good
SIDE CRASH TEST	Average
AIRBAGS	Dual Only
ANTI-LOCK BRAKES	4-wheel (optional)
DAY. RUNNING LIGHTS	Standard
BELT ADJUSTORS	Front
BUILT-IN CHILD SEAT	None
PRETENSIONERS	None

General Information	
WHERE MADE	U.S./Canada
YEAR OF PRODUCTION	Third
PARKING INDEX	Average
BUMPERS	Strong
THEFT RATING	Very Low
TWINS	
DRIVE	Front

Specifications		
FUEL ECONOMY (cty/hwy)	28/39	Good
DRIVING RANGE (miles)	411	Average
SEATING	5	
LENGTH (in.)	176.9	Short
HEAD/LEG ROOM (in.)	39.3/42.5	Roomy
INTERIOR SPACE (cu. ft.)	91.0	Cramped
CARGO SPACE (cu. ft.)	12.1	Small

Specifications may vary.

Prices		
Model	**Retail**	**Mkup**
SL	10,595	15%
SL1	11,595	15%
SW1	12,295	15%
SW2	14,255	15%

Competition	POOR ... GOOD	Pg.
Saturn SL/SW		**208**
Ford Escort		143
Honda Civic		150
Hyundai Elantra		155

*A version of this vehicle is scheduled to be tested later this year. Results are expected to be similar.

Subaru Impreza

Subcompact

The Impreza is the smallest offering from Subaru and it comes in a wide variety of models: the sedan comes in a L model, the coupe in a L or RS, and the wagon comes in L or Outback. Little changes for the Impreza in 1998. The interior, including front dash, has been revised. Standard on the Impreza are dual airbags and ABS.

All-wheel drive now comes standard on all models, which should please cold weather drivers. There are as many engines to choose from as there are trim levels. The base model's engine is a 2.2-liter 4-cylinder engine that produces 137 hp. A 2.5-liter, 15 hp engine is available on the coupe RS. Front seats are comfortable; the back seat is the typical subcompact squeeze, and trunk space is only adequate. The Impreza is one of the top subcompacts on the road.

The Ratings

	POOR — GOOD
COMPARATIVE RATING	□□□□□□□□■□
FRONTAL CRASH TEST	□□□□□□□■□□
SAFETY FEATURES	□□□□□■□□□□
FUEL ECONOMY	□□□□□■□□□□
PM COST	□□□□□□□□■□
REPAIR COST	□□□□■□□□□□
WARRANTY	□□□■□□□□□□
COMPLAINTS	□□□□□□■□□□
INSURANCE COST	□□□□■□□□□□

Safety

FRONTAL CRASH TEST	Good
SIDE CRASH TEST	No government results
AIRBAGS	Dual Only
ANTI-LOCK BRAKES	4-wheel
DAY. RUNNING LIGHTS	None
BELT ADJUSTORS	Front
BUILT-IN CHILD SEAT	None
PRETENSIONERS	None

General Information

WHERE MADE	Japan
YEAR OF PRODUCTION	Sixth
PARKING INDEX	Very Easy
BUMPERS	Strong
THEFT RATING	Very Low
TWINS	
DRIVE	AWD

Specifications

FUEL ECONOMY (cty/hwy)	23/30	Average
DRIVING RANGE (miles)	356	Very Short
SEATING	5	
LENGTH (in.)	172.2	Very Short
HEAD/LEG ROOM (in.)	39.2/43.1	Roomy
INTERIOR SPACE (cu. ft.)	84.4	Vry. Cramped
CARGO SPACE (cu. ft.)	11.1	Very Small

Specifications may vary.

Prices

Model	Retail	Mkup
Impreza L 2dr	15,895	10%
Impreza L 4dr.	15,895	10%
Impreza RS 2dr.	19,195	6%
Impreza Outback Sport	17,995	10%

Competition

	POOR — GOOD	Pg.
Subaru Impreza	□□□□□□□□■□	**209**
Chevrolet Cavalier	□□□□□□□■□□	122
Ford Escort	□□□■□□□□□□	143
Honda Civic	□□□□□□■□□□	150

Subaru Legacy

Compact

Nine Legacy models are available for 1998. You can choose between a sedan, coupe and wagon, each with various trim levels. The fresh styling the Legacy received in 1995 has helped make this car a good seller. The Legacy Outback has become Subaru's prime seller. ABS is optional and dual airbags are standard across the board. 1997 model is pictured.

You have two engines to choose from: a 2.2-liter 4-cylinder or a 2.5-liter 4-cylinder with 30 more horses. Both engines will deliver decent gas mileage. All-wheel drive is standard on all the models which will make the Legacy popular in the colder climates. The GT model should please sportier buyers. Ride and comfort are both good and the Legacy performed well on government frontal crash tests.

The Ratings	POOR … GOOD
COMPARATIVE RATING	□□□□□□□□■□
FRONTAL CRASH TEST*	□□□□□□□□■□
SAFETY FEATURES	□□□□■□□□□□
FUEL ECONOMY	□□□□□■□□□□
PM COST	□□□□□□□□■□
REPAIR COST	□□□□□□■□□□
WARRANTY	□□□■□□□□□□
COMPLAINTS	□□□□■□□□□□
INSURANCE COST	□□□□■□□□□□

Safety	
FRONTAL CRASH TEST	Very Good
SIDE CRASH TEST	No government results
AIRBAGS	Dual Only
ANTI-LOCK BRAKES	4-wheel (optional)
DAY. RUNNING LIGHTS	None
BELT ADJUSTORS	Front
BUILT-IN CHILD SEAT	None
PRETENSIONERS	None

General Information	
WHERE MADE	Japan/U.S./Canada
YEAR OF PRODUCTION	Fourth
PARKING INDEX	Easy
BUMPERS	Strong
THEFT RATING	Low
TWINS	
DRIVE	AWD

Specifications		
FUEL ECONOMY (cty/hwy)	23/30	Average
DRIVING RANGE (miles)	429	Average
SEATING	5	
LENGTH (in.)	181.5	Short
HEAD/LEG ROOM (in.)	38.9/43.3	Roomy
INTERIOR SPACE (cu. ft.)	92.1	Cramped
CARGO SPACE (cu. ft.)	13.0	Small

Specifications may vary.

Prices

Model	Retail	Mkup
Legacy L	19,195	11%
Legacy GT	22,795	12%
Legacy Outback Wagon	22,495	11%

Competition

	POOR … GOOD	Pg.
Subaru Legacy	□□□□□□□□■□	**210**
Ford Taurus	□□□□□□■□□□	145
Oldsmobile Achieva	□□□□□□□□□■	192
Pontiac Grand Am	□□□□□□□■□□	201

*A version of this vehicle is scheduled to be tested later this year. Results are expected to be similar.

Suzuki Esteem

Subcompact

The Esteem, the larger of Suzuki's two cars, is their first entry into the compact-sedan market, a very competitive and crowded market. It comes standard with dual airbags and optional ABS. Daytime running lamps are standard.

You can choose between the base model or the upgraded GLX, though both come with the same engine. The standard 1.6-liter 4-cylinder engine offers poor power and little excitement, though you will get 30 miles to the gallon in the city. The interior promises to be tight as the car is nearly 20 inches shorter than the already small Ford Contour; trunk space will not be any better. Noise levels should be comfortable inside. While its price may be enticing, you can definitely get more for your money elsewhere.

The Ratings

	POOR — GOOD
COMPARATIVE RATING*	
FRONTAL CRASH TEST	
SAFETY FEATURES	
FUEL ECONOMY	
PM COST	
REPAIR COST	
WARRANTY	
COMPLAINTS	
INSURANCE COST	

Safety

FRONTAL CRASH TEST	No government results
SIDE CRASH TEST	No government results
AIRBAGS	Dual Only
ANTI-LOCK BRAKES	4-wheel (optional)
DAY. RUNNING LIGHTS	Standard
BELT ADJUSTORS	Front
BUILT-IN CHILD SEAT	None
PRETENSIONERS	None

General Information

WHERE MADE	Japan
YEAR OF PRODUCTION	Third
PARKING INDEX	Very Easy
BUMPERS	Weak
THEFT RATING	
TWINS	
DRIVE	Front

Specifications

FUEL ECONOMY (cty/hwy)	30/37	Good
DRIVING RANGE (miles)	459	Long
SEATING	5	
LENGTH (in.)	165.2	Very Short
HEAD/LEG ROOM (in.)	39.1/42.3	Average
INTERIOR SPACE (cu. ft.)	97.9	Average
CARGO SPACE (cu. ft.)	12.0	Small

Specifications may vary.

Prices

Model	Retail	Mkup
Esteem GL	11,999	5%
Esteem GL Wagon	12,499	5%
Esteem GLX	13,099	5%
Esteem GLX Wagon	13,599	5%

Competition

	POOR — GOOD	Pg.
Suzuki Esteem		**211**
Chevrolet Cavalier		122
Dodge/Plym. Neon		137
Honda Civic		150

*Due to the importance of crash tests, cars with no results as of publication date cannot be given an overall rating.

Suzuki Swift

Subcompact

Like its twin the Chevrolet Metro, the Swift is inexpensive, small and gets fantastic mileage. But, don't expect much room inside. Dual airbags are standard and those awful door-mounted belts are gone. ABS is optional.

The Swift offers a fairly puny 1.3-liter 4-cylinder engine — thus, the great fuel economy. However, efficiency suffers dramatically at the hands of the optional automatic transmission, so stick to the standard 5-speed. Room for two is tight; the rear seat is really only for children. Handling is quick and precise, but crosswinds and large trucks can pose a problem. The starting price is under $10,000, you can get many options and the Swift comes with a great complaint rating. On the other hand, its tiny, light and not a terrific handling car. This is basic transportation.

The Ratings

	POOR — GOOD
COMPARATIVE RATING	□□□□□□□■□□
FRONTAL CRASH TEST	□□□□□□■□□□
SAFETY FEATURES	□□□□□■□□□□
FUEL ECONOMY	□□□□□□□□□■
PM COST	□□□■□□□□□□
REPAIR COST	□□■□□□□□□□
WARRANTY	■□□□□□□□□□
COMPLAINTS	□□□□□□□□□■
INSURANCE COST	■□□□□□□□□□

Safety

FRONTAL CRASH TEST	Good
SIDE CRASH TEST	No government results
AIRBAGS	Dual Only
ANTI-LOCK BRAKES	4-wheel (optional)
DAY. RUNNING LIGHTS	Standard
BELT ADJUSTORS	Front
BUILT-IN CHILD SEAT	None
PRETENSIONERS	None

General Information

WHERE MADE	Japan/U.S./Canada
YEAR OF PRODUCTION	Fourth
PARKING INDEX	Very Easy
BUMPERS	Weak
THEFT RATING	
TWINS	Chevy Metro
DRIVE	Front

Specifications

FUEL ECONOMY (cty/hwy)	39/43	Very Good
DRIVING RANGE (miles)	422	Average
SEATING	4	
LENGTH (in.)	149.4	Very Short
HEAD/LEG ROOM (in.)	39.1/42.5	Average
INTERIOR SPACE (cu. ft.)	85.8	Cramped
CARGO SPACE (cu. ft.)	8.4	Very Small

Specifications may vary.

Prices

Model	Retail	Mkup
Swift man.	9,099	8%
Swift auto.	9,749	8%

Competition

	POOR — GOOD	Pg.
Suzuki Swift	□□□□□□□■□□	**212**
Honda Civic	□□□□□□■□□□	150
Hyundai Accent	□□□□□□■□□□	154
Toyota Tercel	□□□□□□■□□□	219

Toyota Avalon

Intermediate

Except for a redesigned front grill, there are no changes for the Toyota Avalon for 1998. With more interior room and a higher price tag than the Camry, the Avalon is more upscale in design, competing with models like the Mercury Sable and Nissan Maxima. Dual airbags, side airbags, and seat belt pretensioners are standard, but ABS will cost extra on the XL. 1997 model is pictured.

The Avalon's extra length makes the ride a bit smoother, but it weighs about the same as the Camry, so the handling is just as responsive. The Avalon comes in two trim levels, base XL and deluxe XLS, both with the same powerful 3-liter V6 and automatic transmission. Fuel economy is merely average. Five adults will be comfortable, but don't count on fitting three adults comfortably on the front bench seat. The Avalon is a safe choice but beware of the high maintenance costs.

General Information

WHERE MADE	U.S.
YEAR OF PRODUCTION	Fourth
PARKING INDEX	Average
BUMPERS	Strong
THEFT RATING	Average
TWINS	
DRIVE	Front

Prices

Model	Retail	Mkup
Avalon XL (bucket)	24,278	14%
Avalon XL (bench)	25,108	15%
Avalon XLS	28,128	15%

The Ratings

	POOR … GOOD
COMPARATIVE RATING	□□□□■□□□□□
FRONTAL CRASH TEST*	□□□□□□□□■□
SAFETY FEATURES	□□□□□■□□□□
FUEL ECONOMY	□□□□□■□□□□
PM COST	□■□□□□□□□□
REPAIR COST	□□□■□□□□□□
WARRANTY	□■□□□□□□□□
COMPLAINTS	□□□□□■□□□□
INSURANCE COST	□□□□■□□□□□

Safety

FRONTAL CRASH TEST	Very Good
SIDE CRASH TEST	No government results
AIRBAGS	Dual/Side
ANTI-LOCK BRAKES	4-wheel (optional)
DAY. RUNNING LIGHTS	None
BELT ADJUSTORS	Front
BUILT-IN CHILD SEAT	None
PRETENSIONERS	Standard

Specifications

FUEL ECONOMY (cty/hwy)	21/31	Average
DRIVING RANGE (miles)	481	Very Long
SEATING	5/6	
LENGTH (in.)	191.9	Long
HEAD/LEG ROOM (in.)	39.1/44.1	Very Roomy
INTERIOR SPACE (cu. ft.)	120.9	Very Roomy
CARGO SPACE (cu. ft.)	15.4	Average

Specifications may vary.

Competition

	POOR … GOOD	Pg.
Toyota Avalon	□□□□■□□□□□	**213**
Ford Crown Victoria	□□□□■□□□□□	142
Mercury Sable	□□□□□□□■□□	179
Nissan Maxima	□□□■□□□□□□	188

*A version of this vehicle is scheduled to be tested later this year. Results are expected to be similar.

Toyota Camry

Intermediate

America's newest best-selling car is now the Camry — step aside Ford Taurus. The Camry's redesign last year was a huge hit. You have your choice between three trim levels: CE, LE and XLE and there are many option packages. Dual airbags are standard and 4-wheel ABS is optional. The optional side airbags are highly recommended.

The CE comes standard with a 2.2 liter 4-cylinder engine with 133 hp. Most will prefer the more powerful 3.0-liter V6 engine with a slight loss in fuel economy. The handling is crisp and responsive. Controls are well designed and easy to use and the interior is comfortable for both driver and passengers. The Camry faces tough competition with the redesigned Accord and the boldly shaped Taurus. High repair and maintenance costs plus a lousy warranty hurt the Camry.

The Ratings

	POOR — GOOD
COMPARATIVE RATING	
FRONTAL CRASH TEST*	
SAFETY FEATURES	
FUEL ECONOMY	
PM COST	
REPAIR COST	
WARRANTY	
COMPLAINTS	
INSURANCE COST	

Safety

FRONTAL CRASH TEST	Good
SIDE CRASH TEST	Good
AIRBAGS	Dual/Opt. Side
ANTI-LOCK BRAKES	4-wheel
DAY. RUNNING LIGHTS	None
BELT ADJUSTORS	Front
BUILT-IN CHILD SEAT	Optional
PRETENSIONERS	None

General Information

WHERE MADE	U.S./Japan
YEAR OF PRODUCTION	Second
PARKING INDEX	Average
BUMPERS	Strong
THEFT RATING	
TWINS	Lexus ES300
DRIVE	Front

Specifications

FUEL ECONOMY (cty/hwy)	23/31	Average
DRIVING RANGE (miles)	500	Very Long
SEATING	5	
LENGTH (in.)	188.5	Average
HEAD/LEG ROOM (in.)	38.6/43.5	Roomy
INTERIOR SPACE (cu. ft.)	96.9	Average
CARGO SPACE (cu. ft.)	14.1	Average

Specifications may vary.

Prices

Model	Retail	Mkup
Camry CE	16,938	13%
Camry LE	20,218	13%
Camry LE V6	22,558	13%
Camry XLE	22,628	13%

Competition

	POOR — GOOD	Pg.
Toyota Camry		**214**
Ford Taurus		145
Oldsmobile Cutlass		194
Pontiac Grand Am		201

*A version of this vehicle is scheduled to be tested later this year. Results are expected to be similar.

Toyota Celica

Compact

Expect a redesigned Celica to be introduced mid-year 1998. For now, the '97 model will carryover into 1998. The Celica is a mid-priced sports car, especially popular with women. You can choose between a liftback, a coupe or a convertible. Dual airbags are standard and four-wheel ABS is optional.

The base model ST gets a 1.8-liter 4-cylinder engine that's meek for a supposed performance car, although fuel economy is pretty good. The up-level GT coupe and convertible get a slightly more powerful 2.2-liter 4-cylinder engine that's not quite as economical. The standard suspension handles well, but the sport suspension available on the GT is even better. The dashboard is functional and intelligently laid out. The interior has room for two; the rear seat is a joke. Low complaints make the Celica worth looking at.

The Ratings	POOR — GOOD
COMPARATIVE RATING*	
FRONTAL CRASH TEST	
SAFETY FEATURES	
FUEL ECONOMY	
PM COST	
REPAIR COST	
WARRANTY	
COMPLAINTS	
INSURANCE COST	

Safety	
FRONTAL CRASH TEST	No government results
SIDE CRASH TEST	No government results
AIRBAGS	Dual Only
ANTI-LOCK BRAKES	4-wheel (optional)
DAY. RUNNING LIGHTS	None
BELT ADJUSTORS	None
BUILT-IN CHILD SEAT	None
PRETENSIONERS	None

General Information	
WHERE MADE	Japan
YEAR OF PRODUCTION	Fifth
PARKING INDEX	Easy
BUMPERS	Strong
THEFT RATING	Average
TWINS	
DRIVE	Front

Specifications		
FUEL ECONOMY (cty/hwy)	29/35	Good
DRIVING RANGE (miles)	509	Very Long
SEATING	4	
LENGTH (in.)	174.2	Short
HEAD/LEG ROOM (in.)	34.3/43.1	Vry. Cramped
INTERIOR SPACE (cu. ft.)	77.0	Vry. Cramped
CARGO SPACE (cu. ft.)	16.0	Large

Specifications may vary.

Prices**

Model	Retail	Mkup
Celica ST	17,548	15%
Celica ST Hatchback	17,908	15%
Celica GT Convertible	24,798	15%

Competition

	POOR — GOOD	Pg.
Toyota Celica		**215**
Acura Integra		103
Eagle Talon		139
Ford Mustang		144

**1998 prices not available at press time. Prices based on 1997 data.

*Due to the importance of crash tests, cars with no results as of publication date cannot be given an overall rating.

Toyota Corolla

Compact

Bigger and faster, the Corolla, with its renamed twin the Chevy Prizm, gets a makeover for 1998. Safety was a priority with this latest redesign and the Corolla can come loaded with safety features. Dual airbags and daytime running lamps are standard; ABS and side airbags are optional. 1997 model is pictured, but the Prizm photo (p.127) will give you a good idea of the Corolla's looks.

A new engine is a 1.8-liter, 4-cylinder with 120 hp, which is more powerful than the previous 1.6-liter. The new Corolla's base VE is almost $1,000 less than last year's version. Yet, the Corolla still has lots of great features including a bigger glove box, a cloth-lined case for sunglasses on the dash, and a redesigned instrument panel with an optional outside temperature meter. Scheduled for crash testing next year, the Corolla looks to be a safe choice.

The Ratings

	POOR — GOOD
COMPARATIVE RATING*	
FRONTAL CRASH TEST	
SAFETY FEATURES	
FUEL ECONOMY	
PM COST	
REPAIR COST	
WARRANTY	
COMPLAINTS	
INSURANCE COST	

Safety

FRONTAL CRASH TEST	No government results
SIDE CRASH TEST	No government results
AIRBAGS	Dual/Opt. Side
ANTI-LOCK BRAKES	4-wheel (optional)
DAY. RUNNING LIGHTS	Standard
BELT ADJUSTORS	Front
BUILT-IN CHILD SEAT	Optional
PRETENSIONERS	Standard

General Information

WHERE MADE	U.S./Canada
YEAR OF PRODUCTION	First
PARKING INDEX	Very Easy
BUMPERS	Strong
THEFT RATING	
TWINS	Chevy Prizm
DRIVE	Front

Specifications

FUEL ECONOMY (cty/hwy)	31/38	Very Good
DRIVING RANGE (miles)	462	Long
SEATING	5	
LENGTH (in.)	174.0	Short
HEAD/LEG ROOM (in.)	39.3/42.5	Roomy
INTERIOR SPACE (cu. ft.)	88.0	Cramped
CARGO SPACE (cu. ft.)	12.1	Small

Specifications may vary.

Prices

Model	Retail	Mkup
Corolla VE	11,908	9%
Corolla CE	13,788	9%
Corolla LS	14,798	9%

Competition

	POOR — GOOD	Pg.
Toyota Corolla		**216**
Chevrolet Cavalier		122
Honda Civic		150
Saturn SL/SW		208

*Due to the importance of crash tests, cars with no results as of publication date cannot be given an overall rating.

Toyota Paseo

Subcompact

The Paseo is basically a Tercel, pretending to be a sports car. 1998 is a pivotal year for the Paseo — either a midyear redesign will appear or '98 will be the Paseo's final year. For now, the 1997 model continues into 1998 unchanged. The Paseo comes standard with dual airbags and ABS is optional.

The 1.5-liter, 4-cylinder engine cranks out only 93 horsepower, not exactly what you want in a sports car. Both the standard manual and optional automatic transmissions are fairly fuel efficient. If you're tall, you won't fit inside comfortably and forget about the rear seat. The ride is smooth on good roads, but the handling doesn't match up with the sporty looks. Expect a noisy ride. There are plenty of options to choose from which can really push the price upward. You'll find more performance and a better value with the Dodge/Plymouth Neon Sport or Saturn SC.

The Ratings

	POOR ... GOOD
COMPARATIVE RATING	
FRONTAL CRASH TEST	
SAFETY FEATURES	
FUEL ECONOMY	
PM COST	
REPAIR COST	
WARRANTY	
COMPLAINTS	
INSURANCE COST	

Safety

FRONTAL CRASH TEST	Good
SIDE CRASH TEST	No government results
AIRBAGS	Dual Only
ANTI-LOCK BRAKES	4-wheel (optional)
DAY. RUNNING LIGHTS	None
BELT ADJUSTORS	None
BUILT-IN CHILD SEAT	None
PRETENSIONERS	None

General Information

WHERE MADE	Japan/U.S.
YEAR OF PRODUCTION	Eighth
PARKING INDEX	Very Easy
BUMPERS	Strong
THEFT RATING	
TWINS	
DRIVE	Front

Specifications

FUEL ECONOMY (cty/hwy)	31/37	Good
DRIVING RANGE (miles)	405	Short
SEATING	4	
LENGTH (in.)	163.6	Very Short
HEAD/LEG ROOM (in.)	37.8/41.1	Vry. Cramped
INTERIOR SPACE (cu. ft.)	74.0	Vry. Cramped
CARGO SPACE (cu. ft.)	8.0	Very Small

Specifications may vary.

Prices**

Model	Retail	Mkup
Paseo	13,628	12%
Paseo Convertible	17,148	12%

Competition

	POOR ... GOOD	Pg.
Toyota Paseo		**217**
Chevrolet Metro		125
Dodge/Ply. Neon		137
Hyundai Accent		154

**1998 prices not available at press time. Prices based on 1997 data.

Toyota Sienna

Minivan

For 1998, Toyota drops the Previa and introduces the Sienna, the 'Camry of minivans.' The Sienna is a direct shot at the Chrysler minivans, the philosophy being that if you can't beat 'em, copy 'em. The safety features are numerous. Dual airbags, height adjustable seats belts and pretensioners are standard. ABS is optional. An optional built-in child seat is a must for parents. The Sienna photo was not available at press time; pictured is the '97 Previa.

The Camry's 3.0-liter V6 powers the Sienna. The interior is just as roomy as the Previa was, but getting in and out is much easier on the Sienna. The bench seating is easy to remove, but the optional captain's chairs are more comfy. A powered fourth door is on its way midyear 1998. Due to be crash tested next year, the Sienna looks to score as big as its sibling sedan, the Camry.

The Ratings

	POOR □□□□□□□□ GOOD
COMPARATIVE RATING*	□□□□□□□□□□
FRONTAL CRASH TEST	□□□□□□□□□□
SAFETY FEATURES	□□□□□□■□□□
FUEL ECONOMY	□□□■□□□□□□
PM COST	□■□□□□□□□□
REPAIR COST	□■□□□□□□□□
WARRANTY	□■□□□□□□□□
COMPLAINTS	□□□□■□□□□□
INSURANCE COST	□□□□■□□□□□

Safety

FRONTAL CRASH TEST	No government results
SIDE CRASH TEST	No government results
AIRBAGS	Dual Only
ANTI-LOCK BRAKES	4-wheel (optional)
DAY. RUNNING LIGHTS	None
BELT ADJUSTORS	Front
BUILT-IN CHILD SEAT	Optional
PRETENSIONERS	Standard

General Information

WHERE MADE	U.S./Japan
YEAR OF PRODUCTION	First
PARKING INDEX	Hard
BUMPERS	Strong
THEFT RATING	
TWINS	
DRIVE	Front

Specifications

FUEL ECONOMY (cty/hwy)	18/24	Poor
DRIVING RANGE (miles)	441	Average
SEATING	7	
LENGTH (in.)	193.5	Long
HEAD/LEG ROOM (in.)	40.6/41.9	Roomy
INTERIOR SPACE (cu. ft.)		
CARGO SPACE (cu. ft.)	131.0	Very Large

Specifications may vary.

Prices

Model	Retail	Mkup
Sienna CE	21,140	14%
Sienna XLE	27,100	14%

Competition

	POOR □□□□□□□□ GOOD	Pg.
Toyota Sienna	□□□□□□□□□□	**218**
Chevrolet Venture	□□□■□□□□□□	128
Dodge Caravan	□□■□□□□□□□	135
Honda Odyssey	□□□□□□■□□□	152

*Due to the importance of crash tests, cars with no results as of publication date cannot be given an overall rating.

Toyota Tercel

Subcompact

Look for a redesigned Tercel to appear midyear 1998, although this could be the Tercel's final year. In either case, the 1997 model enters 1998 with no changes. Dual airbags are standard on the Tercel, though you'll still have to pay extra for ABS.

The 1.5-liter, 4-cylinder engine does a decent job at powering the vehicle, but it only offers 93 horsepower. What you lose in power, you gain in fuel efficiency, but only with the manual transmission. You can choose standard or DX trim levels in two- or four-door models. Interior room is not as large as other vehicles in its size class and it is rather noisy inside during hard accelerations. A sound, economical choice, but watch the options as they can quickly inflate the price tag. The Tercel coupe, with its good crash test performance, is a Best Bet this year.

The Ratings

	POOR □□□□□□□□□□ GOOD
COMPARATIVE RATING	□□□□□□■□□□
FRONTAL CRASH TEST	□□□□□■□□□□
SAFETY FEATURES	□□□□■□□□□□
FUEL ECONOMY	□□□□□□□□■□
PM COST	□■□□□□□□□□
REPAIR COST	□□□□■□□□□□
WARRANTY	□■□□□□□□□□
COMPLAINTS	□□□□□□□■□□
INSURANCE COST	□□□□□□□□□■

Safety

FRONTAL CRASH TEST*	Average
SIDE CRASH TEST	No government results
AIRBAGS	Dual Only
ANTI-LOCK BRAKES	4-wheel (optional)
DAY. RUNNING LIGHTS	None
BELT ADJUSTORS	None
BUILT-IN CHILD SEAT	None
PRETENSIONERS	None

General Information

WHERE MADE	Japan
YEAR OF PRODUCTION	Fourth
PARKING INDEX	Very Easy
BUMPERS	Strong
THEFT RATING	Average
TWINS	
DRIVE	Front

Specifications

FUEL ECONOMY (cty/hwy)	32/39	Very Good
DRIVING RANGE (miles)	428	Average
SEATING	5	
LENGTH (in.)	161.8	Very Short
HEAD/LEG ROOM (in.)	38.6/41.2	Cramped
INTERIOR SPACE (cu. ft.)	81.0	Vry. Cramped
CARGO SPACE (cu. ft.)	9.0	Very Small

Specifications may vary.

Prices**

Model	Retail	Mkup
Tercel CE 2dr	11,068	8%
Tercel CE Deluxe 4dr.	12,528	8%

Competition

	POOR □□□□□□□□□□ GOOD	Pg.
Toyota Tercel	□□□□□□■□□□	**219**
Chevrolet Cavalier	□□□□□□□■□□	122
Hyundai Accent	□□□□□□■□□□	154
Suzuki Swift	□□□□□□□■□□	212

**1998 prices not available at press time. Prices based on 1997 data.

*Data given for sedan. Frontal crash test for coupe is Good for an overall rating of 8.

Volkswagen Golf

Compact

Variety is what you'll find when shopping for a Golf. There is the Golf, the sportier Golf Sport, or the GTI VR6. The Golf TDI, or turbo direct engine, joined the lineup last year. They vary in character, but all have the same basic specifications and components. For 1998, no changes were made. There is a possible redesign in the works for 1999. Dual airbags and daytime running lamps are standard, ABS is optional. Traction control is a great feature available on the GTI VR6 model.

The basic Golf offers a 2-liter 4-cylinder engine or a 2.8-liter V6 on the GTI VR6. All models come with 5-speed manual or automatic overdrive. In addition to the industry best 10-year/100,000 mile power train warranty, VW now includes all service, repairs and parts up the entire duration of the basic warranty of 2-years/24,000 miles. The Golf is one of this year's top picks.

The Ratings	POOR □□□□□□□□□□ GOOD
COMPARATIVE RATING	□□□□□□□■□□
FRONTAL CRASH TEST	□□□□■□□□□□
SAFETY FEATURES	□□□□□□□■□□
FUEL ECONOMY	□□□□□■□□□□
PM COST	□□□□□□□□□■
REPAIR COST	□□□□□□■□□□
WARRANTY	□□□□□□□□■□
COMPLAINTS	□□□□■□□□□□
INSURANCE COST	■□□□□□□□□□

Safety	
FRONTAL CRASH TEST	Average
SIDE CRASH TEST	No government results
AIRBAGS	Dual/Opt. Side
ANTI-LOCK BRAKES	4-wheel (optional)
DAY. RUNNING LIGHTS	Standard
BELT ADJUSTORS	Front
BUILT-IN CHILD SEAT	None
PRETENSIONERS	Standard

General Information	
WHERE MADE	Mexico/Germany
YEAR OF PRODUCTION	Fifth
PARKING INDEX	Very Easy
BUMPERS	Weak
THEFT RATING	Very Low
TWINS	VW Jetta
DRIVE	Front

Specifications		
FUEL ECONOMY (cty/hwy)	24/31	Average
DRIVING RANGE (miles)	406	Short
SEATING	5	
LENGTH (in.)	160.4	Very Short
HEAD/LEG ROOM (in.)	39.2/42.3	Average
INTERIOR SPACE (cu. ft.)	87.6	Cramped
CARGO SPACE (cu. ft.)	16.9	Large

Specifications may vary.

Prices

Model	Retail	Mkup
Golf GL 4dr.	13,495	8%

Competition	POOR □□□□□□□□□□ GOOD	Pg.
Volkswagen Golf	□□□□□□□■□□	**220**
Buick Regal	□□□□□■□□□□	114
Ford Contour	□□□□□□■□□□	141
Hyundai Sonata	□□■□□□□□□□	156

*A version of this vehicle is scheduled to be tested later this year. Results are expected to be similar.

Volkswagen Jetta

Compact

The Jetta, like its close sibling the Golf, enters 1998 with no changes. Pick from the Jetta GL, the mid-level Jetta GLS, or the up-level Jetta GLX. The Jetta GT was added last year. They vary in character, but all have the same basic specifications and components. A possible redesign is in the works for 1999. Dual airbags and daytime running lamps are standard; ABS and side side airbags are available.

The Jetta offer a 2-liter 4-cylinder engine. The GLX gets a 2.8-liter V6. All models come with 5-speed manual or automatic overdrive, and a 10-year/100,000 mile power train warranty. VW now includes all service, repairs and parts up the entire duration of the basic warranty of 2-years/ 24,000 miles. Handling is responsive, and the seats are comfortable. A Best Bet for 1998.

The Ratings

	POOR ... GOOD
COMPARATIVE RATING	□□□□□□□■□□
FRONTAL CRASH TEST*	□□□□■□□□□□
SAFETY FEATURES	□□□□□□■□□□
FUEL ECONOMY	□□□□□■□□□□
PM COST	□□□□□□□□□■
REPAIR COST	□□□□□□■□□□
WARRANTY	□□□□□□□□■□
COMPLAINTS	□□□□■□□□□□
INSURANCE COST	■□□□□□□□□□

Safety

FRONTAL CRASH TEST	Average
SIDE CRASH TEST	No government results
AIRBAGS	Dual/Opt. Side
ANTI-LOCK BRAKES	4-wheel (optional)
DAY. RUNNING LIGHTS	Standard
BELT ADJUSTORS	Front
BUILT-IN CHILD SEAT	None
PRETENSIONERS	Standard

General Information

WHERE MADE	Mexico/Germany
YEAR OF PRODUCTION	Fifth
PARKING INDEX	Very Easy
BUMPERS	Weak
THEFT RATING	Average
TWINS	VW Golf
DRIVE	Front

Specifications

FUEL ECONOMY (cty/hwy)	24/31	Average
DRIVING RANGE (miles)	406	Short
SEATING	5	
LENGTH (in.)	173.4	Very Short
HEAD/LEG ROOM (in.)	39.2/42.3	Average
INTERIOR SPACE (cu. ft.)	87.5	Cramped
CARGO SPACE (cu. ft.)	15.0	Average

Specifications may vary.

Prices

Model	Retail	Mkup
Jetta GL	14,595	10%

Competition

	POOR ... GOOD	Pg.
Volkswagen Jetta	□□□□□□□■□□	**221**
Buick Regal	□□□□□■□□□□	114
Ford Contour	□□□□□□■□□□	141
Hyundai Sonata	□□■□□□□□□□	156

*A version of this vehicle is scheduled to be tested later this year. Results are expected to be similar.

Volkswagen Passat

Intermediate

Redesigned for 1998, the Passat is based on the Audi A4. VW claims the Passat gives car buyers the excellence they expect from a German automobile with a low price tag. Safety features abound. Dual airbags are standard, as is traction control and ABS. Side airbags are a welcome standard feature.

Only one trim level is available, the GLS. It is powered by a 1.8-liter 4-cylinder engine. Last in 1998, a V6 and a turbodiesel engine are expected to be available. Inside, the new Passat has more interior room than its predecessor. Along with VW's industry best 10-year/100,000 miles powertrain warranty, VW now includes all service, repairs and parts up the entire duration of the basic warranty of 2-years/24,000 miles. Unfortunately, the Passat is not scheduled for crash testing next year.

The Ratings

	POOR — GOOD
COMPARATIVE RATING*	□□□□□□□□□□
FRONTAL CRASH TEST	□□□□□□□□□□
SAFETY FEATURES	□□□□□□■□□□
FUEL ECONOMY	□□□□□■□□□□
PM COST	□□□□□□□□□■
REPAIR COST	□□□□■□□□□□
WARRANTY	□□□□□□□□□■
COMPLAINTS	□□□□■□□□□□
INSURANCE COST	□□□□■□□□□□

Safety

FRONTAL CRASH TEST	No government results
SIDE CRASH TEST	No government results
AIRBAGS	Dual & Side
ANTI-LOCK BRAKES	4-wheel
DAY. RUNNING LIGHTS	Standard
BELT ADJUSTORS	Front
BUILT-IN CHILD SEAT	None
PRETENSIONERS	Standard

General Information

WHERE MADE	Germany
YEAR OF PRODUCTION	First
PARKING INDEX	Average
BUMPERS	Strong
THEFT RATING	
TWINS	
DRIVE	Front

Specifications

FUEL ECONOMY (cty/hwy)	23/32	Average
DRIVING RANGE (miles)	518	Very Long
SEATING	5	
LENGTH (in.)	184.1	Average
HEAD/LEG ROOM (in.)	39.7/41.5	Average
INTERIOR SPACE (cu. ft.)	95.0	Average
CARGO SPACE (cu. ft.)	15.0	Average

Specifications may vary.

Prices

Model	Retail	Mkup
Passat GLS	20,750	11%

Competition

	POOR — GOOD	Pg.
Volkswagen Passat	□□□□□□□□□□	**222**
Ford Taurus	□□□□□□■□□□	145
Oldsmobile Cutlass	□□□□□■□□□□	194
Toyota Camry	□■□□□□□□□□	214

*Due to the importance of crash tests, cars with no results as of publication date cannot be given an overall rating.

Volvo C70/S70/V70

Intermediate

Volvo's replacement for the 800-Series comes in three flavors: coupe (C70), sedan (S70) and wagon (V70). Despite the new name, the sedan and wagon aren't much different from the old 850, although the exteriors have been revamped. The C70 coupe, however, is a departure for Volvo with aggressive and sporty styling. Safety is still Volvo's strength. Dual airbags, side airbags, daytime running lamps, pretensioners and ABS are all standard. Parents will want the optional built-in child seat.

The standard engine is a 2.4-liter, inline five that produces 168 hp. Turbo versions are optional and provide more power. You can get all-wheel drive on the V70 wagons. Interior room is still roomy and comfortable, but five is a squeeze. The trunk space remains quite generous. Unfortunately, crash tests are unavailable.

The Ratings	POOR ... GOOD
COMPARATIVE RATING*	□□□□□□□□□□
FRONTAL CRASH TEST	□□□□□□□□□□
SAFETY FEATURES	□□□□□□□■□□
FUEL ECONOMY	□□□□■□□□□□
PM COST	■□□□□□□□□□
REPAIR COST	□□□□■□□□□□
WARRANTY	□□□□□□□□■□
COMPLAINTS	□□□□■□□□□□
INSURANCE COST	□□□□□□□■□□

Safety	
FRONTAL CRASH TEST	No government results
SIDE CRASH TEST	No government results
AIRBAGS	Dual & Side
ANTI-LOCK BRAKES	4-wheel
DAY. RUNNING LIGHTS	Standard
BELT ADJUSTORS	Front
BUILT-IN CHILD SEAT	Optional
PRETENSIONERS	Standard

General Information	
WHERE MADE	Germ./Canada/Sweden
YEAR OF PRODUCTION	First
PARKING INDEX	Easy
BUMPERS	Weak
THEFT RATING	
TWINS	
DRIVE	Front

Specifications		
FUEL ECONOMY (cty/hwy)	20/28	Average
DRIVING RANGE (miles)	444	Long
SEATING	5	
LENGTH (in.)	185.9	Average
HEAD/LEG ROOM (in.)	39.1/41.4	Average
INTERIOR SPACE (cu. ft.)	111.5	Very Roomy
CARGO SPACE (cu. ft.)	15.1	Average

Specifications may vary.

Prices

Model	Retail	Mkup
S70	26,985	9%
V70	28,285	8%
C70	38,995	12%

Competition	POOR ... GOOD	Pg.
Volvo C70/S70/V70	□□□□□□□□□□	**223**
BMW 3-Series	□□□□□□□□□■	108
Lexus ES300	□□□□□□□□■□	162
Merc.-Benz C-Class	□□□□□□□■□□	174

*Due to the importance of crash tests, cars with no results as of publication date cannot be given an overall rating.

Volvo S90/V90

Large

The largest car Volvo offers in the U.S. gets a name change and makeover for 1998. Formerly the 900-Series, the replacement comes in two iterations: a sedan (S90) and wagon (V90). Once again, safety is Volvo's main priority and the S90/V90 is no exception. Dual airbags, side airbags, daytime running lamps, pretensioners and 4-wheel ABS are all standard. The wagon gets an optional integrated child seat.

These rear wheel drive cars are powered by a 2.9-liter inline 6 engine. Only one trim level is offered, but it comes fully loaded with luxury features like power windows and locks, heated outside mirrors, front and rear fog lamps, a premium sound system, an alarm system, and simulated wood throughout the interior. A strong competitor, but no crash tests results are available.

General Information

WHERE MADE	Germany/Sweden
YEAR OF PRODUCTION	First
PARKING INDEX	Easy
BUMPERS	Weak
THEFT RATING	
TWINS	
DRIVE	Rear

Prices

Model	Retail	Mkup
S90	34,300	9%
V90	35,850	8%

The Ratings

	POOR — GOOD
COMPARATIVE RATING *	
FRONTAL CRASH TEST	
SAFETY FEATURES	
FUEL ECONOMY	
PM COST	
REPAIR COST	
WARRANTY	
COMPLAINTS	
INSURANCE COST	

Safety

FRONTAL CRASH TEST	No government results
SIDE CRASH TEST	No government results
AIRBAGS	Dual & Side
ANTI-LOCK BRAKES	4-wheel
DAY. RUNNING LIGHTS	Standard
BELT ADJUSTORS	None
BUILT-IN CHILD SEAT	Optional
PRETENSIONERS	Standard

Specifications

FUEL ECONOMY (cty/hwy)	18/26	Poor
DRIVING RANGE (miles)	447	Long
SEATING	5	
LENGTH (in.)	191.8	Long
HEAD/LEG ROOM (in.)	37.4/41.0	Vry. Cramped
INTERIOR SPACE (cu. ft.)	106.9	Roomy
CARGO SPACE (cu. ft.)	16.6	Large

Specifications may vary.

Competition

	POOR — GOOD	Pg.
Volvo S90/V90		**224**
Acura TL		105
Cadillac DeVille		117
Merc.-Benz C-Class		174

*Due to the importance of crash tests, cars with no results as of publication date cannot be given an overall rating.